Waking from the Dream

MEXICO'S MIDDLE CLASSES AFTER 1968

Louise E. Walker

STANFORD UNIVERSITY PRESS

STANFORD, CALIFORNIA

Stanford University Press
Stanford, California

© 2013 by the Board of Trustees of the Leland Stanford Junior University.
All rights reserved.

Printed on acid-free, archival-quality paper

Printed and bound in Great Britain by
Marston Book Services Ltd, Oxfordshire

Library of Congress Cataloging-in-Publication Data

Walker, Louise E., author.
  Waking from the dream : Mexico's middle classes after 1968 / Louise E. Walker.
       pages cm
  Includes bibliographical references and index.
  ISBN 978-0-8047-8151-0 (cloth)
  ISBN 978-0-8047-9530-2 (pbk.)
    1. Middle class—Political activity—Mexico—History—20th century.
2. Mexico—Economic conditions—1970–1982. 3. Mexico—Economic conditions—1982–1994. 4. Mexico—Economic policy—1970–1994. 5. Mexico—Politics and government—1970–1988. I. Title.
  HT690.M4W35 2013
  305.5'509720904—dc23
                                                    2012037022
  ISBN 978-0-8047-8457-3 (electronic)

Typeset by Bruce Lundquist in 10.5/12 Sabon

For my grandmothers,
Louise Kathleen Walker (in memoriam)
and
Elizabeth Olivine Frances Stephens

algún día hemos de llegar . . .
después sabremos a dónde.

we'll get there some day, maybe . . .
later, we'll find out where.

José Hernández, *Martín Fierro*

Contents

Illustrations

Acknowledgments

I began this book more than ten years ago, and many people and institutions have been a part of its—and my—life. My first thanks are to Gilbert Joseph. I am deeply grateful to Gil for his sharp insight, his generosity, and his sense of humor. Gil trained me to think critically about Mexican and Latin American history and helped me figure out how to become a historian on my own terms and in my own rhythm. Without him, I would not have survived in the academy for very long. I want to thank several other mentors who have encouraged me, and this project, in important ways. Stuart Schwartz helped me to think historically about the bigger picture and set an example by asking the sort of questions I aspire to ask. Michael Denning helped me to think creatively; I always left our conversations inspired, with a fresh perspective on whatever it was I was working on. Pablo Piccato helped me grapple with several methodological challenges, and his research suggestions sent me in unexpected and productive directions. I also want to thank Ariel Rodríguez Kuri, whose advice about research questions and archival sources shaped this project at several key moments. Catherine LeGrand sparked my interest in Latin American history and helped me get started on this path; I am forever thankful.

This book would not have been possible without the support of many institutions. In Mexico, the Centro de Estudios Demográficos, Urbanos y Ambientales at the Colegio de México generously provided a home for two years. Research and writing were funded by the Yale Graduate School, the Yale Center for International and Area Studies, the Fox Foundation at Yale University, the Mellon Foundation, the Ministry of Foreign Relations of Mexico, and the Social Science and Humanities Research Council of Canada, and by faculty research support from Louisiana State University, the New School for Social Research, and Northeastern University.

The on-the-ground help and humor of archivists and librarians made research not just productive but enjoyable. I am especially grateful to the archivists in Galleries One, Two, Three, and Six at the Archivo General de la Nación, and to the librarians at the Miguel Lerdo de Tejada, Banco de México, Biblioteca Nacional, and Colegio de México libraries.

I have special debts to Alexander Aviña, Ingrid Bleynat, and Tanalís Padilla. Alex helped me to articulate the underlying arguments of this project. Tanalís helped me to think through the methodological challenges of writing recent history. And Ingrid helped me to think more analytically and more historically and, in the broadest sense, to understand Mexican history. I have learned more from these three friends and interlocutors than I can ever express. Their incisive comments on countless drafts, while invisible to the reader, remain visible to me on every page.

Many people have generously read earlier versions of these chapters, and the book is much improved for their suggestions. I would like to thank Gustavo del Ángel, Jeffrey Bortz, Christine Kooi, Luis Martín-Cabrera, Manuella Meyer, Daniel Noemi Voionmaa, Paul Paskoff, Anne Rubenstein, Tatiana Seijas, Kirsten Weld, and Eric Zolov for their thoughtful feedback on different chapters. I am especially indebted to Jürgen Buchenau, Lyman Johnson, and an anonymous reader for comments on a previously published version of Chapter 6. And all parts of this book have been improved by the advice of colleagues at innumerable conferences and presentations. Errors of fact and interpretation are, of course, my own.

Becoming a historian is a lonely endeavor, and it might have been intolerable without the many great friends that I have made along the way. Sobeeh, David, Claudia, Haralampos, and María: thank you for the world of Edgewood Avenue. Ryan, Manuella, Camilla, Tatiana, and Kirsten: I could not have asked for better friends on this journey. Luis and Daniel: I am glad I was pulled into the vortex. The organizers of the Graduate Employees and Students Organization at Yale University, and especially Alison Bruey, taught me more about how power works than I have learned from any book. Roberto Frau's friendship, the warm and caring home of the Arceo Gómez family, and my friends in the archives—especially Ingrid, Ryan, Raphael, and Amara—helped me survive the vagaries of research. As I began writing, I found a community, and great potlucks, with historians in the Toronto Latin American Research Group. And, throughout everything, I have relied on the support and good cheer of my family and friends in Ireland and Canada, especially Allison Black, Ruby and Enright Clarke, Margaret and Sidney Cooper, Rosemary and Mervyn Elder, and Michael Wheeler. I want to thank everyone for the fun, the inspiration, and the friendships.

My colleagues at Louisiana State University provided a welcoming home during my first years after graduate school. I am especially grateful to Maribel Dietz, Gaines Foster, Christine Kooi, Leonard Ray, and Victor Stater for their mentoring and friendship. I am also indebted to my colleagues in the Committee on Historical Studies at the New School for Social Research for their encouragement, bonhomie, and counsel, with special thanks to Federico Finchelstein, Oz Frankel, Jeremy Varon, and Eli Zaretsky. I am fortunate to have found another nurturing environment in the History Department at Northeastern University, and I want to thank Laura Frader, Tom Havens, and Uta Poiger for their support and enthusiasm.

I am deeply grateful to my editor, Norris Pope, for believing in this project and for guiding me through the process. Also at Stanford University Press, Emma Harper and Carolyn Brown patiently answered many questions, and Christine Gever's copyediting refined the style and content of the text. Two anonymous readers offered insightful feedback and cogent suggestions, which significantly improved the book. Camila Vergara and Marcelo Villagrán Álvarez provided excellent research assistance. Constance Hale, wordsmith and shrewd reader, helped me sharpen the prose and structure.

My family has helped me become a historian in unexpected ways. My mother, Carol Stephens, showed me how to take a chance and enter a new world. I hope to be a historian with some of her independent spirit. My father, Charles Walker, taught me about the importance and danger of history in Belfast, with passion and humor. My sisters, Clare and Gillian, humble me with the work that they do. I dedicate this book to my grandmothers, who set high standards for insight and gave me an appreciation of irony.

Daniel Noemi Voionmaa has been with me through so much of this journey, and I could not have gotten here without his love, his support, and his jokes. *Compañero* and critic, he has read more of this book than I might have expected, and on many, many evenings he indulged my desire to talk Mexican history. He also takes me away from the books, and makes sure that I enjoy our life. As we close one chapter, I look forward to more.

Abbreviations

CNC   Confederación Nacional Campesina
National Peasant Confederation

CNOP   Confederación Nacional de Organizaciones Populares
National Confederation of Popular Organizations

CTM   Confederación de Trabajadores de México
Confederation of Mexican Workers

CUD   Coordinadora Única de Damnificados
Overall Coordinating Committee of Disaster Victims

FDN   Frente Democrático Nacional
National Democratic Front

Fonacot   Fondo Nacional para el Consumo de los Trabajadores
National Fund for Worker Consumption

Fonhapo   Fondo Nacional de Habitación Popular
National Fund for Popular Housing

Inco   Instituto Nacional del Consumidor
National Institute for the Consumer

INEGI   Instituto Nacional de Estadística, Geografía e Informática
National Institute of Statistics, Geography, and Information

IPN   Instituto Politécnico Nacional
National Polytechnic Institute

ISI   Industrialización por Sustitución de Importaciones
Import Substitution Industrialization

IVA   Impuesto al Valor Agregado
Value-Added Tax

PAN   Partido Acción Nacional
National Action Party

PEMEX   Petróleos Mexicanos
Mexican Petroleum

PRD   Partido de la Revolución Democrática
Party of the Democratic Revolution

PRI   Partido Revolucionario Institucional
           Institutional Revolutionary Party

Profeco   Procuraduría Federal del Consumidor
           Office of the Federal Attorney for the Consumer

SHCP   Secretaría de Hacienda y Crédito Público
           Ministry of the Treasury

SIC   Secretaría de Industria y Comercio
           Ministry of Industry and Commerce

SPP   Secretaría de Programación y Presupuesto
           Ministry of Programming and Budget

UNAM   Universidad Nacional Autónoma de México
           National Autonomous University of Mexico

WAKING FROM THE DREAM

Introduction

THE MIDDLE CLASSES AND THE CRISIS
OF THE INSTITUTIONAL REVOLUTION

This is the story of how the Mexican middle classes made history during several decades of economic and political upheaval. A midcentury boom, so impressive that it was dubbed the Mexican Miracle, came to an end in the late 1960s. Illusions of prosperity and stability, which had seemed possible during the Miracle, dissipated. At the same time, the political hegemony of the Institutional Revolutionary Party (Partido Revolucionario Institucional, or PRI), the heir to a political dynasty that had governed Mexico since 1929, dissipated as well. We can see, with hindsight, major changes in the economy and the political system in the late twentieth century, from the 1960s through the 1990s, as state-led development was replaced by neoliberalism and the de facto one-party state gave way to procedural democracy. But these were messy processes, and the period is best understood as several decades of economic and political turmoil.

At the center of these changes were Mexico's misunderstood middle classes, whose reactions to crisis shaped recent history. During the Mexican Miracle, PRI politicians and bureaucrats had prided themselves on the country's rigorous growth and political stability. They saw the economic well-being and political quiescence of the middle classes as an outgrowth of their stewardship.[1] But if the middle classes were symbols of the PRI's success, they were also harbingers of its decline. As the segment of the population that had most benefited from the boom, they were also the most buffeted by the difficult process of economic change, from the everyday experience of unpredictable inflation and unexpected peso devaluations to major changes in philosophy and policy. The middle classes—doctors and lawyers, laboratory technicians and engineers, shopkeepers and civil servants—acted out the stresses of this economic history: they protested in the streets and in the corridors of power; they suffered alienation, hope, and fear. Whether they formed groups of armed rebels, suffered malaise silently, or gossiped about a coup d'état, their actions signaled that the PRI's one-party system was in crisis. The beleaguered PRI struggled to recoup support and to contain the political upheaval on the left and the right, but ultimately the party split under the pressure.

The desires and fears of the middle classes, as well as their actions, shaped the economic and political history of late twentieth-century Mexico. Most scholars have pointed to the 1968 student movement as the beginning of the end of PRI's hegemony, but this was only one symptom of a larger upheaval. The emphasis on the student movement has eclipsed a more important historical point: that the most consequential struggles over the future of the PRI's system took place among the middle classes. The leftist students who took to the streets to protest the authoritarianism of the PRI can and should be analyzed alongside conservative housewives enraged at the rising cost of living, alienated engineers suffering ennui, consumers falling into debt to support their lifestyle, yuppies who believed the world was their oyster, and angry homeowners struggling to defend their privileged access to housing. These reactions to crisis, which span the political spectrum, represent different threads by which the one-party system was coming undone.

The Middle Classes

Who were these middle classes? Professionals such as lawyers and doctors; intellectual workers such as university professors, teachers, and artists; white-collar workers such as administrators, secretaries, and clerks; and technical workers such as photographers and sound engineers belonged to the middle classes. So too did small business owners, merchants, and supervisors.[2] Importantly, most PRI functionaries, from civil servants to party officials, formed part of these middle classes. These are the people who benefited from the midcentury economic boom. They had relatively high levels of education, engaged in nonmanual or technical work, and lived in urban environments where they had access to cultural, leisure, and health services.[3]

"Middle class" refers to a set of material conditions, a state of mind, and a political discourse. As a set of material conditions it can be measured by income and class stratification. (Please see the Appendix for a description of various attempts to quantify the middle classes and delineate their social reality in twentieth-century Mexico.) As a state of mind, it is an identity, lifestyle, and cultural world that can be longed for—and lost. Some of the fiercest political battles in twentieth-century Mexican history are struggles to acquire and defend the socioeconomic and cultural markers of class, which do not always coincide, as illustrated by the popular descriptions *con dinero sin cultura* (with money but without culture) and *con cultura sin dinero* (with culture but without money).[4] Middle class is also a political discourse. Ideas about the nature and function of this group have been used (usually by cultural, political, and academic élites) to create influential narratives about Mexico's past, present, and future—narratives that serve ideological and political purposes. For example, the middle classes have been the premier protagonists in narratives about capitalist economies since at least the nineteenth century, and vociferous debate continues, in Mexico and elsewhere, about their historical role. They have been described as harbingers of modernity and economic progress and as actors in political chaos. They have been alternately characterized as apathetic and alienated, productive and parasitic, conservative and revolutionary. This three-pronged approach to studying class—socioeconomic, cultural, and political—is present throughout the book, although different dimensions are emphasized in different chapters. The plural, "middle classes," is intended to convey the array of indicators, identities, and ideas that define this protean group of people who have been both idealized and reviled.

How big—or how small—are these multifarious middle classes in Mexico? One estimate puts them at 8 percent of the national population in 1895, 16 percent in 1940, 20 percent in 1950, 22 percent in 1960, 29 percent in 1970, 33 percent in 1980, and 38 percent in 1990.[5] According to this estimate, by the 1980s they constituted as much as one-third of the national population. Other, more conservative measures describe them as one-quarter of the population in that decade.[6] Most measures of class stratification in twentieth-century Mexico, though, indicate an overall trend whereby the middle classes increased as a proportion of the national population, even during the crisis years of the 1970s and 1980s.[7] This trend defies some popular and scholarly assumptions. As several leading experts argue, statistics on class stratification have often been miscalculated and misinterpreted to advance political arguments about inequality in Mexico.[8] But bureaucrats and business owners, airline pilots and movie projectionists, stockbrokers and students did not belong to a small or disappearing class. They belonged to a rapidly changing world.

Related to the question of how big the middle classes are is the question of location. "Middle class" does not describe those in the middle of the income distribution. Instead, they reside in the top deciles, between the poor majority and an extremely small, wealthy minority. The middle classes and the PRI, then, together constituted an élite realm. In one study of class stratification and income distribution, for example, an analyst argued that, in 1977, they occupied the eighth, ninth, and first half of the tenth deciles of Mexico's income distribution.[9] But the boundaries between the poor, the middle classes, and the wealthy are far more complicated than income deciles, as the myriad labels for this group suggest. "Middle-class," "bourgeois," "petit bourgeois" and an array of other "smalls" and "mediums"—such as proprietors, merchants, and industrialists—all refer to an intermediary group between the poor and the wealthy. Some terms are associated with economic differentiation, others evoke cultural criteria.[10] While these designations are often used interchangeably, this book uses "class" for two related reasons: it refers to a social position that is made rather than inherited, and its making (and endless unraveling and remaking) is a political and historical process.[11] Much of this book examines how individuals and groups struggled to erect, maintain, break down, cross over, or ensconce themselves within class boundaries.

The history of the middle classes is a political, economic, and cultural story that requires methodological creativity to uncover.[12] In many ways, economic crisis appears as the primary driver of historical change in this book. But economic crises are political and cultural crises. They disrupt established patterns of class domination, necessitating class reconfiguration—a political, economic, and cultural process.[13] An underlying assumption in this book is that capitalism generates economic growth, trade, and profit but also social and cultural relations, dreams and nightmares.[14] Studying the middle classes in their many dimensions is an opportunity to combine the methodological tools of the cultural turn, political economy, bottom-up history, and economic history.[15] In some chapters, "middle class" is primarily defined by education. In other chapters, the middle classes are studied in their places of everyday consumption (such as gas stations); through their income levels and family finances; according to the neighborhood in which they live; and as they are portrayed in Mexico's public sphere, from novels and television programs to press accounts and political speeches.[16] This methodology unearths a broad range of middle-class experiences and relationships. It underscores the tensions and contradictions within the middle classes and emphasizes the dynamic and central role of these groups in recent Mexican history.[17]

Miracles

Writing in 1970, historian John Womack Jr. argued that "the business of the Mexican Revolution is now business." He described a Mexico City full of "shimmering new buildings [that] teem with transactions and accountings into the future" and remarked that Mexicans "run up bills on three credit cards." The Mexican Revolution, which commenced in 1910, began as a struggle for justice and became the foundational narrative for twentieth-century Mexican history. "Why," Womack asked, "did the old struggle for justice—violent, confused, but intent—turn into the new drive for development? How did the Revolution become a bonanza?"[18] This midcentury bonanza—the so-called Mexican Miracle—was intimately connected to the expansion of the middle classes and the postrevolutionary state apparatus.

The PRI's rule has been described as the "perfect dictatorship."[19] After the Revolution, political leaders faced the challenge of ruling a territory that had nearly been pulled apart during the upheaval. In the early postrevolutionary years, different interest groups jockeyed for power, and the PRI eventually emerged from this intense process.[20] Although it was officially founded in 1946, the PRI was the heir to a political dynasty that began in 1929. Scholars often use the earlier date to underscore the continuity and longevity of the political system: after all, the PRI and its precursors ruled Mexico from 1929 to 2000.[21] Ostensibly democratic, a presidential term was limited to four (later, six) years, and presidents were limited to one term. Elections were meant to be open and democratic. In reality, though, the PRI held tight control over the electoral process, limited the number and power of registered opposition parties, and resorted to fraud to ensure its continued victories at the polls. In order to maintain social control, the PRI relied upon large groups to represent campesinos, such as the National Peasant Confederation (Confederación Nacional Campesina, or CNC); workers, such as the Confederation of Mexican Workers (Confederación de Trabajadores de México, or CTM); and the middle classes, such as the National Confederation of Popular Organizations (Confederación Nacional de Organizaciones Populares, or CNOP). These state-affiliated confederations of unions and associations lobbied for the interests of their constituents, to be sure, but they also ensured that their members would support official policies. In this corporatist system, mandatory business chambers represented industrialists, merchants, business owners, and other important groups of the private sector.

The party resembled a negotiation table, balancing the competing interests of these different organizations. The church, social organizations, small opposition parties, and voluntary business organizations also participated in the limited space allowed for pluralism within the one-party state. And, like most ruling parties, the PRI itself was not a monolith but rather an association of different interests and power brokers occupying positions in different ministries.[22] The party held in balance these varied and conflicting interests in the context of regional, national, and international pressures. Importantly, when consensus could not be reached by mutual accord, bribery, or carrot-and-stick negotiation, the PRI found recourse in violence (most often against workers and campesinos).[23] Ideally, this system worked as a welfare state, in which state institutions guaranteed the social and economic well-being of citizens; in reality, it functioned as a welfare state that could never meet the needs of all its citizens, as one in which one party exchanged resources for political loyalty. Though by no means a perfect system (or dictatorship), the PRI's Institutional Revolution provided a certain amount of stability.[24]

The political system consolidated in the context of a midcentury economic boom from 1940 to 1970, when Mexico's economy grew at an average annual rate of more than 6 percent. Mexican and foreign observers began to talk about the "Mexican Miracle."[25] This growth resulted from a prosperous world economic context (especially following the Second World War) and an internal economic strategy known as Import Substitution Industrialization, or ISI. In Mexico, ISI can be described as a mixed economy, with both public and private investment and a large amount of state involvement. Mexican leaders sought foreign investment to promote domestic industrial manufacturing and implemented high tariffs on imported goods to protect these fledgling industries. The ISI strategy was intended to counter the structural inequality of the international economy; it was designed to give Mexico the breathing space to "catch-up" with the developed world. In this endeavor, the state wholly owned certain strategic industries (such as oil extraction) but also heavily subsidized domestic private-sector industrialists, either directly or through subsidized services. Although the terms "miracle," "ISI," and "state-led development" have become shorthand for thinking about the economic boom, it remains unclear whether there was a coherent and consistent development policy, never mind an economic model, during those years; these terms might obfuscate more than they explain. It is more likely that economic policy resulted from ad hoc and self-interested compromises among business, labor, and political élites at regional, national, and international levels.[26]

The growth of the postrevolutionary state apparatus, from the 1920s onward, bolstered the middle classes.[27] A reciprocal relationship between the middle classes and the state emerged: the middle classes studied in the public education system and then, drawing upon the cultural capital they had accrued, filled the ranks of the growing state's bureaucracies.[28] Increased access to public education was one of the postrevolutionary state's most prominent social commitments. Despite important successes, especially regarding access to primary school, education remained a marker of privilege. For instance, of the population over fifteen years of age living in Mexico City, only 41 percent had completed primary school in 1970; this figure decreased to 34 percent in 1980.[29] Further, as the public education system grew (the number of high schools doubled between 1940 and 1960), so too did the value placed on education, and poverty began to be explained by low levels of education.[30] As a result, despite the efforts of politicians and policymakers, the education system ended up reinforcing middle-class privilege.[31]

After 1940, Mexico's political leaders, especially those who worked for the federal government and lived in the main cities, came predominantly from the ranks of the middle classes. Members of the middle classes found employment not only at the highest levels of the government but also as civil servants and midlevel supervisors.[32] The middle classes consolidated their position in 1943 with the creation of the CNOP (National Confederation of Popular Organizations), an umbrella organization that represented many middle-class associations and unions.[33] This confederation brought together state employees, professionals, intellectuals, soldiers, small merchants, small farmers, and small and medium industrialists. It also represented the urban poor, including shantytown dwellers and shoeshine boys.[34] Though heterogeneous, it was dominated by middle-class state employees. Its principal goal was to provide a corporatist representation for the middle classes within the regime, similar to large organizations that represented campesinos and workers. Although bureaucrats constituted the core of this "popular sector," the strength of the organization (and its usefulness to the PRI) was its ability to function as a brokering device between different middle-class interests, providing the PRI with remarkable institutional flexibility.[35] The dynamism of the "popular sector" also helped the PRI to balance the power of the worker and campesino sectors—the inclusion of the urban poor, for example, lent revolutionary legitimacy to the popular sector and the PRI.[36] This was especially important as the CNOP quickly superseded the campesino and worker organizations in terms of political clout and power.[37] Thus, the middle classes and the PRI forged a mutually beneficial relationship that served to protect and reproduce their privilege. The economic boom fortified this relationship during the midcentury decades.[38]

As the middle classes grew, the PRI developed infrastructure to feed, house, and entertain them. Massive, modernist, high-rise apartment complexes were built with great fanfare, in the style of Le Corbusier, to provide nurses and accountants with all the accoutrements of modern life, including parking spaces for their cars, indoor plumbing, electricity, multiple bedrooms, kitchen appliances, and even carpeting and window drapes. The Tlatelolco apartment complex, perhaps the most emblematic of all these housing projects, is the subject of Chapter 6. The National Autonomous University of Mexico (Universidad Nacional Autónoma de México, commonly known as UNAM) was moved from its original location in downtown Mexico City to a sprawling suburban zone in the south of the city, which became known as University City. New suburbs, in an American style, were developed, and entertainment and shopping complexes sprang up for the leisure pursuits of these residents.[39] The formation of an identity of this burgeoning class was greatly influenced by American consumption patterns and culture. Social status became tied to appliances, clothes, and electronic gadgets imported from the United States or to their nationally manufactured equivalents (which denoted less status, to be sure).[40] During the midcentury boom, then, being middle class meant to have privileged access to education, to live in a modern apartment, and to enjoy a certain lifestyle.

Being middle class implied having hope for the future. As the middle classes grew and gelled, they came to expect upward mobility. A 1959 civic culture survey found that nearly 80 percent of middle-class respondents expected to be better off economically in ten years (compared with only 60 percent of other urban respondents). For example, "Mr. C," a forty-year-old radio operator and technician, felt satisfied with his salary and working conditions. In his spare time, he took care of his car, read newspapers and magazines, and listened to the radio. Mr. C lived with his wife and four children in a medium-sized city, where their neighbors were mostly business owners, professionals, and office workers. Mr. C completed primary school and trade school, took advanced training courses in the evenings, and enjoyed thinking of future opportunities, even if his plans did not materialize. "I had planned to open up a radio store," he told the interviewers. "I had to postpone it, hoping that business conditions would become more favorable, but it has not been feasible so far."[41] Mr. C believed that his children would be more successful than he was, because of growing educational opportunities.[42] In the 1960s, sociologist Pablo González Casanova argued that such expectations for upward mobility constituted a powerful "hope factor" by which "the peasants of yesterday are the workers of today and the sons of those workers can be the professionals of tomorrow."[43] If these aspirations overestimated the real possibility of social mobility (the middle classes, after all, constituted an élite minority), in doing so they fostered a degree of political moderation and social conformity among the believers; as González Casanova argued, these aspirations were "powerful palliatives of inequality."[44]

Scholars have questioned the political stability and economic prosperity of the midcentury decades. The so-called Mexican Miracle was miraculous only for a privileged few.[45] Its darker side included economic desolation and political repression. The murder of campesino activists in the state of Morelos during the 1940s and 1950s and the repression of railway workers in Mexico City in 1958–59, among other examples, reveal the violence upon which the PRI's rule depended.[46] But whether this period should be understood in terms of its stability or its violence, or some combination of the two, remains an open question; an interpretive framework is still emerging.[47] The significance here is not the accuracy of the Miracle narrative but rather the fact that PRI functionaries, and others, believed it. It may be true that this dream never existed in reality, but stability is often a state of mind, and in the early 1970s a perceived stability began to unravel. Thus, the argument here is not that a Pax Priísta did or did not exist but that we need to analyze the belief in it.

In this belief, the middle classes came to represent the modern, developed Mexico, symbolizing the goal toward which all Mexicans ought to strive. Their role in maintaining the status quo was legitimated by the authority that their education and their political position gave them. A midcentury pact emerged, whereby the middle classes provided ideological legitimacy to an authoritarian system in exchange for economic prosperity and political stability. Mr. C., quoted above regarding his optimism about the future, described elections as "fraudulent." He supported the PRI but with some resignation: "Of all the bad [parties], I think the least bad one is the PRI."[48] His cynicism notwithstanding, Mr. C's political quiescence buttressed the midcentury pact between the state and the middle classes, and he enjoyed the benefits it conferred. It must be stressed that while the middle classes became the ideal of the postrevolutionary state, they were not always discussed as such in public. The PRI cultivated a folk archetype which was meant to represent the authentic or the indigenous.[49] Nevertheless, the PRI wanted the nation to move toward an ideal of urban middle-class living. In the consolidation of the postrevolutionary state, the middle classes came to stand for the nation.[50] Because this was a predominantly urban ideal, it centered on the middle classes who lived in the country's main cities, especially Mexico City. If the visibility and influence of the middle classes far exceeded their proportion of the national population, this was especially true of those living in the capital and other major cities—yet another example of how Mexico City has sometimes stood for the nation.[51]

The vision of an urban middle-class Mexico might have been a fantasy of PRI functionaries, but the idea stuck, so to speak, because of the glue of economic prosperity. In turn, this fantasy buttressed the prolonged period of economic boom and relative political stability from 1940 to 1970 and helped to fill in the fissures of discontent. When the Miracle began to fade, fantasies became nightmares.

1968 *and Writing Recent History*

On the rainy evening of 2 October 1968, government forces massacred hundreds of students in Tlatelolco, a plaza in the heart of Mexico City. This massacre put an end to the student movement, which had gathered momentum throughout the summer as students organized marches to protest the authoritarianism of the PRI. The conflict began with a seemingly apolitical, routine skirmish between students from several *preparatorias* (higher-education institutions between high school and undergraduate studies) and vocational schools. On 22 July a fight broke out between students from Vocational School 2 and the Isaac Ochoterena Preparatoria. The next day, there was another fight. There was nothing particularly unusual about any of this. But on 23 July, the city government sent in two hundred riot police, who confronted students with violence and arrested approximately twenty. In the following days, street battles occurred in the center of Mexico City. Prepa and vocational students, now joined by students from UNAM and the National Polytechnic Institute (Instituto Politécnico Nacional, or IPN), fought the police, riot police, and military. Students blockaded avenues and the military barricaded streets, and on 30 July government forces occupied several secondary schools. Although precise numbers are unknown, newspaper reports estimated that, by the end of July, four hundred students had been injured and one thousand arrested; students claimed that over fifty students had been killed, disappeared, or jailed. In less than ten days, a wide array of middle-class students found themselves in direct confrontation with the government.[52]

In the following weeks, student groups from various schools issued several demands, including freedom for political prisoners; elimination of Article 145 of the penal code, which mandated a sentence of two to twelve years for spreading sedition; abolition of the riot police (*granaderos*); dismissal of the Mexico City police chief; indemnification for victims of repression; and justice against those responsible for the repression.[53] Student groups also organized tactical responses to the aggression. Young men and women formed unarmed guard units to protect their schools from invasion. Student strikes began on the IPN and UNAM campuses, then spread to other schools in the capital city and beyond. Eventually the National Strike Council was established. Committees of Struggle (Comités de Lucha) formed to discuss events and plan strategy.[54] And Lightning Brigades emerged as young people fanned out across the city to communicate the students' position to the broader public.[55] Margarita Isabel, a student actress who joined a brigade after riot police invaded the National Institute of Fine Arts, described the political effervesence in the city's streets: "We organized encounters—happenings, you know what I mean? I'd go up to a newspaper stand, for example, and ask for a newspaper." At the same time, another member of the brigade, dressed up as a "very 'square,' very middle-class matron, wearing earrings and a little pearl necklace" would also approach the kiosk. Then Isabel (wearing boots and a miniskirt) and her actress comrade would stage an argument about the student movement and its demands, drawing in bystanders who gathered as the argument escalated. "Our audience wouldn't say anything at first, but then suddenly, without even realizing it, they'd begin to take sides and some man in the crowd would say, 'Listen, *señora*, this young lady is right, you know, because you don't even know what the students' six demands are."[56] The actors' brigade staged these encounters in markets, cafés, restaurants, factories, and plazas across the city, to publicize the students' demands and shape public opinion. The bridgades, committees of struggle, and strike council were the infrastructure for what would become known as the 1968 student movement.

Conflict escalated in August and September. The army invaded and occupied the UNAM campus, but students successfully defended the IPN. Riots erupted in several areas of the city, and violent confrontations between students and government forces led to deaths and injury on both sides.[57] Galvanized into action, growing numbers of citizens joined the demonstrations, protesting the undemocratic nature of the one-party state and the brutality of the police. Womack described the movement two years later: "This was at heart a civic movement for civil liberties. . . . Not only students but also their parents, their teachers and many tens of thousands of office workers, housewives, shop workers, professionals and petty merchants marched in massive demonstrations to protest official abuse of civil rights."[58] By the end of the summer, the number of protestors was in the hundreds of thousands.

From solemn silent marches to the energetic lightning bridgades, the student movement threatened the PRI. Mexico was hosting the Olympics that month, the first third-world nation to do so, and the opening ceremonies were scheduled for 12 October in Mexico City. Such widespread protest would undermine the image the PRI had been cultivating as an effective government for a prosperous Mexico.[59] On the evening of 2 October, just ten days before the opening ceremony, hundreds of students gathered peacefully in the plaza of the Tlatelolco apartment building complex, to discuss strategy and plan their next steps. Instead, when government forces began shooting from the rooftops, the movement was quashed in a few bloody hours. The details of the massacre are murky: How did it begin? Who were the snipers on the rooftops and plainclothesmen on the ground? How many people died? The official death toll is 49, but international journalists who had been in the plaza that evening reported upwards of 325 dead.[60]

One year after the events, Nobel laureate and poet Octavio Paz wrote, "The second of October, 1968, put an end to the student movement. It also ended an epoch in the history of Mexico."[61] The student movement, and especially the Tlatelolco massacre, has become a defining moment in narratives about recent Mexican history. Scholars, public intellectuals, and journalists use the events of 1968 to explain the arc of twentieth-century Mexican history. For Paz, the massacre was the end of an era. Others describe 1968 as a turning point, between the midcentury Miracle and a period of generalized crisis in the late twentieth and early twenty-first centuries.[62] The events also laid the foundation for origin stories, whether those narratives describe the beginning of the end of the PRI's rule, the heroic birth of the New Left, or the initial impetus for a prolonged transition to electoral democracy.[63] The Second of October is also understood as an instance of anagnorisis, a moment of tragic recognition, when those who had gathered in the Tlatelolco plaza realized the full extent of the darker side of the Miracle.[64]

It is time to de-center the 1968 student movement in explanations of Mexican history. It is intellectually irresponsible to lionize the student movement; doing so magnifies its significance and distorts our understanding of Mexico's recent past. The crucial story is the historical arc of the middle classes, of which the students were only one part. In the late 1960s and early 1970s, crisis began to diffuse throughout the middle classes: students, certainly, but also doctors, detectives, and dentists, as well as many others, found themselves in uncertain times. The future of the PRI's Institutional Revolution actually turned on how a broad spectrum of the middle classes would react.

The End of the Miracle

In the late 1960s, the boom began to falter. On one level, it had always been unstable. For many, midcentury capitalist growth had been anything but miraculous. In 1970 Octavio Paz described how the boom had produced "two Mexicos, one modern and the other underdeveloped." Paz wrote that "half of Mexico—poorly clothed, illiterate, and underfed—has watched the progress of the other half."[65]

On another level, by the mid-1960s, prominent economists and observers commented on the exhaustion of the ISI (Import Substitution Industrialization) strategy. The belief was that the easy stage of ISI had ended. It had successfully generated domestic industries, but only for simple goods. Moreover, internal demand for these goods was relatively small, and they were not competitive on the world market.[66] Other economists, though, warned against extreme prognoses, suggesting that policymakers had pinned unreasonable expectations on ISI. When disappointment ensued, it was tempting to succumb to failure complexes, or "fracasomania."[67] A less dramatic explanation was that ISI had simply passed its first, exciting stage and that the slowdown was cause for concern but not a calamity.[68] Despite this caution, a "gloomy vision" took hold. In fear that the ISI model had failed, policymakers, politicians, and industrialists were galvanized into action, attempting to forge another economic strategy—a political, socioeconomic, and cultural process in which the middle classes had much at stake.[69]

By the mid-1960s, the middle classes began to experience the contradictions that had long been inherent in the so-called miraculous midcentury capitalist growth. Doctors, teachers, and students mobilized to demand better wages and working conditions, as well as greater transparency and more meaningful democracy. The 1964–65 doctors' strike, for example, revealed the tension between young doctors' middle-class aspirations and the material limitations they confronted.[70] During the midcentury boom, Mexico's public health-care system expanded rapidly, and so did the numbers of doctors graduating from UNAM and the IPN, as well as other institutions. But it had become increasingly difficult for the state to provide health care to more and more citizens; likewise, the state struggled to pay its doctors a salary that adequately reflected their education and the services they offered.[71] A gulf had emerged between the prestige of being a doctor and the inability of many doctors to earn even a marginally middle-class salary. In late 1964, when a rumor circulated that end-of-year bonuses would be withheld, doctors went on strike to demand their bonuses and to protest unsanitary living quarters, low pay, and underemployment. Invoking the prestige conferred by their profession, their rallying cry was "Dignity for the medical class."[72] These young doctors, who should have belonged to the middle classes, had come up against the limits of the Mexican Miracle.

The doctors' frustrated aspirations were part of a broader trend. The privilege conferred by education—not only medical education—had come under threat. Francisco López Cámara, an official in the CNOP and a scholar who counseled the PRI regarding the middle classes, described the process as "Malthus and Darwin against Marx and Freud."[73] A growing number of educated professionals faced an increasingly saturated job market.[74] Education was no longer a guarantee of upward mobility as the likelihood of a secure job in the state bureaucracies diminished. Growing expectations of consumption, compensation, and upward mobility came under threat just when they were at their highest ever in postrevolutionary Mexico. Writing in 1966, López Cámara describes how middle-class students felt cheated ("defraudado") of their privilege.[75] The best-known manifestation of this feeling of having been "defrauded" came with the 1968 student movement, but scholars and public intellectuals have mostly focused on its political and cultural dimensions; its structural context has received less attention. The student movement, though, is also an economic story. Structural economic crisis generated widespread discontent, and citizens across the political spectrum began to protest. Certainly, in

1968 the students—and the other participants—were deeply frustrated by the authoritarianism of the PRI's system. But fear of losing class status was another motivation for taking to the streets.

Octavio Paz foretold "great political battles" in the realm of the middle classes.[76] The PRI worried intensely about continuing middle-class discontent. Indeed, Francisco López Cámara, in his capacity as scholar of the middle classes with connections to the party, argued that their discontent represented the biggest threat to Mexico's political and social stability. The middle classes, worried López Cámara, were "threatening to become the great unknown of the 1970s."[77] He urged the PRI to develop a coherent political and economic policy to avert what seemed to be a looming disaster. Importantly, both Paz and López Cámara connected middle-class discontent to the exhaustion of the ISI model and growing economic instability.

The fundamental precariousness of their privilege makes economic instability especially threatening to the middle classes. Even in times of economic boom, the basis for their privilege is shaky. Theorist Immanuel Wallerstein describes the middle classes as being condemned to live in the present—their privilege might disappear with the next crisis.[78] Paz described the effects of this existential instability on the middle classes: "[The middle class] constitutes a mobile stratum which, though relatively satisfied from an economic point of view, is aware that the situation could change overnight. This insecurity inspires an aggressiveness and unrest that is not found among the workers."[79] After more than a generation of economic boom, during which middle-class habits and hopes became expectations, students and doctors, housewives and engineers, small business owners, car owners, and customers in dry cleaning shops, among others, were confronted by their structural instability, and they reacted in myriad ways.

The Great Unknown

This book begins in the early 1970s, when instability takes center stage. It addresses two central questions: What happened to the political relationship between the middle classes and the PRI when the boom ended? And, how did neoliberalism (with its theoretical and policy emphasis on private enterprise, free markets, and free trade, in contrast to state-led development) emerge from the debris of the Mexican Miracle? These questions are closely connected. During the 1970s and 1980s, the middle classes and the PRI experienced the end of the boom, experimented with economic alternatives, and negotiated the birth of a neoliberal paradigm. Through the tumultuous history of economic change, political crisis pervaded the élite realm of the PRI and the middle classes, which was constantly being reconfigured. At times, there seemed to be an echo of the midcentury pact, as when the PRI provided consumer credit and the middle classes paid higher taxes. In other moments, neoliberal economists and policymakers broke from the state-led development model that had principally benefited the middle classes, a move that created cleavages both within the party and within the middle classes. These economic and political crises occurred in tandem and led to the end of the "Institutional Revolution" from which the party derived its very name.

The new landscape of the 1970s and 1980s was one of crisis.[80] Cultural critic José Agustín described the mood toward the end of the year 1970: "On the surface, everything appeared normal despite the hard proof of 1968," he began. "But in many people, there existed a vague impression of having woken from a dream to face a reality that they had previously avoided. The cracks in the system were everywhere to be seen for those willing to look; the negative traces of 'developmentalism' or the 'Mexican miracle' were now perceivable."[81]

Mexico had experienced economic ups and downs earlier, but during these decades crisis became the backdrop of everyday life. Indeed, aside from the brief interlude of an oil boom, the term became virtually synonymous with the normal state of affairs. The economic (and political) crises of these decades were, in part, routine crises, necessary to ongoing capital accumulation, but they led to a profound shift from the midcentury state-led development to the neoliberalism of the late twentieth century.[82] The theorist Antonio Gramsci defines crisis as consisting "precisely in the fact that the old is dying and the new cannot be born; in this interregnum a great variety of morbid symptoms appear."[83] This book explores that ambiguous moment between two modes of capitalist accumulation.

This book tracks the middle classes and the PRI through the convulsions of crisis. Part I, "Upheavals," focuses on the political activities of the middle classes in the early 1970s, in the shadow of 1968. Chapter 1 outlines the spectrum of leftist politics, from moderate students to radical urban guerrillas, and examines how leftists struggled to come to terms with their middle-class status. It also analyzes the PRI's attempts to reach out to the discontented students. Chapter 2 documents a wave of destabilizing rumors, as the conservative middle classes worried about peso devaluations, rising inflation, and a possible leftward turn in Mexican politics. The chapter then examines the PRI's reaction to conservative protest and traces the escalation of these rumors to whispers of a coup d'état in 1976. Together, Chapters 1 and 2 demonstrate widespread discontent, protest, and even rebellion among the middle classes.

Part II, "The Debt Economy," analyzes how the PRI and the middle classes tried to exit economic crisis by moving Mexico toward a debt economy. Chapter 3 focuses on the short oil boom from 1977 to 1981 and analyzes "middle class" as a political discourse in the public sphere. It examines the hopes (and fears) that politicians, scholars, and public intellectuals pinned on the middle classes. Chapter 4 studies the effects of inflation, which began increasing significantly and erratically in the early 1970s. It documents a changing economic relationship between the middle classes and the PRI, with a focus on consumer credit, consumer rights, and taxation. Chapters 3 and 4 together outline the emerging debt economy at the national and household levels, whereby national debt funded oil extraction and consumer credit mitigated the effects of inflation on household consumption.

Part III, "Fault Lines of Neoliberalism," studies the social and political effects of the 1980s economic crisis and Mexico's transition to neoliberalism. When oil prices collapsed and interest rates rose in 1981 and 1982, Mexico entered an economic crisis known as "the lost decade." Chapter 5 analyzes the emergence of neoliberal ideology and policy and its impact on different segments of the middle classes. The chapter charts how the élite realm of the PRI and the middle classes split between the advocates and critics of neoliberalism. Chapter 6 begins with the September 1985 earthquake that devastated Mexico City. It examines the pivotal role of middle-class residents in the protest movement that emerged after the natural disaster, focusing on the massive Tlatelolco apartment building complex. The chapter also analyzes how the postearthquake landscape of Mexico City functioned as a sort of crucible for neoliberalism. Chapters 5 and 6 demonstrate how a series of crises facilitated Mexico's shift to neoliberalism.

The history documented in these chapters challenges our understanding of postrevolutionary Mexico. The middle classes, as the segment of the population that had most benefited from the Mexican Miracle, offer a premier vantage point from which to examine the end of the boom and the end of the PRI's one-party state. Yet there is remarkably little historical scholarship on the middle classes. This might be because the postrevolutionary state appeared to be dominated by the large and powerful corporatist associations representing workers and campesinos; significantly, the CNOP (National Confederation of Popular Organizations) has received less attention than its counterparts, the National Peasant Confederation and the Confederation of Mexican Workers.[84] This could be an effect of official rhetoric: while the PRI may have moved closer to the interests of the middle classes, it needed to present the regime as the embodiment, or revindication, of the campesinos and workers who fought and died in the Mexican Revolution.[85]

The lack of attention to the middle classes, however, might also reflect the scholars who have analyzed postrevolutionary Mexican history and society. Considering a similar lacuna in historical scholarship on the United States, one historian argues that it is related to a discomfort of the Left, and especially leftist academics, with the category "middle class."[86] Many scholars explicitly describe their work as a political project. Middle-class fears and insecurities do not fit well with a romantic, revolutionary narrative of political change. Many politically motivated scholars who analyze social movements, among other topics, have become invested in these narratives and consequently focus on the poor and marginalized as vehicles for social change from below.[87]

No doubt, the middle classes appear in many studies as artisans, merchants, professionals, bureaucrats, teachers, Catholic activists, students, and countercultural aficionados. Few works, though, explicitly address questions of middle-class formation, politics, or cultures in Mexico. Often historians use the term "middle-class" as a descriptive adjective rather than a historically contingent category requiring analytical engagement. Indeed, some scholars perform strenuous contortions to *not see* the middle-class status of those they study.[88] Theorist Immanuel Wallerstein argues that the middle classes tend to function as a deus ex machina: like the literary device that suddenly—and inexplicably and unsatisfactorily—resolves the plot, they are reified, unexamined, and mystified.[89] Whatever the reason, the politics of writing about the middle classes have shaped the scholarship on modern Mexico, in which the middle classes are conspicuous by their absence.

But the middle classes can be apprehended in the historical record through an array of primary and secondary sources. Newly released government spy reports provide a window onto the political activities of parties, groups, associations, and individuals. These documents come from two intelligence agencies that operated under the Secretaría de Gobernación (Ministry of the Interior): the Directorate of Federal Security and the General Directorate of Political and Social Investigations.[90] While these spy reports offer richly detailed accounts of public meetings and private conversations, excitement over this historical source must be tempered; the reports are sometimes inaccurate, and the analysis they provide often only scratches the surface. Many spies came from the ranks of the police or military, and it was virtually impossible to become an intelligence agent without a personal recommendation from someone within the intelligence agencies. A culture of secrecy pervaded the agencies, and agents were chosen and rewarded for their loyalty rather than their experience or ability in surveillance.[91] In his study of Mexico's intelligence apparatus, Sergio Aguayo describes how reporting agents would sometimes exaggerate the threat posed by groups or individuals in an effort to curry favor with their superiors and justify increased government funds for the Ministry of the Interior.[92] In the late 1970s, the Directorate of Federal Security ordered a psychological study of a sample of its agents whose jobs were to infiltrate organizations and follow individuals. The report was damning: psychologists found that agents had low levels of both formal education and general intelligence, and they described agents as "vain, wasteful, and self-indulgent" as well as "egotistical and superficial."[93] The experts also found that agents were "not worried about societal morals and norms" and had "little contact with reality."[94]

In theory, intelligence organizations should serve the state and not any one party or politician. But in Mexico, the agencies served the PRI and the president.[95] From their beginnings in the 1920s, the intelligence agencies functioned as a political police—shadowing friends and enemies of the regime—and Aguayo describes how their activities often reflected the personal interests and insecurities of the president.[96] In the 1960s, it seems that President Gustavo Díaz Ordaz's anticommunist paranoia sparked a massive growth in the number of DFS agents and informants, from approximately 120 agents with some informants in 1965 to 3,000 agents with 10,000 informants in 1981.[97]

These growing numbers of government spies focused much of their attention on rebellions against the regime, such as the 1968 student movement and the leftist and conservative protests of the 1970s. Agents watched individuals and groups (the list of targets was often full of suggestions from the president and his highest advisors): they eavesdropped on private conversations in streetcars and other public places, as well as infiltrating opposition groups, tapping telephones, intercepting letters and telegrams, and controlling a network of informants.[98] On occasion agents acted on the surveillance information, harassing and even eliminating perceived enemies of the regime.[99]

These intelligence reports, then, often reveal as much about state obsessions as they do about the activities of groups deemed subversive. The documents tell us at least two stories. They capture middle-class political culture, together with the worry that it caused the PRI.

Documents from the presidential archives, which include economic data on consumer credit and taxation, internal political strategy documents, and official speeches and propaganda, provide another important source for studying the middle classes. So, too, do press accounts. This book further benefits from the vibrant tradition of social commentary by public intellectuals, writers, and scholars. These works serve as both primary and secondary sources—primary, because they illustrate the contemporary intellectual climate; secondary, because they often offer important historical analyses. Finally, popular culture, especially hard-boiled detective fiction, offers a unique perspective within contemporary social criticism.

· · ·

Leftist students, conservative car owners, alienated detectives, indebted families, optimistic yuppies, and protesting homeowners: in the late 1960s, these protean middle classes awoke from a dream. For over two decades, they experienced the transition pains of major economic change. Their histories tell the story of how a miracle ended and how the PRI's Institutional Revolution, which had prided itself on the robustness of the middle classes, came undone.

Part 1

On 17 September 1973, one of Mexico's leading industrialists died in a botched kidnapping attempt. The radical urban guerrilla group, Liga Comunista 23 de Septiembre (Communist League 23rd of September), attempted to kidnap Eugenio Garza Sada in order to secure the release of political prisoners, raise funds, and announce the arrival of the Liga as an important player on the national stage. Garza Sada's bodyguard fought back, and the ensuing shoot-out killed the patriarch of the Monterrey Group, one of Mexico's most powerful family dynasties.

A few days later, Luis Echeverría Álvarez, president of Mexico from 1970 to 1976, attended the funeral. He sat in the front row as prominent business leaders blamed him personally for the death of their colleague. These leaders believed the president was too tolerant of the radical Left. From the podium, Ricardo Margáin Zozaya, a representative of the Monterrey Group, accused the president of "encouraging deliberate attacks on the private sector, in order to foment division and hatred between social classes. We have suffered kidnappings, dynamite explosions, bank robberies, destruction and death."* This public excoriation of the president by some of the most powerful economic groups in the country, televised across the nation, was unprecedented in Mexican history.

Perhaps more than any other event, the funeral epitomized the political upheaval of the 1970s. Across the political spectrum, radicals and conservatives challenged the PRI's one-party system. Dramatic rupture between the PRI and the middle classes occurred when university students joined armed guerrilla groups. A more mundane form of protest manifested in the jokes, rumors, and whispered threats of car owners at gas stations.

---

* Agustín, *Tragicomedia mexicana* 2, 89.

These forces collided at the Garza Sada funeral, where the president seemed caught in the middle of escalating tensions between the Left and the Right. The event revealed a weakened PRI, struggling to reestablish its midcentury pact with the middle classes.

1   Rebel Generation

BEING A MIDDLE-CLASS RADICAL, 1971–1976

On 14 March 1975, President Luis Echeverría visited Mexico's leading university to inaugurate the spring semester classes. Only a few years after several massacres of peaceful student protestors by police and military forces, this was a gesture of goodwill to a student population rife with political discontent. In preparation for the presidential visit, workers at the UNAM (National Autonomous University of Mexico) in Mexico City cleaned up the campus, scrubbing graffiti off the buildings. But on the morning of Echeverría's visit, small groups of students nervously attacked the walls once more: "Repudiate the assassin," read one graffito; "LEA out of the UNAM," read another, using the initials of the president's full name, Luis Echeverría Álvarez.[1] Perhaps the most provocative jabs were made by flyers that circulated in the university bus station: they featured an image of Echeverría with a falcon near his head and a puppet of the university rector hanging from his right hand. A chain linked the rector to a gorilla, symbolizing his complicity with the *porra* (individuals and groups funded by the government to intimidate students in the university).[2] The image of the falcon referred to the Halcones, a paramilitary force trained by the city government and responsible for a massacre of students on 10 June 1971. "LEA Halcón, Ave de Rapiña," the graffiti read: Echeverría is a falcon, a bird of prey. Police and riot troops circled the university but did not enter the campus.[3]

In the large auditorium of the medical school, Echeverría spoke to students about his program of *apertura democrática*—a program of "democratic opening" to lower voting ages and grant amnesty to students jailed in the 1960s and 1970s student movements. In turn, students took the microphone and accused the president and the university rector of being responsible for massacres in 1968 and 1971. Echeverría listened to these accusations and then insisted that he had come to establish a dialogue with the students. While some students seemed willing to engage with the president, they were drowned out by boos, hisses, and shouts of "Assassin!" from other, more radical students. Divisions that riddled the UNAM emerged for all to see.

As Echeverría left the auditorium, students crowded the doorway chanting: "Che Che Che Guevara, Echeverría a la chingada [go fuck yourself]!" A large banner greeted the president as he exited: "Echeverría is an assassin; fascism will not prevail; we revolutionary students do not deal with assassins; students do not want dialogue, we do not want opening, we want revolution."[4] A fight broke out between these radical students and those who supported dialogue with Echeverría; rocks flew through the air and one hit the president in the forehead. With difficulty, his bodyguards rushed the president, blood dripping down his face onto his suit, through the riotous crowd.[5]

After the stoning of the president at the UNAM, government spies—some were former police officers, others had worked in government bureaucracies—set about to gather reactions from the student body, sometimes by direct eavesdropping and other times through informants. Many students described Echeverría as valiant for coming to the university. Some accused him of planning the event to generate publicity and claimed it was nothing more than a premeditated farce. Others claimed that the debacle was the work of provocateurs who had infiltrated the Left and purposely pushed the situation too far. The spies also reported that a significant portion of students showed very little interest in the event.[6] Journalists, on the other hand, reported that all sectors of society were calling for an exhaustive investigation to determine those responsible for the shameful acts, and some in society raised the possibility of CIA involvement.[7] The remarkable events on campus demonstrated the difficulty of establishing common ground—between those students interested in dialogue and those who refused to grant Echeverría any legitimacy. The latter accused the former of allowing themselves to be co-opted by Echeverría's symbolic gestures.

The fissures among students extended beyond the UNAM campus. The rebel generation—politically active leftist students in the late 1960s and early 1970s—was divided between moderates and radicals.[8] During the early 1970s, in an environment of political and economic instability, these middle-class students had to decide whether to accept Echeverría's offer of dialogue. To accept would mean letting go of a past in which the PRI's highest-ranking politicians had ordered the massacre of peaceful protesters; to accept would mean accepting that the PRI could change. To refuse would mean rejecting the moral authority of the president and the legitimacy of the one-party system; to refuse would mean disavowing the PRI as the legitimate custodian of the Mexican Revolution. While some students responded to Echeverría's democratic opening by attempting revolution, others attempted reform. Still others sank into resignation.

The middle-class backgrounds of these students defined the parameters of their response, whether it was action or inaction. Some students, ashamed of their middle-class identity, opted to *proletarizarse*, to "become proletarian," as they mobilized workers and shantytown residents. A few students reformulated revolutionary theory so that they themselves—students— would supplant workers or peasants as the vanguard of a socialist revolution, and, within this theoretical framework, formed armed guerrilla groups to overthrow the state. Still others sought to protect their middle-class status and worked for reform. These moderate students worked with the PRI to rebuild bridges between the party and the student population more generally, while demanding material improvements in their schools as well as respect for the rights guaranteed in the 1917 Constitution.

Banishing the Emissaries from the Past

Why was Echeverría in the UNAM in March 1975? His appeal to students was part of his prolonged endeavor to mend the relationship between the PRI and the middle classes. After the 1968 massacre, many within the PRI worried about left-leaning, intellectual middle-class discontent. One consultant to the party described the middle classes as "aggressive, violent, unsatisfied, [and] critical," worrying that they represented a "social bomb whose ultimate consequences are still unforeseeable."[9] In this context, the party chose Echeverría as its candidate in the 1970 elections. He had one foot inside the conservative PRI, owing to his role in the Tlatelolco massacre on 2 October 1968 (as minister of the interior, he condoned the attack on students). But he was also considered a liberal, because his brother-in-law had been jailed in the 1959 railway worker conflict.[10]

Echeverría designed a series of reforms meant to reach out to the students, teachers, and young professionals who had taken to the streets in 1968. His so-called democratic opening granted amnesty for many political prisoners arrested during the student movement. He lowered the voting age as well as the minimum age for congressmen and senators, a move he hoped would placate students and intellectuals. He also sought to increase the political representation of the middle classes. In theory, the CNOP (National Confederation of Popular Organizations) ought to have advocated for the interests of everyone from shopkeepers to civil servants, because it had been created in 1943 to represent them within the PRI's corporatist system. The confederation, however, had become a powerful lobbyist for bureaucrats; many nonbureaucrat members of the middle classes might have felt marginalized within both the CNOP's and the PRI's corporatist structures (indeed, several analysts point to the late 1960s as the beginning of the CNOP's decline).[11] Echeverría attempted to reform the CNOP from within by incorporating new cadres of professionals, often from the ranks of formerly discontented students.[12]

In addition to the democratic opening, the Echeverría administration attempted to reconcile with students through his educational reform program, an ambitious set of initiatives that culminated in the 1973 Federal Law of Education. This program meant a fourteenfold increase in the education budget, the opening of new schools and university campuses, higher salaries for professors, and new financial resources for students, especially scholarships to study abroad.[13] By shoring up support for education, Echeverría and his advisors hoped to appease students.[14]

The president also emphasized his leftist heritage in symbolic ways. He attempted to ingratiate himself with the leftist students and the burgeoning hippie movement and wove indigenous tropes into this image: he had the presidential residence decorated with Mexican furniture and handicrafts and drank *agua de horchata* instead of brandy at official parties. In popular revolutionary style, he referred to his wife, María Esther Zuno de Echeverría, as "la compañera Esther." (She referred to him by his surname.) Echoing her husband's sometimes backfiring efforts, Zuno de Echeverría wore traditional indigenous clothes. This style, though, did not always remind people of Frida Kahlo, as may have been intended, but rather called to mind the elaborate uniforms of waitresses in the middle-brow Sanborns restaurants; consequently, the waitresses were often referred to as "las Esthercitas" (the little Esthers).[15]

Echeverría cast himself as the defender of the weak against imperialism on the international stage. He envisioned Mexico as the leader and protector of the developing world—a radical shift from the first-world ambitions of earlier administrations. During his presidency, which ended in 1976, Mexico welcomed leftist political exiles from other Latin American countries. Echeverría even imagined himself a candidate for secretary-general of the United Nations. But his third-worldism, which coincided with the growing internationalism of the student movement, had greater impact within Mexico than abroad. Some activists accused the president of organizing the Vietnam solidarity protests, to demonstrate the alignment between student demands and official policy.[16] Among leftist students, solidarity with Vietnam was manifest and students drew connections between Ho Chi Minh's guerrilla war and guerrilla movements in Mexico, as demonstrated by this chant connecting the Vietnamese leader with Lucio Cabañas in the state of Guerrero: "Ho Ho Ho Chi Minh; Echeverría go fuck yourself; Lucio Lucio give it to them hard; we will triumph."[17]

Echeverría's rhetoric and reforms marked a significant change in PRI policies—the supposedly all-powerful party had acknowledged its weakness and curbed its power in response to popular pressure. As Porfirio Muñoz Ledo, one of Echeverría's chief advisors, put it, Echeverría was the first president willing to admit that the Mexican Miracle had a darker side: Echeverría was working "to dispel the persistent myth developed over many years of the so-called 'Mexican Miracle,' and not because he [was] unaware of the real achievements which [had] been made, but rather because he [felt] that the persistence of such a myth, in the final analysis, can only favor those sectors that have obtained the greatest benefits from this growth." Muñoz Ledo argued that complacency had given way to self-criticism: "The ritualistic exaltation of the achievements of the government," he said, "is being replaced by a more rigorous analysis of the functioning of institutions."[18]

But the president soon encountered serious resistance within the PRI to these political reforms and symbolic gestures. Old-guard Priístas, under the influence of former president Gustavo Díaz Ordaz and with the support (and funding) of many leading businessmen, organized against the president. CNOP veterans did not welcome the infusion of leftist students into their ranks and were angered by cuts to their discretionary budgets. Furthermore, Echeverría created new structures for citizens to file complaints against government administrators. These reforms were designed to limit corruption in the bureaucracies, especially the solicitation of bribes.[19] This could not have sat well with those who had used bribes to accrue small fortunes.

Echeverría's compromise potential was doomed from the outset. He had been charged with resolving the tensions between the PRI and the middle classes. Whenever he attempted to do so, though, he angered sectors within the PRI. In the context of cold war politics, conservative sectors of the PRI rejected rapprochement with leftist students and intellectuals, whom they accused of communism. Caught between student discontent and stubborn resistance within his own party, Echeverría had little room to maneuver. This became undeniable on the afternoon of 10 June 1971, when the clandestine paramilitary group, the Halcones (Falcons), killed fifty students at a peaceful demonstration in Mexico City, which came to be known as the Corpus Christi Massacre, or simply 10 June.

The demonstration had been organized as a show of solidarity by Mexico City students with counterparts in the northern state of Nuevo León, where a heated political situation had erupted involving the state governor, the university administration, and the private sector industrialists regarding the composition of the University Council. That conflict was resolved by 5 June, but student leaders in Mexico City decided to go ahead with the demonstration anyway, hoping to rekindle the student movement in the capital, which had suffered a severe setback after the 1968 massacre. In the UNAM, the National Polytechnic Institute (IPN), and the *preparatorias*, signs and banners invited students to the march: "The student movement ended in Tlatelolco, but the movement in Nuevo León is just beginning," said one. "The assassins of students can't be our leaders," argued another.[20]

On the afternoon of that day, from 3:30 p.m. on, students gathered at the National School of Biological Sciences in the city center.[21] Specialized units of riot police known as *granaderos* (literally, "grenadiers") watched from across the road, shouting insults and trying to provoke the students. As the number of protestors grew by the thousands, one government spy described a red sea of banners and flyers. The protestors called for an end to repression and declared their support for the students in Nuevo León. Busloads of *granaderos* arrived and anti-insurrection tanks patrolled the streets. The police announced they would block the march; students responded that they would not be stopped. The march began at 5:10 p.m., with more than five thousand students and workers moving toward the Monument to the Revolution. The *granaderos* threw tear gas at the marchers and ordered them to disperse.[22]

One thousand Halcones arrived at 5:15 p.m. and began shooting into the air. The clandestine paramilitary group had been formed in 1968, organized and subsidized by the Mexico City government through its various bureaucracies, such as the Department of Parks and Gardens. It seems that between 1968 and 1971 the Department of Parks and Gardens had received disproportionate budget increases that were funneled directly to the Halcones; the city government supplied their material needs, and their salaries varied according to their courage and savageness. In 1968, the Halcones comprised seven hundred members; by 1971 they boasted one thousand. Military men headed the group and recruited members from city unions—such as the police or the cleaning services—as well as city gangs. Other members had been taxi drivers, soldiers, or boxers. At their base in the San Juan de Aragón zoo, they were trained in gymnastics, karate, kendo, and firearms. Many were given fake credentials and student cards and entered the UNAM and IPN campuses to infiltrate student groups as agitators and provocateurs.[23]

As the crowd pressed forward, groups of students were squeezed onto the surrounding side streets, where they encountered the Halcones. The regular city police observed, passively, from the sidelines as the *granaderos* and Halcones beat the students. The Halcones attacked students with guns, bats, cattle prods, bayonets, and other instruments. When they cornered a group of students in a side street, another group of students organized a counterattack to rescue their friends; a gun battle erupted. The

Halcones retreated and the students sought refuge with the injured in the nearby National Teachers College. Fifty students had been killed.[24]

By 8:00 p.m., according to the reports of government spies, there was general calm. Demonstrators had abandoned the streets and the riot police patrolled the Zócalo, the city's main plaza, to prevent students from staging a protest. At the Teachers College, students insisted on accompanying ambulances. They wrote down the names of the paramedics and took pictures of the injured. From the outset, there was an urgent sense that they needed to document proof of repression; almost immediately rumors circulated that corpses had gone missing. Students followed the dead and injured to the hospitals, to ensure that their bodies did not disappear. Many of the demonstrators headed to the UNAM campus, where the Comités de lucha (Committees of Struggle, formed during 1968 to shape the student movement) held emergency meetings. In the immediate aftermath of the repression, families and friends of missing students desperately sought their loved ones. They held meetings in parking lots and tried to determine the last known locations of missing students. Small groups of five or six set off to search hospitals and city offices for the missing.[25]

That evening, an outraged Echeverría appeared on television. "If you are infuriated, I am even more so," he told Mexicans. Five days later, he fired the city's mayor and police chief.[26] The Halcones were disbanded. Importantly, the mayor, Alonso Martínez Domínguez, had ties to the old-guard PRI factions and had worked against Echeverría since the beginning of his administration; the 10 June massacre was, in part, a strategy to undermine Echeverría's entreaties to students.[27] The events of 10 June provided Echeverría with a politically expedient opportunity to eliminate a rival.

When Echeverría announced the dismissal of the mayor and police chief on television and radio, he described Mexico as living in uncertainty. Truth and clarity, he said, were in danger of disappearing. He urged respect for the government, the student, the common citizen, the reporter, the intellectual, and the teacher. Echeverría attempted to calm the nation by declaring that "we will close the door on emissaries from the past," referring to old-guard Priístas such as Martínez Domínguez.[28]

Echeverría's decision to fire the mayor and police chief represented a major change in Mexican politics. After all, in 1968 the PRI had refused to acknowledge that a much larger massacre had even occurred; indeed, evidence of the repression had been more or less erased in time for the Olympic games. When he dismissed the mayor and police chief, Echeverría offered an olive branch to the students. This gesture, doubtless combined with a grim fear of massacre in the streets of the capital city, dissipated the student protest. Students would not mobilize again en masse, forcefully and consistently, until the late 1980s.

That said, Echeverría's dismissal of the mayor and police chief did not eliminate student discontent. The violence and repression of the late 1960s and early 1970s had exposed the corruption, inequality, paternalism, and antidemocratic foundations of the so-called Mexican Miracle. Certain middle-class groups who before 1968 might have ignored the darker side of the PRI's system perceived it more readily in the 1970s. Echeverría was keenly aware of this small but important shift and aimed his rhetoric—and reforms—at those who, in the words of cultural critic José Agustín, felt as though they might have awakened from a dream.[29]

With his democratic opening, Echeverría sent a message to detractors on both the left and the right, inside and outside the party: the executive power had established a dialogue, and protest must be directed through this new channel. By banishing the "emissaries from the past," Echeverría proclaimed an end to the old way of doing politics—repression—and announced that politics would now embrace dialogue. Repression continued but more subtly, at least in the main cities (massacres of peaceful demonstrators ceased).[30] Implicit in Echeverría's democratic opening, however, was another form of oppression: once again, the PRI was attempting to define and delimit the parameters of politics.

Fissures within the Student Population

After the 10 June massacre, many moderate students expressed anger, uncertainty, and apathy toward the student movement and its leaders. No doubt, after the massacre some students continued to participate in the movement and others became increasingly radicalized, but many students accepted, if tentatively, Echeverría's olive branch. In an article for a university newspaper, one student expressed hope and skepticism: "[Echeverría] seems like an honest man but, you know, it's a question of waiting to see if his actions live up to his words." This student noted, however, that with Echeverría's banishment of emissaries from the past, Mexico had entered a period of calm.[31]

Ambivalence toward the student movement within some sectors of the UNAM had, of course, existed before 10 June. In the days before the massacre, government spies had reported the opinions of anonymous UNAM students. Many students, according to the spies, had opposed the demonstration. These students argued that it was too dangerous to take to the streets with riot police waiting for them; they claimed it would only lead to blood, tears, and prison. They accused the leaders of the student movement of wanting to tell heroic anecdotes about confrontation with police. Leaders, they claimed, had felt frustrated by the floundering student movement following the 1968 massacre and wanted to provoke another confrontation with police so they might return to the UNAM campus as heroes. They resented how leaders lured students to the demonstration with slogans; once there, the students would likely face police bayonets and clubs. It was not worth it, they said, to be beaten, go to prison, and lose a year of study—only to satisfy the "vanity of a few."[32]

After the massacre, government spies continued to report on anonymous student opinion, canvassing students in the UNAM and other schools and through their informants. Some students, the spies reported, argued that because the situation in Nuevo León had been resolved prior to the march, the tragic events of 10 June were the result of agitation by the Communist Party, whose influence among the student body was waning ("que no tenía bandera"). They accused the Communist Party and student leaders of wanting to provoke conflict between students and the police in order to infuse the student movement with new life.[33]

Divisions between moderate students and their more radical peers became sharper during the 1970s.[34] Some students were frustrated by the growing militancy of the radical student leaders. For example, in the Committees of Struggle, the more radical students argued that they should organize a seminar on guerrilla warfare.[35] And in one of the *preparatorias*, government spies reported teachers giving lessons in guerrilla tactics: in chemistry they taught students how to make Molotov cocktails and nitroglycerin bombs; in history they asked students to do projects on Marxism and the Mexican student movement; in languages, they taught Russian and Czech; in psychology, they discussed how to resist different methods of torture.[36] At some demonstrations, individuals actively recruited students to join urban and rural guerrilla groups.[37]

A few weeks after 10 June, government spies found an open letter to students circulating in the UNAM, supposedly written by a former Halcón. He asked the students for forgiveness and a kind of intervention: "Save us from ourselves! You are the only social class who can, at this moment, put strong pressure on the government so that we will not be forced to kill our own children. When you guys decide to act, we will help you."[38] This letter underscores the challenges of using spy reports. It is plausible that a former Halcón penned it, and it is consistent with other testimonies by former Halcones arrested after bank robberies. However, student activists may have written and circulated it to generate support for their movement, since the letter addresses students as a powerful force for change. It suggests that they might count on the support of well-trained former paramilitaries who might have access to arms. Above all else, it gives the students the moral high ground, confirming their status as victims of repression and conferring upon them the capacity to forgive. It might offer a glimpse into how activist students perceived themselves and designed creative strategies to foment support among the wider student population.

While some considered taking up arms, moderate students accepted Echeverría's olive branch and began to organize for improvements in their schools. For many, their protest was fundamentally about middle-class insecurity and responsibility, and their demands were liberal democratic in nature, not radical.[39] After all, university and *preparatoria* students either belonged to or aspired to join the status quo. Taking advantage of Echeverría's increased education budget, they demanded more teachers and staff; higher salaries and better training for teachers; buses for the schools; more scholarships; more books, calculators, and other equipment; and new classrooms. They also demanded more participation in decisions about the budget and the curriculum.[40] These moderate students wanted reform, not revolution. According to one historian, most students felt they had an obligation to ensure that political leaders acted responsibly and for the betterment of conditions for all; their middle-class status "filled them with a sense of purpose and obligation to the social order."[41]

Echeverría's reforms mollified many of the student protestors. By creating new jobs in the state bureaucracies and increasing funds for education, along with some political reforms, the president addressed the material and political concerns of many students—some of whom were incorporated not only into mainstream channels of negotiation but also into the PRI itself. In doing so, Echeverría continued one of the PRI's most entrenched hegemonic strategies: to co-opt dissent. Since the 1920s the PRI and its precursors had sought to incorporate dissent into the party, thereby undermining support for radical change. Echeverría's reforms were part of this longer tradition.[42] Through the democratic opening and other strategies, Echeverría preyed upon divisions between the students and sought to bring many of the more moderate, reform-minded students (back) into the party. The Left excoriated this tactic, as it undermined their support among students. For example, the urban guerrillas, discussed below, described education reform as a bourgeois project that enabled capitalist exploitation.[43] But, despite many points of contention, there was a good deal of overlap between the PRI and moderate student protestors. (Importantly, only some sectors of the PRI and some sectors of the student population shared this common ground; the consensus was neither stable nor all-encompassing. The president may have espoused a conciliatory rhetoric, but he continued to rely upon repressive tactics when he met resistance). Reform-minded students negotiated and compromised with the president and his administration, often benefiting from the process.[44]

While some students accepted Echeverría's olive branch, others "dropped out." As the student movement waned, some were drawn to the burgeoning countercultural movement. After the massacres, one participant described a "terrible sense of frustrated impotence."[45] Into this bleak landscape danced the *jipitecas*. Unlike the moderate students who worked within the framework of Echeverría's education reform and democratic opening, the hippies rejected the status quo and abandoned interaction with the state. As historian Eric Zolov argues, the counterculture offered an escape from familial and societal pressures, especially in terms of patriarchal and religious values.[46] The hippies repudiated society, retreating from traditional politics.

Many in the Mexican Left criticized this move. Cultural critic José Agustín described Mexico City in the early 1970s as alive with *peñas*, little cafés or bars where folk musicians performed. At meetings, artists and singers attacked the middle classes (usually using the term "bourgeoisie"), satirized Echeverría, and made vague gestures toward guerrilla leaders such as Lucio Cabañas in Mexico and others abroad.[47] Agustín decried this urban middle-class phenomenon as a shallow protest and accused its followers of believing that they had done their revolutionary duty by sitting down and listening to protest songs.[48] And leftist activists at the UNAM argued that Echeverría preferred the youth to channel their discontent through cultural expression and lifestyle because "the state prefers a drug-addicted youth to a revolutionary youth."[49]

Debates over the significance of these cultural politics turned on the class identities of the hippies. They rejected their own privilege, a move that some leftist critics found politically troubling. The hippie movement had emerged in the industrialized first world, where it was an expression of malaise and anomie among the middle classes of Anglo/Franco North America and western Europe. While the middle-class Mexican hippies might have challenged gender norms and traditional authority, many leftists questioned what privilege, exactly, they were rejecting. Leftists emphasized the irony of mental colonialism in the act of imitating American protest: "What great [material] abundance can the Mexican hippies [claim to] deny? Against which high technology do they protest in the name of love?" asked cultural critic Carlos Monsiváis.[50]

Although many students had accepted Echeverría's olive branch or had dropped out of traditional politics into the counterculture, the PRI remained preoccupied with middle-class leftist discontent. Other students had been politicized by continuing state-sponsored violence; they rejected what they saw as empty rhetoric or symbolic gestures by the president. But the lines dividing moderates, hippies, and radicals were not rigidly drawn: most of them came from the same middle-class world, and individuals often engaged in different kinds of protest. Molotov cocktails and marijuana, as Zolov describes, were often found side by side at house parties in the 1960s and 1970s.[51]

The Shame of Being Middle Class

Two days after the 10 June massacre, the National Teachers College, where the students had taken refuge from the Halcones, was closed. A floral offering lay on its front steps. Banners decorated the front doors: "Mr. President, we have been familiar with this dialogue you propose since Tlatelolco 2 October" and "Honor the dead students. A minute of silence—no; a life of struggle—yes."[52] Many radical students took this "life of struggle" to factories and shantytowns. They left the universities and sought contact with workers and residents to organize a broader coalition against the PRI. When they did so, their middle-class backgrounds generated tension for the radicals. While reform-minded students sought to protect their privilege and hippies rebelled against the accoutrements of their class status, radicals faced difficult questions about revolutionary "authenticity." Outside the arena of the university, they encountered resentment from workers and from the urban poor, who accused students of casting themselves as leaders of the revolution, of acting as though they owned the Marxist knowledge necessary to make revolution.[53]

These students also confronted their own existential insecurities. Questions of moral legitimacy arose, as the radicals fretted over their relationship to the Marxist or socialist revolution they wanted to foment. Obsessions over authenticity begin with the act of reading Marx: a certain amount of education is required to grapple with *Das Kapital*. (In the late 1960s and early 1970s, leftist students began to read Marx in earnest, in both informal reading groups and in their classes. Changes in the curriculum of the economics faculty at the UNAM gave Marx a sudden prominence in the syllabus.)[54] But, within a classical Marxist framework, it is ultimately the workers (or, in a Maoist framework, the peasants) who are at the forefront of historical change; ideological identity and class position are at odds. Radicals, militants, and the denizens of the Far Left were not proud to be middle class. Indeed, according to revolutionary theory in the 1960s and 1970s, a middle-class individual would have to renounce his or her background in order to develop a revolutionary consciousness. Radical agronomist and Guinean and Cape Verdean independence leader Amílcar Cabral argued this in an important speech in Cuba in 1966: "The petite bourgeoisie has only one choice: to strengthen its revolutionary consciousness, to reject the temptations of becoming more bourgeois . . . to identify itself with the working classes." Then Cabral went further: "The revolutionary petite bourgeoisie must be capable of committing suicide as a class in order to be reborn as revolutionary workers."[55] In Mexico, radical students undertook various strategies to shed their class condition; committing class suicide meant living in a turmoil of doubt, shame, arrogance, and self-loathing.

Groups of students, sometimes organized by the Committees of Struggle, channeled their political activism into proletarian neighborhoods. They went to the "lost cities," the large shantytowns on the periphery of the capital and other cities. These neighborhoods often lacked basic services such as electricity and clean water. The public health situation was dire.[56] The contrast between the shantytowns and the students' home neighborhoods cannot be overemphasized, nor can the rampant paradoxes created. Groups of students would often meet at an outlying metro station and take buses to the shantytowns. En route they sang protest songs against the government. Other times they would drive to the neighborhoods in cars, sometimes luxury brands like Mercedes Benz (although it is most likely that few students came from truly wealthy families). Once they arrived, they helped build or improve houses and gave out clothes and toys. Students who had been trained as engineers worked on the design and layout of newly formed squatter settlements. As they did this work, they told residents that the government had forgotten them and that it was only the students who worried about them.[57]

Students in the *preparatorias* and universities either came from or aspired to join the middle classes. Education enabled upward mobility, and during the midcentury Miracle it had become an important marker of privilege, as only a minority of citizens completed basic schooling. In the context of such inequality, students who made it to postsecondary institutions were either maintaining their middle-class condition or entering the middle classes (though a small number would have belonged to the wealthy).[58] Through education, students acquired cultural capital; as theorist Pierre Bourdieu argues, education is a material and symbolic good that is sought after and exchanged, ultimately conferring power and status.[59] When they entered the shantytowns, students became uncomfortably aware of their privilege.

In the shantytowns, questions about the complicated position of the middle classes in the revolution emerged (not the Mexican Revolution, whose legacy the PRI claimed to represent, but the socialist revolution that students and residents were making). At one community meeting, residents complained about how these students imagined themselves as the leaders of the revolution. And one of the community leaders accused the intellectuals of claiming theoretical ownership of Marxism: "These illusions are a result of the Marxism taught in the universities, because Marxism is in the hands of the petty bourgeoisie or middle class."[60] Faced with this criticism, students responded by attempting to deny their middle-class condition. They decided that it was necessary to "live like and with the working class in proletarian neighborhoods."[61]

Conflict over class identity also erupted when students and leftist leaders contemplated forming a political party and entering electoral politics.

This was a significant move toward engagement with the state. In a series of meetings in November 1971, prominent intellectuals, student leaders, and labor activists—including Octavio Paz, Carlos Fuentes, Demetrio Vallejo, Carlos Sánchez Cárdenas, Heberto Castillo, and Tomás Cervantes Cabeza de Vaca—gathered to discuss forming a political party. In these meetings, student leaders admitted a general feeling of frustration within the movement; they described weariness among the student population, who, they claimed, were tired of being manipulated by existing political groups.[62] At one of the meetings, a cobbler challenged the intellectuals present to "set aside their vanity" and approach the workers and the campesinos as equals, so that these groups might teach the intellectuals about revolutionary struggle. Students and intellectuals, he argued, had much to learn from workers. In response to this challenge, labor activist Heberto Castillo argued that the best option would be for students, intellectuals, and some sectors of the bourgeoisie to integrate into the worker sector, to *proletarizarse*, or "proletarianize themselves."[63]

When students and intellectuals faced class resentment from workers and the urban poor, their response was to purge themselves of their class identity, to become proletarians. This solution was met with skepticism. No doubt, class structures can change over time, and some individuals might lose privilege. But moving down from the middle classes to the lower classes as a political choice is hardly the same as being forced down by economic realities. The complex matrix of cultural components that make up a social class, such as education, values, and expectations, cannot simply be discarded. Leaving aside the question of whether it is possible to proletarianize oneself, middle-class leftists attempted to do so in various ways. It was part of a political strategy to challenge the authoritarianism of the PRI that they embraced after other forms of political action—such as student demonstrations and protests—had met with repression.

In his memoir, former guerrilla Alberto Ulloa Bornemann describes how activists competed among themselves to be less bourgeois. Some strategies were relatively superficial, such as his adoption of "'proletarian' attire"—denim shirts of the sort worn by railroad workers.[64] Other strategies involved inconvenience and discomfort. For example, Ulloa Bornemann elected to take the bus rather than driving his car, even when it entailed catching three buses followed by a long walk to attend his guerrilla warfare training sessions. "All of these complications," he wrote, "stemmed from a guilty eagerness to proletarianize myself and to provide an unsolicited demonstration of revolutionary political decisiveness in the face of [a fellow guerrilla's] accusations of my petty-bourgeois behavior."[65] In another instance, Ulloa Bornemann, dirty and dusty after changing a flat tire, expressed relief when he washed his hands and face in a nearby stream; his companion "went nuts, going on and on about how I should not clean up and should avoid all such 'bourgeois impulses.'"[66]

At times, the ways in which middle-class students tried to "be poor" provoked disbelief among those whom they were trying to organize. For example, Ulloa Bornemann describes how the campesinos they were working with looked on in "astonishment" when two activists opted to return to Mexico City by bus rather than by automobile, at night and with a newborn child.[67] In a chronicle of political movements in proletarian neighborhoods, public intellectual Elena Poniatowska describes the work of university students in the Rubén Jaramillo neighborhood in the state of Morelos. There, students sold their newspaper *El Chingadazo* (which roughly translates as "The Big Punch" but also carries the obscene connotation of "The Big Fuck") on street corners, shouting: "Buy your *chingadazo*; thirty cents, a *chingadazo*." Residents, although smiling when they heard this, commented to Poniatowska: "With all their education they end up shouting obscenities on the street corner; just because we speak like that, doesn't mean they have to."[68] These students faced the daunting task of convincing the workers and urban poor (as well as themselves) of their authenticity.

Armed Rebellion

The most radical students formed urban guerrilla groups. Like the students who organized in the factories and shantytowns, the guerrillas had been politicized by continuing state-sponsored repression and the apparent elimination of legal means of social change. The guerrillas rejected Echeverría's olive branch, turning to violence to achieve a socialist and egalitarian society. Clandestine revolutionary guerrilla activity erupted in the streets of Mexico's main cities during the early and mid-1970s. Bombs went off in banks and bomb threats disrupted events; men and women assaulted city police officers and stole their weapons; groups of students, divorced housewives, and workers robbed pharmacies, "expropriating" money for their revolutionary aims; and factories became sites of intense political struggle as students, who had joined groups such as the Liga Comunista 23 de Septiembre (Communist League 23rd of September), clashed with private security and the police while they distributed pamphlets and newsletters to workers. Though only a very small number of students joined guerrilla cells (the Liga likely had no more than five hundred members), they acquired national significance through their dramatic acts.[69]

The Far Left guerrillas came of age during an international moment when decolonization movements inspired middle-class youth around the world. Régis Debray's *Revolution in the Revolution?* was read in Latin America and beyond and became a manual for a struggle based upon armed insurrection.[70] The Cuban Revolution, Salvador Allende's Path to Socialism in Chile, and the Sandinista Revolution in Nicaragua animated leftists across Latin America—and, in the process, generated high expectations for social change.[71] In Mexico, these high expectations generated tensions for many radicals who confronted disturbing contradictions between their class background and their Marxist or Maoist political ideologies.

The Far Left guerrillas attempted to resolve the tension between their class position and their ideology by reformulating revolutionary theory. They proposed what they called the university-factory thesis (*tesis universidad-fábrica*).[72] In their analysis, the university became an arena of capitalist mass production, another sector of the economy alongside extraction and manufacturing. According to the thesis, moderate students ("bourgeois democrats") who participated in Echeverría's democratic opening and education reform were the enemy: "bourgeois democrats—always conciliatory and opportunistic with regard to the one-party system—argue that students are petit bourgeois; bourgeois democrats emphasize the class origin of the students and the 'democratic' and 'progressive' character of the student movement as a fight for 'respect for the 1917 Constitution and bourgeois law.'"[73] In contrast, the university-factory thesis posited the university as a factory; education was the commodity produced. Students, who had previously simply consumed this commodity, became, in the late 1960s and early 1970s, workers who produced it. Students were transformed from passive consumers into producers through their participation in seminars, in social service, in practicums, and in laboratories; in the university-factory, students and professors were the primary labor force.[74] Through this reformulation of revolutionary theory, students joined the proletariat: "students are part of the proletariat, and as such have the same needs and face the same fundamental problems as the rest of the working class."[75] The university-factory thesis proposed a new revolutionary protagonist: the middle-class student. In this regard, the guerrilla groups were more creative than those who advocated proletarianization.

Many members of guerrilla groups had first participated in reformist politics; they began their careers as students demanding constitutional rights. One example from the hundreds of arrests illustrates a typical process of politicization. The Peruvian doctor "Esteban" (his alias), who was arrested in late 1973, testified that he had moved to Mexico City to study medicine in 1966.[76] His father had wanted him to study in Spain, where he believed there was less chance of his son's being corrupted by leftist political activism. Esteban, though, wanted to go to Mexico, which he considered a socialist country.[77]

Esteban did not participate directly in the student movement, for fear of being deported, but by 1972 he had graduated from medical school and found himself economically pressured because his father, who had been sending him money, had passed away. The economic crisis meant few available jobs; Esteban was forced to take work as a nurse. He married "Luisa" (alias), a Mexican from the state of Guerrero, who shared his belief that worldwide social change must occur through violent means. In 1973, Esteban was working for free in a clinic in Nezahaulcóyotl, a working-class area of Mexico City, when he met "Ernesto" (alias), a fellow Peruvian with whom he discussed the political situation in their home country. Esteban had been involved with leftist groups at the San Marcos University in Peru, but he had felt frustrated because, in his view, they focused on propaganda at the expense of concrete actions. After a number of casual meetings, Ernesto told Esteban that he was part of a clandestine revolutionary organization in Mexico; shortly thereafter Esteban and Luisa joined the Liga. He treated injured members in a network of clandestine surgical clinics throughout the city and with Luisa distributed propaganda and attended meetings in middle-class neighborhoods such as Tlatelolco. The cell-like structure of the Liga prevented members from knowing more than a handful of others. Only after awhile did Esteban realize that his brother-in-law, a student in economics at the UNAM, was the director of the Liga in Mexico City.[78]

On 30 November 1973, the city police attempted to detain five individuals in a downtown neighborhood of the capital city. There was a gunfight on the street, killing one police officer. The five fled, leaving behind a suitcase containing surgical equipment and various revolutionary political documents. From this evidence, police arrested a few members of the Liga, including Esteban.[79]

Much of the information about the Liga and other groups comes from the interrogation of captured members. Often acquired by the use of torture, these testimonies must be read with caution. While it may be impossible to ever gauge the truth of such accounts, they do illustrate the realm of the plausible. They reveal what those captured believed the Ministry of the Interior agents wanted to hear; they also reveal what the agents considered plausible—at least plausible enough to send these reports to their superiors.[80]

The ultimate goal of most of the urban guerrilla groups was to overthrow the government and install a socialist system in Mexico.[81] One of these groups had actually received training in North Korea. In a press release in March 1971, the PRI announced the capture of nineteen guerrilla fighters, including three women, who belonged to the Revolutionary Action Movement (Movimiento de Acción Revolucionaria, or MAR). According to the press release, the goal of this group was to implement a Marxist-Leninist regime. They had received training near Pyongyang. Their contact with North Korea began through cultural exchange events and the embassies of North Korea and the USSR in Mexico. In October 1968, they traveled to West Berlin, crossed over to East Berlin, and went to the North Korean embassy, where they were given North Korean passports. They traveled to Moscow and continued to Pyongyang, where they trained in the arts of sabotage, firearms, explosives, terrorism, robbery, and guerrilla warfare. They returned to Mexico City in 1969 and divided themselves into three groups: robberies, recruitment, and training schools. They also established a guerrilla school in the Roma neighborhood. They were caught with a significant amount of equipment, including money, guns, automatic rifles, stolen cars, short-wave radios, wireless communication devices, video cameras, mimeograph machines, and binoculars. They also had surgical equipment, official uniforms and badges, wigs, and fake mustaches.[82]

Some members of these groups had the financial resources to fund the purchase of dynamite, detonators, and other bomb-building equipment. The bombs helped to distract police while the insurgents robbed banks and businesses to acquire money to purchase more arms. Other tactics included the kidnapping and ransoming of wealthy public figures. According to the unpublished testimony of one former member, in 1973 the Liga planned an operation called "Asalto al Cielo" (Assault on the Sky). This plan involved a series of "spectacular actions" such as kidnapping prominent targets including Anthony Duncan Williams, the British consul; Nadine Chaval, the daughter of the Belgian ambassador to Mexico; Eugenio Garza Sada, patriarch of the powerful Monterrey Group, which represented private sector business owners; Fernando Aranguren, a wealthy young businessman; and Antonio Fernández, an important functionary in the Modelo beer company, which had been in labor conflict with its workers. In 1976, they unsuccessfully attempted to kidnap Margarita López Portillo, the sister of the president-elect, José López Portillo. The audacity of this last attempt met with outrage and was followed by repression sufficient to end the Liga.[83]

The repression was carried out by the Brigada Blanca, a paramilitary police force similar to the Halcones and created expressly to fight the Liga.[84] Agents were told to get information "by whatever means."[85] Often relying upon torture, the security forces interrogated captured Liga members about these kidnappings and future plans. They wanted to know about the ideology of the guerrilla group, internal ideological disputes, relations with other clandestine groups, funding sources, distribution of funds, and the funds needed to sustain basic operations. They also questioned captured members about their support among workers and students.[86]

The urban guerrillas had ties to similar groups in Latin America and elsewhere. An intelligence report detailing the activities of a young couple from Mexico City, Alfonso and Jazmín, illustrates how this international context informed many urban guerrillas and set them apart from their rural counterparts. In April 1971, intelligence agents intercepted a love letter from Alfonso to Jazmín, who was studying English in New York City. After professing his love and erotic desire, he asked her to buy guns and books on guerrilla campaigns and Far Left ideologies. One week later, when government spies arrested Alfonso and searched their Mexico City apartment, they found a mimeograph, walkie-talkies, tape recorders, maps, and "communist propaganda."[87]

Alfonso and Jazmín saw themselves as part of an international revolutionary vanguard, not a provincial Mexican movement. Their self-fashioning did not always square with their Maoist-inspired ideology, and sometimes led to tensions with the contemporaneous rural guerrilla movements in Mexico. For instance, Alfonso and Jazmín, together with colleagues, made a film about Genaro Vázquez Rojas, one of Mexico's most prominent rural guerrilla leaders, intending to showcase it at a youth film festival in West Germany. If these urban guerrillas sought membership in an international cultural politics, their rural counterparts had other things on their minds. While urban guerrillas often turned to their counterparts in the countryside in search of support, training, approval, and legitimacy, they also derided the rural guerrillas as unsophisticated and lacking ideology.[88]

The period of guerrilla insurgency in Mexico—and Latin America more generally—still needs more historical attention.[89] Each individual formed political beliefs and joined groups in his or her own way, although many had been active in or had contact with the student movement. A number of guerrilla fighters were murdered, tortured, jailed, or disappeared. Almost all of the urban guerrilla groups were made up of middle-class youth disposed to sacrifice their lives to redress conditions of exploitation in Mexico.

The urban guerrilla groups belong to a national history of the middle classes. They also belong to a history of the rebel generation, alongside the more moderate students who accepted Echeverría's olive branch, the student leaders who continued to organize in the student movement, the hippies who retreated from politics into the countercultural movement, and the activists who organized in shantytowns and among workers. These students and former students all struggled with their middle-class identities, and it shaped their decisions and strategies, as well as their desires and their shame.

The history that emerges here is one of self-doubt, anxiety, and contradictory paths. Indeed, many students felt caught in the middle, frustrated by the political extremes. A ballad called "Los delirantes" (The delirious) handed out in the main streets of Mexico City in November 1973 captures this sentiment, pointing to the "delirium" and "insolence" of both the Left and the Right. Some of its verses include:

LOS DELIRANTES

Nuestro gobierno ha auspiciado
El diálogo y la apertura
Pues sabe que así asegura
La paz que hemos conservado
No todos han aceptado
La democrática norma
Y a veces la prensa informa
De varios enfrentamientos
De fondo y también de forma

Una izquierda delirante
—Y que no es toda la izquierda—
Por sus actos nos recuerda
Vieja línea anarquizante
Una agitación constante
Mueve esta banda anarquista
Con método terrorista,
Asalta, roba y secuestra
Y da una imagen siniestra
A la izquierda progresista

Cuando un grupo delincuente
Asesinó a un empresario
Que era un hombre extraordinario
Filántropo y eminente
Quiso el Sr. Presidente
Asociarse al común duelo
Tratando de dar consuelo

En el triste funeral
Al que asistió el presidente
Habló en un tono insolente
Un lider empresarial
Y al gobierno nacional
Culpó de gran tolerancia
Con la extrema militancia
De los grupos izquierdistas

Hay derechas delirantes
Como izquierdilla insolante

¿Castigo? A los delirantes
Sean de izquierda o derecha
Pero no abrir más la brecha
Entre pobres y pudientes[90]

THE DELIRIOUS

Our government has sponsored
Dialogue and an opening
In order to maintain
A peace that we have conserved
Not all have accepted
The norm of democracy
And sometimes the press reports
On various confrontations
Both profound and superficial

The delirious Left
—Not all the Left—
With their actions remind us
Of old anarchists
And constant agitation
Out with this anarchist gang
And their terrorist methods
Of assault, robbery, and kidnapping
That give a sinister image
To the progressive Left

When a group of delinquents
Murdered a businessman
Who was an extraordinary man
An eminent man and philanthropist
The president wanted
To share the common grief
And tried to give his condolences

At the sad funeral
Which the president attended
A business leader
Spoke in an insolent tone
And blamed the government
For being too tolerant
Of the extreme militancy
Of leftist groups

Just as parts of the Right are delirious
Some of the Left is insolent

Who to punish? All the delirious
Be they on the Left or the Right
But don't open any more the breach
Between the poor and the rich

While the source of this ballad is unknown (it might have been produced and circulated by members of Echeverría's administration to generate sympathy for the president), the lyrics speak to the frustration felt by those caught between the Far Left and the Far Right. It would capture the frustration of the president's allies, too, as they were caught between political extremes. Starting in 1973, in the aftermath of Garza Sada's murder by the Liga Comunista 23 de Septiembre and the "sad funeral" described by the ballad, the president faced mounting recalcitrance from the political Right. Throughout his presidency, Echeverría struggled to find a compromise between political extremes, but by 1975, when he visited the UNAM, he was unable to create common ground among students.

Toward a Critical History of the Rebel Generation

The middle-class background of the leftist students, and the tensions it generated, is an important part of the history of the rebel generation. Given the educational inequality in 1970s Mexico, there can be no doubt that the vast majority of university students belonged to the middle classes (or, by virtue of attending university, were entering the middle classes). The public intellectual Elena Poniatowska's collection of testimonies concerning the 1968 student movement, now a classic, abounds with examples of the privilege enjoyed by the students and the resentment it generated among some members of the broader public. "They're so thick between the ears! What a laugh—politicizing workers!" said one student.[91] "Workers don't know the first thing about anything," said another participant.[92] A bus driver, however, complained, "I didn't get any kind of formal education because my folks couldn't afford to send me to school. But if education nowadays is the sort that produces students like that, I'm glad I didn't go to school. I've never in my life seen such disrespectful, vulgar, foul-tongued people."[93] Likewise, a restaurant owner felt that students should be grateful for their privilege: "University students are the future solid middle class of the Mexican Republic. So what reason do they have to be doing all this?"[94] At a demonstration in 1968, students carried a banner with the following offer, which, depending on one's perspective, could be considered generous or condescending: "Free tuition for *granaderos* [riot police] enrolling in literacy classes."[95]

While former student activists and former guerrillas have willingly discussed the class tensions that pervaded leftist politics in the 1960s and 1970s, these tensions are not privileged in academic and popular analyses of this history. Scholarly reluctance to analyze the students as middle-class historical actors might be connected to a reflexive association of "middle class" with conservative politics or the status quo (as though the term itself were an insult, as it was for many radicals at the time). But students' struggles to square their class status with their politics shaped the everyday history of the rebel generation. Their doubts and frustrations shed light on the political context in which they lived and help to explain the decisions that they made. It is especially important to tease out this tension and turmoil, because the student movement has become one of the most written about events in modern Mexican history. Accounts of the movement, most of them focused on the events of 1968, exert a major influence on how we understand the rebel generation more broadly—from the moderate to the radical students, from the countercultural hippies to the armed guerrillas. Almost immediately after the Tlatelolco massacre, a series of books were published, forming the basis of what would become the 1968 canon. The custodians of this canon are former student leaders, activists, and sympathizers, many of whom became Mexico's leading public intellectuals in subsequent decades.[96] In this narrative, heroic young people took to the streets against an ossified regime, challenging the established political system and conservative social and cultural norms. Faced with the possibility of arrest, injury, and even death, their enthusiasm grew until the tragic evening of 2 October. In many ways, this is an accurate interpretation; its enduring power is a testament to its precision. Its enduring power is also a testamant to political imperatives—to hold the PRI accountable for the repression, to uncover the details of the massacres and other incidents, and to sustain the political longings of the people who joined the protests in 1968.[97]

It is time, however, to move beyond this heroic narrative. At the fortieth anniversary of the 1968 student movement, there were hundreds of talks by academics and public intellectuals, artistic events, and marches to commemorate the student protests. While a few individuals, mostly from the public, asked provocative questions about the events of 1968 and their legacy, most speakers reproduced the heroic narrative.[98] On the morning of 2 October 2008, around one hundred people had gathered in the UNAM's cultural center for a program of academic discussion, and in a revelatory moment one young woman in the audience lamented that we might need to wait until the fiftieth anniversary for a critical history.[99] With the opening of new archives, it is a good moment to begin this endeavor, to work toward a critical history of the rebel generation and its legacy—not a history that is necessarily critical of the leftist students, urban guerrillas, and countercultural hippies but one that critically analyzes them as historical actors in a historical moment.[100]

The leftists of the rebel generation were not saints. The moderates were not sell-outs, and the radicals were not deluded. They were middle-class students, full of doubt and frustration, who tried, in different ways, to improve the world in which they lived.

2 Cacerolazo

In late 1973, a wave of rumors swept the middle classes. They gossiped in cafés, restaurants, taxicabs, and supermarkets. They whispered about a possible coup d'état and about the threat of peso devaluations; they ridiculed President Luis Echeverría and laughed at his wife's clothes. Listening to these casual conversations were government spies, the secret police who eavesdropped or used informants to report on the political activities of citizens and groups. This marked a significant change in the focus of these intelligence agents, which had been, since at least 1969, primarily centered on students, unions, and official organizations.[1] By 1973, the crisis in the economic strategy of ISI (Import Substitution Industrialization) manifested in rising inflation, made worse by the 1973 OPEC oil strike, which generated the "oil shock" and the first worldwide recession since the Second World War. In Mexico and other Latin American countries, this generated uncertainty, and the conservative segments of the middle classes reacted against perceived threats to their economic well-being. In tandem with élite monopoly capitalists—the oligarchs of northern Mexico—they purposely fomented a sense of instability through a campaign of destabilizing rumors.

Until recently, the Right has been underanalyzed in historical studies of Latin America, with a disproportionate focus on the Left or progressive forces.[2] This has led to an incomplete understanding of power relations in the region and in Mexico. Derogatory and dismissive labels often applied to rightist historical actors—especially accusations of fascism by the PRI and the Left—are unsatisfactory. Instead, the conservative middle classes and leading businessmen struggled to make sense of the rapidly changing economic and political landscape. They employed the weapons of both the strong and the weak to protect their interests.

In cafés, cabs, and dry cleaning shops, customers engaged in everyday political banter. Fears of gas shortages, frozen savings accounts, or a devalued peso (which would make the cost of imported leisure goods prohibitively high for many of them) reflected concerns over maintaining a certain level of consumption.[3] The stories told in these establishments illustrate how the middle classes coped with growing economic troubles. While the very wealthy might have frequented such establishments, they likely would not have complained about the rising cost of dry cleaning their suits; at the other end of the class spectrum, the cost of such goods and services would have excluded most of the poor and working classes—not just from the cafés but from the conversations.

Through the everyday politics of jokes and rumors, the conservative segments of the middle classes struggled to defend their class position. They had carved out a space for themselves in a highly unequal society and they fought to defend it.[4] On one level, car owners and housewives protested the economic turmoil and the president's policies through gossip, as well as through economic strategies such as withdrawing their savings from bank accounts. On another level, wealthy industrialists, merchants, and business owners—leaders of the private sector—also disgruntled by Echeverría's leftist rhetoric, circulated propaganda and engaged in massive capital flight. The power of private sector businessmen to destabilize the government was, of course, much greater than that of housewives with modest bank accounts; they had much more money to divest from the national economy. That said, the atmosphere of uncertainty perpetuated in everyday places by denizens of the middle classes worried the government intensely, as the voluminous production of spy reports about their conversations illustrates. Combined, these various levels of protest presented a formidable challenge to the legitimacy of Echeverría's administration.

Establishing direct connections between middle-class individuals and the leaders of the private sector, such as the members of the Garza Sada family dynasty, proves elusive. Rather than a cohesive group mobilized against the state, the Right constituted a fluctuating network of alliances, to which sections of the middle classes were attracted in the 1970s.[5] While important distinctions exist between middle-class individuals and leading businessmen, their interests and actions also overlapped, which threatened the PRI and challenged the Left. In these years, it was widely believed that private sector leaders deliberately fueled the insecurities of middle-class individuals and directly funded their protests (either by organizing campaigns of telephone calls or by financing propaganda). The PRI and various leftist groups perceived an emerging, if heterogeneous, threat from the Right.

1973: Economic and Political Watershed

The year 1973 deserves a place in Mexico's pantheon of recent "crisis" years, alongside the student massacre of 1968, the economic crash of 1982, the earthquake of 1985, the fraudulent elections of 1988, and the inauguration of NAFTA and simultaneous outbreak of armed resistance in Chiapas in 1994. In particular, 1973 is fundamental to the history of conservative protest, marking the beginning of a middle-class and élite rebellion against the PRI. As Echeverría sat silently suffering accusations from business leaders during Eugenio Garza Sada's funeral in September 1973, the war between the president and the private sector solidified. In that moment, as cultural critic José Agustín writes, the war between them was "frank, open and boded ill of things to come."[6]

This political tension occurred in a period of general economic downturn. Mexico's ISI model had begun to show signs of exhaustion, and from the mid-1960s onward the size of Mexico's foreign debt grew substantially, putting pressure on the government to meet payments as it invested in infrastructure (such as the arenas and housing required for the 1968 Olympic games). Inflation began to increase significantly and sometimes erratically, starting in 1973, and families struggled to stretch their budgets. (This will be discussed more fully in Chapter 4.) The October 1973 OPEC oil embargo, which generated inflation and recession around the world, accelerated Mexico's economic instability and exacerbated everyday discontent with the economic situation.

In a press conference during the summer of 1973, a spokesman for the Ministry of Industry and Commerce emphasized that the economic uncertainty must be seen within a global context and insisted that the Mexican government could not be blamed for it. He described the rising prices and growing scarcity throughout the world. He condemned price speculation, calling upon the *empresario nacionalista* (nationalist businessmen) to invest capital in the Mexican economy and work with the government. "The nationalist businessman is also a product of the Mexican Revolution," he observed, calling upon individuals to curb unnecessary consumption. "We have created a set of consumption habits, that if we examine them rationally, we will see as superfluous," the spokesman continued. "If beef is expensive, buy pork or chicken. If it is sardine season, buy sardines instead of sea bass."[7] Government spies began compiling reports on the cost of living in the neighborhoods of the *popular* (poor and working classes) and in those of the *clase acomodada / clase media* ("comfortable" middle classes). These weekly studies tracked changes in the prices of goods such as tortillas, fruit, beans, coffee, meat, oil, cleaning products, and so on. In addition to reporting prices in neighborhood stores, the spies asked housewives and shopkeepers their opinions on the prices. Their reports reflect the government's desire to have a sense of the on-the-ground economic reality among different social strata.[8] Intelligence agents took special care to document these opinions concerning the economic turmoil and the PRI's handling of it overheard in local shops and cafés.

By the fall of 1973, the secret police were reporting, systematically and in copious detail, on the insecurities of middle-class individuals. Intelligence agents began to gather the jokes, rumors, and threats spoken in middle-class shops and gathering places, using informants (such as taxi drivers) or by eavesdropping directly. The shift in the activity of government spies—from gathering information on unions and student organizations, among other groups, to recording anonymous conversations—revealed a change not only in the political foment among the middle classes but also in the PRI's perception of its own vulnerability.

In the context of mounting economic and political instability, Echeverría promoted a new economic approach, which he termed "desarrollo compartido," or shared development. With this move, the president acknowledged the failures of so-called "desarrollo estabilizador," or stabilizing development, which had dominated Mexican economic planning since the 1950s and had prioritized growth over equality. During the 1950s and 1960s, Mexico's annual economic growth had averaged over 6 percent and inflation remained low, leading observers to speak of a Mexican Miracle. But the apparent success of stabilizing development masked underlying problems, including growing underemployment, inequality, and a trade deficit, as well as an anemic public-sector revenue base.[9] Political protests, especially during the 1960s, had called attention to the structural problems inherent in stabilizing development.[10] In his inaugural address, Echeverría described these problems: "Grave deficiencies and injustices [continue], which could endanger our accomplishments: overconcentration of income and the underprivileged situation of large groups are a threat to the harmonious continuity of our development."[11] "Shared development," in contrast, prioritized distribution, equality, employment, and quality of life—a radical reconfiguration of economic theory.

The Echeverría administration focused economic policy on distributive justice and independent economic growth. The central policy goals were to increase employment, to maintain the high growth rate of the Mexican Miracle, to improve Mexico's balance of trade, and to prioritize the needs of the majority of the population.[12] Shared development included programs to combat the effects of inflation and protect real salaries, such as subsidized consumer credit, greater focus on minimum wage policy, and the creation of more worker stores. Jobs were created in the public sector, as well as indirectly in the universities as a result of increased government funding in education.[13] This was growth by public spending, and a robust public sector was the bedrock of the new economic philosophy. Public investment increased by 516 percent between 1971 and 1976 (266 percent in real terms).[14] During the Echeverría administration, the balance between public and private investment changed with the state's increased role in the economy, a move that alienated the private sector: in 1970, there were 84 state enterprises; in 1976, these numbered 845.[15]

Although shared development was a promising program, one of its centerpieces—to generate public revenue through tax reform—failed. The reform would have increased taxation on the richest Mexicans in order to finance public spending, with a goal of income redistribution. In addition to a small increase in tax rates, the proposed reform would have reduced the anonymity of wealth by taxing assets as well as income, thus altering the established rules of the game (something that worried members of the private sector and high-ranking PRI officials). Faced with political opposition from the private sector and from within the PRI, Echeverría dropped the reform before it reached Congress.[16] That Echeverría abandoned progressive tax reform is a testament to how political considerations limited his ability to push through economic changes. Without additional revenue from taxation, the administration relied increasingly on foreign loans to fund the growing public sector and subsidize domestic economic programs; the public external debt more than quadrupled, from 4.7 billion American dollars in 1970 to 21.6 billion in 1976.[17] So Echeverría's administration led Mexico's shift to a debt-based economy. The government's foreign debt increased, but so did business borrowing and household debt.

In short, this was not a propitious time for an ambitious economic philosophy and policy plan. Shared development was put into practice as the underlying problems of the midcentury Miracle were becoming manifest and in a budgetary situation of failed tax reform and growing dependence upon credit, especially foreign credit. This exacerbated the trade deficit, increased public debt, and contributed to rising inflation, which, ironically, increased the need for social programs.[18] And political crisis converged with economic crisis, when increased state participation in the economy and the rhetoric of distributive justice angered private sector business owners.

Echeverría may have reestablished some legitimacy with the intellectual dissidents, but the leftist rhetoric of shared development worried the country's leading businessmen, industrialists, and merchants. Ironically, however, in Echeverría's program the state intervened in the economy to support national industry, which benefited many industrialists. Echeverría's policies, in general, continued to favor the economic interests of the big companies and medium-sized businesses of the private sector.[19] And indeed, business pressure forced Echeverría to backpedal on some of his more progressive policies. For example, powerful construction consortiums in Mexico City pressured the president to reverse his initial stance against expanding the metro system; these consortiums then won lucrative contracts to build more subway cars and tracks.[20] Leading businessmen may have feared that the president's rhetoric signaled a more radical policy shift to come. They may have been worried that they had little sway over the administration's future economic policies.[21] In this regard, Echeverría's administration marked a major turning point in relations between the state and the private sector.

Groups of business owners made up the private sector. There was a wide array of compulsory organizations and voluntary associations. All medium and large industrialists were required by law to join an industrial chamber. In the 1970s, the two most powerful groups of industrial entrepreneurs were the Confederation of Industrial Chambers (Confederación de Cámaras Industriales, or Concamin), created in 1918, and the National Chamber of Manufacturing Industry (Cámara Nacional de la Industria de Transformación, or Canacintra), created in 1941. Many of the Monterrey-based industrialists, such as the Garza Sada dynasty, belonged to the latter.[22] Merchants were required to join the Confederation of National Chambers of Commerce (Confederación de Cámaras Nacionales de Comercio, or Concanaco). Far from constituting a monolithic block, Mexican business owners formed a private sector with internal divisions and differences. From the 1940s until the 1970s, these groups enjoyed a mutually beneficial—if occasionally tense—relationship with the state, and their members benefited from the ISI policies. This changed in the 1970s, however, when these business chambers became outspoken critics of President Echeverría.[23]

At moments of tension between the private sector and the state, business leaders formed cross-industry voluntary associations, which allowed them to organize effectively for their interests. The Mexican Employers Association (Confederación Patronal de la República Mexicana, or Coparmex) emerged in 1929 as a response to state-sponsored organized labor. The Mexican Council of Businessmen (Consejo Mexicano de Hombres de Negocios) formed in 1962 as a response to left-leaning policies of President López Mateos. And in 1975 the Mexican Council of Businessmen created the Business Coordinating Council (Consejo Coordinador Empresarial, or CCE) in response to Echeverría's leftist politics and rhetoric.[24] The Monterrey industrialists played important roles in all of the voluntary associations.

These business chambers and voluntary associations had contradictory relationships with the government. While many private sector leaders often complained that the state was an incompetent and corrupt business partner, some of them were financially dependent upon it, through direct subsidies, low interest rates, or subsidized services. Many leading business owners preferred the idea of a mixed economy, driven by both state and private investment.[25] When Echeverría began to alter the balance between state and private investment in the economy, coupled with his leftist rhetoric, leaders of the private sector retaliated.

In addition to his leftist economic programs, Echeverría's ambitions to become a leader of the third world—through his presentation of the Charter of Economic Rights and Duties of States to the UN, his support of Salvador Allende's socialist government in Chile, and his advocacy for China's entry into the UN—all raised the ire of private sector leaders, who in no way fancied themselves as "third-worldists." Rankled by Echeverría's rhetoric and worried about the international economic climate, leaders of the private sector took action. The so-called Monterrey Group, the powerful and very public industrialists based in that northern city, whose patriarch, Eugenio Garza Sada, had been killed by the Liga Comunista 23 de Septiembre, was perhaps the most vocal critic of Echeverría, and the secret police reported disproportionately on its political activities.

The private sector retaliated by engaging in capital flight by purchasing dollars and cutting back on their investment in the domestic economy, as well as raising the prices of goods and services. These actions only worsened the economic situation.[26] In late 1973, when rancor was at a height following the Garza Sada murder and Echeverría's perceived tolerance for guerrilla activities, the Monterrey Group fueled a campaign of rumors to destabilize Echeverría's administration.

The Rumor Mill

In the famous blue-tiled Sanborns on Madero Street, in the historic center of Mexico City, government spies eavesdropped on the clientele's negative comments about Echeverría. Patrons consisted primarily of journalists, politicians, and white-collar employees working in the public and private sectors. "Amazingly," reported the spies, discontent raged even among federal government bureaucrats—an employee of the attorney general's office was overheard commenting that someone should blow up Echeverría's car because of the scarcity of sugar and the rising price of gasoline. The spies reported a wave of malicious jokes that attacked the intelligence of Echeverría and his officials, lampooned his reckless spending, and commented on his growing legion of critics. For example, in Sanborns, the spies overheard a joke about how the city government would have to build extensions onto the presidential residence, Los Pinos, to house all the women who wanted to shout insults at the president.[27] In another Sanborns café, a journalist asked his companions if they knew why the Ministry of the Interior had prohibited jokes about Echeverría in public places. Because, the journalist continued, they finally understood them![28]

Rumors are a critical part of everyday political culture, especially during times of discontent. They are weapons that may be used by the state or against the state. Although Mexico has a long and vibrant tradition of political humor, contemporary experts agreed that, during Echeverría's administration, jokes and rumors captured the public imagination and acquired a greater symbolic importance than political humor had enjoyed during previous administrations.[29] The veracity of these rumors is uncertain; likely they mixed fact and fiction. But for a rumor to spread—and for the secret police to consider it enough of a political threat to record it in their reports—it had be credible to those who received and repeated, and sometimes acted upon, the information.[30] Likewise, the jokes were appreciated by the intended and unintended audiences (friends and acquaintances, government spies and their informants) for their cleverness, and also because they expressed a shared perception of political and economic instability.

Government spies were especially interested in the morning gatherings at the Madero Street Sanborns of a group of engineers, journalists, economists, and former student leaders who had been in prison. This group commented that even though the cost of gasoline was rising, the government supplied gas to many of its bureaucracies, and the bosses, their wives, their lovers, and the "juniors" (the spoiled children of high-level PRI functionaries) were all happily filling their tanks. One engineer noted that he had it from a good source that a movement against Echeverría was developing because of the price hikes in basic and luxury goods. Using the example of soda pop, he added that many in Mexico now considered luxury goods a necessity because Mexico had become a consumer society that was controlled by the American bourgeoisie.[31] The engineers discussed how the government should start an education campaign about consumption, to teach people not to make luxury purchases and thus better manage their budgets. They spoke about how the desire for these luxury products was manipulated, even produced, by American psychological techniques and stressed that middle-class Mexicans needed to kick their addiction to luxury goods.[32]

This group of men who met for morning coffee concurred that Echeverría should beware of a possible violent change in government because he was angering both the poor and the middle classes. Sooner or later, they thought, the people would react against their exploiters. These men also criticized the Left for infusing students with false illusions and luring them into guerrilla groups: "We shouldn't make assholes [*pendejos*] of ourselves because America won't allow its neighbor to become a socialist country." The Left, they claimed, "isn't worth shit [*vale mierda*], and most students have lost faith in it, especially the Communist Party and those false leaders who in '68 led them like sheep to the slaughterhouse and now work in the government."[33]

These sardonic speculations provided a channel for middle-class anxieties amidst a worsening economic situation. The secret police fanned out to glean middle-class reaction to the growing instability from the sectors of the middle class not represented (and thus, to a degree, controlled) by the CNOP (National Confederation of Popular Organizations). While these spy reports must be read with caution, they provide a window into what the PRI was concerned about. For instance, the Que Ricos Tacos shop near the Insurgentes metro stop was alive with worries and conjectures about Echeverría and the economic downturn. The owner of the shop joked that the previous night someone had attempted to assassinate Echeverría by throwing salt in the president's bed, since that was the best way to kill a moron.[34] He continued with a play on words, asking his customers if they had heard that Echeverría had ordered the closure of all taco stands because the president wanted Mexico to be an outstanding (*destacado*) country. (*Destacado* translates as "outstanding"; the play on words suggests that the president wanted to de-taco the country.)[35]

The spies also collected information in supermarket chains where the middle classes shopped, banks where they did their business, gas stations where they filled their cars, *taxis de sitio* (a more expensive and secure network of taxis operating out of a base, as opposed to the taxis that could be hailed on the street), and in dry cleaning shops. The decision by the state-owned oil company Petróleos Mexicanos (PEMEX) to suspend production of certain grades of gasoline—and to raise the prices of others—angered middle-class car owners at gas pumps. Car owners accused PEMEX of robbery and only purchased small amounts of gas. Some became aggressive with the men working in gas stations; one car owner asked sarcastically whether the gasoline had turned to gold overnight. Class tensions quickly emerged: a man who owned a small car complained that the government had given workers a 20 percent salary increase and had raised the price of gas to counter the cost, which only squeezed the middle classes. In another gas station, the owner of a large car carped that it was becoming very expensive to drive, that the price hike was too high, and that the government's only solution to the economic problems was to raise prices. Another person, not a car owner, argued that the gas price hike was positive because it helped ensure a social balance, by harming those who enjoyed extravagant luxury goods. Gas station owners and workers groused that consumption was down—and so were their tips—as consumers started cutting corners to manage their budgets.[36]

Polls of people leaving banks captured them complaining that the situation was worsening daily. They fretted that industrialists were not investing for fear of a peso devaluation and that the government was not doing what it should to calm these fears. Not surprisingly, individuals were withdrawing their money from their accounts, anticipating a run on the banks.[37] Throughout the capital city there was a shortage of twenty-peso bills, which caused problems because market vendors, taxi drivers, and bus drivers demanded exact change. A journalist described the atmosphere: "The only thing that is certain is ruin or bankruptcy, and across the city everyone is angry."[38] In a survey by government spies of various small businesses that catered to the middle classes in Mexico City, including American fast-food chains, air-conditioning companies, sporting goods stores, and shops selling imported luxury beauty products, many owners complained about the salary increases for workers, the higher cost of production, the dwindling customers, and the diminishing access to credit. The spies concluded that alarmism in city newspapers was spawning a general state of "psychosis."[39] Journalists reported that rumors circulated throughout the city alleging that the private sector was bent on discrediting the government to encourage a coup d'état.[40]

Cacerolazo

Cultural critic Carlos Monsiváis blamed this rumor mill on groups of women tied to ultrarightist Catholic organizations. He suspected them of spreading these and other destabilizing rumors through a myriad of telephone calls.[41] According to him, these women fomented fear of scarcity and encouraged panic purchasing, which added to the economic pressure on the government—all of which drew comparisons with the roughly contemporaneous *cacerolazo* protests in Chile. (*Cacerolazo* refers to the protests of middle-class and élite women in Santiago de Chile, who banged on their pots and pans—their "cacerolas"—to protest shortages and inflation; their protests heralded the coup d'état against Salvador Allende's government and the beginning of General Augusto Pinochet's military dictatorship.)[42] In Mexico, such stories spread quickly. Writer José Agustín contends that the middle classes accepted them almost without question, repeating them with the morbid pleasure of divulging juicy gossip and the dubious prestige of being "in the know." As an illustration of the atmosphere he cites the popular rumor about a sex-strangler on the loose in Mexico City. This mysterious psychotic was rumored to rape then murder (or was it murder then rape, they whispered?) his victims in commercial warehouses in the northern parts of the city (or could it be in the city's southern environs?). Agustín describes these rumor-mongering middle classes as those who went to the movies, attended theatres, frequented nightclubs and restaurants, and vacationed abroad. Although they prided themselves on being "in the know," Agustín argues that they were being manipulated by national and international private capital. Conservative segments of the middle classes began to feel politicized, as empowered to change their situation as were the *cacerolazo* protestors in Chile.[43]

The references to Chile were not merely rhetoric; events there affected policymakers, powerful business owners, and ordinary citizens in Mexico. President Salvador Allende's "Path to Socialism" reminded the Mexican Right of Echeverría's populism. While the comparison between Allende and Echeverría was overdrawn (Echeverría's policies and rhetoric had little in common with Allende's plan to advance socialism in Chile), many in Mexico connected the two leaders in a broader Latin American political configuration. Private sector leaders gauged the moment as one of potential change, a moment auguring a move to the left across Latin America. In the context of cold war politics, they wanted to preempt such a shift in Mexico.

For their part, PRI officials also had the Chilean example on their minds. They payed attention to the conservative *cacerolazo* protests in Santiago de Chile and worried that a similar movement might grow in Mexico. The middle-class and élite women who led the protests in Santiago played a significant role in the Chilean coup d'état, by providing a moral justification for military intervention. The food shortages and the long lines for goods—from basic necessities to electronics—struck at their identities as women and mothers. Their inability to provide adequately for their children inspired feelings of anger and anxiety, which fueled their protest.[44] This was particularly true of the middle-class women who joined and often led the protests; élite women, after all, could afford to shop on the expensive black market. Though some poor and working-class women did participate in the *cacerolazo* protests, they more commonly cast their lot with Allende's government.[45] The Chilean economic crisis was due to several factors, including the international economic downturn and mismanagement of the economy by Allende's administration. But the Chilean conservative opposition, in alliance with the American government, curtailed investment, encouraged hoarding and speculation, and sabotaged production—all to undermine Allende.[46] It would seem that the Mexican private sector had learned some important lessons from the Chilean model. Indeed, just as the Mexican student uprisings were part of a pivotal moment for the Latin American Left, the wave of destabilizing rumors was part of a key moment in the history of the Latin American Right.[47] In the early 1970s, the PRI worried intensely about increased politicization on both the left and the right.

In the context of rising inflation and increased radical violence, the ranks of conservative middle-class Mexicans criticized Echeverría's economic policies and complained about his leftist rhetoric. They worried that Mexico was turning socialist, and the Chilean example loomed large in their minds. Many made direct or thinly veiled references to Allende's fall and warned that, if Echeverría did not change his tune, a similar series of events could occur in Mexico. Echeverría had made a significant gesture to the Left by criticizing the Chilean coup d'état and welcoming Chilean exiles, including Allende's widow, Hortensia Bussi de Allende. The lyrics of a ballad found circulating in the Centro Médico hospital complex in Mexico City excoriated Echeverría and his policies. One verse specifically targeted Allende's widow:

Ya ciérrale el pico a tu amiga Hortensia
que con discursillos de líder barata
solo incita al pueblo hacia la violencia
para ensangrentarlo como fue su patria.

Tell your friend Hortensia to shut up
because with her little speeches and her second-rate leadership
she is only inciting the people to violence
to start a bloodbath, like the one that was unleashed in her country.[48]

In a dry cleaning shop, customers criticized the government's policies and worried that Mexico was on a path to socialism, adding that the Chilean exiles should not interfere with Mexico's internal politics. In their view, the Echeverría administration was on the same path as Allende's—and they even dared say, according to one spy, that Echeverría should not forget what happened to Allende.[49] When canvassed for their opinions in supermarkets, housewives blamed Echeverría personally for the rising cost of living. If it continued, they threatened, more serious unrest could result; the people might get tired and give the government a scare. One supermarket shopper complained that "we have never had a president like this one, who doesn't understand or care about the people," observing that if things did not change, a coup d'état could happen in Mexico, as it had in Chile.[50] There were persistent rumors of an imminent middle-class strike against inflation and the rising cost of gasoline. Rumored to be organized by word of mouth, it was believed that car owners would simultaneously stop wherever they happened to be driving and honk their horns. The idea was to refer to the "casserole strikes" in Chile.[51]

In the pricier *de sitio* taxis, customers complained vociferously to their cab drivers about the cost of living. Because the PRI helped taxi drivers acquire vehicles, most drivers were PRI supporters and some of them worked as informants, reporting the opinions of their customers to the secret police. According to these drivers, customers complained about the rising cost of food and clothing. Some customers claimed that leftist groups were taking advantage of the discontent to discredit the government and attack big capitalists. They complained to their drivers that the education system discouraged freedom of expression and that students were forced to adhere to a Marxist line of thought. The taxi drivers described how their fares accused Echeverría of demagogic populism and of wasting scarce government resources on the construction of prisons, hospitals, and schools. According to the drivers, customers also complained about the cost of admitting foreigners, like Chilean exiles, who were ungrateful and acted as subversives in Mexico.[52]

Criticism also came from organizations and political parties on both the left and right. In the aftermath of the Garza Sada murder, a group calling itself "Madres Mexicanas," whose members hailed mostly from the northern state of Nuevo León, published an open letter to Echeverría demanding a climate of security, peace, liberty, and moral recuperation. They accused the president of imposing his personal sentiments upon the nation, which went against those of most Mexicans, especially regarding Allende and Chile. They demanded to know why he was concerned about the disappeared in other countries when in Mexico people disappeared through kidnappings, robberies, and assassinations. Indeed, many worried that their own children would be kidnapped for ransom. Why, they asked, did Echeverría force Mexicans to accept "unpleasant elements" as exiles in their country? These mothers opposed "imported ideologies" (read: Chilean socialism or communism) that might contaminate Mexico.[53]

An urban movement called Cívico Familiar (Civic Family) handed out magazines, flyers, pamphlets, and newspaper articles repudiating socialism and communism. Its members criticized Echeverría for his "socialist tendencies" and generally tried to make him look ridiculous, according to a Ministry of the Interior spy report. In its propaganda, the Cívico Familiar blamed the president for the economic turmoil and complained about the embarrassing image Echeverría cultivated abroad (as he campaigned to be the leader of the third world). They also referred to the open conflict between the president and the private sector and argued that he would not be able to win over the nation's leading industrialists. According to the spy report, Cívico Familiar had close ties to a pro-Pinochet group called Solidaridad Orden Libertad (Solidarity Order Liberty), which was based in Santiago de Chile and whose members favored a militaristic, American-leaning government. The spy report claimed that many of Solidaridad Orden Libertad's leaders were Chileans who had lived or studied in the United States or had some association with American political groups. Their goal was to extend an ideology favorable to American interests to all parts of Latin America, with Mexico a key part of the endeavor. According to the report, some Chileans had joined the Mexican Cívico Familiar movement, but most members were middle-class Mexicans; its leaders were primarily based in the northern cities of Monterrey and Guadalajara, with some living in middle-class neighborhoods in Mexico City, such as Del Valle and Roma.[54] Both Cívico Familiar and the Madres Mexicanas illustrate that the reactionary middle-class protest extended beyond individual complainers and gossips to organizations with national reach and perhaps international influence.

Political parties also participated in the rumor mill. In a press release shortly after the Garza Sada murder, the president of the conservative National Action Party (Partido Acción Nacional, or PAN) pointed out that, in the fifteen days after the fall of Allende, Mexico's Far Left had issued proclamations that violence was the only path of change and that a wave of violence had begun to wash over Mexico. (Allende was overthrown on 11 September and Garza Sada was killed on 17 September.) The most established opposition party, the PAN drew much of its support from middle-class Catholics and the owners of small and medium-sized businesses, who gravitated to its defense of private property rights, its promotion of civic engagement in municipal politics, and its opposition to excessive state intervention in the economy.[55] The prominence of the PAN in the *cacerolazo* protests serves as one indicator of the protests' national importance. The PAN argued that the death of Allende served as a pretext for "morbid intellectuals" (*intelectuales enfermizos*) to seize upon the Chilean events to incite "false, mercenary, and selfish rage" against the Mexican state. They accused Marxist intellectuals of obfuscating the lessons that the events in Chile might hold for Mexico. These intellectuals, the PAN complained, ignored the fact that, under Allende, Chile had suffered political and economic chaos. The economy could not be directed with declarations and discourse, the PAN maintained, warning that Mexico ought to meditate upon these lessons to avoid the "contagion" of historical disasters—a veiled threat from the most prominent opposition party that what happened in Chile could occur in Mexico. The PAN pointed out that the most vocal sector against Allende had been middle-class housewives protesting rising inflation, which the party compared with the Mexican protests.[56] Government spies noted in 1974 that the PAN had covered Mexico City with flyers pointing to the cost of gasoline and encouraging a protest against inflation.[57]

For the conservative middle classes in Mexico, such fliers—whether or not they came from the PAN—expressed very real threats to their lifestyle.

It is possible that these café-goers, taxicab customers, and supermarket shoppers were manipulated by the private sector, as the PRI believed at the time and as several public intellectuals have suggested. No doubt, the insecurity generated by the economic instability and threats to their purchasing power—and identity—would have made them vulnerable to such machinations.[58] The *cacerolazo*-style rumor mill reflected the intersection of economic and political crises. In their precarious position, fearing falling into the working classes and hoping to join the ranks of the wealthy, members of the middle classes experienced the growing instability on both practical and emotional levels.

Chairman Mao, El Che, and Sex Ed

This crisis also pervaded the intimate world of middle-class family and sexuality, when Echeverría's administration—in an attempt to reach out to the Left—introduced an updated version of free school textbooks that affronted the social conservatism of some members of the middle classes. The new textbooks were at the heart of Echeverría's educational reform policy, a program that included increased funds for education.[59] The controversy surrounding the textbooks illustrates how conflicts over how one divides the world and assigns roles—to men and women, for instance—infused the battle between the conservative middle classes and the government.

This was not the first controversy over textbooks. Polemics over the free and obligatory textbooks began in 1958, when the administration of President Aldolfo López Mateos inaugurated a new education plan to provide primary education to all children. Alongside teacher training and the construction of schools, the plan included free and mandatory textbooks for all public and private primary schools. The National Commission of Free Textbooks (Comisión Nacional de los Libros de Texto Gratuitos) was created by presidential decree and charged with developing content. The rationale behind the free textbooks was largely economic: most families could not afford to purchase books each year. However, the ideological aim of standardizing content to promote national unity provoked resistance. Middle-class parents worried that, through these textbooks, the state would impose an official version of Mexican history. At its height, this protest movement drew crowds of several hundred thousand to public demonstrations.[60] The National Union of Parents (Unión Nacional de Padres de Familia), an ecclesiastical organization created by the Catholic Church in the 1920s to defend "liberty of teaching" (*libertad de enseñanza*), led the charge.[61] After several years of conflict, a compromise emerged in the early 1960s whereby schools could recommend or use alternative textbooks alongside the official one.[62]

Textbooks were once again at the center of controversy from 1973 through 1976, when the new Federal Education Law reasserted the power of the state over private initiative in education. Among other regulations, Article 5 of the new law stated that only the government could authorize educational material (read: textbooks) in public and private schools.[63] When the updated and strictly obligatory primary textbooks were introduced in 1972 and 1973, they sparked outrage. Conflict centered on the social science and natural science material. The National Union of Parents led the protest on the right, denouncing what they saw as the promotion of birth control and family planning, a Marxist bias in the historical and political content, and sections on the evolution of the species that contradicted Church dogma.[64] In particular, sections on sexual education infuriated parents, who felt it was their duty, not that of the schools, to teach their children about reproduction. They charged that the references to extramarital sex and the discussion of masturbation as a natural act threatened the morality of their children. They also criticized the portrayals of such figures as Fidel Castro, Che Guevara, and Mao Tse-tung. Parents complained that the textbooks were intended to produce "little Marxists" and train their children to hate the rich; instead, they insisted, their children must learn the importance of both the rich and the poor. They worried that exaltations of socialism would lead their children to negatively characterize the wealthy and the first world.[65]

The textbook conflict reflected changing social and cultural mores. Since at least the 1960s, a polarization of values had taken hold among the urban middle classes in which progressive, secular attitudes challenged conservative, religious views.[66] The difficult and intimate nature of the changes underway is perhaps best illustrated by attitudes toward birth control. Two surveys of middle-class Catholics, from 1966 and 1969, reveal a population divided on the purpose of marriage and sexual relations. Men and women both declared the ideal number of children to be significantly higher than the size of their own families; likewise, while over half of the women interviewed agreed with the Catholic Church's prohibition of birth control (aside from the rhythm method and abstinence), the number of interviewees using the birth control pill increased from almost 14 percent in 1966 to over 33 percent in 1969.[67]

These contradictions led to controversy in the 1970s, when the federal government began a major family-planning campaign.[68] Official policy shifted radically: Luis Echeverría's 1969 campaign slogan "To govern is to populate" was replaced by the catchphrases of the family planning campaign, "Responsible parenthood" and "A smaller family lives better."[69] Anthropologist Matthew Gutmann describes the policy shift as "the 1973 about-face": Article 24 of the Constitution, which banned the sale of contraceptives, was abolished; Article 4 was amended to read "Every person has the right to decide, in a free, responsible, and informed manner, the number and spacing of their children"; and in December 1973, the Mexican Congress approved the new Population Law (Ley General de Población).[70] The new policy direction was the result of feminist arguments that the number and timing of children was a personal choice and that women should have contol over their bodies, as well as growing concern in development and planning circles over high population rates and economic growth.[71] As a consequence of these policy and legal changes and as part of an international trend, the use of contraceptives, especially the pill, became widespread in Mexico during the 1970s.[72] But social and cultural values could not be easily changed, and when new attitudes toward sexuality and reproduction appeared in school textbooks, conservative parents protested.

In middle-class and wealthy Mexico City neighborhoods, such as Roma, Condesa, Napoles, and Polanco, parents distributed flyers against these textbooks. They claimed that communists had infiltrated the Ministry of Public Education (Secretaría de Educación Pública) and that traitors to Mexico (*vendepatrias*) were working hard to undo the country's tradition of liberty and unity. They called upon Christians to attend a protest in the Roma neighborhood, in defense of parents' rights to protect their children and in defense of Catholicism. "Death to Communism," their flyer cried; "Mexico will always be Catholic."[73] At the demonstration a few days later, speakers argued that Mexican education should not be imported from socialist countries; they accused government functionaries responsible for these textbooks of being anti-Mexican. Toward the end of the protest, they invoked the Cristero War of the 1920s, when Catholics revolted against the government's anticlerical actions, hinting that more general unrest might emerge against a government that they perceived as pandering to the Left.[74]

The Minister of Public Education, Víctor Bravo Ahuja, defended the government's position on the textbooks. The state's aim, he argued, was to make better citizens. He emphasized that the government did not intend to replace old dogmas with new ones and that the textbooks were not inspired by one particular ideological current; instead, they were intended to encourage a critical revision of all ideologies. The new textbooks explained the historical context of important figures such as Castro, Che, and Mao, among others, so that students would not ignorantly carry banners with the names of these leaders, failing to understand their political and historical significance. Bravo Ahuja accused the clergy of instigating this controversy because the educational reform policy aimed to reduce the role of the clergy in education.[75]

The PRI hoped to use educational reform to generate support for the party, to combat the influences of both the Right and the Left. On the right, the PRI wanted to curb the influence of the private sector and the clergy over certain educational institutions. On the left, the party wanted to ingratiate itself with students, teachers, and scholars by increasing the education budget. According to the CNOP, which represented many of the middle classes within the PRI, the aim of education was to make students into "productive young people for the development of the country." CNOP officials saw the program of educational reform as a possible solution to the kinds of problems that had emerged in 1968 and argued that the PRI needed to rescue the educational system from dangerous revolutionary influences and its "dark and murky" situation (*de las tinieblas y de la situación tenebrosa*). Basically, they hoped to infuse the educational system with patriotism and, in turn, generate support for the state: "Being revolutionary does not mean taking up arms, but to revolutionize the education system that speaks much more about other people's history," asserted one CNOP bureaucrat. Referring to the Mexican philosophers and politicians José Vasconcelos and Antonio Caso, the bureaucrat lamented: "Never in a primary school do you hear talk of Vasconcelos or Antonio Caso; it is necessary to know our own history and our own needs."[76]

Just as Echeverría's administration struggled to defend the educational reform program against conservative, middle-class protest, many on the Far Left also rejected it. The Revolutionary Teachers Movement (Movimiento Revolucionario del Magisterio, or MRM), a group of politically radical teachers, believed that education should have a progressive social aim. They envisioned teachers as social leaders who taught Marxist analysis and politicized their students. Education, according to these radical teachers, should benefit the exploited classes, not the bourgeoisie, and they rejected the educational reform program on the premise that it was modeled to suit the needs of the dominant classes. Instead, they proposed the formation of revolutionary brigades to politicize the people and to elaborate a radical theory and policy of education, alongside more material goals such as structural improvements for rural schools and better training and pay for teachers.[77]

Political struggles over public education have emerged at key moments in the negotiation of power and hegemony between the state and various social sectors, with the middle classes often leading the charge.[78] What children learn in school shapes their identity as citizens and Mexicans; conflicts over curriculum are ultimately conflicts over questions of *mexicanidad* (Mexican-ness). In the mid-1970s, conservative parents perceived threats not only to their class status, owing to the economic and political turmoil, but also to their social and cultural identity. They fought for their right to teach their children themselves about reproduction, sexuality, and gender roles. They wanted to pass on their worldview to their children, sharing with them their understanding of how the world was—or should be—ordered. Men and women, the rich and the poor—all had their place in life and history. At the time, many on the left dismissed this worldview as outdated, reactionary, and dangerous. Certainly, these protestors fought to maintain the status quo and to protect their privilege, but the nature of their discontent was profoundly intimate. Like most parents, they wanted to give their children tools for understanding the world. Their experience was their most valuable bequest and the new textbooks threatened to undermine it. These parents worried that the textbooks fostered class antagonism and challenged sexual norms and would alienate their children from them; thus, while they fought for the status quo, they also fought to preserve their bonds with their children.

Fascism and Conspiracy Theories

Personal, political, and economic concerns all drove conservative middle-class protest. The PRI responded with heated accusations and conspiracy theories, increasingly desperate to reassert its hegemony in the context of growing discontent. The PRI accused the conservative protestors of fascism and worried about the susceptibility of the middle classes to reactionary ideas. One senator, at a breakfast meeting of the CNOP, argued that, because they feared falling into the proletariat and wanted to join the privileged élite, the middle classes were vulnerable to manipulation by certain groups (read: private sector business leaders). He stressed that the PRI would have to develop programs to combat the corruption of the middle classes.[79]

PRI party president Jesús Reyes Heroles spoke in public about the "new fascism" in Latin America, to which Mexico was susceptible: "The world today, in crisis with inflation and unemployment, is a good breeding ground [buen caldo] for a new fascism." Consequently, he argued, the middle classes should be on guard because they were the object of a campaign to attract them to causes that were not their own. He warned that the middle classes should not confuse their interests with those of the "oligarchic groups of ultramontane inspiration." He claimed to be confident, though, that the middle classes would not be tricked by fascist instigations, the "cacerolismo," which was not an authentically Mexican phenomenon. However, Reyes Heroles's rhetoric masked his worries. He urged the middle classes to join in a project for Mexico's future, attempting to convince them, somewhat desperately, that they would not be sacrificed or lose their identity—as some of the destabilizing rumors contended.[80]

The director of the CNOP, David Gustavo Gutiérrez Ruiz, argued that the national and transnational Right had initiated an ideological confrontation by fomenting hatred and a sense of impotence among the middle classes, "from the campaign of malicious rumors to terrorist attempts, in a brazen attempt to impose solutions by force."[81] The CNOP accused powerful business owners of leading a smear campaign against the government and of spreading unfounded, malicious rumors. This antigovernment campaign did not come from artisans or workers, they argued, but emanated from high society, "where the rich toasted with champagne and imported wine and wanted to take over the country and run it to their advantage."[82]

Accusations of fascism often invoked references to Nazi Germany or Mussolini's Italy, but there is little accuracy in such comparisons. Francisco López Cámara, a scholar of the middle classes and an official of the CNOP, described how vulgar, banal, and simple classifications of the middle classes abounded in the 1970s: "If the ideologues of the Right . . . judged the student movements as the fruit of international 'communist' conspiracies, the leaders and ideologues of the student movements, forgetting their own class condition, qualified—without further analysis—the middle class as conservative, reactionary, authoritarian, and, with resounding condemnation, fascist."[83] No doubt, the label was an attempt to write off these protestors: comparing them to Nazi Germany or Mussolini's Italy invalidated their protests.[84]

Within the Echeverría administration, analysts worked furiously to document private sector machinations. They examined newspaper articles that quoted business leaders threatening to obstruct the government's anti-inflationary plans—the price controls that were designed to protect the poor.[85] And government spies traced ties between the private sector and various newspapers, which became vehicles for attacking Echeverría's administration. Articles that defended Nixon or attacked leftist groups in Mexico were considered to be discreet attacks on the president.[86]

Conspiracy theories about private sector plots to foment instability abounded. The line between conspiracy theories and actually existing conspiracies is fuzzy. In Mexico, where semiclandestine networks of the wealthy or influential scheme to advance political aims on both the right and left, there are many actually existing conspiracies.[87] Conspiracy theories, on the other hand, reflect a desire for narrative. In societies with opaque political systems and a history of actually existing conspiracies—such as Mexico in the 1970s—this desire often manifests in unnecessarily complicated explanations involving deliberate collusion.[88] Theorist Fredric Jameson argues that, in the last third of the twentieth century, conspiracy theories and their popular manifestations (such as spy novels and cyberpunk science fiction) were attempts to conceptualize the institutions that governed the globalized world of the late twentieth century. In a world in which power networks became "enormous and threatening, yet only dimly perceivable," conspiracy theories were "as much an expression of transnational corporate realities as . . . of global paranoia itself."[89]

In Mexico, many on the left speculated about connections between the CIA and the private sector. For instance, in an assembly at the UNAM one student claimed that the educational reform program emanated from the CIA, which, he argued, viewed all students of the humanities as potential enemies. The CIA, they claimed, wanted to "tecnificar" all of Latin America; to curb the revolutionary potential of knowledge, the CIA would replace teachers with computers and televisions.[90] In another example, the Socialist Workers Party (Partido Socialista de los Trabajadores, or PST) accused the private sector, especially the Monterrey Group, of fueling the textbook scandal and sponsoring terrorism.[91]

At other times, accusations came from leftist parties with ties to the PRI, such as the Popular Socialist Party (Partido Popular Socialista, or PPS). The PPS accused the PAN of conspiring against Mexico and of spreading rumors to paint a picture of discord between the government and the people. The PPS argued that the government had undertaken a battle for the "true independence of Latin America." According to the PPS, the provocations, kidnappings, dynamite explosions, and assassinations were all part of a plan organized by the forces of the Right—the "agents of imperialism."[92] These claims were a bit far-fetched, since leaders of the private sector, such as Eugenio Garza Sada, suffered from the radical violence that they were accused of financing.

To counteract these accusations, various business organizations took out ads in major newspapers defending themselves.[93] In September 1976, the secret police eavesdropped on a telephone call between Carlos Sparrow Sada, president of the Chamber of Commerce of the state of Sonora, and other leading businessmen in which they discussed the best strategy for attacking the government. These private sector leaders debated the wording of a petition in which they demanded similar subsidies for their companies as those enjoyed by state-run stores that sold goods at subsidized prices to PRI corporatist groups. These stores did not pay taxes or utilities, which allowed them to undercut independent businesses. The business leaders decided that the first version of their petition was too sarcastic and sounded insincere (*se va al lado de la burla*); they did not want to risk angering the public. They decided it was better to present an image of good faith and resigned themselves to more moderate wording, even as they lamented losing an opportunity to "stick it to the government [*darle en la torre al gobierno*]." In the end, they considered it more important to combat their negative image as speculators who caused inflation and, ultimately, hunger.[94]

In this telephone conversation, leading business owners engaged in a war of words against the government, fighting for the hearts of Mexicans. Indeed, a few days after the conversation, at a meeting of business leaders in Acapulco, Carlos Sparrow Sada asked: "What is happening in Mexico? Are we becoming communist? Mexico is on the edge of moral destruction because for many years the government has been plundering the country's wealth." He deplored the influence of "pernicious Chileans" on Echeverría's policies and accused the president of demagogy.[95] That same day, in an interview with Ministry of the Interior agents, Sparrow Sada called Echeverría an inept thief and referred to his "cowardly [*gallina*] advisors who are unconditionally submissive to the government and its henchmen."[96]

The war between the president and the private sector, now personal, vicious, and public, only added to a generalized feeling of instability. Leftist parties contributed to the panic. In their meetings, the Mexican Labor Party (Partido Laboral Mexicano, or PLM) called for a coup d'état and exhorted Mexicans to support a moratorium on external debt. The secret police reported that merchants, office employees, and young people with a "hippie aspect" attended these meetings. A flyer distributed by the Labor Party conveys their agitation: it accused the *Financial Times* journalist Alan Riding—"CIA agent, prostitute, pig"—of embedding instructions in his articles to the Monterrey Group to commit a "Pinochetazo" (a military coup similar to Pinochet's coup against Allende). This sort of propaganda sparked a wave of rumors among housewives, employees, workers, activists, and leaders of political organizations.[97] The Labor Party accused the Monterrey Group of allying with American president Jimmy Carter to kill Mexicans, in order to pay off their debts to their "masters," the Wall Street bankers:

This morning the bastards of the Monterrey Group make public their alliance with the nuclear psychotic Jimmy Carter. Their plan is to assassinate 30 million Mexicans. Carter will close the border and kick out 10 million Mexicans. Hundreds of thousands will be sent to the southeast [in Mexico] to work in slave camps. These plans are public and evident and nobody can ignore or negate them. The survival of every Mexican [*todo mexicano*] depends upon us moving quickly to detain this gang of assassins. The Monterrey Group has a gun pointed at your family. Will you let them shoot?

We can stop them. We know who they are. They aren't many. Some of the bastards are: Marcelo Sada, Guajardo Suárez, Humberto Serrano, Sansores Pérez, Santiago Roel . . .

They believe you are stupid and cowardly.[98]

Crescendo

By 1976, the battle between Echeverría and the private sector had intensified, as the result of both the worsening economic situation and the growing personal rancor between the president and the country's leading businessmen. On 31 August 1976, Echeverría was forced to float the peso, which had been pegged to the American dollar since 1954. For the first time in more than twenty years, Mexicans could not count on a fixed exchange rate. A generation of Mexicans for whom twelve and a half pesos equaled one American dollar experienced the peso devaluation in both practical and symbolic terms. The devaluation was a major blow to the economic security of the middle classes—and thus to the president's legitimacy. The decreasing value of the peso threatened savings and undermined purchasing power, especially for imported goods. Because their social identity depended on a certain purchasing power, the devaluation had significant emotional impact. Without the stability of a fixed exchange rate, the collapse of the Mexican Miracle became undeniable. After decades of relative growth and upward mobility, in 1976 the middle classes' economic dreams became nightmares.

In the third week of September 1976, rumors circulated that the government would freeze bank accounts. Government spies monitored banks in middle-class neighborhoods of the capital city, such as Roma, Condesa, Coyoacán, Del Valle, Narvarte, Lindavista, San Ángel, and Napoles. They noted a moderate level of panic, with an increase in withdrawals and longer-than-usual queues. Waiting in line, customers repeated rumors that bank accounts would be frozen and griped at the paperwork required for withdrawing large sums. There was a general consensus that no one should believe official declarations—that indeed it was best to believe the opposite. Government spies overheard speculation about a coup d'état. As a counterpoint, they noted that banks in Iztapalapa, a working-class area, were functioning normally.[99] The panic appeared to be confined to middle-class neighborhoods.

Throughout the fall of 1976 the peso floated, which led to a rise in almost all prices. Fear of a hike in gasoline prices festered. Though the government promised there would be no such increase, few believed it. And, in November, gas prices rose. Once again, intelligence agents monitored public sentiment in gas stations in middle-class neighborhoods. Gas-station owners reported congestion and panic purchases.[100] The spies visited public markets, schools, churches, and companies, as well as groups of campesinos, industrialists, bureaucrats, workers, and professionals, in order to get a sense of public reaction (*el pensar del mexicano*) to the spiraling economic crisis. Their reports illustrate the mounting frustration in all sectors of society. "The country is bankrupt, and we owe this to Echeverría. It's a product of his recent demagogic declarations against the United States and the Mexican private sector," commented one anonymous individual. Another declared: "The devaluation is a result of the loans Echeverría gave to the Chileans, Cubans, Argentines, and others, as well as his ostentatious trips. His wife also helped him bankrupt the country."[101]

While this might seem like a repeat of the 1973 rumor wave, the peso devaluation exacerbated the tensions between the government and business leaders. PRI deputies accused Andrés Marcelo Sada (a member of the Garza Sada dynasty) of causing a wave of tendentious rumors across the country. They called him a traitor and accused him of working against the textbooks, of fomenting gossip about a coup d'état, and of personally spreading rumors from his office telephone.[102] Intelligence agents reported on conversations of individual business leaders and detailed the activities of private sector organizations across the republic.[103] By 1976, the president and the country's leading business owners seemed to be engaged in a personal struggle.

While Echeverría might have had little choice but to float the peso, given international and domestic economic pressure, some of his other actions in the fall of 1976 can be interpreted as personal revenge against the Monterrey Group. After enduring ridicule throughout much of his administration, in 1976 he was forced to commit the ignominious act of devaluing the peso and to acknowledge the end of an era of prosperity. Echeverría retaliated against those he believed were responsible for the country's troubles. Exercising Article 27 of the Constitution, which granted the government broad powers to expropriate private property for reasons of "public interest," on 20 November—only ten days before leaving office—he expropriated one hundred thousand hectares of land in the Yaqui Valley in the northern state of Sonora.

This was the culmination of an ongoing battle between Echeverría and Sonoran businessmen over land invasions in the state. At the beginning of his presidency, Echeverría had been close to Sonoran governor Carlos Armando Biebrich, but as Biebrich became increasingly involved with businessmen and wealthy ranchers, the president distanced himself. In 1975 campesinos invaded these lands and Biebrich ordered the military to remove them forcibly; in the confrontation seven campesinos died. In response, Echeverría forced Biebrich to resign and replaced him with a closer ally, to the ire of local business leaders. Led by Carlos Sparrow Sada, they organized strikes and roadblocks. Many within the PRI, including the president of the party, Jesús Reyes Heroles, complained that while the private sector was certainly out of order, so, too, were the backhanded politics behind the land invasions. It seems likely that the supposed campesino-invaders were encouraged by Echeverría and his allies; many of these so-called campesinos later appeared as deputies in the Chamber of Deputies.[104]

Businessmen across the republic reacted to the Yaqui Valley expropriation with fury. They attempted to organize a general strike of industrialists and threatened to suspend payment of taxes.[105] Women shopkeepers in Sonoran cities created window displays filled with symbols of grief: "This mourning is a symbol of our sadness for the way our constitution was violated and our liberty limited [read: their right to private property]."[106] For their part, PRI senators demanded that the attorney general investigate the "oligarchic mafia" of the Garza Sada dynasty.[107]

There was more at stake, though, than personal vendettas. Business leaders wanted to flex their muscles for the benefit of President-Elect José López Portillo, who would take office in December 1976. López Portillo made no comment on Echeverría's final actions and waited on the sidelines. His old friend, oilman Jorge Díaz Serrano, had confided that American technicians were certain that Mexico had tremendous unexploited oil reserves. After the escalation of political and economic turmoil throughout Echeverría's administration, López Portillo hoped to use the promises of these oil revenues—promises of black gold—to mollify all sides.

"Six Years of Craziness"

Echeverría remains one of Mexico's most controversial presidents. His attempts to please all sides, his ambition to become the leader of the third world, and his hubris (illustrated by his expropriation of one hundred thousand hectares of land as an act of personal revenge) all provoked cutting sarcasm, frustration, and rage during his administration and in the years that followed. A ballad, found circulating in Mexico City in August 1976, captures the resentment Echeverría inspired:

SIN REMEDIO	WITHOUT REMEDY
Un médico dio el consejo que Uri Geller nos diría como quitar lo pendejo y lo loco a Echeverría.	A doctor recommended we ask Uri Geller how to cure Echeverría of his stupidity and craziness.
Presurosos consultamos al mago de tanta fama, confiados como lo estamos le ofrecimos buena lana.	Quickly we consulted the famous magician, being so confident that we offered him quite a sum.
Lo pendejo, se lo quito con mucha facilidad	The stupidity I can cure quite easily

la locura, ni un poquito la tiene a perpetuidad.	but the craziness, not even a little he has that forever.
Sin perder la esperanza de quitarle la locura, con promesas y alabanzas llamamos al señor cura.	Without losing hope of curing his craziness, with promises and praises we called the priest.
El sacerdote y la bruja lucharon en buena lid y voltearon boca abajo al pendejo de don Luis.	The priest and the witch fought a good fight and flipped that idiot Mr. Luis face down.
Pero nada consiguieron a pesar de su talento, la locura, nos dijeron, la trajo de nacimiento.	But they could do nothing with all their talents; this craziness, they told us, he was born with.
Quizá nos hiciera burradas, no ayudando su mujer, pero muchas pendejadas las sugiere doña Esther.	Maybe he did foolish things to us, his wife didn't help, but Mrs. Esther suggested so many stupid things.
Luego, . . . con esa mujer que escogió por compañera; la acabamos de joder, . . . con facha de tamalera.	Later, . . . with that woman who dressed up like a tamale vendor whom he chose for his partner; then, we were really screwed.
Se disfraza de Adelita también de China Poblana; ella cree que es muy bonita y se ve de la chingada.	She dresses like Adelita and also like China Poblana; she thinks she is very pretty but she looks fucking awful.
Don Luis se pasa las noches redactando disparates, legislando a trochemoche con su cerebro de orate.	Mr. Luis spends his nights writing nonsense, legislating without rhyme or reason with his lunatic's brain.
Buena vida, sí se da y pasea a nuestras costillas, Europa, África y más allá terminando en la Antillas.	He's got a nice life and travels on our penny, Europe, Africa, and farther away ending up in the Antilles.
En su locura don Luis queriendo el mundo arreglar, al radio Oriente, feliz, al judio fue a visitar.	In his madness Mr. Luis wants to fix the world; he's happy in the East, and he went to visit Israel.
Nada se metió en hora mala el caso de Belice	He took part at a very bad moment in the situation in Belize

viajando hasta Guatemala	and traveled to Guatemala
como un perfecto metiche.	like a real busybody.
Al pobre quiso ayudar	He wanted to help the poor
con una vida mejor,	to achieve a better life,
y lo acabó de fregar;	but he ended up annoying them
encareciendo el frijol.	by making beans more expensive.
Pudo conseguir	He could have made a difference
pues solo metió la pata,	but he only put his foot in it,
pero les fue a presumir,	and he went on presuming,
gastándose nuestra plata.	wasting our money.
Si Dios quisiera llevarlo	If God wants to bring him
a la gloria, que se fuera;	to glory, let him go;
pero San Pedro al mirarlo,	but Saint Peter just by looking at him,
nos lo devuelve a la tierra.	would send him back to earth.
Y si al infierno llegara	And if he goes to hell
el mismito Lucifer,	even Lucifer himself
al momento lo hecha fuera	would throw him out
pues no lo quiere ni ver.	because he doesn't want to see him.
Quieras o no; lo toleras	Like it or not; you tolerate
seis años sus locuras	six years of his craziness
después, haces una hoguera	after they're over, build a bonfire
y lo quemas como el Judas.	and burn him like Judas.

The following exhortation appeared at the bottom of the page: "If you love Mexico, make five copies and give them to five friends."[108]

Echeverría may have been doomed from the outset. As the party's "compromise candidate," the PRI wanted him to pull the country (and especially the middle classes) back together and back into the fold of the party after the tumultuous events of 1968. Charged as he was with an impossible task, Echeverría's policies oscillated between attempts to placate the Left and moves to appease the Right. On the one hand, Echeverría faced mounting leftist middle-class discontent; on the other, he had to contend with conservative middle-class and private sector antipathy. As the textbook scandal illustrates, any gesture in the direction of one side alienated the other. Contrary to the rhetoric of the private sector and the conservative middle classes—and, likely, contrary to Echeverría's own inclinations, at least initially—the president backpedaled on many of his left-leaning policies and moved toward the Right throughout his administration.

Echeverría's presidency could be seen as a lost opportunity. His programs of democratic opening, educational reform, and shared development were milestones in PRI policy and perhaps could have generated a more equitable social structure. But Echeverría did not have the political capital to push for real change. He was unable to generate consensus and reform the party in the context of economic instability. Consequently, the president's reforms did not satisfy the Left, and they infuriated the Right.

At Eugenio Garza Sada's funeral, Echeverría sat in the front row, caught between the Left and the Right. This symbolic moment augured a new era of crisis in Mexican history. While it might be tempting to put students, laboratory technicians, economists, and engineers into separate categories, a glance at Mexico during the early 1970s suggests that analyzing them together, as a dynamic and volatile middle class, allows for a fuller understanding of the forces of historical change. Together, their protests constituted a formidable challenge to the state. Without the analgesic of the economic boom, the middle classes rebelled, exposing the limits of the PRI's one-party system.

Part II

THE DEBT ECONOMY

"Every month it was the same. On the twenty-fourth, Sofía became tense. On that day, religiously, a big white envelope arrived from American Express. . . . If she didn't have her payment ready by the deadline, her stress level was un-i-ma-gi-na-ble."[*] Sofía, the protagonist of a series of novels about consumerism, captures the contradiction between comfort and crisis experienced by many in the middle classes: she enjoys the privileges of an affluent world, yet she is terrorized by her American Express bill.

Through the booms and busts of the 1970s, policymakers experimented with strategies to escape economic and political crises. The prosperity that crested in 1973 evaporated. An oil boom began in 1977, then went bust in 1981. During these years, massive structural change occurred at the national and household levels, as the nation began to rely on foreign loans to fuel oil extraction and families coped with inflation by turning to consumer credit. A debt economy emerged. Caught at the center of these changes, in terms of political narratives and policy programs, were the middle classes. Politicians and analysts, concerned with spurring development, debated the role of middle-class families and consumers in the nation's economy and politics. Various policies targeted the middle classes and brought them, for better or worse, into a life of material comfort and mounting bills.

The shift to a debt economy was, in part, an attempt to return to the midcentury boom, a world that receded with the political and economic upheavals of the 1970s. As the PRI and the middle classes struggled with the end of the Mexican Miracle, they tried to re-create the past through structural change. But in doing so, they ushered in a new world. Whether

---

[*] Loaeza, *Debo, luego sufro*, 25.

it was through foreign loans, an American Express card, or government-issued credit, the debt economy signaled profound policy and cultural changes, as Sofía, high-level politicians, and families across the republic grappled with new ways of understanding money, time and value, and the changing economy.

3 The Power of Petróleo

Televisa, Mexico's largest television network, aired a series of educational programs about the middle class in 1979.[1] The narrative was pessimistic, if not damning: the middle class supports authoritarianism, it betrays progressive movements, and its members are alienated and morally weak. Only a few years earlier, in 1975, PRI presidential candidate José López Portillo had declared, "I am, in reality, a typical member of the middle class," and he described how "the fundamental aspiration of an independent people is located in the middle class."[2] These were very different arguments about the historical role of the same group of citizens, each of which had an urgent relevance in times of boom and bust as intellectuals, journalists, and politicians sought to explain the role of the middle class in Mexico's economic development and underdevelopment.

In the midst of an economic boom, the Televisa series accused the middle class of sucking up the country's resources at the expense of the working classes and the poor. The discovery of significant oil reserves in 1976, off the shores of the states of Veracruz, Tabasco, and Campeche, had created an oil boom. Oil, it seemed, had endless possibility; for José López Portillo, who succeeded Echeverría and was president from 1976 to 1982, oil offered a panacea for many of the country's problems. And from 1977 to 1981, during the four short years of the oil boom, the president and his highest advisors converted Mexico into a rentier state (a state that derives a substantial, often excessive portion of its revenue from a natural resource), as Mexico became dependent on oil. Black gold seemed to offer them an escape from the tumult of the Echeverría administration. In the words of López Portillo, it constituted an "exit" from underdevelopment and instability.[3] The newfound oil reserves would facilitate Mexico's transition to modernity and prosperity, a transition to be spearheaded by the middle class, to which he proudly belonged. The host of the Televisa series, in contrast, argued that the middle class resisted change and lacked a national project. She decried "the historical and political disarticulation of the middle class."[4]

Ideas about the middle class were central to debates about the oil boom and Mexico's political economy more generally. "Middle class" is a socioeconomic category and a state of mind that individuals may achieve, experience, and lose. It is also a political narrative, produced by cultural, political, and academic élites to advance arguments about economic development and underdevelopment. In speeches, newspaper articles, television programs, academic analyses, and popular literature, journalists, politicians, and cultural critics expressed ideas about the meaning of the middle class. Some celebrated small business owners, students, and technicians for their productivity and considered a robust middle class to be crucial for a prosperous and stable nation. Others, however, connected engineers, civil servants, and teachers with excess, corruption, and political instability. Since at least the nineteenth century, philosophers and intellectuals have cast the middle class as the protagonist in narratives about capitalism in Mexico and beyond.[5]

During the oil boom, two contending narratives emerged about the historical role of the middle class. In one, the black gold put an end to the instability that began in 1968 and thus allowed Mexico and the middle class to resume progress toward first-world capitalist modernity. This view revived fantasies of stability that had flourished in the so-called miraculous midcentury decades. In the second vision, the middle class emerges as a corrupt parasite in a rentier state, betraying its historical responsibility to establish a liberal, bourgeois democracy and suffering the consequences of its failure. The newfound oil, then, generated fantasies of prosperity as well as nightmares of corruption and injustice.

These narratives had power. The remarkable consistency in the terms of agreement and disagreement—for example, even though they reached opposite conclusions, López Portillo and the Televisa host referred to a similar set of ideas and used a similar language to advance their arguments—transformed what might otherwise have remained isolated narratives into a broader discourse (a normative framework for thinking and talking about the middle class).[6] The formation of a discourse about the middle class was a contentious process that occurred in Mexico's public sphere, in television shows, novels, academic writing, press accounts, and political speeches.[7]

This discourse could be used as a political tool. Many different people, including the president and a writer of popular detective fiction, used ideas about the middle class to make arguments concerning development and underdevelopment in Mexico, and their arguments most likely impacted policy decisions, political strategy, and public opinion. There is, however, no clear-cut cause-and-effect in discourse analysis. It is difficult to gauge, for example, the degree to which the president and popular writers actually shaped public opinion, to know how middle-class individuals reacted to television shows, novels, or political speeches.[8] Instead, what emerges is a set of powerful ideas about the role of the middle classes in Mexico's past, present, and future.

The Midas Touch

López Portillo remembered the moment when he realized that Mexico's oil reserves were not moderate but extraordinary: "Everything changed," he recalled at a press conference in Mexico City on 3 December 1979.[9] The optimism that pervaded López Portillo's rhetoric marked a drastic shift away from Echeverría's public battles. In his first State of the Union address on 1 September 1977, López Portillo declared that "in the present era, countries can be divided into those that have oil and those that do not. We have it. . . . Once again in our history, oil has become the biggest factor in our economic independence and the answer to our problems."[10]

From the moment Lázaro Cárdenas nationalized Mexico's petroleum reserves and expropriated the equipment of foreign oil companies in 1938, oil served as a powerful symbol of nationalism, economic autonomy, and political independence in Mexico. Cárdenas decreed that the country's reserves would be managed by Petróleos Mexicanos (PEMEX), a state-owned company that became one of the largest oil companies in the world and one of the most important sources of income for the Mexican state.[11]

The discovery, in the mid-1970s, of new oil fields reinvigorated such oil-based nationalism. López Portillo declared that oil offered Mexico a chance for economic self-determination, an opportunity to reduce the country's dependence on external financing and to improve international relations. According to the president, oil revenues would facilitate industrial planning and improve the country's transportation, housing, education, worker training, social development, and agriculture.[12] Oil was transformed from one base of economic development among several, providing hydrocarbons for domestic use at reduced prices, to the central axis of national economic development.[13] From the moment satellites confirmed the Cantarell Complex oil field in the southern Gulf of Mexico—before drilling had even begun—the anticipated reserves had been imagined as a panacea for Mexico's material and existential problems.

Mexico's oil reserves skyrocketed. In 1975, Mexico had about six billion barrels in proven reserves; these rose to forty billion in 1978 and more than seventy billion in 1982. At the same time, the average price of crude oil went from approximately US$13 per barrel in 1977 to more than US$30 per barrel by 1980.[14] The economic woes of 1976 receded, and the government began massive infrastructure projects. In effect, Mexico went on a spending spree to spur economic growth and placate political discontent. And this government-sponsored growth produced impressive results: among other indicators, between 1977 and 1981 the annual average GDP growth was 8.4 percent.[15] Much of this growth was financed by foreign loans based upon projected oil revenues.

International creditors and commercial banks clamored to extend credit to Mexico. Even though the country had the good fortune of discovering significant reserves when oil prices were at an all-time high, the investment required to extract the crude overshadowed the profit during the first several years. Consequently, between 1976 and 1982 Mexico's total external debt increased from US$27.5 billion to US$92.4 billion.[16] Instead of diversifying the economy, Mexican policymakers intensified rent-seeking behavior, relying increasingly on revenue from its natural resources. Put simply, the ISI (Import Substitution Industrialization) economic strategy, which had promoted a mixed and diversified economy during the midcentury decades, was replaced by one that relied excessively on revenue from oil extraction. Mexico became increasingly dependent on oil: in 1976 oil exports constituted 15.4 percent of total exports; by 1981 this number had climbed to 72.5 percent.[17]

Mexico became a "petro-state," which political scientist Terry Karl describes as a nation in which a "petrodollar deluge gave rise to new aspirations—for prosperity, national greatness, equity, and autonomy."[18] The term conveys more than "rentier state," which refers to the economic basis of public revenue; "petro-state" also evokes the political and cultural dimensions of overdependence on oil. In a petro-state, anticipated prosperity puts pressure on the government to meet rising expectations. Policymakers feel a historical imperative to advance in great leaps: suddenly, existing trajectories are placed on "a grander, more accelerated and ultimately unmanageable scale."[19] Adding to the instability of high expectations, foreign loans, which help finance these expectations, begin to exceed oil revenues. According to Karl, countries as diverse as Venezuela and Nigeria came to believe that they could "sow the petroleum" and "catch up" with the developed world. Instead, "petro-mania" and a "petrolization" of policy decisions emerged, in which all plans and programs took oil as their starting point.[20]

At times, López Portillo expressed concern about becoming too dependent on oil. He had not forgotten the 1973 oil shock and the ensuing economic turmoil, and he warned Mexicans of another energy scare.[21]

Nevertheless, he did not imagine an imminent danger; he anticipated decades of oil-based growth. This optimism seemed well founded. In 1979, production raced ahead of schedule: the target of producing fifty thousand barrels per day by 1982 would be achieved by 1980. PEMEX was exceeding even its own expectations.[22] Furthermore, international forecasts were positive: Lloyd's Mexican Economic Report forecast that the year 1978 "would be written in oil."[23]

This optimism pervaded the very language used to discuss the economy. The president's oft-repeated mantra, "administering abundance," underscored his belief that the biggest challenge would be to manage the wealth. "Administering abundance is sometimes more difficult than managing misery," he told the PEMEX administrative council in 1977. "The prodigal son risks squandering."[24] Economic realities that had previously been considered the cause of instability, such as inflation, were now described in more positive terms. Certainly, the economic problems of the early 1970s did not disappear when the first oil well was drilled, but their cultural meanings shifted radically. Official speeches moved away from Echeverría's direct attacks on the private sector as the cause of inflation; instead, López Portillo reflected upon the effects of inflation in an abstract manner. The promise of oil revenues allowed the president to enjoy a more relaxed attitude toward a seemingly temporary economic problem: "A large part of inflation is subjective; it comes from expectations, from two fundamental psychological factors: ambition and fear of insecurity," he assured those who listened to his State of the Union address on 1 September 1980. "Psychological factors can only be overcome by conviction, serenity, and reflection. Only the mind can overcome the mind."[25] This description of the emotional and cultural dimensions of inflation seems almost luxurious compared with Echeverría's battle cries. Where Echeverría had portrayed himself under siege by a hostile domestic private sector and a dire world economic situation, López Portillo had a meditative relationship with inflation. It would seem that the promise of oil had transformed economic problems into emotional states. This transformation was especially remarkable given that inflation continued to undermine consumer purchasing power throughout the late 1970s.

When addressing concern over the size of PEMEX's—and the country's—debt, the president and his highest functionaries argued that this debt was positive. Jorge Díaz Serrano, the director of PEMEX, called his detractors alarmists. In a rebuke to those who expressed concern, he argued that PEMEX's debt was comparable to that of other large global companies, such as Exxon. He derided the "provincial and timid" attitude that reflexively cast debt as negative. By contrast, he considered debt to be an asset, because it helped finance subsidies to domestic consumers.[26]

(Some of these subsidies are analyzed in the next chapter.) López Portillo defended his policy of accepting foreign credit and increasing Mexico's debt. At a 1979 press conference in Mexico City, he argued that international credit was part of Mexico's patrimony and that, as president, he was obligated to take advantage of it to finance the country's development.[27] In another meeting with the press, he denied that Mexico's foreign loans had made the country too dependent on foreign creditors. After all, Mexico was capable of paying them back. Instead, he heralded the value of foreign loans: "Credit is one of the values of an individual and a society."[28]

López Portillo entered the 1980s confident. He believed that Mexico had been rescued from the brink of disaster and could finally leave behind the crisis that "began in '68 and worsened over the course of the 70s."[29] He was confident that the country could use black gold to "exit" underdevelopment. The official mood was sanguine: "Mexico, luckily, is living in times of hope, and we can be confident that if we organize ourselves well . . . we have exits, and this is the most fundamental."[30] Newspaper articles described how the official optimism was contagious. One journalist reported that his interviewees had begun to calculate their share of the wealth by dividing the oil potential per capita.[31] Another journalist described how the man in the street—Juan Pueblo—had started to take a greater interest in oil. Previously, Juan Pueblo had been poor or working class; now he was a car owner who tracked the politics of oil. Beyond filling up his gas tank, Juan Pueblo had become interested in the "magical aspects" of production—the sophistication of the refineries and the complicated distribution network. According to this journalist, Juan Pueblo was seduced by the "magic" of oil modernity.[32]

At times, official rhetoric assumed almost philosophical dimensions. In 1978, Díaz Serrano claimed, "the production and consumption of petroleum are the most accurate indicators of the prosperity and well-being of humanity in the modern period."[33] The following year, at a speech in Mexicali, the director of PEMEX explained how the oil boom had allowed the country to "move toward complete modernity."[34]

The boom also brought pressure to succeed. In December 1978, López Portillo described the devastating cost of failure: "That a country without oil fails," he told PEMEX workers, "is lamentable, yet understandable; but in these times, in the last third of the twentieth century, it would be very grave if a country with oil could not resolve its social and economic problems. Such a country would destroy its historical project; it would not deserve a dignified place in history."[35]

The middle class was central to this "historical project." From the beginning of his administration (which might be extended to include his campaign, as López Portillo was the only contender in the 1976 presidential election), he had placed a premium on unity between the PRI and the middle class. He described 1968 as the "crisis of conscience" of the middle class and applauded Echeverría's attempt to reach out to students and bring them into the PRI: "[It was] a rescue and incorporation of the middle class into the revolutionary institutions." In his 1975 speech to the executive committee of the National Confederation of Popular Associations— the CNOP, which represented many of the middle classes within the PRI's corporatist system—López Portillo identified himself as squarely in the middle class. He located the fundamental aspiration for Mexico's future in the middle class:

I am, in reality, a typical member of the middle class. . . . I am the son of an intellectual, a modest employee and historian who educated me in the moral, responsible, modest, and austere strength of the provincial middle class. . . . A professional, like many of you here today . . . I experienced and I understand the tremendous, complicated problems of a growing middle class. . . . The middle class has a fundamentally revolutionary destiny, which we have to organize and care for. . . . The fundamental aspiration of an independent people is located in the middle class.[36]

The middle class and the PRI had reconciled and could now march together toward modernity and economic development. The future president had declared his allegiance to the middle class, a group that, in the same speech, he described as the "basic and critical class in the country."[37]

Beyond official rhetoric, the administration used black gold to court the middle classes. Much of the economic growth, fueled by foreign loans, benefited this crucial sector of the population. The boom was a brief golden age that provided the middle classes with new infrastructure projects, such as the construction of the Cultural Center (Centro Cultural Universitario) at the UNAM, and allowed them to escape the turmoil of the mid-1970s.[38] The middle classes now intensified their consumption patterns: imported consumer goods increased approximately sixfold from 1976 to 1981, when they fell to preboom levels.[39] Expectations of upward mobility increased during the oil boom years. Many workers believed they could join the middle classes; civil servants, lawyers, and laboratory technicians were confident that they could maintain their income and privileges; others aspired to join the wealthy.[40] Aspirations forged during the midcentury Miracle came to seem like acquired rights during the oil boom.[41] According to one consultant to the PRI, the president and other high-ranking party members believed that they could seduce the middle classes into political complacency, under the *embrujo*, or "spell," of black gold.[42] Perhaps emboldened by the seemingly mollified middle classes, López Portillo extended Echeverría's democratic opening by legalizing the participation of smaller political parties, including the Mexican Communist Party. And, although the causes are much debated, urban public protest did decline during the oil boom years.[43]

The PRI believed that oil wealth had invigorated its political hegemony, its Institutional Revolution. But competing narratives of the oil boom emerged. Official optimism was thrown into bold relief when newspapers revealed corruption in the public bureaucracy charged with managing the newfound revenue, and when hard-boiled detective fiction portrayed injustice and alienation throughout society. In these narratives, members of the middle class—from cops to bureaucrats—wasted the nation's resources and self-destructed in the process. If direct political protest diminished during these years, ennui, cynical satire, and noir culture expressed the zeitgeist. Twin visions—one bright, the other dark—each cast the middle class as the protagonist in a historical narrative about capitalist development and democratic stability.

The Dictatorship of the Civil Servants

In newspaper articles during the oil boom, journalists and public intellectuals accused middle-class civil servants of siphoning off wealth. Attacks on bureaucrats were attacks on the state itself because, for many, bureaucrats represented the embodiment of the state. In their day-to-day dealings with the state apparatus, most citizens interacted with low- and midlevel public employees. Bureaucrats, therefore, nicely illustrate the intersection between the state and the middle class.

One of the most pernicious effects of "petrolization" is increased official corruption. Countries awash in petrodollars—loans given on the projected oil revenues—spend fortunes purchasing loyalty from citizens, which in the long run undermines political authority. Vested interests that reap the benefits of the boom work to reinforce this petrolization of the economy. The petro-state itself becomes a barrier to change as it begins to rely upon petrodollars.[44] For example, one journalist took issue with Jorge Díaz Serrano's statement that Lázaro Cárdenas had given Mexico the gift of oil. Díaz Serrano had emphasized oil as part of the revolution's great legacy. In response, Jesús Guisa y Azevedo, writing in *El Universal*, invoked the wisdom of the poet Ramón López Velarde, who had described oil as a gift from the devil: poets often penetrate the truth of the things, Guisa y Azevedo noted. "Petroleum can lead to division, even bitter division, an occasion to squander, to waste, as if we had won the lottery. . . . It can lead to an abundance of money, an exaggerated cost of living; it can foment vice, dissipation, momentary wealth, and subsequent poverty."[45]

Journalistic criticism of bureaucrats during the oil boom ranged from satirical anecdotes to diatribes to more profound examinations of the bureaucrat's psychology. Journalists expressed concern that the oil wealth would remain under the control of the PRI, in the coffers of the one-party state's institutions and ministries, and that any citizens who wanted a taste of it would have to "resign themselves to becoming public employees."[46] In scathing critiques, journalists complained about the ineptitude and laziness of public employees, as illustrated in Figure 1, which satirizes their work schedules.

Satire went hand in hand with unremitting concern that a materialistic middle class would squander oil revenues. Journalists expressed anger at extravagant, unsustainable consumption patterns. One article described the "Ridiculous Class"—the class of "I want but cannot have" (*la del quiero y no puedo*). This class was prone to being lured by advertising (and promises of easy credit) to buy unnecessary goods such as cars, televisions, and window drapes. Only credit gave them the ability to buy these goods. The article derided those who spent more on one meal than people need to spend on food for an entire month. Members of this class, the journalist contended, take mortgages to go on vacation, living on loans drawn against an uncertain future. They were thus condemned to the most alienating of all alienations: the servitude of unattainable desires. They were also condemned to rumor mongering, stubborn discontent, and catastrophism; they held the country back.[47]

Journalists argued that oil money should not be funneled directly into government-owned companies. Government agencies, they charged, had begun to fantasize about prosperity, and state employees speculated about where the anticipated millions would land. In the meantime, the various bureaucracies competed to maximize their budgets.[48] As these agencies lobbied for increased funds, many journalists worried that bureaucrats and PEMEX workers would be the only ones, besides the political élite, to reap the benefits of the boom.[49] These concerns provoked sharp criticisms of middle-class public employees and of corruption in the state apparatus. "There is an inflation of ideas, when it is said that we will be rich because of oil," wrote Jorge Eugenio Ortiz in *El Universal*. "We should not let ourselves be convinced by this fantasy. We need to be precise about who will become rich, and we must begin with the principle that oil is a national resource and not the personal resource of any individual or group."[50] Because public employees embodied the petro-state, critiques of bureaucrats were attacks on the state and its economic model and demonstrated the limits of López Portillo's populism (of the "embrujo").

It is difficult to know how the newspaper-reading public reacted to these articles. In fact, the Mexican press has been accused by public intellectuals of being uncritical and co-opted by the PRI. But newspaper accounts of the oil boom, many of them critical of the PRI and the status quo more

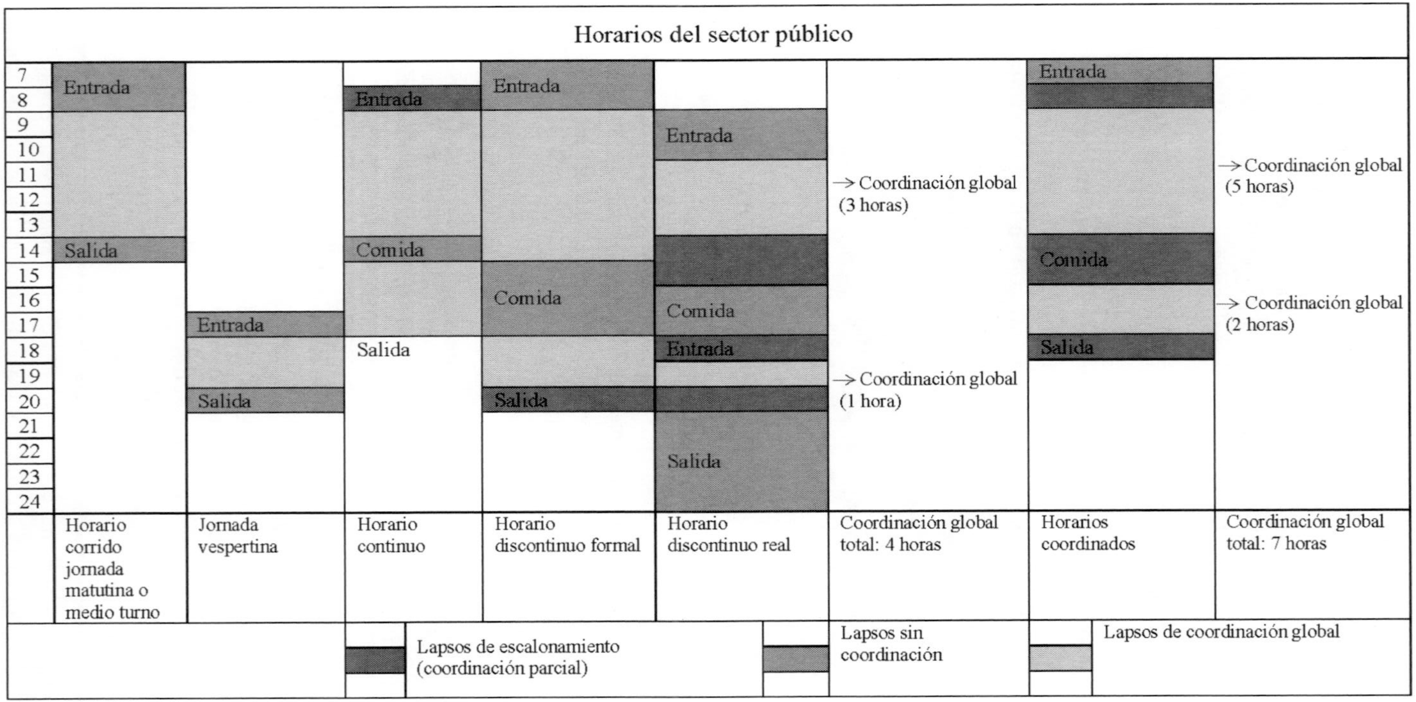

FIGURE 1. A bureaucrat's work schedule. According to this chart, the bureaucrat spends most of his or her time arriving and getting settled, eating, and getting ready to leave. In the office, large segments of time are spent in organizational meetings. From "Horarios del sector público," *El Sol de México*, 28 January 1977.

generally, suggest that this was not always the case.[51] Indeed, advocating for the power of the public sphere, the journalist Ana Mairena suggested that readers write letters to the editor and op-ed pieces to condemn the "ridiculous class," to "make its members face themselves in the mirror of public opinion."[52]

Newspaper articles often contained anecdotes about the frustrations of dealing with bureaucrats, especially those who held their job because of a powerful relative. These anecdotes invoked a guileless citizen attempting to process paperwork who was confronted by the intransigence of a bureaucrat; in the process, the naïve citizen quickly learns the efficiency inspired by a five-hundred-peso bill.[53] Writers occasionally distinguished between helpful bureaucrats and those who avoided doing their jobs. The writer Paco Ignacio Taibo told an anecdote about a bureaucrat—an "astute" bureaucrat—who avoided all work.[54] At first, this specimen pretended to read a document, then hid behind some file cabinets, feigning not to notice people queuing at the window. Taibo's aunt happened to be in the queue and demanded to know why this man was not attending to the public. When she learned that he was a cousin of the boss's wife, she became infuriated and demanded to be served by him. Another bureaucrat, who had been attending to the queue, became nervous and offered to assist the aunt. But she refused, indignant: "I want him, the one hiding behind the file cabinet, to come out so we can see what he's doing. I want to know if my taxes are working or if they're hidden behind a file cabinet." Soon, others in the queue joined in, shouting: "Get out from behind the file cabinet! Get out from behind the file cabinet!" This moment of collective action, Taibo wrote, did not come to much because the "astute" bureaucrat fled and locked himself in the bathroom. This anecdote—apocryphal or not—illustrates the rage inspired among the public by everyday encounters with nepotism.

Debates about bureaucrats did not cast them as a homogeneous group. Many journalists drew distinctions between different groups within the middle class; one article contrasted the "common, everyday" bureaucrats with the "petulant technocrats." According to this journalist, the former were second-class citizens: "They eat *chilaquiles*, not snacks of Roquefort cheese sprinkled with walnuts; they pass their vacations—patriotic vacations—in Oaxtepec [a tourist area near Mexico City]; they do not drink champagne in luxury jets." This article illustrates nuances in the stereotype of the bureaucracy, underscoring the division between high-level officials with their luxuries and lower-level, middle-class state employees, with their modest albeit comfortable homes, medical care, access to credit, and protection by strong unions.[55]

When citizens came into contact with the state bureaucracy, the split personality of the middle class became clear. Its members filled the ranks of the state agencies but also suffered the effects of corruption and nepotism. Figure 2 shows a cartoon that captures this tension, with its queue of middle-class citizens trying to process paperwork, being treated with disdain by the middle-class bureaucrat who is attending to them.

Sometimes journalists analyzed the psychology of these civil servants and explored the motivations of the iconic lazy bureaucrat. One journalist described how bureaucrats sought clever, discreet forms of pleasure in everyday acts, to compensate for feelings of frustration and impotence. (Mario Sepúlveda Garza's "discreto encanto" made a clever pun on the 1972 film by Luis Buñuel, *Le charme discret de la bourgeoisie* [*The Discreet Charm of the Bourgeoisie*].)[56] They created a world in which their influence mattered. Other writers showed how bureaucrats themselves felt alienated from their insignificant workplaces, where they were nothing more than cogs in the machine, in "the system."[57] This existential malaise was one of the prominent themes of the Televisa series: condemned to unrewarding work, alienated from their creative potential, many members of the middle class sought escape through consumerism, sports, and comic books, all of which reinforced conformism and mediocrity.[58]

Certainly, critiques or laments over the political, economic, and psychological condition of bureaucrats were not limited to Mexico or to the

FIGURE 2. What's happening to us? The clothing they wear suggests that the man in line and the woman behind the window at the clerk's office belong to the same class. Indeed, they look as though, in another set of circumstances, they could be married. By Leonardo Martínez Aguayo, reprinted in Galico, *Los 80's*, 62.

1970s and 1980s. They belong to a tradition that examines the historical role of the middle class; social scientists and analysts have long grappled with the political and economic role of this pivotal social group in Latin America and other developing regions. Some analysts argue that the existence of a robust, reformist middle class is a requirement for a stable democracy; others view the middle class as inclined toward authoritarianism, militarism, and revolution.[59]

In postrevolutionary Mexico, newspaper accounts from the 1930s through the 1960s underscore both the hope and the fear that the middle class inspired.[60] Positive portrayals cast the class as the achievement of the Mexican Revolution. In newspaper accounts from the 1930s through the 1960s, many journalists commended the middle classes for their intellectual preparation, technical skills, and social background, as well as for their constant desire to better themselves, their assiduousness, and their perceived innate passion for work. Some journalists referred to the redistributive capacity of the middle class, as a social equalizer between the wealthy and the poor. Many articles highlighted not only the role of the middle class in bringing economic progress but also the role it played in the liberal-democratic regimes in the United States and much of Europe, and regarded the class as crucial to the development of democracy in Mexico. In negative accounts, journalists often derided members of the middle class for being apolitical, attributing this to the unstable limbo they lived in, caught between the desire to emulate upper-class lifestyles and the dread of falling into the working classes or poor. This precarious position between privilege and poverty inspired fear. Journalists noted how the middle class had supported totalitarian regimes in Germany and Italy; and many expressed concern that bureaucrats and businessmen were vulnerable to radical ideologies.

Evaluations of the middle class in the developing world often compared it with the European bourgeoisies and found the former lacking.[61] One of the most damning comparisons came from Frantz Fanon, a scholar of dependency, decolonization, and postcolonialism in Africa.[62] In his classic *The Wretched of the Earth* (1961), Fanon argues that the European bourgeoisies, which he describes as dynamic, educated, and secular, had succeeded in establishing stable liberal democracies and prosperous capitalist economies. In contrast, the middle class in underdeveloped countries—a "little greedy caste, avid and avaricious, with the mind of a huckster"—failed to establish bourgeois states based upon liberal ideas of democracy and equality.[63] Instead, the middle class created the one-party state, which transformed democracy into a blatantly corrupt system in which the ruling party became a means for personal advancement (just as journalists complained that a surefire way to get a share of the Mexican oil wealth was to become a public employee).[64] In Fanon's analysis, the middle class constituted a profiteering élite of civil servants—a "dictatorship of the civil servants"—whose privileges were based upon their role as intermediaries (either between foreign investors and the nation or between the state and the people).[65] Comfortable in this lucrative position, they did not rise to the role of a national and patriotic bourgeoisie.[66] They governed through fear, farce, and demagogy, unlike the western European bourgeoisies that governed through law, order, and justice.[67] Fanon's conclusion was one of clear condemnation: "the single party is the modern form of the dictatorship of the bourgeoisie, unmasked, unpainted, unscrupulous and cynical."[68] To be sure, Fanon may have idealized the role of the bourgeoisie in Europe, but his writings offer a glimpse into the expectations placed upon the middle class in the developing world at midcentury. His work is a lament for squandered potential: the middle class failed itself and the nation by betraying its own historical responsibility. It also provides a framework for understanding criticisms of corruption among public employees in the PRI's one-party state, which belong to a broader tradition of disappointment with the middle class across the developing world.

In 1979 the six episodes in Televisa's series condemned the role of the middle class in Mexican history, and in sweeping terms. The television series gave few positive examples of the middle class in Mexican history. Those examples it did give came from the colonial and early national period, with the middle class appearing as a classic bourgeois force, in the European mold, during the struggle against the colonial regime and the nineteenth-century civil war between the liberals and conservatives. But when it came to appraising the middle class's role in modern history, the series was censorious: responsible for the dictatorship of Porfirio Díaz and the betrayal of the Mexican Revolution, the middle class sought alliance with the wealthy and worked against progressive change.[69] After the Revolution, according to the series, the middle class appropriated the benefits of social programs intended for the working classes, peasants, and poor. And, during the Mexican Miracle, the middle class overdetermined social and cultural norms, becoming more than just a powerful social group but also an influential ideology, hegemonic and conservative.[70]

During the oil boom, criticisms of public employees provided an alternative to official optimism. The narratives of corruption formed a political discourse about middle-class failure: when José López Portillo and his top advisors converted Mexico into a petro-state, the middle class had undeniably failed to assume its historical responsibility to establish a liberal, bourgeois state. Because the oil was a state-run industry, petrolization increased the PRI's political control (especially after the shaky Echeverría administration) and fortified Mexico's one-party system. And the influx of petrodollars intensified the day-to-day corruption of civil servants. Instead of being agents of dynamic capitalist growth, the members of the middle classes were unproductive parasites in a debt economy. For example, the upswing in imported consumer goods, most of which ended up in the shopping carts of middle-class consumers, was contrary to the López Portillo administration's Global Development Plan (Plan Global de Desarrollo), which aimed for greater domestic production of consumer goods, to reduce nonproductive imports.[71] Indeed, in 1981 Leopoldo Solís, a prominent economist at the Bank of Mexico and, for a time, an important member of López Portillo's team, argued that the middle class's taste for imported goods threatened economic growth and social welfare.[72]

Criticism of bureaucrats exposed the folly in idealizations of the middle class and underscored a burgeoning crisis. Bureaucrats, who had embodied the fantasies of the midcentury miracle—of a state-led prosperity and a stable middle class—became, during the oil boom, a corrupted version of the ideal. The middle class failed in the role that had been imagined for it. What happened to the middle class when it failed? It went hard-boiled.

Middle-Class Noir

The middle class went noir in the late 1970s. In the novels of Paco Ignacio Taibo II, the corrupt world of middle-class Mexico emerges as the antithesis to the idealized middle class as a harbinger of liberal democracies. The novels are a political narrative from the radical left, in which the very notion of a bourgeois, liberal democracy in Mexico is, at best, an ideological fantasy and, at worst, a cruel joke. Instead, Taibo advances a narrative about middle-class failure in his hard-boiled detective fiction (unsentimental crime stories that portray brutality and social corruption).[73] Part of the generation of intellectuals who came of age during the 1968 student movement, Taibo is one of Mexico's most prominent writers and activists, known for his caustic wit and political activism. His Belascoarán detective series, first published in 1976, constituted a significant intervention in the public sphere, exposing the grim underbelly of the oil boom. His middle-class characters, from cops and customs officials to shopkeepers and movie stars, have created a world permeated by official corruption and existential malaise. Justice and redemption are impossible. Amid the corrupt police and juridical bureaucracies of the capital city, Taibo's middle-class characters are disillusioned refugees from their own fantasies.[74]

Detective fiction is a rich source for a social and cultural history of the middle class. Theorist Ernest Mandel argues that detective fiction (and the mystery novel) capture the essence of bourgeois society. Mandel charts the history of detective fiction from its origins in early modern European stories of the noble bandit and populist petit bourgeois such as Robin Hood (heroes in revolt against feudalism) through the nineteenth-century evil criminal who threatens the bourgeois order. The rise of detective fiction in the mid-nineteenth century in England, France, and the United States, he argues, came about at "a particular point in the development of capitalism, pauperism, criminality, and primitive social revolt against bourgeois society. . . . With the rising need of the bourgeoisie to defend instead of attack the social order, the noble bandit is transformed into the evil criminal."[75] Mandel traces the evolution of detective fiction from the parlor games of eccentric élites making deductions from clues to plodding police detectives tracking criminals through scientific analysis in the novels of the 1930s and 1940s.

Throughout this evolution of the detective story, the crime was solved, justice was usually served, and the bourgeois social order survived. This began to change as the lines between the criminal, on the one hand, and law and order, on the other, became murkier in the noir novels of Raymond Chandler and Dashiell Hammett, written during the 1920s and 1930s and increasingly popular in the postwar period. Their detectives are cynical, tragic heroes, "operating within the framework and in the service of an Establishment in which they believe less and less, which they even begin to hate and despise."[76] In this ambiguous space between crime and the established order, the possibility of justice is cast into doubt.[77] The genre of detective fiction, then, has from its inception explored the intersection of the law, justice, and the social order.

Latin American writers have further subverted the norms of the genre by pointing to the state as the source of criminality. In the Latin American *novelas neopoliciacas*, the detective is no longer a superhero but a frail and flawed character. The criminal is no longer an individual; instead, crime originates in political institutions. And the narratives are driven less by a need to resolve the mystery than by an imperative to expose social, ideological, and political problems.[78] The Latin American *novela neopoliciaca* emerged in the wake of political failure. By the 1970s, coup d'états against democratically elected leaders, state-sponsored genocide, and the disappearance of tens of thousands of citizens had come to characterize the history of cold war Latin America. In this political landscape of failure, the *novelas neopoliciacas* offered sharp and incisive social criticism.

Paco Ignacio Taibo II is a pioneer of the genre in Latin America. The novels in his Belascoarán series name the corruption in Mexican society rather than focusing on solving the crime. Certainly, these novels retain some of the forms of a whodunit and solving the mystery remains an imperative throughout, but the resolution is often unsatisfactory because the system that generates the crimes—the corrupt world of Mexico City—survives unperturbed. By pitting his detective, Héctor Belascoarán Shayne, against the police and other state officials, Taibo depicts law in the service of corruption, emphasizing the impossibility of justice and the instability of the social order. In the words of cultural critic Luis Martín-Cabrera, hard-boiled detective fiction in Latin America gives the lie to the "ideological fantasy" of a liberal state and its promises of justice.[79]

Taibo's Belascoarán series belongs to a Mexican intellectual tradition of writing about the middle classes. In the aftermath of the Mexican Revolution, an imperative to understand national culture emerged, as intellectuals (and politicians) attempted to forge a nation after nearly ten years of violent struggle. In this context, some of the country's most prominent intellectuals produced a series of writings on *lo mexicano* (the Mexican) or *mexicanidad* (Mexican-ness), which grapple with questions about the historical role of the middle class.[80] In *Profile of Man and Culture in Mexico* (1934), one of the foundational texts of the "lo mexicano" literature, humanities scholar Samuel Ramos wrote, "The middle class has been the backbone of our national history and is still its real substance."[81] Yet, according to Ramos, the middle-class Mexican (always a man in Ramos's analysis) suffers from a psychological inferiority complex regarding his national identity: he is overly sensitive about being Mexican. This insecurity leads the middle-class Mexican to "debility, self-denigration, feelings of incompetence and of vital deficiency."[82] Ramos traces the origin of this disjuncture, between the prominent historical role of the middle class and this sense of national inferiority, to a European education. It was in European schools (and in Mexican schools with European curricula), he argues, that middle-class Mexican students began to resent their national identity. For Ramos, this inferiority complex might be resolved through a nationalist education program that emphasized the study of Mexico.[83] In Ramos's analysis, then, the middle class constituted the prime mover and "real substance" of Mexican history, but its historical actors were hampered by an inferiority complex.

In contrast, Octavio Paz argued that the middle class had never really existed in Mexico. In his seminal essay *The Labyrinth of Solitude* (1950), Paz described how nineteenth-century liberals had hoped to break with the colonial system; they hoped that a democratic constitution "would almost automatically produce a new social class, the bourgeoisie."[84] As a new social class, the bourgeoisie would lead Mexico out of the feudal legacy of the colonial period. It is possible that Paz subscribed to a historical narrative that pinned the hopes for democracy, modernity, and capitalism on a European-style, classic bourgeoisie.[85] Like Ramos, Paz attributed a determining historical role to the bourgeoisie; unlike Ramos, however, Paz wrote of the absence of such a historical actor in Mexico.[86] Neither the

War of Independence, nor the War of Reform, nor the dictatorship of Porfirio Diaz produced a bourgeoisie (in the European mold).[87] Paz attributed the failure of the Mexican bourgeoisie—its failure to exist, its failure to emerge, its failure to assume its historical role—to the constraints of imperialism: "[The liberal plan] should have brought a bourgeoisie into power. Thus our evolution would have followed the same stages as that of Europe. But our progress is erratic. Imperialism has not allowed us to achieve 'historical normality.'"[88] Mexico's colonial and, later, neocolonial position in the world economy encouraged the would-be bourgeois to act not as a harbinger of capitalism but as an intermediary for foreign interests, similar to Fanon's "huckster" civil servants.

Paz is more equivocal on the existence and nature of the middle class in postrevolutionary Mexico. On the one hand, he accuses the bourgeoisie of abdicating its historical role in favor of the role of the intermediary: "Their methods would not be much different from those of the great landholders under Díaz: they would govern from behind the mask of the Revolution, just as Díaz governed from behind the mask of liberalism."[89] On the other hand, Paz describes how the Revolution "tried to complete a task that had taken the European bourgeoisie more than a hundred and fifty years."[90] And Paz describes some of the ways in which the Revolution succeeded in moving Mexico closer to "historical normality." He describes how the Revolution produced, albeit under the umbrella of the state, a working class, a bourgeoisie or middle class, and a national capitalist class.[91] In Paz's analysis, it remained to be seen if one of these two different middle-class archetypes—the neocolonial intermediary or classic bourgeois—might dominate the postrevolutionary political landscape.

For Paz, the potential of the middle class (and the other modern classes that emerged after the Revolution) hinged on whether it could achieve some autonomy from the corporatist structures of the PRI's Institutional Revolution. Writing *Labyrinth of Solitude* in 1950, Paz seems uncertain whether the middle class wanted to or could establish such autonomy. He describes how the PRI's system impeded the potential of the middle class: "Suddenly we have reached the limit: in these few years we have exhausted all the historical forms Europe could provide us. . . . The sterility of the bourgeois world will end in suicide or a new form of creative participation."[92] But there was a glimmer of hope in the second possibility. (And, in the years after 1950, these modern classes did agitate for their constitutional rights and for a degree of autonomy from the one-party state—such as the railway workers movement of the late 1950s, the doctors movement of the mid-1960s, the peasant movements for local democracy of the 1950s and 1960s, and the student movements of the late 1960s—their "creative participation" ended not in suicide but in state-sponsored massacre.)[93]

Paz's apparent indecision regarding the potential of the postrevolutionary middle class found no place in the work of later Mexican writers. Novelists such as Carlos Fuentes belonged to a generation of Mexican and Latin American writers who came to prominence during a period that cultural critic Carlos Monsiváis has termed the "years of confidence"—a period bookended by the 1959 Cuban Revolution and the 1968 Tlatelolco massacre.[94] During these years of confidence, Mexican cultural production exploded with energy, which manifested itself in experimental cinema, new publishing houses, mass media techniques, milestone projects such as the Museum of Anthropology in Mexico City, and a new, critical cosmopolitanism.[95] During this brief decade of confidence, novelists critiqued the middle-class world produced by the Mexican Miracle. Carlos Fuentes's *Where the Air Is Clear* (1958) and *The Death of Artemio Cruz* (1962) are perhaps most emblematic of this trend; these novels portray a corrupt, vapid, consumerist, and self-indulgent middle class that embodies the betrayal of the Mexican Revolution.[96] Writers like Fuentes boldly challenged both the cultural nationalism promoted by the PRI and the American way of life embraced by the middle class.[97] Their novels were grand narratives, "total novels" (*novelas totalizadoras*), that attempted to rewrite history; their subject was the urban middle-class world (to the extent that Mexico City is the main character in *Where the Air Is Clear*).

The Tlatelolco massacre marked the end of these years of confidence. It was at once an epilogue that confirmed the corruption of the middle-class world exposed in *Where the Air Is Clear* and *The Death of Artemio Cruz* and also the beginning of what Carlos Monsiváis called "dissidence as atonement."[98] In 1976, Monsiváis commented on the absence of a critical and perceptive literature after 1968 (notwithstanding several notable exceptions).[99] By 1976, the corruption portrayed by writers like Carlos Fuentes had been made manifest by the state-sponsored violence of the late 1960s and early 1970s. In his indictment of the rotting system, Fuentes was proven correct. After 1968 the question was, what more would be said? or, what literature would be written?

Paco Ignacio Taibo II's Belascoarán series appeared amid the political desolation of the post-1968 Mexican landscape. By 1976, the student movement had been repressed, the urban guerrilla movement had been squashed, and any compromise or reconciliation that Luis Echeverría's administration might have promised had evaporated. In this political and cultural landscape, the Belascoarán series restored critical vitality to representations of the middle class in Mexican literature. Taibo offered one strategy for writing after 1968: in his novels, the middle class went hard-boiled.[100] Whereas Fuentes took the middle-class world as his subject, in the Belascoarán series Taibo focused on the inner turmoil that this corrupt world generated among the middle classes themselves.[101]

Literary scholars argue that the Belascoarán series captures the failure of the Mexican state, the corruption of the Mexican Revolution, and the postapocalyptic urban environment of Mexico City.[102] But who failed whom? This is a failure of the middle class: instead of establishing a progressive democracy, it helped to create the so-called Institutional Revolution and one-party state. The Belascoarán series charts how this failure impacted middle-class individuals, showcasing themes of complacency, alienation, disillusionment, guilt, despair, and politicization.

The premise of the series is the end of middle-class aspirations, dreams, and contentment. Héctor Belascoarán Shayne abandons his comfortable middle-class life, his job as an engineer, and the apartment where he has lived with his wife and, after a three-week correspondence course, becomes an independent detective. His alienation propels the series.

The first four novels of the Belascoarán series are set during the oil boom: *Días de combate* (1976), *Cosa fácil* (1977), *No habrá final feliz* (1981), and *Algunas nubes* (although written in 1985, the action takes place in 1978).[103] In *Días de combate*, Héctor pursues a strangler who murders women in the city streets. In *Cosa fácil*, he solves three mysteries simultaneously—the murder of an engineer in a steel company, the mystery behind a teenage girl in danger, and the question of whether or not Zapata is still alive. In *No habrá final feliz*, he follows a trail of official violence and corruption to the Halcones. And in *Algunas nubes*, Héctor investigates the brutal murder of two brothers linked to the corruption and extralegal activities of government officials.

Muy Mierda

No habrá final feliz begins with a note from the author: "Evidently, the story and names in this novel are purely fictional. The country, however, even though it is hard to believe, is absolutely real."[104] In this novel, Héctor Belascoarán investigates the Halcones, the paramilitary police force supposedly disbanded after the massacre of students on 10 June 1971. In the novel, following the massacre the Halcones have been employed by the city government in the guise of subway security but continue to work (the novel is set in 1979) as a private paramilitary force for city politicians. As he gets closer to the truth, Héctor finds himself without recourse. Even if he had documented proof of the existence of the Halcones and their crimes, no one could help him—not the media, not the Communist Party, no one.[105] At the end of the novel, Héctor articulates a philosophy of the state, a theory of good and evil. Until *No habrá final feliz*, he had been able to dance with the state on the edge of the system, but in this novel the one-party state emerges as totalitarian—there is no room for maneuver. He pictures the state as "the great castle of the witch in Snow White, out of which came not only the Halcones, but also engineering degrees and Televisa programming. There were no nuances. It was an infernal machine that you had to stay away from. . . . [He imagined] epic duels. He thought of Bakunin against the State, of Sherlock Holmes vs. Moriarty. There was no middle ground."[106]

At the end of *Días de combate*, Héctor admits to the strangler that, in fact, "the Great Strangler was the System. . . . You're right; you're not the only one. From higher levels, others are playing chess with us. But I can't reach those levels. One day the sky will be taken by assault."[107] Héctor confesses to the strangler that the system itself is perhaps more dangerous than one sociopath. The phrase "assault on the sky" refers to a 1974 uprising led by the Liga Comunista 23 de Septiembre. By referring to the urban guerrilla movement, Héctor suggests that a more radical, organized, and violent challenge to the system would be necessary to redress corruption at the highest levels. Nevertheless, he insists on his mission to stop the strangler—a futile insistence, for after all, if the ubiquitous state is the originator of crime, Héctor's individual campaign against the strangler would not challenge the system.

In *Algunas nubes*, a storeowner works as a money launderer for PRI officials through family connections (specifically, his brother-in-law, a corrupt police commander who got his start repressing leftist activists). When the storeowner dies of natural causes, nefarious forces working outside the law murder his children and almost kill his daughter-in-law, the only one left to inherit the sizeable fortune that had been hidden in his name. The novel is set in December 1978, at the height of the oil boom. It depicts how money can be siphoned into the coffers of state employees and how this corruption can destroy the middle class. In the novel a character named La Rata (the rat) works for state officials as a run-of-the-mill gangster, on the margins of the system. La Rata began his career intimidating students in the UNAM and in 1968 had personally met the mayor of the city. When the student movement lost steam and thus ceased to provide lucrative opportunities for gangsters like La Rata, he worked as a bodyguard for state functionaries.[108] When Héctor meets him in his office, his desk is covered with letters bearing the PRI's official logo.[109] While the dirty money in *Algunas nubes* comes from drugs and bank robberies, the money-laundering system and the violence perpetrated in the name of the PRI serve as a critique of corruption during the oil boom.

The series traces the despair and alienation that this failing system causes among the middle class. Early in the first novel, *Días de combate*, Héctor has dinner with a couple, friends from his former life, and tries to explain to them his decision to abandon his comfortable existence and become a detective. As his friends question him, he looks out their window and sees "the diminutive and soft, soggy and weak [*blandengue*], rose-colored city; the slow city of the affable middle class. The city invented for those who live on the seventh floor." He feels a pang of envy for these friends and, as they question him, the material goods of their lives taunt him. His internal monologue rattles off a list: the nice dinner table set, the bossa nova music in the background, the "ordered disorder of books that form piles in discrete corners." He watches as Ana María, with a gesture and a condescending smile, forbids her husband to light his pipe. His friends cannot accept his motives, and Ana María questions how serious his decision is: "It sounds very New York, very cosmopolitan, not very Mexican. I suspect it's not very serious." Héctor leaves abruptly, before dinner, and these friends do not reappear in the novels.[110]

Shortly thereafter, Héctor meets his brother, Carlos, whom he has not seen in several years. They have coffee in Carlos's small room. Much of Héctor's political schooling happens through Carlos, and this meeting serves as a transition from his old world to his new one. Héctor enters his brother's world, describing Carlos's room as inviting. For Héctor, it suggests a life of listening to records, smoking pipes, drinking coffee, reading books, and sipping sherry. It is full of books by or about Marx, Trotsky, Lenin, Mao, Ho Chi Minh, and Che, as well as anthologies of Cuban poetry, books from Latin American presses, volumes on contemporary history, detective novels, and the classics of science fiction.[111] Juxtaposed with his internal catalogue of the possessions in Ana María's house, his brother's room illustrates, through contrast, the differences within the middle class.

Héctor explains his decision to his brother: "I am dying at the bottom of a canyon and I have no idea where all this will take me. . . . The strangler is a pretext." He describes the moment his transformation began, after having seeing a film about Sherlock Holmes:

I was leaving the cinema with Claudia. . . . But it wasn't the movie, although it helped. . . . I was looking for a pretext; nothing was rational. . . . We left the cinema and a kid sold me a copy of *Extra*. That afternoon the strangler had appeared in the newspapers for the first time. And Claudia said that she liked the movie. And I agreed. But I didn't say anything about what was going on inside me, and I spent the night tossing and turning in bed. And that's how it began. Three days later we separated and I quit my job.[112]

Carlos embraces his brother's metamorphosis. He admits that he had cast Héctor as the conservative sibling, part of "the Establishment," who excelled at being petit bourgeois. Although pleased with Héctor's new persona, Carlos warns his brother about playing on the edge of the system because the police chief, the president, the factory owners, "they're all there [as well]; but they're playing on the edge of *their* system."[113] Héctor can accept the dangers, which he prefers to the monotonous routines of his old life: "Better than the marathon for a new car every year, the slow even life [*vida a cuentagotas*], the middle-class security, the symphony, the tie, the cardboard relations, the cardboard bed, the cardboard sex, the wife, the Mrs., the future children, climbing the ladder, the salary, the career, all that he escaped to pursue a strangler."[114]

Héctor walks the city incessantly. His roaming takes him to the parks and streets of middle-class neighborhoods, such as Roma and Condesa, and his internal monologue provides a commentary on this world. He notices "kids playing football, old men re-reading the *Iliad* or the *Odyssey*, teenagers listening to rock on their radios, the ice-cream man, bicycles. It made him smile, reminded him of a Lelouch movie; it was a world that, lamentably, was full of shit [*muy mierda*]."[115]

Most of the principal characters enter the narrative through their own disillusionments. Irene, Héctor's elusive love interest, seeks out the strangler in the hope of being his next victim. She comes from an élite political family, one permeated by desperation, loneliness, boredom, and incest. Her father had been a union leader, and at university she learns of his corrupt practices. The 1968 student movement "exploded inside her." She participates in demonstrations and hides a mimeograph machine in her garage. She experiences *azoro*, "a confused excitement, surprise, the fight, and hope." But this does not last, and on 2 October, the day of the Tlatelolco massacre, she is sunbathing at her family's summer home in Cuernavaca. Her boredom intensifies; she drops out of university and travels around the world. But affairs with exiled Czech radicals in Paris and long trips to India do not cure her "profound loneliness." One night after Irene returns to Mexico, her sister, on a drunken binge, climbs into their father's bed, naked. He responds to her sexual overtures and, soon afterward, Irene's sister shoots herself. This incest and its tragic outcome drive Irene to despair. After these events, at the beginning of *Días de combate*, Irene takes to the streets in search of the strangler, to offer him her neck. Instead, she meets Héctor, in his own search for the strangler.[116]

The strangler's story is also one of desperation. A businessman who owns three import companies, he studied accounting at the UNAM and later completed a graduate degree in Geneva. He speaks French well and plays squash at a private club. He derives pleasure from owning things and wears monogrammed clothing. He uses watermarked paper and stamps his personal seal in his books. His diary, which Héctor uncovers, is a class confession. He is a member of the upper echelons of the middle class and commits his crimes to access the elemental part of life, to feel alive. Creating fear gives him pleasure, and he notes with pride that the topic of conversation at his dinner parties has switched from debates over the virtues of different brands of cognac to the grisly murders.[117]

Guilt permeates Héctor's disenchantment. In *Cosa fácil*, he agrees to work for the director of a steel company, to investigate the murder of an engineer. He does this so he can redress his past behavior, when, as an engineer for General Electric, he had treated the workers with disdain.[118] The steel factory is in the northern part of the city, near General Electric. He recalls how he used to drive past working-class and poor neighborhoods,

> trying to look as little as possible to both sides, hating the dust and the market, the public works and the masses that assaulted the buses at 5:30 a.m. He had tried to ignore that all this existed as he headed for the comfortable, pestilent security of the middle-class Napoles neighborhood. . . . He didn't have anything to do with the industrial zone . . . the misery of the immigrants from the countryside, the pools of sulfur, dry dust, and the drunken police. The land frauds, the illegal slaughterhouses, the salaries below minimum wage, the cold air from the east and the unemployment. . . . He had closed his eyes and ears.[119]

Now, as a detective, he takes the bus, but he cannot avoid a feeling of middle-class guilt for his past behavior: "Because of this, when he got off the bus, a vague feeling of guilt invaded him."[120] When he meets with the directors of the factory, Héctor comes face-to-face with his old life; in the tidy white-collar offices, he recognizes his old world. He wonders if he can ever truly escape the life he had so desperately fled: "Would he forever be condemned to live on the same side of the fence? Could he ever erase the mark, that sort of Masonic stamp imprinted on him when he entered the Faculty of Engineering, which made him an overseer and accomplice of the bosses for life?"[121]

In his ongoing struggle to escape his middle-class life, Héctor often conflates the lower classes with a stronger sense of *mexicanidad* and wants to experience life as an "everyday Mexican." His three officemates serve as foils for his endeavor: Gilberto the plumber, Carlos the carpenter, and "El Gallo" the sewage engineer. For example, at the beginning of *Días de combate*, Héctor describes a feeling of alienation from "los mexicanos" about whom Gilberto the plumber can speak so readily.[122] Héctor needs these men to help keep him Mexican and believes that, with them, "he was another artisan, with less training, with less professional capacity. He was a Mexican in the Mexican jungle and had to make sure that the myth of a detective, full of cosmopolitan and exotic suggestions, did not eat him alive."[123] Importantly, however, it is with El Gallo, who comes from a middle-class neighborhood in a northern city, that Héctor has the most meaningful conversations. In *Cosa fácil*, Héctor decries the rising cost of Pepsi due to inflation. But money is not the issue, because he has just inherited a sizeable estate from his mother. Héctor associates complaining about prices with being Mexican:

> He took a sip of the sweet liquid. In his mind, he complained about the price. Motherfuckers. [*No tenían madre*.] He still remembered when soda pop cost forty-five cents, not too long ago.
>
> This was his way of remaining Mexican. An everyday Mexican, sharing the complaints, protesting the rising price of tortillas, getting pissed off at the increase in bus fares. . . . If only by joining his brothers in complaint, scorn and pride . . . Belascoarán won his right to continue being Mexican, his chance to avoid becoming a *vedette* or a Martian; it was his chance to stay close to the people.
>
> He dedicated an obscene gesture to whoever was responsible for the hike in soft drink prices and returned to his desk.[124]

Through Héctor's struggle to abandon his world, the series advances a critique of middle-class complacency in the face of official corruption. The novels serve as a condemnation of political quiescence in the midst of a rotting system. To some extent, the very condition of being middle class implies complacency. For example, Elisa, Héctor's sister, returns to Mexico after a failed marriage in Canada just as Héctor begins his hunt for the strangler. She had been a housewife in the first world, but that comfortable life had left her empty and apolitical: "In the end, [I was] a housewife, dependent, even useless. If I had even known how to do anything, it was almost forgotten. And now I'm 24 years old, single again, without children, ragged, lonely, with some rudimentary knowledge of typing, de-politicized because Canada makes you middle class to the core. Everything I experienced in '68 is now hidden in my memory."[125]

For Héctor to escape from his middle-class condition and its inherent complacency, he must undergo a process of politicization; he needs to be schooled in the workings of the system to solve the mysteries. Héctor receives most of his political education from his brother Carlos. In *Cosa fácil*, Carlos explains to Elisa and Héctor what happed to the 1968 student movement. Carlos describes how Echeverría co-opted the generation of '68; half of them, he says, took well-paid jobs in state institutions: "Echeverría re-invented the country to give them jobs." Carlos acknowledges that many wanted to make a difference when they started but soon lost that commitment, falling for the "elegant bureaucracy of intellectual expertise." He notes sarcastically that they now work in absurd state institutions pushing initiatives such as the "National Organization for the Development of Cherries" or the "Trust for the Utilization of Bananas."[126]

The author appears as a character in *Algunas nubes*. In the course of his investigation into official corruption, Héctor comes across the name of a detective fiction writer, Paco Ignacio Taibo II, and seeks out the writer to warn him he is in danger—La Rata is after him. When Héctor and Taibo meet, two distinct political experiences stand in contrast with one another. Héctor barely noticed 1968, while Taibo participated in it. Taibo warns Héctor of trying to take on the system alone: "This country kills you, Héctor. . . . It kills you in lots of different ways. Through corruption, boredom . . . hunger, unemployment. . . . I've been fighting for the last 13 years. I was there in '68, joined a leftist party, went into union organizing, worked with industrial workers. . . . I didn't dedicate myself to making money, I never worked for the PRI, I owe nothing, or almost nothing. . . . But I am not willing to start a solitary war against the system. . . . Those wars you don't win or even fight."[127] In these novels, however, Héctor does fight a solitary war against the system. He had missed the radical, antiauthoritarian fervor of the late 1960s and early 1970s; by 1975, when he abandoned his old life, there were fewer spaces left for challenging the system.

At times, Carlos expresses frustration at Héctor's cynicism. Carlos, the radical activist who tries to change the system through political action, accuses his brother of having a vision of the "middle class prostituted by the violence of the system."[128] In Carlos's view, Héctor's cynicism—illustrated by his futile, individual struggle against the state—becomes yet another form of middle-class complacency. Instead of joining Carlos, who seeks change by organizing workers, Héctor sacrifices himself (over the course of the novels his body deteriorates and he loses sight in one eye; his body is absorbing the virulence of the system). Héctor tries to explain his one-man campaign to Taibo: "Listen Paco . . . '68 passed me by. . . . I read Che when I was 30, and only because I was stuck in a house with nothing else to read. I studied engineering to make bridges, cathedrals, and sport complexes, but I ended up in the asshole of General Electric."[129]

In the Belascoarán series, middle-class complacency functions as a litmus test of the PRI's hegemony. If the characters had remained complacent (in their tidy apartments, in Canada, with their monogrammed clothing), PRI politicians might have interpreted it as support for the Institutional Revolution. But instead of living in denial, under the illusion of democracy and justice, Héctor, his sister Elisa, his lover Irene, and other victims of corruption and injustice—even the strangler himself—abandon their illusions. For many of them, the middle-class political radicals Carlos and Paco Taibo become their mentors and critical guides to the underbelly of the oil boom, to the darker side of the PRI's official optimism, to the corrupt and rotting system that holds their world in place.

What is at stake in this test? In *Cosa fácil*, one of the mysteries Héctor is charged with solving is whether Emiliano Zapata is alive. Héctor accepts the job because he "wanted to see Zapata's eyes; he wanted to see if the country that the man had dreamed was possible. He wanted to see if the old man could communicate something of the passion, of the faith, that had animated his crusade."[130] Héctor narrows his search for Zapata to an old man living in a cave in the mountains of Morelos. As his search for Zapata nears an end, Héctor ruminates upon the corruption of the country. The two other mysteries in the novel involve a police commander black-mailing high-level functionaries in a steel company over contraband precious metals, and a teenager in danger because she has found pictures of politicians in compromising positions with her mother, a film star and mistress to some of the country's top officials.[131] Héctor laments this corruption and acknowledges that his own impunity is part of the problem—he has avoided arrest after gunfights in the streets.[132] When he meets the old man in the cave, the old man tells him: "[Zapata] is dead, I know what I'm talking about. He died in Chinameca, assassinated by traitors. The same rifles would appear today; the same men would give the order. The people cried then, they don't need to cry twice."[133]

The stakes are high in these novels: the corrupt one-party system alienated the once-complacent middle class. The failure of the PRI's Institutional Revolution (which, from the perspective of this old man, had been doomed from the beginning) drove the characters into desperate action and melancholic inertia.

Héctor dies at the end of *No habrá final feliz*, murdered by the Halcones, shot down as he crosses the street in front of his office. In an ultimate example of the arbitrary nature of violence in Mexico, Héctor's involvement with the Halcones begins with a misunderstanding: their captain incorrectly believes that Héctor has been investigating them. Héctor understands that his death is imminent because he has finally pushed too far against the edge of the system. As he lies dying in the gutter, he remembers his brother's advice, proffered when he began his career as a detective: "Carlos had been right, a few years ago, when he said Héctor wouldn't be able to skate on the edge of the system." In the battle between the forces of good and the forces of evil, "the spoils went to evil . . . and the country sent the fallen into the sewers."[134]

The Devil's Excrement

Whether in hard-boiled detective fiction or in searing newspaper critiques of bureaucrats, in the 1970s culture the term "middle class" became code for corruption and disillusionment. Fantasies about the middle class as the "fundamental aspiration" for Mexico's future had no place in these narratives: instead of producing a stable, bourgeois nation of law and order, the Mexican middle class created a world "full of shit." At midcentury

Octavio Paz had seen some promise in the postrevolutionary emergence of a Mexican bourgeoisie. But with the petrolization of the nation-state, Paz's fledgling middle class began to look more like an aristocratic rentier class than a classic bourgeois one. The rentier economy underscored the neo-colonial intermediary function of the middle class that both Paz and Fanon had decried. Petrolization thus impeded the possibility that Mexico might reach the (imagined) "historical normality" of a developed, bourgeois nation. And during the oil boom years, novelists and journalists hammered the petro-state and the middle class through the idiom of corruption and injustice. The official optimism about the oil boom and the censure by social critics both came out of an intellectual tradition that grapples with the historical role of the middle class, a tradition with a long history in Mexico.

In Mexico, Latin America, and beyond, "middle class" is an element of political discourse that generates powerful fantasies and fears. Ideas about what the middle class should be and do exert an almost centripetal force in discussions about political economy, development, and underdevelopment. Celebrated by some, excoriated by others, the middle class is a fundamental category in both radical and conservative analysis. In the late 1970s, narratives about the middle class were deployed in debates about the promise and danger of the oil boom and the PRI's one-party system more generally.

The so-called black gold quickly became, as Venezuelan OPEC founder Juan Pablo Pérez Alfonzo famously said in 1976, the "Devil's excrement."[135] With the promise of revenue from rent, the PRI gambled on the price of a single commodity. Mexico became dependent upon oil prices and vulnerable to fluctuations in the interest rate on its foreign debt. In 1981, when oil prices began to fall and interest rates rose, Mexico found itself in a severe economic crisis that would later become known as the "lost decade."

López Portillo and his top advisors had fallen for a classic dependency trap: they had mortgaged Mexico's future on the assumption that the market price of a single commodity would continue to rise or at least remain stable. As private bankers lined up to lend Mexico money, another dependency emerged—debt dependency. International bankers, awash with petrodollars from the Middle East, needed a good investment bet. On the belief that a government would not default, they were eager to lend Mexico money against her future oil reserves.

Why did the president and his advisors fall into this trap? After all, they might have mitigated the effects of any bust by holding oil revenues outside the domestic economy and building foreign currency reserves. They could have introduced petrodollars into the domestic economy at a gradual pace, which might have protected industry and agriculture from an inflated exchange rate.[136] Certainly, it is impossible to say whether such measures could have kept the "lost decade" at bay, but this alternative version of history raises a simple question: Why did the López Portillo administration embrace the petrolization of the Mexican economy?

Mexican policymakers believed in the magic of oil.[137] It is tempting, with hindsight, to view their optimism as either empty rhetoric or deluded fantasy. But cynical histories do not help us understand the historical mechanisms that produce dreams and visions. Uruguayan essayist Eduardo Galeano writes that Latin America's poverty is due to its natural wealth; but we cannot see Mexico as a victim of its oil reserves—commodities themselves do not make decisions.[138] They do, however, have the power to seduce. And for those ready and willing to be seduced, the black gold seemed to offer the world.

The black gold seemed to offer an easy way out of economic uncertainty, but the petrolization of the economy did not address the underlying structural problems in Mexico's mode of capital accumulation. These problems had been growing since the late 1960s; they were evident in 1973 and were undeniable by 1976. The oil boom, it turned out, was little more than an intoxicated interregnum between crises, in which the optimistic imbibed the black gold and the pessimistic were soused in melancholy and apathy. All the while, Mexico's economy underwent massive structural and symbolic transition.

The problems in the Mexican economy were far too profound to be resolved by the petroleum bonanza. As the government took massive loans to finance its populism, middle-class consumers also turned to debt to subsidize their lifestyles.

4 Consumer-Citizens

INFLATION, CREDIT, AND TAXING
THE MIDDLE CLASSES, 1973–1985

In the 1970s, the middle classes acquired a new collective political identity, at least from the perspective of the PRI: they became consumer-citizens. Beginning with the economic instability of the early 1970s, and through the oil boom later in the decade, Presidents Echeverría and López Portillo increasingly relied on foreign loans, promoting debt-based growth at the national level. During these years, the PRI also made a debt economy possible at the household level, to mitigate the effects of inflation on middle-class consumption. In broad terms, the shift to a debt economy was an attempt to defy the economic crisis and return to the prosperity of the Mexican Miracle. In this attempt, a new economic relationship emerged between the PRI and the middle classes, and the one-party state created a new political subject: the consumer-citizen.

"Political subject" refers to a formally represented group within the PRI's institutional corporatist system. The Confederation of Mexican Workers (Confederación de Trabajadores de México, or CTM) represented workers, and the National Peasant Confederation (Confederación Nacional Campesina, or CNC) represented peasants. While the middle classes had acquired representation in the 1940s with the creation of the National Confederation of Popular Organizations (Confederación Nacional de Organizaciones Populares, or CNOP), in the 1970s consumers became political subjects with the creation of a public institution for consumer credit, together with new consumer rights legislation and a new tax on consumption. In December 1973, the National Fund for Worker Consumption (Fondo Nacional para el Consumo de los Trabajadores, or Fonacot) was created, which provided consumer credit to qualified salaried workers. In February 1976, the Federal Law for the Protection of the Consumer (Ley Federal de Protección al Consumidor) came into effect, protecting consumers from abuses by private and public providers of goods and services and consecrating the political subjecthood of consumers as law. The PRI thus established a classically paternalistic relationship—it subsidized and protected the consumer. This relationship acquired a new dimension in 1980 when the López Portillo administration succeeding in passing a new tax law. The new value-added tax (Impuesto al Valor Agregado, or IVA) levied a 10 percent tax on consumer goods.[1]

With these initiatives, the consumer-citizen emerged. Until the legislative changes of the 1970s, consumers had, of course, existed as economic and social subjects, but their political status had been ambiguous.[2] By regulating the relationship between consumers and merchants, as well as the relationship between consumers and the state, the PRI officially recognized consumers as political subjects. Consumers became consumer-citizens when they gained representation and protection within the PRI's one-party state.[3]

The consumer-citizen was connected to two phenomena: an increasingly sophisticated consumer economy and rising inflation. With regard to the former, Fonacot and the consumer rights law were indicators of a complex consumer society that offered a seemingly endless array of goods and credit schemes but in which the consumer was virtually defenseless (it was very expensive to take a merchant to court over a minor sale). In the 1970s, the PRI became concerned with worker welfare not only at the point of production but also at the point of consumption. With Fonacot, the PRI offered an alternative to private sources of credit such as credit cards; with the new law, the PRI created a legal mechanism whereby consumers could denounce merchants. Simply put, the increasingly complex consumer economy propelled the party into creating support mechanisms for consumers.

Fonacot and the consumer rights legislation were also reactions to rising inflation in the 1970s, which threatened middle-class consumption. During the Mexican Miracle, middle-class prosperity—as well as aspirations—had depended on increasing purchasing power. From the late 1940s through the early 1970s, real wages steadily rose, permitting teachers, pharmacists, and engineers to acquire the goods necessary to maintain their class status. This salary boom was the result of the state's minimum wage policy and the capacity of unions to push for wage increases.[4] In the context of global recession and the exhaustion of the ISI (Import Substitution Industrialization) model, in the 1970s minimum wage policy and union power were not sufficient to protect salaries. In 1973, Mexico's inflation rate began to rise erratically and sometimes dramatically. This marked a major change from the low and comparably stable inflation rates of earlier decades, as can be seen in Table 1.[5]

Being middle class involves both earning a certain income and using that income to underwrite a middle-class lifestyle, whose markers constantly

TABLE 1. Annual inflation rate, 1951–2000

Year	Inflation rate	Year	Inflation rate	Year	Inflation rate
1951	23.36	1968	2.11	1985	63.75
1952	3.54	1969	2.52	1986	105.75
1953	−1.26	1970	4.97	1987	159.17
1954	9.33	1971	5.60	1988	51.66
1955	13.50	1972	4.85	1989	20.01
1956	4.48	1973	12.13	1990	29.93
1957	4.45	1974	23.74	1991	18.79
1958	5.00	1975	14.97	1992	11.94
1959	0.51	1976	15.75	1993	8.01
1960	4.39	1977	29.21	1994	7.05
1961	1.02	1978	17.41	1995	51.97
1962	2.36	1979	18.16	1996	27.70
1963	0.29	1980	26.36	1997	15.72
1964	4.18	1981	27.92	1998	18.61
1965	2.17	1982	98.84	1999	12.32
1966	1.04	1983	80.78	2000	8.96
1967	2.79	1984	59.16		

Source: Messmacher and Werner, "Inflación en México: 1950–2000," 54, table 3.

Note: Estimates of inflation vary depending on source and method. A comparable series can be found in Moreno-Bird and Ros, *Development and Growth in the Mexican Economy*, 269–270, tables A.11 and A.12. Various series can be consulted on the Bank of Mexico website.

shift.[6] In the postrevolutionary decades, urban middle-class consumer culture expanded significantly. The arrival of American department stores and the construction of modern apartment complexes, for example, changed the way people lived and shopped—and the goods they purchased.[7] Consumer culture was defined by constant change: a clothes-washing machine might have indicated middle-class status in 1960s Mexico, but by the 1980s this was not necessarily the case. Declines in purchasing power could prevent a middle-class family from keeping up with the Joneses—or the Castros, to take the name of the nouveau riche family in Oscar Lewis's *Five Families*. And this could have political consequences, such as the *cacerolazo* protests of the early 1970s. Facing economic and political pressure, the Echeverría and López Portillo administrations forged new, innovative strategies to mitigate the effects of instability.[8] Fonacot and the consumer-rights law were part of the PRI's strategy to help the middle classes weather the effects of inflation by buttressing purchasing power, as well as to attract popular support for the party. In the 1970s, then, for consumer culture to continue expanding (or even to maintain established expectations), middle-class consumption needed to be subsidized.

Fonacot and the new consumer-rights law demonstrated the structural instability of the middle classes, especially for those at the lower end of the income spectrum. (Please see the Appendix for analysis of middle-class incomes.) The need for Fonacot demonstrated that the middle classes could no longer rely on their salaries alone to maintain their lifestyles, and many went into debt to purchase a television or to cover educational expenses. Consumer debt thus began to replace decent salaries. And the need for consumer-rights legislation demonstrated the weak position of some middle-class consumers vis-à-vis merchants: in their desire to acquire symbols of middle-class status, many consumers accepted unethical and even illegal prices and terms of credit. The new law also exposed another sort of middle-class instability: that of small business owners, who protested that the legislation would endanger their livelihoods, forcing them to spend time and money defending themselves against false claims.

For their part, the middle classes turned to consumer credit in order to realize their expectations. By doing so, people mortgaged their futures to protect their dreams—dreams that belonged to a past golden age. When the debt economy became the debt crisis of the 1980s, these consumer-citizens found themselves in an even more tenuous position than in 1973 or 1976.

Mortgaging the Future to Save the Past

On 30 December 1973, the Mexican Congress passed reforms to the Federal Labor Law (Ley Federal de Trabajo) to create Fonacot.[9] The government now provided credit to individuals for private consumption. Fonacot lent money for the purchase of goods ranging from refrigerators to stereo equipment to king-size beds, and for services that included funerals, family vacations, and the printing costs of undergraduate theses. Individuals had to meet a series of requirements to access this credit. These requirements, and the approved goods and services, essentially limited qualified recipients to members of the lower-middle classes. As part of the Federal Labor Law, Fonacot was designed to "protect the purchasing power of workers and facilitate their access to the goods and services that would satisfy their material, social, and cultural needs."[10] Accordingly, a worker's real wage was considered insufficient to satisfy his needs. Labor Minister Porfirio Muñoz Ledo heralded Fonacot as an important step beyond an exclusive focus on raising salaries: "Salary protection is not only about defending salaries at their source [at work], but also defending salaries when they are spent by defending workers as consumers."[11]

Inflation had hit the salaried middle classes hard. Fonacot is only one example of the various ways the state began to subsidize middle-class consumption in the 1970s.[12] During the same period the state dramatically increased subsidies for home ownership, and public institutes such as the National Workers' Housing Fund (Instituto del Fondo Nacional de la Vivienda para los Trabajadores, or Infonavit) provided subsidized mortgages to qualified workers. (Prominent PRI economist and politician Jesús Reyes Heroles González Garza connected Infonavit and other programs to the consumer credit provided by Fonacot as part of a broader official policy to redistribute resources to the middle classes).[13] Fonacot worked in tandem with the endeavors of Infonavit and other initiatives. The rationale was stated by one journalist this way: "If Infonavit constructs houses for a salaried worker, it would be incongruent not to give that same worker the economic capacity to furnish the house."[14]

To apply for credit, salaried workers filled out a request form available at their place of work or union or in the Fonacot offices. Employers then certified that the information was correct. With this certification, the employee submitted the form to a selected provider or directly to Fonacot, along with recent pay stubs, social security information, and evidence of residence. Applicants also indicated which goods, from an established list, they wished to purchase. Once the credit was issued, monthly payments were deducted from the worker's paycheck.[15]

Although the official description of Fonacot called it a fund for low-income, economically needy workers, it ended up benefiting those with middle-class salaries.[16] To qualify for credit, an applicant had to be formally employed, to have worked for at least one year in the same job, and to earn a salary that fell between two and five times the minimum wage. In Fonacot's own literature, applicants were invariably described as salaried workers (*asalariados*).[17] Fonacot's income range fits scholarly and official estimates of a middle-class income (see Appendix). For example, the National Minimum Wage Commission (Comisión Nacional de Salarios Mínimos) estimated that, in 1977, a middle-class income ranged from 2.6 to 4.3 times the minimum wage.[18] The wage criteria for Fonacot credit changed over time; by 1993 the salary requirement was one to ten times the minimum wage, which corresponds to estimates of a middle-class income at that time.[19] From its inception in the mid-1970s through at least the mid-1990s, Fonacot provided credit to consumers who earned a middle-class salary, helping some families protect their middle-class status and aiding others to acquire that status. Even though policymakers tried to target the working classes, the middle classes captured much of the benefit.

The goods and services bought with Fonacot credit included family vacations to national destinations, as well as education and funeral services. The educational services, in particular, link credit and class. For example, a recipient could be an undergraduate student in the Faculty of Economics at the UNAM who had completed both the coursework and the required thesis. After successfully finishing the rigorous program—which only a few in Mexico even had a chance to begin—the student might not have the funds to print and bind the thesis, as required by the degree program. Such a student could apply to Fonacot for credit to cover these final requirements of the undergraduate degree. Students who could not afford to print and bind their theses lived in the liminal space between the middle and lower classes. By granting credit for finishing undergraduate theses, Fonacot fortified—and facilitated access into—the lower ranks of the middle classes. The fund, then, was one strategy by which the Echeverría and López Portillo administrations tried to continue the state's commitment to education as a means of social mobility.

Fonacot's list of approved goods and services reflected the wide range of middle-class needs and desires. From the beginning, major household appliances had been a central part of the Fonacot list—the "línea blanca" goods such as refrigerators and stoves (referred to as "white line" products because they were originally white in color). Such products, which made life much more agreeable, had, since midcentury, been a feature of modern, urban, middle-class homes. Families could apply for credit to purchase stereo equipment, queen- and king-sized mattresses, bicycles, and motorcycles. They could also use the credit to pay for car repairs.[20] Over time, the list of approved products grew, keeping pace with changing technology and material culture. For instance, clothes washing machines were approved in 1982 but dryers were not until 1988, when a family could purchase a dryer with a capacity of five kilograms. Likewise, many small household appliances, such as toasters, coffee makers, and vacuums, did not appear on the 1982 list but were permitted by 1988.[21] These goods and services were trophies in the daily struggle to acquire or maintain class status, and they reflect the spectrum of middle-class realities—from borrowing money to print a thesis or buy a bicycle to taking a loan for a family vacation or a new motorcycle.

The inconsistency between official rhetoric that proclaimed Fonacot a service to lower-income groups and the reality that it benefited the middle classes was perhaps a matter of practicality. The minimum salary requirement for credit recipients was some guarantee that Fonacot would be repaid. This in turn meant that more affluent "workers" were served. Policymakers did in fact try to target those at the lower end of the salary range.[22] But sometimes they were stymied by the fuzzy boundaries between different social groups, which frustrated their efforts. The difficulty of differentiating income groups came out in a 1982 report, when a functionary in the Ministry of the Treasury (Secretaría de Hacienda y Crédito Público, or SHCP) complained that even categorizing necessary and luxury goods was impossible: "We thought that color televisions were luxury goods, but after we conducted a study we realized that there is a high percentage of color televisions in urban areas that are generally considered to be marginal neighborhoods. The same thing happened with several other goods."[23] (In this instance, the ministry decided that a seventy-five-centimeter color television was a luxury good, whereas smaller sets were considered to be more commonplace.) While there were real practical considerations and challenges, this inconsistency might also indicate a more systemic challenge for social policy: that the middle classes tended to appropriate social benefits intended for the lower classes. That policymakers could not prevent this suggests that, just as the idea of "middle class" exerted a centripetal force in political economic theory, the middle classes functioned as a kind of vortex in social policy, even radical social policy. Fonacot was, after all, part of the shared development program for distributive justice.[24] One anonymous critic suggested that the middle classes were not the inadvertent beneficiaries of shared development but that it "was designed to increase the representation of the small and medium bourgeoisie within the dominant block."[25]

Not only did Fonacot provide credit, it provided cheap credit. In the 1970s, the interest rate offered by Fonacot was lower than that of other credit providers, a point emphasized in official propaganda for the program. For example, in 1978 Fonacot's interest rate was 18 percent, while the commercial interest rate was 24 percent.[26] Indeed, as shown in Table 2, Fonacot's interest rate remained close to the average percentage cost (*costo porcentual promedio*, or CPP). The CPP measures the cost of accepting deposits and thus represents the minimum interest that could be charged without losing money on the transaction.[27] That said, the interest rate remained stable only for the first few years; Fonacot, unsurprisingly, was unable to offset the economic turmoil of the 1980s. As shown in Table 2, from 1976 to 1981 the interest rate hovered fairly close to the proclaimed 18 percent, varying between 16 and 21 percent; but by 1982 it had climbed to almost 28 percent, and by 1987 it had reached over 90 percent.

TABLE 2. Fonacot interest rates, 1976–1987

Year	Fonacot average interest rate	CPP average
1976	15.83	11.84
1977	17.75	12.88
1978	18.00	15.13
1979	18.00	16.35
1980	20.25	20.71
1981	21.00	28.58
1982	27.75	40.40
1983	50.65	56.65
1984	41.43	51.10
1985	51.40	56.07
1986	74.14	80.88
1987	91.46	94.64

Source: Secretaría del Trabajo y Previsión Social, "Fondo de Fomento y Garantía para el Consumo de los Trabajadores, Memoria Institucional 1983–1988," MMH, 14.10.01.20, c. 1, exp. 8, pgs. 112–115, AGN.

Note: The Bank of Mexico's historical CPP rate, available on its website, is slightly different from the one recorded by Fonacot.

The dramatic increase in interest rates limited Fonacot's ability to protect middle-class consumption. In its official publications, Fonacot acknowledged that increased interest rates had raised the cost of credit "beyond all of the principles and objectives of the Fund to provide workers with timely and <u>cheap</u> credit."[28] The fund struggled to provide its social service throughout the 1980s. Several times it reduced interest rates, eliminated fees, expanded the amount of credit given to an individual, and periodically slashed the interest rates for specific goods and services, such as education expenses; starting in 1984, it offered lower interest rates to lower-income applicants, to offset the rising cost of the credit.[29] Fonacot made these changes amid severe budget constraints caused by peso devaluations and more generalized economic instability. For example, the fund set the prices for approved goods and services in advance: the 1982 prices, set in 1981, were out of date by early 1982, and the fund entered into disputes with suppliers when it refused to renegotiate prices. Likewise, it struggled to maintain the interest rates that it had agreed to with workers.[30] At the end of 1982, journalists reported rumors that Fonacot had stopped functioning altogether; representatives insisted that they were still in operation.[31]

Beyond the struggle to cover basic operational costs, the appeal of Fonacot's services diminished during the crisis of the 1980s, the lost decade. In an environment of currency devaluation and skyrocketing inflation, the value of money was uncertain: one week, five hundred pesos might get you a toaster; the following week it might only cover the cost of a loaf of bread. In the best of times, money is an abstraction of value that functions on several levels: as an IOU, or promise, from the government; as a store of value; and as an agreed-upon fiction to which everyone subscribes—so much so that the fiction takes on the appearance of fact.[32] And if paper money is an abstraction of value, credit is an abstraction of paper money.[33]

Inflation and currency devaluations erode confidence in the value of money and credit. Manuel, a worker in a large company, explained to *El Día* his reluctance to apply for Fonacot credit in 1983: "The thing about Fonacot is that you lose a lot of time. First you have to fill out lots of forms. Then you have to wait a few weeks until your credit is approved. While all this is happening, the value of money is going down because the peso is always being devalued, and so the cost of the furniture has gone up."[34] Manuel told the journalist who interviewed him that he would rather save his money and purchase the item without credit, which, for him, was less risky. Manuel might have been wrong in his judgment. Had he taken out a loan in pesos that were later devalued, he would have repaid the loan in the newly devalued pesos, which presumably would have been easier to come by. Alternatively, if Manuel's salary was not completely indexed to inflation (likely it was not), then his judgment might have been economically sound.

The rationality of Manuel's economic behavior notwithstanding, his calculations reveal how the credit economy and the economic crisis altered everyday understandings of the relationship between time, money, and value.

Manuel's skepticism toward government credit betrayed a crisis more profound than increased inflation. Government consumer credit was a relatively new economic phenomenon for the Mexican middle classes, and when combined with unpredictable inflation—also a new economic reality—it seemed risky. The "fact" of the value of money and the value of government credit had come into question. And when the value of legal tender and government credit came into question, popular confidence in the government that issued the paper money and the credit reached a low.

While Manuel was reluctant to use Fonacot credit, many middle-class families relied on Fonacot during the lost decade. As other sources of credit dried up or became too expensive, Fonacot became the only option for many members of the salaried class, including bureaucrats and teachers, who had previously had access to other sources of credit through their unions.[35]

The uncertain economic prospects of these members of the middle classes were reflected in the goods and services approved for credit. Whereas during the oil boom Fonacot functionaries considered expanding credit to include automobiles, during the lost decade the fund provided emergency credit for food at lower interest rates.[36] But despite the challenges that the 1980s crisis presented, both for the fund and for middle-class families, the system functioned. As Table 3 illustrates, throughout the 1980s an increasing number of people applied for greater and greater amounts of credit. And the rate of repayment during the 1980s suggests that most recipients could, in general, afford the credit they were issued.[37]

TABLE 3. Fonacot credit granted and repaid, 1975–1987

Year	Number of credits granted	Total value of all credit granted (thousands of pesos)	Total amount of credit repaid (thousands of pesos)	Average value of individual credits (pesos)
1975	172,355	1,481,179	516,700	8,594
1976	215,767	1,268,928	344,400	5,881
1977	140,625	1,006,760	1,177,400	7,159
1978	269,339	2,359,644	1,643,400	8,761
1979	282,589	3,091,563	2,396,300	10,940
1980	305,295	4,148,807	3,229,100	13,590
1981	376,896	5,538,035	4,283,000	14,694
1982	245,968	5,155,645	6,023,500	20,961
1983	191,459	5,711,942	8,128,100	29,834
1984	198,094	10,093,408	9,088,000	50,953
1985	225,416	17,595,953	15,256,000	78,060
1986	246,186	28,014,764	28,327,000	113,795
1987	254,942	71,613,600	51,368,800	280,902

Source: Secretaría del Trabajo y Previsión Social, "Fondo de Fomento y Garantía para el Consumo de los Trabajadores, Memoria Institucional 1983–1988," MMH, 14.10.01.20, c. 1, exp. 8, pg. 150, AGN.

Healthy Family Budgets

The creation of Fonacot was, in part, a government response to an over-all increase in consumer credit. Through the 1950s, access to consumer credit had been fairly limited. Some department stores began issuing store credit in the 1950s, and some state workers had access to short-, me-dium-, and long-term loans through their unions or their work contracts. Banks would, on occasion, lend money to their wealthier clients. And the poor had access to informal credit through savings clubs or savings pools (*tandas*), small credit unions (*cajas de ahorro*), pawnshops, and credit granted by merchants at neighborhood shops, as well as from moneylend-ers who targeted the poor.[38] With the appearance of bank-issued credit cards in 1968, credit for private consumption became more widely avail-able to middle-class Mexicans.

Credit cards altered the role of credit in consumption. Suddenly, the middle classes had easier access to credit. (Figure 3 depicts how credit cards became a coveted commodity.) The first credit card, "Bancomático," was put into circulation in January of 1968, and within a few months two other cards appeared. By June 1971, approximately six hundred thousand Mexicans had these credit cards.[39] In November 1971, at an international conference of central bank technicians, the Bank of Mexico representa-tive described how consumer credit had been "revolutionized" in less than four years. He warned, though, that the bank credit cards needed a large number of active cardholders in order to be profitable.[40] The advent of credit cards occurred in tandem with the computerization of the bank-ing system and extension of banking services to increasing numbers of citizens (although this "massification" was generally limited to the urban middle classes and wealthy), all of which led to a growing number of cardholders: for example, in 1970 Banamex (National Bank of Mexico) issued approximately two hundred thousand cards; by 1980 this number had reached over one million, and by 1985 Banamex had issued two mil-lion cards.[41]

In the early 1970s, the minimum monthly income required for a credit card was 5,000 pesos.[42] This would include many, though not all, of the members of the middle classes (see Appendix). Fonacot targeted those ex-cluded from the credit card market. From 1976 to 1982, for instance, over 45 percent of the Fonacot credits were granted to workers who earned less than 6,000 pesos per month; 35 percent were granted to workers earn-ing less than 9,500 pesos per month.[43] In 1979, the number of salaried workers in Mexico reached 10,400,000. Only 6.5 percent of these workers qualified for bank credit (including credit cards); 18.5 percent qualified for credit from commercial firms (such as department store credit); and nearly

FIGURE 3. Coveting a credit card. From "La lámpara maravillosa," *Expansión,* 7 April 1980.

50 percent qualified for Fonacot credit.[44] Fonacot was thus a government strategy to broaden the availability of credit.

Three undergraduate economics theses from 1970 analyze how the middle classes used consumer credit.[45] The studies defined poor families as households that earned under 2,000 pesos per month; middle-class families earned 2,000 to 5,000 pesos; and wealthy families earned over 5,000 pesos per month. The data presented in these theses, however, indicate the need for another category, that of families who earned between 5,000 and 12,500 pesos per month, which could be called upper-middle class. Indeed, the study of wealthy families divided that group into two categories, at the monthly income level of 12,500 pesos. The results indicate that families earning 5,000 to 12,500 pesos had more in common with families in the 2,000 to 5,000 bracket than with families who earned over 12,500 pesos.[46] The authors found that the poor had access to credit in neighborhood shops for staples such as corn, beans, coffee, eggs, bread, oil, and soda pop. Twenty percent of poor families surveyed had used credit to purchase furniture and 30 percent had used credit to buy large household appliances ("línea blanca"). Among the poor, the families with incomes closer to 2,000 pesos had the greatest access to credit, for both perishable and nonperishable goods.[47] Compared with the poor, the wealthy (with a monthly income over 12,500 pesos) had relatively little use for credit, with the exception of credit cards. Many of the wealthy families surveyed considered credit cards to be symbols of prestige and used them widely in restaurants, bars, and hotels and at travel agencies.[48] Between the wealthy and the poor, the middle classes (families with monthly incomes between 2,000 and 12,500 pesos) had the most use for consumer credit. Families in this stratum had access to short-term credit from their workplaces, commercial firms, and department stores; those who earned above 5,000 pesos had access to bank credit and credit cards. Middle-class families used credit for large household appliances, vacations, and, especially those with incomes above 5,000 pesos, for automobiles.[49]

Credit, as a concept and a social relation, provokes moral arguments: credit is often viewed as liberating and productive while debt is considered debilitating and dangerous.[50] The undergraduate studies reveal contemporary attitudes toward credit (and debt) as it became more widely available. The authors all express concern about the capacity of families to control themselves; they worry that, without guidance, families might succumb to conspicuous consumption and fall into a downward debt spiral. One of the authors, for example, observed that middle-class families did not pay close attention to interest rates.[51] This concern over the dangers of credit appears even stronger in a fourth undergraduate economics thesis from 1970 on the effects of credit cards; the author concludes that credit cards pose a danger to all social strata except the very wealthy.[52] This student argues that the poor lack the self-control required to manage credit cards, and that "because of their lack of education and culture, the poor are unable to comprehend the problems that could accompany the misuse of a credit card."[53] The lower-middle classes fare only slightly better in his analysis. If the head of a family exercises strict control, a credit card could be an important resource in a lower-middle-class family's budget. Without such control, however, families risk falling into penury. Upper-middle-class families, according to this student, tend to use their credit cards for amounts greater than they earn, in a desperate effort to keep up appearances. Credit cards, he concludes, could precipitate the descent of an upper-middle-class family into the ranks of the lower-middle classes or even the poor. In view of these dangers, the author advocates government regulation of credit. With strong regulation, credit cards could be a resource for the Mexican population; without such regulation, credit cards could become "a weapon the population might use against itself."[54] Without government intervention, credit card misuse could negatively impact the national economy.[55] These four undergraduate theses suggest a common perception that credit was both desirable and dangerous.

With the creation of Fonacot, the government provided credit and protected consumers from the dangers of overextending themselves, for the good of both the household and the nation. At the household level, Fonacot's mandate included protecting citizens from usurers as well as from themselves. The strict salary requirements ensured that a family would only receive the credit it could afford, while deducting the monthly payments from the worker's paycheck guaranteed that a family would not fall into arrears as the result of irresponsible budgeting. Fonacot also used its list of approved goods and services as a tool to protect consumers in various ways. First and foremost, the list limited the use of credit to goods and services deemed reasonable, thus avoiding the possibility that a family would go into debt because of an addiction to luxury goods. Second, the fund used the list to negotiate below-market prices. Producers would grant discounted prices in exchange for getting onto Fonacot's list of approved goods. On occasion, the fund acquired these discounts by directly subsidizing the production and distribution of specific goods. Fonacot also stimulated production by informing producers of products that borrowers desired but were not yet available at affordable prices. And, in the 1970s, Fonacot participated directly in production by holding several design competitions, run through the School of Design at the UNAM. Competitors designed products, especially furniture, with the dual goal of reducing production costs and increasing style by imitating (with cheaper materials, to be sure) high-end products.[56]

At the level of the national economy, the government hoped that consumer credit and increased consumption would function as an economic stimulus. As conceived in the 1970s, Fonacot was part of Mexico's ongoing industrialization. The theory went that workers with greater purchasing power constituted a stronger internal market for domestically produced goods. Greater demand, in turn, would generate production and employment.[57] This formula would only work, however, if individuals and families could balance their budgets.

Healthy family budgets would translate into a healthy national economy. Importantly, starting in the 1970s, healthy family finances meant sound management of debt: the debt economy permeated the household level. Thus, while Fonacot constituted an innovative attempt by the PRI to mitigate the effects of economic instability, it was ultimately an insufficient stopgap. The debt economy left consumers (and the nation) vulnerable to hikes in interest rates and other variables that were often beyond their control. But as a stopgap, Fonacot represented a significant change in the economic relationship between the state and the middle classes. The PRI had begun to interact with the middle classes as consumers. Shortly after creating Fonacot, the government passed radical consumer rights legislation intended to protect and educate these consumers (to whom it had lent money) from the abuses of public and private providers of goods and services.

Vulnerable Consumers and Voracious Merchants

"The old aphorism that the consumer is the supreme king of the market, of which liberal thinkers are so fond, is no longer accurate—if it ever was accurate," argued José Campillo Sainz, Mexico's Minister of Industry and Commerce (Secretaría de Industria y Comercio), before the Chamber of Deputies on 28 November 1975.[58] He urged the deputies to approve a new law protecting consumer rights. Consumers, he argued, experienced a double pressure: on the one hand, inflation and general economic instability undercut their purchasing power; on the other hand, their vulnerability increased as Mexico's consumer economy became more sophisticated. Campillo Sainz expressed the PRI's concern that the improved production and distribution of goods had incorporated growing numbers of citizens into a mass-market economy, creating a consumer society. In this new economic landscape, citizens were susceptible to manufactured desire, and consumers were in a weak position vis-à-vis producers and distributers.[59] The proposed law would protect consumers from themselves and from unscrupulous providers. The consumer rights legislation passed, and in February 1976 the Federal Law for the Protection of the Consumer (Ley Federal de Protección al Consumidor) came into effect.

This law protected consumers from misleading advertising, from defective goods or services, and from unethical payment and credit agreements.[60] Articles 5 through 10 established the following rights regarding publicity: the customer had the right to true and sufficient information regarding goods and services; providers who failed to give such information would be liable for damages; it was specifically prohibited to advertise that a product was "made for export" or "export quality." As Campillo Sainz outlined in his speech to the Chamber of Deputies, such labels encouraged a "malinchista" attitude in which the Mexican consumer did not merit the same level of quality as consumers in other countries.[61] ("Malinchista" refers to

La Malinche, an Aztec woman who aided Spanish conquistador Hernán Cortés in the sixteenth-century conquest of Mexico; in this context, "malinchista" is intended as an insult, referring to a Mexican who demeans or betrays Mexico.)[62] The law also established a consumer's right to change his or her mind: Articles 18 and 19 guaranteed the consumer's right to return merchandise for store credit within three working days, and Article 48 allowed five working days for a consumer to return any goods bought from a door-to-door salesman. Campillo Sainz described these provisions as the "derecho a rajarse" (the right to back out or "chicken out").[63]

Mexico's consumer rights legislation was pioneering in its regulation of credit arrangements.[64] Articles 20 through 29 established the regulations for credit and installment purchases. Consumers had the right to accurate information as to the cash price of a good versus the total that would be paid according to the credit or installment agreement, including the interest rate, the number of payments to be made and their frequency, the total interest to be paid over the amortization period, and the possibility of early liquidation. The Ministry of Industry and Commerce would set maximums on both interest rates and fees, to be published in the *Diario Oficial* and major newspapers; any person or business that violated these maximums would be subject to prosecution for usury.[65] Article 1 established these and others rights in the interests of the social good: consumer rights were social rights. Inalienable, they could not be affected by laws, customs, practices, or contract stipulations to the contrary.

In his presentation before the Chamber of Deputies, Campillo Sainz described how the consumer rights initiative shared the same spirit as legislation that protected workers and campesinos.[66] Consumers, Campillo Sainz argued, needed to be protected by the government as much as workers and campesinos did: "Just as the worker should not be forced to accept deplorable working conditions, just as the campesino should not be forced off his land or find himself without a market for his produce, the consumer should not be forced to accept the conditions and the prices imposed by the merchant."[67] Until now, continued the minister, the government had regulated relations between workers and employers and between campesinos and landowners (*detentadores*); with the new legislation, the government would regulate relations between consumers and providers.

The middle classes were among the beneficiaries of the new legislation. While Fonacot primarily benefited the middle classes because of the salary requirements, the new law targeted a broader audience—consumers who had complaints against merchants—that included the lower, middle, and upper classes. The promoters of the consumer rights legislation, however, emphasized the benefits to the middle classes. In his speech, Campillo Sainz relied exclusively on examples from the middle classes. For instance, he outlined how the new law would protect consumers from poor services: "Those Mexicans who own only one car—and I'm speaking here about the middle classes, not only the wealthy—those Mexicans understand the inconvenience and costs of being without a car."[68] Campillo Sainz argued that if a car owner sent his or her car for repairs which later proved to be ineffective and he or she was forced to leave the car once again with the mechanic, then the mechanic should provide an alternative vehicle. Other services to be regulated, such as travel agencies, tourist services, restaurants, and hotels, all illustrate different ways in which the middle classes would benefit from the new legislation.[69] Finally, given that the middle classes depended on credit to sustain their lifestyles, they would benefit from the regulation of credit arrangements.

Articles 57 through 75 created two new institutions to implement the law and educate consumers, the Office of the Federal Attorney for the Consumer (Procuraduría Federal del Consumidor, or Profeco) and the National Institute for the Consumer (Instituto Nacional del Consumidor, or Inco), both of which came into existence in February 1976. The former was charged with protecting consumer rights, the latter with educating consumers. At the inauguration of these institutions, Campillo Sainz declared that the government could no longer permit the "arbitrary game of a liberalism that limits and enslaves men."[70]

Profeco was the muscle behind the new legislation. It would represent the consumer against all offenders, from individual merchants and service providers to government agencies. Profeco was a decentralized agency with its own funds and considerable juridical power. Campillo Sainz underscored Profeco's power when he pointed out to the Chamber of Deputies: "The agency would protect consumers from the government; that is, it would protect consumers from ourselves; indeed, it would even protect consumers from the Ministry of Industry and Commerce [which sponsored the legislation]."[71] Profeco opened offices across the republic, concentrated mainly in urban areas, where consumer-citizens could seek recourse.

Not surprisingly, many objected to the creation of Profeco. Business leaders protested, but Campillo Sainz described their denunciations as "a futile rebellion of the minority, of the oligarchic groups."[72] The timing of the new law, which came toward the end of Echeverría's administration, put it in the middle of the battle between the president and the private sector industrialists, merchants, and business owners. Leaders of private sector organizations publicly declared that they would not respect the law.[73] In this context, the creation of Profeco might have been, in part, a strategy by Echeverría to address the *cacerolazo*-style protests that had emerged in 1973, when inflation, declining purchasing power, and general economic instability fueled on-the-ground discontent in Mexico's cafés, gas stations, and taxicabs. By protecting middle-class consumption, the president and his top advisors likely sought to stem the waves of rumor and gossip.

Take, for example, dry cleaning: customers in dry cleaning shops complained in one breath about the rising costs of cleaning their suits and, in the next, gossiped about a possible coup d'état.[74] In his speech to the Chamber of Deputies, Campillo Sainz spoke personally of the abuses suffered by consumers at the mercy of dry cleaners: "Another frequent case of abuse in the provision of services—and something that we have all experienced—occurs when you drop off an article of clothing for cleaning or repair, and they destroy it. This happens to our shirts, our suits, and all our other garments that we send to the dry cleaner."[75] The new law would protect consumers from the abuses of dry cleaners, forcing the latter to pay for any damages (instead of performing a quick and shoddy repair of the damaged article). Perhaps then the dry cleaning clientele might be less inclined to join the *cacerolazo* protest.

But merchants—not only those who belonged to the private sector élite but also small and medium business owners—had reason to be concerned. They worried that a bureaucratic and inefficient state agency would interfere with their business.[76] José Luis Ordóñez, president of the National Chamber of Commerce (Cámara Nacional de Comercio, or Canaco) and leader of over thirty-eight thousand merchants in Mexico City, complained that merchants suffered from negative stereotypes that portrayed them as speculators: "The Mexican merchant is hurt by these accusations. It's ungrateful to accuse us of being hoarders or price-gougers . . . when we supply everyone's needs."[77] He worried that the new law would promote such stereotypes. His concern was not unfounded; indeed, the new director of Profeco proclaimed that he would work toward eliminating the "venal merchant."[78] Such statements caused intense concern among merchants, who feared a "witch hunt."[79]

Campillo Sainz attempted to assuage small and medium-sized merchants. When discussing the right to "chicken-out," for example, he anticipated their concerns: "What if someone buys a stereo for a party that night and then returns it the next day?"[80] He explained that the consumer would only receive store credit for the returned merchandise; the merchant would still benefit. Moreover, he argued that the new law would protect small merchants who found it difficult to compete with larger companies. For example, the new legislation prevented anyone from offering free gifts to consumers; many small and medium-sized businesses had been unable to compete with this sort of promotion. The law also prohibited promotions on foreign-produced goods, which most small and medium-sized businesses did not sell; instead, they would be able to attract more customers through promotions on Mexican products.[81] Ultimately, Campillo Sainz and others relied on a simple defense of the new legislation: "In what way do we hurt honest and honorable merchants by asking them to not deceive the public?"[82]

The first three complaints that Profeco received exposed an array of dishonest practices. The first complaint involved an orphanage that had received tax benefits as a nonprofit charity. Apparently, though, the so-called orphanage actually rented its rooms to adult tenants; a woman who claimed to be renting a room filed the complaint. The second complaint involved impurities in Coca-Cola products at a neighborhood miscellaneous shop. The third complaint came from a man who had purchased a television on a credit arrangement whose terms were illegal. Later on that first day, another man filed a complaint against a construction company that was supposed to install a new kitchen; a year later he was still waiting for them to finish the job.[83] Once Profeco received a complaint, the procedure could include summoning both parties for arbitration (with the threat of a significant fine for nonattendance), investigation of the business establishment, possible legal action against the establishment, and, if warranted, public denunciation of the establishment.

The first big scandal created by the denunciations carried a moral weight that helped to legitimize Profeco as a social service for all citizens. It concerned the age-old practice of fiddling with measurements. In this case, milk distributors sold nine hundred milliliters of milk in one-liter bottles; by cheating consumers out of ten milliliters of milk per bottle, distributers netted a huge profit bit by bit. These distributors were excoriated in the press and fined heavily by Profeco.[84] This first scandal, which played on long-standing associations of milk with purity and innocence, imbued Profeco's mission with a moral righteousness that enhanced its public image. Denunciations of false measurement remained a constant complaint.

Recurring issues emerged in denunciations to Profeco throughout the 1970s and 1980s, including many complaints about middle-class goods and services.[85] Consumers denounced shoddy service by mechanics, scams in time-share vacation agreements and fraud at travel agencies, hikes in private-school tuition, misleading advertisements for "rejuvenating" beauty treatments, illegal terms of service for credit cards, and clothes destroyed by dry cleaners, to give a few examples.[86] In 1981, Señora Lemont, visiting the capital city, complained that a stylist in the salon of the upscale Camino Real hotel had burned her hair during a highlighting treatment. José Ortiz Estrada described how a small shop in the San Jerónimo neighborhood of Mexico City had advertised a bottle of San Marcos brandy for the price of 154 pesos, but at the cash register the clerk charged him 174 pesos. Leonard Becker, from the United States, filed a complaint against a taxidermist whom he had paid to preserve a trophy fish caught on a fishing trip in Acapulco; mounted on his office wall, the trophy had started to crack open only eight months later (this would be the first in a series of complaints against the taxidermy company by American fishermen).[87]

Denunciations of housing developers and others involved in real estate matters were likely the most common complaints brought to Profeco.[88] Consumers filed thousands of complaints against condominium apartments and single-family home developers in middle- and upper-middle-class suburbs of the capital and other cities.[89] Luxury (*super-lujo*) condominiums advertised lovely gardens and two parking spots—false advertising, it turned out, which elicited swift consumer denunciations.[90] Likewise, claims of minimum down payments and long-term financing masked a different reality: hidden fees, sudden changes to contract agreements, price increases, delayed completion, use of lower-quality materials, and exorbitant interest rates, among other common abuses.[91] For example, on 17 February 1981, Irma Fernández Rosas and Martha Fernández Rosas filed a complaint with Profeco about an "infinity of details and defects" in the two-story, two-bath apartment with multiple bedrooms that they had purchased in the San Jerónimo neighborhood of Mexico City the previous year. A broken boiler, broken closet doors, torn carpeting, and pools of stagnant water in the storage room, as well as mold in one of the bathrooms, in the master bedroom, and around the skylight, led the women to Profeco after their developer refused to answer their telephone calls or respond to their letters. Once contacted by Profeco, though, the developer responded quickly, admitting mistakes and promising repairs—their lawyer explained that they did not have enough personnel to attend to these issues. The matter was resolved by 1 June 1981.[92] Although the Fernández Rosas family seems to have received the help they needed, these sorts of problems were so pervasive that, on several occasions, Profeco issued a general advisory to consumers; in 1982 officials described an "epidemic of fraud" in real estate developments.[93]

Profeco's cases also document the difficulties consumers experienced when they participated in the emerging credit economy. In 1981, two women filed separate complaints against credit card companies. María Guzmán López and Silvia Lozano Huertado both described how a salesman had visited them in their workplaces offering "Carnet" credit cards. They both signed up but were surprised when the first bill arrived (before the card had been delivered) with a charge for insurance. María filed her complaint for false publicity, Silvia for wrongful charges. In both cases, Profeco ordered Carnet and the insurance companies to remove the charges. Middle-class consumers like María and Silvia—both of whom earned more than the minimum salary required for a credit card: María was a federal employee in the Ministry of the Treasury and lived in the Mexico City neighborhood of Napoles, while Silvia worked as an administrator for the Institute of Social Security and Services for State Employees (ISSSTE) and lived in Tlatelolco—found recourse in Profeco as they struggled to navigate the new credit economy.[94]

Others were more audacious. On 20 July 1981, Josefina Villagomez Román complained about charges on her Sears Roebuck store credit card. After an initial meeting of Josefina, a Profeco agent, and a Sears representative, the parties determined which charges should be investigated—not all the charges Josefina had listed were considered questionable. At this first meeting, Josefina agreed to make a payment, within ten days, for the items that she had clearly purchased. Another meeting was scheduled to analyze the remaining items. At this point, Josefina disappeared. She did not make the payment, nor did she respond to multiple letters from both Profeco and Sears. In September, Profeco ordered a signature analysis and the expert determined that Josefina had signed for all the purchases. She still did not reply, and the agency closed the case in November 1981 (after suggesting to the Sears representative that the company might pursue legal channels to recuperate the losses). For Josefina, it seems, Profeco provided an opportunity for a small-scale scam.[95]

An everyday history of macroeconomic crisis also emerges from Profeco's case files. After the 1976 and 1982 peso devaluations, real estate developers, travel agencies, car dealers, and credit-card companies all tried to recoup their losses by compelling middle-class Mexicans to pay their debts in dollars.[96] For instance, in 1976 two young women had a debt with an airline, in dollars, for a European tour they had taken the previous year. When they tried to clear their debt with the airline the day before the widely expected peso devaluation, the airline refused to accept their pesos. Having heard rumors of the devaluation, the women wanted to clear their debt before it ballooned into an amount of pesos they could not afford. The airline, it seems, had also heard the rumors of devaluation and refused to accept pesos that would likely be worth much less the following day. The young women sought recourse in Profeco.[97] Profeco fought on behalf of these and other consumers to enforce the law. Mexico's monetary law stipulates that all payment obligations must be settled in pesos, unless the debtor has specifically agreed to repay in a foreign currency (these women had not), and thus the airline could not refuse to accept the pesos offered by the two young women.[98]

But the effects of the devaluations were more complicated when a contract specifically stipulated payment in American dollars. In these instances, the law was less clear; exceptions could be made and citizens could be forced to honor their debts in dollars. In such cases, Profeco could not always protect Mexican consumers, and many found themselves with untenable debts.[99] In late 1982 and early 1983, for example, department stores in El Paso, Texas, canceled more than eighty thousand store credit cards held by Mexican citizens who could no longer meet their dollar obligations.[100]

Although Profeco could do little to help such consumers, it did fight to eliminate any clauses that required payments in dollars. The most outspoken resistance to this change came from upscale housing developers, who wanted customers to sign contracts in dollars. The battle between developers and Profeco raged from 1976 until 1982.[101] These clauses became illegal in 1982, after which Profeco issued warnings to consumers against accepting illegal terms.[102] Despite this, the 1982 devaluations caused "anarchy," with merchants and providers speculating on prices and demanding payment in dollars.[103] Offenders included real estate developers, private schools, car dealers, furniture stores, and travel agencies.[104] According to one Profeco functionary, "The cynicism of some Mexicans has reached the limits of the believable."[105]

Educating Consumers

While Profeco engaged in daily battles to protect consumers during times of boom and bust, Inco (National Institute for the Consumer) had an educational mission. The institute provided cost comparisons for consumers and counseled them on where to find the best deals. It also attempted to cultivate better consumer practices, such as rational budget management, teaching consumers about the dangers of living beyond their means. Inco educated consumers on their role in Mexico's economic development, promoting consumer consciousness and good consumption habits in order to protect both household finances and the national economy, on the theory that sound household finances would help ensure the stability of the family and the nation. According to Campillo Sainz, "illogical consumption practices posed a danger to the individual and the collective."[106] Mexican consumers, the PRI worried, imitated the luxury consumption practices of its neighbor to the north, and Inco fought the development of an American-style consumer society, a task made especially difficult by Mexico's proximity to the United States. Campillo Sainz argued:

It is imperative to fight the development of a consumer society, which induces the consumer to acquire goods that he does not need; which deliberately produces goods that do not last; which makes it acceptable, even necessary, to throw out goods that are useful but have gone out of fashion; and which generates a state of mind whereby social esteem and prestige are measured by how many of the latest products one owns. All of this is aggravated because we are neighbors with the richest country in the world, and we try to imitate a lifestyle that does not correspond to our level of development.[107]

Mexican consumers needed to learn consumption practices appropriate to their household budgets and their nation's level of development. In essence, Inco was charged with the ideological and practical formation of good consumer-citizens.[108]

Among its many projects, Inco published a series known as Books for the Consumer. The novels and essays in this series serve as cautionary tales of a consumer society. The series includes Guadalupe Loaeza's *Compro, luego existo* (*I Shop, Therefore I Am*), published in 1992, with a sequel, *Debo, luego sufro* (*I Owe, Therefore I Suffer*), in 2000. *I Shop, Therefore I Am* documents Inco's educational mission at the end of the 1980s, illuminating the institute's perspective on Mexican consumption patterns approximately fifteen years after the Federal Law for the Protection of the Consumer was passed.[109]

The novels center on a group of four friends, Sofía, Inés, Alejandra, and Ana Paula. Just as Fonacot recipients straddled the fuzzy boundary between the lower ranks of the middle classes and the poor, these women exist in the murky realm of the upper-middle and upper classes.[110] They can afford an occasional vacation to Europe, but they suffer acute anxiety as they wait for their American Express bills to arrive. They are determined to keep up with the latest trends, and they oscillate between shopping–pleasure–social triumph and debt–despair–defeat. *I Shop, Therefore I Am* opens with Sofía returning to her Miami hotel room, laden with purchases (paid for with her American Express card): "For Sofía, shopping meant to vibrate with life, to enjoy life, to feel fulfilled. But then, at the same time, it also provoked an intense feeling of guilt in her, of anxiety and insecurity. When this happened, it was better to not do the math, to not count the cost."[111] Sofía dreaded the twenty-fourth of every month, the day her American Express bill arrived.[112] She lived in terror, waiting for the moment of reckoning. She resorted to hiding the bill when it arrived— from herself and her husband. She went to a psychiatrist for help:

You have to help me, before I end up, again, at the Credit Bureau. That, doctor, is like entering hell. It's like having Damocles' sword hanging above your head. The moment a credit card holder gets on the Credit Bureau's black list, he's lost: at that moment, he ceases to qualify for credit. Do you understand what that means? It's like ceasing to exist. If you don't have credit, you're nobody. Nobody! You don't exist! And I can't allow that to happen to me, doctor.[113]

For Sofía, the value of financial credit surpasses old examples of moral credit, such as chastity, and she describes her satisfaction from paying her American Express bill as orgasmic.[114] Sofía is not alone in her dependence on credit: her friends Inés and Daniel have built their entire lives on credit (for their business, homes, cars, clothes, shoes, jewelry, and so on). From the late 1980s through the mid-1990s, they repeat their mantra: "This is what credit is for." For them, credit had become "the money of the future." They even use credit to meet their minimum-payment obligations. When the peso is devalued in 1994, their interest rates skyrocket and their credit limits are slashed. Their bills accumulate and they can no longer solve their problems by using more credit. Their mantra rings hollow in their memories.[115]

Similarly, one night when he cannot sleep Alejandra's husband, Antonio, reminisces about the booms and busts of the 1970s and 1980s. He and Alejandra survived the 1976 devaluation quite well—they had little debt and, as a lawyer, he made a fortune representing clients, especially airlines, who fought Profeco's crusade against contract clauses stipulating payment in dollars. But the 1982 devaluation hit them hard; indeed, they learned about the peso devaluation in their San Diego apartment (for which they had a mortgage in dollars).[116]

The instability of social standing emerges as a prominent theme in these novels. All of the characters perform their class status through every-day acts. Sofía, for instance, displays her expensive face creams so that the Miami hotel maids will appreciate her good taste; in the sequel, as a recently divorced woman her dependence on her American Express card increases as she feels more pressure to maintain her status.[117] The desperation of these performances is most poignantly captured by the behavior of Ana Paula, who continually struggles to belong to the group—to be a *niña bien* (a well-to-do girl). Unlike the other women, Ana Paula comes from a solidly middle-class background. As her husband, a banker, is increasingly successful, they move up Mexico City's real estate ladder, from a home in the middle-class Narvarte neighborhood to one in upscale Polanco and then to one in the wealthy Las Lomas. Through her friendship with Sofía, Inés, and Alejandra, Ana Paula tries to become a wealthy Mexican. She asks her friends where they buy their furniture, where they buy their clothes, where they buy their flowers, who caters their dinner parties, and to which American summer camp they send their children. The others constantly mock Ana Paula's tackiness, and their disdain suggests the ultimate futility of Ana Paula's efforts: she will never be one of them.[118] In another example of friction between the middle and upper classes, Inés describes her lover, Manuel, as a "C" in terms of socioeconomic status: his monthly income is only 7,000 pesos, he lives in a three-bedroom condominium in Coyoacán, he has one car, and he rarely travels abroad. He owns a VCR, a television, and a stereo (a list of possessions that Fonacot recipients purchased). Inés would never divorce her husband for such a man.[119]

What is the lesson here? The characters never learn from their mistakes; they never develop better consumer habits. Indeed, when Profeco opened its doors to the public, these four women rushed to denounce abuses by dry cleaners (who lost the buttons of their Chanel suits), veterinarians (who caused panic attacks in their imported pedigreed dogs), beauty salons (who did not replicate the Princess Diana haircut as promised), and house-hold appliance stores (that sold imported, state-of-the-art refrigerators with broken ice-cube makers).[120] By drawing attention to unrestrained con-sumerism and unsound financial planning, these novels serve as a warning about the dangers of credit. Sofía, Ana Paula, Inés, and Alejandra embody the upper-middle-class anxieties that the undergraduate theses on consumer credit warned about in 1970: they show the havoc wreaked by a lack of self-control. At one point, Sofía asks an economist friend why "people" (she would never admit the state of her finances to a friend) lacked control with credit cards. He replied: "In Mexico we don't have a culture of using credit cards correctly. The banks haven't created one. Quite the opposite: they almost harass us with their credit card offers. The entire urban middle class in this country receives mail and telephone calls asking, 'Would you like to use this credit card?' The banks bombard us with slogans like 'With the power of the signature.'"[121] The characters suffer from their habits, and they know it. In an internal monologue, Sofía laments: "Your life is bor-rowed. Do you realize what that means? It means that you waste money that is not yours to purchase dreams, status, false satisfactions, to entertain stupid neuroses and to escape from the world."[122]

The purported lesson is straightforward: material things do not lead to happiness. Although these women enjoy considerable material wealth, they are dogged by guilt and fear, they run up debts with credit-card companies, and they owe money to their psychiatrists. These novels, for all their frivol-ity, capture the dark side of unrestrained consumerism. They are didactic novels, part of Inco's mission to educate Mexican citizens about the dangers of materialism. And, by opening a window onto consumption habits in the late 1980s and early 1990s, they also illustrate the almost Sisyphean task with which Inco was charged. After fifteen years of tutelage by Inco, Mexi-can consumers remained susceptible to the dangers of a consumer society.

The Monster Who Turned Out to Be a Dude

Through Fonacot and Profeco, the PRI tried to subsidize middle-class pur-chasing power and influence consumption habits. In theory, the middle classes would repay the PRI with increased political loyalty. As it turned out, though, they would also repay the government with their money: they would be taxed. On 1 January 1980, the value-added tax (Impuesto de Valor Agregado, or IVA) began to be levied on consumer goods.[123] The tax constituted a fiscal victory for the PRI, following a series of failed attempts at tax reform; it was thus not directly related to rising inflation but rather a part of the government's ongoing attempts to levy tribute. Likewise, the tax was not directly related to Fonacot and Profeco but fell under the jurisdiction of the Ministry of the Treasury. As a tax on consumption, however, it directly impacted the economic relationship between the PRI and the middle classes. It added a new dimension to the category of the consumer-citizen: with Fonacot and Profeco the state protected the consumer-citizen; when he or she paid the tax, the consumer-citizen repaid the state.

The value-added tax disproportionately affected middle-class consumers. The poor and lower classes were shielded from the new tax because basic goods such as tortillas, bread, meat, eggs, milk, sugar, salt, and non-carbonated water were exempt.[124] At the other end of the income spectrum, the upper classes were better able to afford the 10 percent cost. The IVA thus raised questions about the political relationship between the PRI and the middle classes: How would middle-class consumers react to the new tax? How would the PRI attempt to convince them to fulfill their obligations as tax-paying citizens?

The new tax replaced a federal tax on commerce, industry, and services (*Impuesto Federal sobre Ingresos Mercantiles*). It also eliminated seventeen other taxes on specific industries or goods, such as the tax on oils, fats, and lubricants and the tax on cloth and upholstery.[125] Because the IVA replaced already-existing taxes, it did not constitute a new burden on consumers. Symbolically, though, it represented a major change. Before the tax, if a consumer purchased a telephone for a retail price of 100 pesos, the bill would show a subtotal of 100 plus a 4 percent tax, totaling 104 pesos. With the new tax, a subtotal of 100 pesos would be taxed 10 percent, totaling 110 pesos. In theory, however, the value-added tax would reduce the final cost of goods. The rationale was that because the old system involved cascading taxes (4 percent was charged at every stage of production and distribution), the retail price of the telephone ended up being higher than it would be with the new tax, which did not levy cascading taxes; possibly, under the new system, the telephone would have a retail price of 90 pesos plus 10 percent tax. The Ministry of the Treasury calculated that, on average, consumers paid a total of 12 percent in taxes under the old system. Importantly, though, most of that 12 percent was hidden from the consumer. With the IVA, the government had to convince consumers that 10 percent was in fact less than 4 percent. Consumers might pay less tax, but they became more aware of the taxes that they were paying, which produced significant political fallout.[126]

Why, then, would the government initiate this new tax? Surely it did not make sense to levy less tax while at the same time angering consumers. At a basic level, the tax was part of an endeavor to modernize Mexico's fiscal system. The old tax on commercial activities and the seventeen specific taxes were outdated and inefficient. The Minister of the Treasury argued that the value-added tax would benefit small and medium-sized businesses and export sales, make tax evasion more difficult, and simplify administra-

TABLE 4. IVA as a source of revenue for the federal government, 1977–1991 (in millions of pesos)

Year	Total revenue for federal government	Total revenue from taxes	Revenue from ISIM-IVA*	ISIM-IVA as a percentage of tax revenues*	Percentage change in tax revenues	Percentage change in ISIM-IVA*
1977	491,903.4	421,692.5	83,228.8	19.7	n/a	n/a
1978	558,087.8	476,707.7	88,911.9	18.7	13.0	6.8
1979	631,828.7	531,421.8	112,039.4	21.1	11.5	26.0
1980	806,042.4	571,821.0	141,452.3	24.7	7.6	26.3
1981	856,747.9	592,752.7	145,371.4	24.5	3.7	2.8
1982	705,884.9	445,652.3	99,965.4	22.4	−24.8	−31.2
1983	810,652.9	468,421.4	138,243.2	29.5	5.1	38.3
1984	796,500.8	488,176.3	150,952.0	30.9	4.2	9.2
1985	781,292.5	475,355.9	144,535.0	30.4	−2.6	−4.3
1986	602,129.0	426,703.1	118,697.9	27.8	−10.2	−17.9
1987	604,627.0	381,793.9	114,899.6	30.1	−10.5	−3.2
1988	822,358.2	572,921.1	169,566.0	29.6	50.1	47.6
1989	911,172.1	617,571.8	171,957.7	27.8	7.8	1.4
1990	915,122.4	616,126.7	207,074.8	33.6	−0.2	20.4
1991	1,160,788.2	665,178.4	212,905.4	32.0	8.0	2.8

Source: Bank of Mexico website. Converted into 2010 real pesos using the Bank of Mexico's consumer price index. I am grateful to Eva O. Arceo Gómez for her help with the data.

*From 1977 to 1979 only, Impuesto sobre Ingresos Mercantiles; from 1980 to 1991 only, Impuesto al Valor Agregado.

tive processes.[127] Mexican policymakers followed the lead of other countries that had instituted a value-added tax, such as France (1954), Brazil (1967), Germany (1968), and Argentina (1975). At the level of socioeconomic justice, the Minister argued that, through the exemption of basic goods and by generating lower prices and a more just tax rate, the IVA would counteract inflation and protect salaries, and thus help to alleviate social tensions.[128] According to official propaganda, the new tax would foster "a socially harmonious development, in which all sectors of the population enjoy increased quality of life."[129] In reality, however, value-added taxes are regressive: they place a greater burden on the poor than on the rich because lower-income households pay a larger proportion of their income toward the tax. While many basic goods were exempt, a middle-class family that purchased a car would have a harder time paying the new tax than a wealthy family would.

The new tax also heralded a symbolic change in the PRI's power vis-à-vis the middle and upper classes. Previous attempts at tax reform had failed. Policymakers had faltered when faced with opposition (real or imagined). In the 1960s, a proposed income-tax reform had been curbed owing to collusion between politicians and those who benefited from low income tax rates; in the early 1970s, Echeverría abandoned a radical tax reform to avoid further alienating private-sector interests.[130] It is possible that, because of the optimism of the oil boom, the PRI did have the political clout in the 1970s to assert its power to tax. The IVA thus represented a political triumph.[131] This symbolic coup was perhaps more important than the fiscal modernization and the revenue generated by the new tax (see Table 4). It constituted one step in a much longer endeavor to reform Mexico's fiscal culture—Mexico had (and still has) one of the lowest tax collection rates in Latin America.[132]

The PRI's attention to consumer needs throughout the 1970s had generated an important amount of political capital that likely allowed the party to push through the new tax. After all, it was consumers who would experience the greatest shock when they went to the shops in January 1980. Through initiatives such as Fonacot and Profeco, the PRI had demonstrated its desire to bolster purchasing power. No doubt, the timing of the reform was also important: at the height of the oil boom many consumers were caught up in the optimism about Mexico's economic development. The combination of policy and rhetoric had generated a certain amount of goodwill for the PRI on the part of middle-class consumers. That said, the government had to mount a considerable public-relations campaign to contain the political fallout from consumers, as well as from producers, distributors, and merchants, all of whom feared higher taxes.

A cartoon pamphlet titled *Las aventuras del Fideo: El caso del monstruo que resultó cuate* (The adventures of Fideo: The case of the monster who turned out to be a dude) is an outstanding example of the Ministry of the Treasury's information campaign.[133] In this pamphlet, two young boys, Fideo and Paco, try to understand the new tax. Paco arrives at Fideo's house and finds him hiding under his bed. Fideo tells Paco that he's hiding from a space monster that is approaching Earth: "Haven't they been talking about this monster in your house? . . . The monster's called IVA. . . . And even my dad, who's big and strong, is scared of IVA," says Fideo.

Paco calls Fideo's mother upstairs to explain what her son is talking about. Here the cartoon reveals several of the ministry's stereotypes, or at least stereotypes that its staff thought might play well with the Mexican public. Fideo's mother is initially confused about this monster. When Fideo explains to her that he overheard his father talking on the phone about IVA, she assumes her son misheard and that her husband is having an affair with a woman named Eva. Her jealous rage is followed by a scene in which the young boys discover a newspaper and realize that IVA refers to a new tax, and then explain to the hysterical mother that her husband is not having an affair with a floozy (*corista*) named Eva.

The boys then seek out their neighbor, Elenita, an attractive (*bien bonita*) accountant, to explain how the IVA will work (see Figure 4). As Elenita explains the IVA to Fideo and Paco, she also spurns the advances of a suitor, Efren, who offends her with his ignorance of the tax. When Efren condescends to the children that the IVA is a trick by the govern-

---

FIGURE 4. Elenita and Efren disagree over the IVA. From SHCP, *Las aventuras del Fideo: El caso del monstruo que resultó cuate*, 1979, JLP, c. 1897, exp. 7, AGN.

Panel 1
Efren: Go play somewhere else, kids.
Juan "Fideo": Elenita, it's a very urgent matter, and you're the only intelligent friend we have . . .
Elenita: What's going on?
Paco: We want you to tell us about the IVA . . .

Panel 2
Juan "Fideo": The tax that'll be in effect in January.
Efren: She doesn't know anything about taxes . . . Can't you see that she's a woman?
Elenita: And what does being a woman have to do with it? Of course I know that the IVA is the value-added tax!

Panel 3
Juan "Fideo": Ah! So IVA are just the initials . . .
Elenita: Exactly . . .
Efren: It's another trick by the government to charge us more taxes.
Elenita: It's the opposite; when the IVA comes into effect we'll all be paying a more just tax.

Panel 4
Efren: How naïve you are, Elenita!
Elenita: I'm not naïve, Efren, I'm an accountant, and I know what I'm talking about . . .
Efren: Are you saying that I don't?

PUES VAYAN A JUGAR A OTRA PARTE MUCHACHITOS.

ELENITA, ES ALGO MUY URGENTE Y ERES LA UNICA AMIGA INTELIGENTE QUE TENEMOS...

¿DE QUE SE TRATA?

QUEREMOS QUE NOS CUENTES DEL IVA...

EL IMPUESTO QUE VAN A PONER EN ENERO.

ELLA NO SABE NADA DE IMPUESTOS... ¿QUE NO VEN QUE ES MUJER?

¿Y QUE TIENE QUE SEA MUJER?... ¡CLARO QUE SE! EL IVA ES EL IMPUESTO AL VALOR AGREGADO.

AH! ENTONCES IVA SON SOLO LAS INICIALES...

EXACTAMENTE...

Y ES OTRO TRUCO DEL FISCO PARA COBRARNOS MAS IMPUESTOS.

POR EL CONTRARIO, CUANDO EMPIECE A FUNCIONAR EL IVA PAGAREMOS UN IMPUESTO MAS EQUITATIVO.

6

¡QUE INGENUA ERES, ELENITA!

NO SOY INGENUA, EFREN SOY CONTADORA Y SE DE QUE ESTOY HABLANDO...

¿QUIERES DECIR QUE YO NO SE?

ment to make them pay even more taxes, Elenita calls him out on his ignorance.

Once Elenita exposes Efren's ignorance (he doesn't understand how the old federal tax on commerce worked), she takes Fideo and Paco to an ice cream parlor to explain the tax. She explains to the children that even though the IVA rate of 10 percent is higher than the old rate of 4 percent, "When the IVA comes into effect, we'll be paying a more just tax." Elenita uses the example of her dress: She paid 663 pesos for the dress, plus the old tax of 4 percent, totaling 689 pesos. In the old system, the price of 663 pesos had taxes hidden in it already (12 percent), so Elena actually paid a 16 percent tax on her dress. Under the new system, there will be no taxes hidden in the price, and she will pay only the 10 percent IVA on the dress.

Meantime, Efren went to ask his brother, a lawyer, about Elenita's claims. Efren catches up with the others at the ice cream parlor, shame-faced (see Figure 5). It turns out, admits Efren, that Elenita was right: "[The IVA] is so good that almost every modern country uses it."

As Elenita, Paco, Fideo, and Efren discuss other benefits of the IVA (such as a reduction in tax evasion and an increased simplicity of paperwork) while enjoying their ice cream, Fideo's father arrives. The father, a successful busi-nessman, agrees with their conclusions: "The IVA, on top of being positive, is absolutely indispensable," he says. "Mexico has great resources, and our economy has grown a lot, and now we need more modern and egalitarian systems." The pamphlet ends with everyone singing together (see Figure 6).

FIGURE 5. Efren arrives at the ice cream parlor, now in agreement with Elen-ita. From SHCP, *Las aventuras del Fideo: El caso del monstruo que resultó cuate*, 1979, JLP, c. 1897, exp. 7, AGN.

Panel 1
Efren: The IVA is a tax that is not added to the cost [at every stage of production, like the previous cascading tax] . . . It is only charged once, openly, to the customer when the prod-uct is purchased . . .
Paco: Efren! It's great that you came!
Juan "Fideo": You missed the explanation of cascading taxes.
Efren: I didn't miss anything because I asked my brother, Enrique, who's a lawyer . . .

Panel 2
Elenita: Is that why you disappeared?
Efren: Elenita, I was ashamed that I didn't know anything about the matter, so I did some research about the IVA . . .
Elenita: Now are you convinced that it's a good thing?
Efren: It's so good that practically every country with a modern economy uses it.

Panel 3
Juan "Fideo": I thought we were going to be the first to use it.
Elenita: No, Juan, the benefits of the IVA have been demonstrated in many other countries.
Efren: France has been using it since 1954 . . .
Juan "Fideo": But I want to know how it works.

14

FIGURE 6. IVA: A song for change and progress. The lyrics read: "We are grow-ing; and we need to change; long live the change so we can progress." From SHCP, *Las aventuras del Fideo: El caso del monstruo que resultó cuate*, 1979, JLP, c. 1897, exp. 7, AGN.

In *The Adventures of Fideo* the characters are all middle class: they're well dressed (Elenita paid 689 pesos for her dress); they have nice homes (Fideo's house is large, with at least two stories, and he has his own bed-room); they live in a nice neighborhood with a lovely park (where Efren was courting Elenita); and they go to an American-style ice cream parlor (not a typical Mexican one). Fideo's father is a successful businessman.

Did this propaganda work? A questionnaire was tucked into the pam-phlet, to be completed and return posted at no cost. In this question-naire, the Ministry of the Treasury asked readers, among other questions: "What is the IVA? What are the differences between the IVA and the old federal tax on commerce? Which do you think is a better system, and why? How do you think the IVA will impact you personally? Do you think that this pamphlet provides sufficient information so that people understand the IVA and its advantages?" Surely the Ministry of the Treasury was concerned that the new tax would generate confusion on 1 January 1980. Indeed, in an intriguing moment of metanarrative, the ministry transcends the plotline in *The Adventures of Fideo* to comment upon its information campaign. Fideo's father refers directly to the cam-paign: "Can you imagine all of the work that the Ministry of the Treasury is doing to inform people and bring the systems up to date? It's tremen-dous!" And the pamphlet depicts the information sessions provided by the ministry to its own staff, to public accountants, and to business own-ers (see Figure 7).

After over a year of information sessions and propaganda pamphlets, on 1 January 1980, the new tax went into effect. In December 1979 and January 1980, newspapers reported great confusion among consumers and merchants, who were uncertain which goods were exempt from the IVA.[134] Consumers denounced merchants to Profeco for what they believed was illegal taxation.[135] Merchants, in turn, complained about unclear guidelines. Many small merchants—*causantes menores* who earned up to 1.5 million pesos annually—were exempt from the tax and worried that their suppliers (larger businesses who were not exempt) would apply the tax on the goods

FIGURE 7. Ministry of the Treasury metanarrative. The person who has fallen asleep in this information session might be a dig at the public in general. Treasury depended on the good faith of citizens to do their part in learning about and adapting to the new tax. From SHCP, *Las aventuras del Fideo: El caso del monstruo que resultó cuate*, 1979, JLP, c. 1897, exp. 7, AGN.

they supplied.[136] The hardware store owner in Figure 8, for example, was worried that her suppliers would charge her the IVA, even though, as a *causante menor*, she was exempt. For small business owners such as this woman, an increased cost from improper taxation could distort budgets.

Merchants also complained of a lack of clarity and last-minute changes to the list of exempted goods. In pharmacies, for example, confusion reigned on 1 January 1980. Initially, only pharmaceuticals for animals were to be exempt, in order to protect farming; on 31 December 1979, however, the Ministry of the Treasury revised the rules regarding drugs and announced that all drugs would be taxed at a reduced rate.[137] In the first few

Ferreterías *con "cuotas fijas", no habrá problemas.*

EXPANSION 6 FEB 1980

FIGURE 8. Hardware store owner worries about IVA. From "¿Qué onda con el IVA?," *Expansión*, 6 February 1980.

weeks of January, many small pharmacies decided to absorb any extra cost generated by the confusion, for fear of a call from Profeco. Pharmaceutical laboratories, too, were caught off guard by the eleventh-hour change and did not have labels or invoices prepared for a different tax rate. All of this led to a temporary shortage of medicine.[138] Other last-minute changes sparked conflict between merchants and the government. More than one million merchants, for example, signed a statement condemning the late December 1979 decision to exclude worker stores from the new tax.[139]

The value-added tax remained controversial during the 1980s crisis. The government faced hostility in 1983, for example, when it introduced new IVA rates. In an attempt to both raise public revenue and alleviate the impact of the debt crisis on poorer consumers, the government eliminated the 10 percent rate and created distinct IVA rates for basic goods (6 percent), regular goods (15 percent), and luxury goods (20 percent). The resulting increased revenue is evident in Table 4 above. Although the 6 percent rate for basic-but-not-exempt goods sought to protect economically marginal consumers, this category excluded necessities such as toothpaste and toilet paper, which would be taxed at 15 percent. Many commentators argued that an income tax would be less regressive, hence fairer.[140] Protests against the tax continued through 1984, when a coalition of leftist parties, workers, and the private sector mounted a campaign to eliminate it altogether.

Although none of the protests succeeded in repealing the tax, the constant protest forced the Ministry of the Treasury to make a major change. At the end of 1984, it announced that, starting in August 1985, the tax would be buried in the retail price. Treasury representatives explained that the tax's unpopularity had forced them to conceal it in the final price.[141] Consumers would no longer receive a bill that listed both the price of the item and the tax; instead, the tax would be hidden in the price. Many accused President de la Madrid and the Ministry of the Treasury of a lack of transparency, but the change did in fact weaken the ongoing protests against the tax. At what expense? One journalist lamented that, by burying the tax, the government reinforced a lack of fiscal consciousness among Mexican consumers.[142]

The Debt Economy

From 1973 to 1985 the economic relationship between the PRI and the middle classes changed significantly. The middle classes acquired a new political identity, that of consumer-citizens. In an environment of rising inflation, the PRI sought to protect their purchasing power by providing consumer credit to salaried workers. And the government consecrated consumer rights into law. Along with these benefits and rights came responsibilities, such as payment of taxes. Consumers took advantage of the benefits by making use of credit from Fonacot and exercised their rights by availing themselves of Profeco's services, but they did not willingly assume their fiscal responsibility. And, by burying the IVA in the price, the Ministry of the Treasury implicitly encouraged such hypocrisy.

It was a difficult time to be a consumer. They had to navigate a series of new economic phenomena, including rapidly rising inflation, public sources of consumer credit, private credit cards, consumers rights, peso devaluations, and taxes on consumption. Many of these indicated an increasingly complex consumer economy. Fonacot, Profeco, and the IVA represented the PRI's attempt to generate a similarly sophisticated financial culture among consumers, and they were promising initiatives. They might have represented the beginnings of a solid financial culture among middle-class (and other) consumers. They might also have forged a more transparent economic relationship between the state and its consumer-citizens. The new institutions and the new tax did generate some movement in these directions, but in the context of economic and political instability, any such movement was limited.

These changes occurred during a remarkable period of boom and bust in Mexico. The oil boom of 1977–1981 was a period of prosperity that was also marred by the profound structural instability of a petro-state. The inflation rate, which continued to rise during the oil boom, belied official proclamations that the newfound petroleum reserves offered Mexico an exit from underdevelopment and economic instability. Many members of the middle classes could no longer sustain their lifestyle with their wages, and the structural shift from decent real wages to consumer credit (and debt) continued during the oil boom. After oil prices crashed in 1981, it became clear that the problems of 1973–76 had not disappeared.

But much had changed since 1973. The debt economy that emerged in the 1970s collapsed in 1981–82, when Mexico faced a balance of payments crisis. Simply put, Mexico could not meet its loan payment obligations.

Part III

FAULT LINES OF NEOLIBERALISM

"From parking space Z-650, at the corner of the Nuevo León building, I saw the tremor unleashed," recalled Salomón Reyes, a Tlatelolco resident in 1985. "I saw as clear as day how the building fell over, but what can you do? Turn into Superman and stop it? My children were waiting for breakfast to go to school," he continued. "The first thing I thought was, 'My children, my children, God of mine!' And the building came down, nothing but a screech, and when it hit the ground as if yanked out from the roots, it raised black smoke, really black smoke."[*]

In September 1985, an 8.1 earthquake struck the heart of Mexico City. Salomón Reyes described watching his apartment building collapse while he worked as a security guard in one of the complex's parking lots. As he "sprinted" from his post—to join crowds looking for "their family, their loved ones, their relatives"—he witnessed the damage done to countless other buildings in the Tlatelolco apartment complex.[**] Built by the government in the 1960s to house the middle classes, Tlatelolco had symbolized the successes of the Mexican Miracle. But by the 1980s, residents in these high-rise apartment buildings no longer represented the postwar economic boom and political stability; instead, they belonged to a middle-class world that had come under threat.

Hope for a return of the midcentury prosperity faded as Mexico had the dubious honor of inaugurating the third-world debt crisis in 1981. The PRI and the middle classes could not—and some did not want to—resuscitate that midcentury world. Instead, a group of policymakers within the PRI looked for a new kind of prosperity. They undertook a neoliberal

---

[*] Testimony collected in Poniatowska, *Nothing, Nobody*, 48.
[**] Ibid.

reordering of the Mexican economy, dispossessing some members of the middle classes and benefiting others. In the face of these changes, the élite realm of the PRI and the middle classes could no longer hold together. Toward the end of the decade, it split into two camps: loyal supporters and vehement critics of neoliberalism.

5 La Crisis

ON THE FRONT LINES OF AUSTERITY AND *APERTURA*,
1981–1988

In the 1980s, "la crisis" initially referred specifically to the economic contraction that was underway, but as all aspects of life began to be affected, the term became a shorthand way of capturing the zeitgeist. By 1981, the oil boom had gone bust and Mexico faced a serious imbalance of payments. What began as a macroeconomic problem quickly permeated the economic, social, political, and cultural realms, and Mexico entered a period that came to be known as the lost decade.[1] Members of the middle classes lost their personal independence, their lifestyles, their future aspirations, and their health. As one journalist described:

Carmen was a seventy-four-year-old woman who lived alone in an apartment, paying the rent with her widow's pension. For her, "austerity" meant abandoning her apartment and moving in with one of her children, a situation she had always wanted to avoid.

For Hermenegildo, a retired seventy-five-year-old man living modestly on his savings, the austerity measures drove him to become a photographer for social reunions.

Pilar and María Veronica were studying in the United States on scholarship, but had to return to Mexico before the end of their courses.

Fernando, a businessman, struggled to refinance his debt after his bank credit dried up and he began to suffer headaches.[2]

For over a decade, Presidents Luis Echeverría and José López Portillo had responded to economic and political instability with public spending, hoping to revive the perceived prosperity of the Mexican Miracle. In this endeavor, the philosophies behind shared development and the petrostate had, perhaps not intentionally, centered on the middle classes. In the 1980s, a new generation of policymakers moved away from the state-led development strategy and set the country on a path toward a neoliberal economic model. Broadly speaking, the proponents of neoliberalism argued that human well-being would be maximized by market forces. The role of the state in the economy, in contrast, should be limited to creating an institutional framework that would allow market forces to dominate.[3]

From mid-1981 to late 1982, Mexico's economy went into free fall. At first, López Portillo, perhaps believing that the crisis would be temporary, took out short-term loans at highly disadvantageous interest rates to pay Mexico's foreign debt, which only exacerbated the situation.[4] When Paul Volcker, chairman of the American Federal Reserve Bank, raised interest rates in 1981, Mexico was unable to meet payments. Toward the end of August 1981, Mexico's minister of the treasury announced that the country was unable to pay its debt, and creditors agreed to a ninety-day suspension of debt service. Mexico's debt crisis, then, was caused by irresponsible borrowing, predatory lending, and Volcker's monetary policy.

As the situation worsened, López Portillo reacted with ever more desperate measures, losing his credibility in the process. In February 1982, he assured Mexicans that there would be no peso devaluation; indeed, he declared that he would "defend the peso like a dog"; only weeks later the peso plummeted. Then, in August 1982, as Mexico's foreign reserves reached a record low, he announced a freeze on all American-dollar bank accounts (individuals could save their money in Mexican banks in either pesos or dollars) and converted these dollars into pesos at below-market exchange rates. Finally, in September of that year, he nationalized Mexico's banking system.[5]

The urgent question, asked around the world, became: Would Mexico pay its debt? This was the context in which President Miguel de la Madrid took office on 1 December 1982. López Portillo's final actions—his declaration to defend the peso like a dog, the freezing of dollar accounts, and the nationalization of the banking system—might have led to an autonomous stand on the question of debt payment. His actions suggested an economic nationalism that would privilege Mexico's autonomy vis-à-vis international creditors; they recalled an earlier debt crisis in the 1930s, when some Latin American countries had defaulted on their foreign debts. Instead, on 10 November 1982, the López Portillo administration signed a letter of intent with the International Monetary Fund (IMF). This was an agreement whereby Mexico's debt repayments would be rescheduled in exchange for widespread structural adjustment of the economy, with a particular emphasis on reduction of the public-sector deficit.[6] When de la Madrid took office, he initially exceeded the IMF targets: one contemporary expert decried how the president "complied excessively" with the IMF agreement; another, though, praised his administration's "overkill."[7]

With his embrace of the IMF program, de la Madrid made clear that his view of the economy, and its relationship to society and state, differed dramatically from the one espoused by the previous administration. López Portillo had attempted to quell political discontent by creating jobs, thereby bringing some of his critics into a growing state apparatus. This populist strategy ended as de la Madrid cut spending in almost every area except debt repayment. Through austerity measures and, later, trade liberalization, de la Madrid shifted from state-led development to neoliberalism. This move produced—and required—radical changes in the élite realm of the PRI and the middle classes. More than declining growth rates or budget imbalances, economic crises rupture established patterns of class domination; likewise, economic transitions require class reconfiguration.

As Mexico's economy underwent massive structural changes, inequality increased within the middle classes: some became richer and others poorer.[8] Some nurses, airline pilots, and small business owners, for example, became poorer and more vulnerable, and many faced unemployment or bankruptcy. On the other hand, some engineers, stockbrokers, and movie producers became richer and moved to gated communities and their children attended private schools. By certain measures, such as the ability to purchase meat without straining the household budget, some families stopped being middle class altogether. If the boundaries between social classes are inherently porous, the lines between the poor, the middle classes, and the wealthy became especially fuzzy during *la crisis*, with families moving up and down the social hierarchy at a heightened pace.

During the 1980s, debates over the structural changes and their effects intensified, and the middle classes and PRI politicians became increasingly divided along the lines of supporters and detractors of neoliberalism. But for most of the decade there were no clear lines in the debate. Some individuals viewed the trade liberalization with optimism and rushed to invest their savings in the stock market, while the austerity measures caused others to entertain thoughts of suicide. One thing was certain: those who had benefited from the oil boom and the midcentury prosperity had much to lose. The middle classes and the PRI together constituted an élite realm, and the economic and political crises that began in the late 1960s and early 1970s had shaken this realm. Structural economic change began in the early 1970s, in the context of intense political upheaval, with a policy of increased debt at both the national and household levels. No doubt the oil boom, for all its instability—and despite the existential malaise that accompanied it—helped avert full-blown political and economic crises. If the oil boom functioned as a brief period of prosperity, it also accelerated structural change as Mexico's leaders converted the country into a petrostate. The forces of structural change, economic turmoil, and political instability met head-on in the 1980s. By the end of the decade, the PRI and the middle classes split under the pressure.

Economic Souls: State and Economy

A questionnaire circulated at a November 1982 meeting of small business owners captures the fervor of the debate over structural economic changes, especially regarding the appropriate role for the state in the economy. This meeting was organized by the Confederation of National Chambers of Commerce (Confederación de Cámaras Nacionales de Comercio, or Concanaco), which represented merchants, and two of the multisector associations, the Business Coordinating Council (Consejo Coordinador Empresarial, or CCE) and the Mexican Employers Association (Confederación Patronal de la República Mexicana, or Coparmex).[9] Shortly after López Portillo nationalized the banks, and only weeks before de la Madrid would take office, leaders and high-level officials of these private sector organizations delivered speeches condemning López Portillo's actions. The questionnaire, which had no author, asked business owners to what extent they agreed or disagreed with the following statements:

a. The government is intervening too much in free enterprise.

b. Mexico is headed more toward totalitarianism than capitalism.

c. In Mexico, the authority does not respect our Constitution.

d. In Mexico, the executive power does not respect the jurisdiction and responsibility of the legislative and judicial powers.

e. In Mexico, politics are not in accordance with our Constitution, but rather with the imposition of foreign ideologies.

f. Business owners ought to participate more actively in politics to defend their principles.[10]

Leaders of these organizations characterized government involvement in the economy as totalitarian, attempting to foment discontent among the small and medium-sized business owners who filled the ranks of their organizations. Other questions in the survey suggested taking action against the growing role of the state in Mexico's economy: "In comparison with one year ago, do you think that there is more or less liberty in Mexico today? Do you believe the government has been acting correctly or incorrectly? What do you think one should do to defend the principles of free enterprise?"[11] During this meeting, several speakers derided the bank nationalization and described the state as fascist and totalitarian. The vice president of the Mexican Employers Association (Coparmex), Jorge del Rincón Bernal, for instance, gave a speech in which he outlined how Mexico was moving toward fascism, which he defined as "nothing without the state; nothing against the state; nothing outside the state."[12]

It would be misleading, however, to characterize the private sector as reflexively opposed to state intervention in the economy. After all, in September 1981 one of the leading private sector groups in Mexico, the Alfa Group (heirs to the Monterrey Group), received a government bailout of approximately twelve million pesos. Scandal erupted when news of the loan was leaked to the Chamber of Deputies. Business leaders supported state action when it was in their interest; when they felt threatened, they accused the state of, at best, impeding free enterprise and, at worst, totalitarianism and fascism.[13]

In his inaugural address, President de la Madrid declared: "We shall not nationalize society; that would be totalitarianism," a clear rejection of López Portillo's policies.[14] In contrast to his predecessor, de la Madrid embraced an economic worldview that minimized state participation.[15] Whereas López Portillo had pinned Mexico's future on a large petro-state, de la Madrid saw the country's future in a trim and unencumbered neoliberal state. In this speech, the new president set the tone for the following six years: "Mexico is undergoing a grave crisis," he began. "The crisis is evident in the expressions of mistrust and pessimism regarding the country's ability to fulfill its immediate requirements." After describing Mexico's macroeconomic situation, he warned: "We are in an emergency."[16] The president then outlined a ten-point plan to address the situation, his Immediate Program for the Reordering of the Economy (Plan Immediato para la Reordenación de la Economía). With it, he laid out the foundations of his economic policy: "I shall propose an austerity budget," the new president announced.[17] Of the ten points, the three that addressed public spending and restructuring the public administration to increase "efficiency" and eliminate "squandering, waste [and] corruption" represented the most significant change introduced by the plan; they constituted the heart of de la Madrid's austerity plan: first point: "reduction of growth in public spending"; fourth point: "strengthening of standards ensuring discipline, proper programming, efficiency and scrupulous honesty in implementation of authorized public spending"; and ninth point: "restructuring of the Federal Public Administration."[18]

In addition to austerity measures, de la Madrid later embraced an economic policy that was referred to as "opening" (*apertura*). The state-led development strategy, which had guided the midcentury Import Substitution Industrialization (ISI) boom and the 1970s oil boom, was gradually replaced by one that increased Mexico's openness to foreign trade and investment; this shift was epitomized by Mexico's 1986 entry into the General Agreement on Tariffs and Trade (GATT), which led to reduced trade barriers. Together, austerity and *apertura* altered the foundation of Mexico's economic development strategy and facilitated the transition from state-led development to neoliberalism. They constituted a massive structural adjustment of the Mexican economy, one required by the IMF in return for the rescheduling of debt payments.[19]

Although austerity and *apertura* together facilitated the emergence of neoliberalism, they do not explain its origins. A reduced state and an un-fettered market may be components of a neoliberal worldview, but they do not explain how such a view takes hold. In retrospect, it seems clear that de la Madrid and his top advisors began a process of privatization and trade liberalization that culminated in Mexico's entry into the North American Free Trade Agreement (NAFTA) under President Carlos Salinas de Gortari (who was president from 1988 to 1994). But this process was a fitful one, and the consolidation of neoliberalism under Salinas was not the natural end of a teleological process.[20] For example, a protest move-ment following a major earthquake forced de la Madrid to find recourse in state-led economic development when he expropriated private prop-erty in the interests of the public good. Likewise, Salinas ran an extensive social-welfare program, called the National Solidarity Program (Programa Nacional de Solidaridad), to reduce poverty and mitigate the effects of the austerity measures.[21] Thus, both de la Madrid and Salinas combined economic liberalization and state-led development strategies, hence it is difficult to pinpoint a precise break from state-led development. The shift in worldviews more resembles an overall trend, with a good deal of messi-ness on the ground; the shift occurred in policy, rhetoric, and ideology and was a political and cultural process as much as an economic one. In the pithy words of one of neoliberalism's most prominent early promoters, British prime minister Margaret Thatcher, "economics are a method; the object is to change the heart and soul."[22]

The shift in worldviews hinged on *la crisis*. Miguel de la Madrid began his presidency with the theme of crisis, overshadowing visions of moder-nity and dreams of prosperity. During the 1980s, the term *crisis* carried several meanings that, together, transformed it into a powerful keyword that defined the decade. Literary theorist Raymond Williams describes key-words as words used to make sense of the major transformations, forma-tive experiences, and consequential concepts of a certain moment: "This, significantly, is the vocabulary we share with others, often imperfectly, when we wish to discuss many of the central processes of our common life."[23] On one level, *la crisis* referred to the socioeconomic crisis that had a drastic and generally negative impact on the standard of living of many cit-izens. The term also became a cultural referent, signaling political paralysis and cynicism. And when de la Madrid, in his inaugural speech, raised the specter of "emergency," he began a process of normalizing the extraordi-nary; *la crisis*—these exceptional circumstances—served as an ideological tool that helped to justify economic restructuring. *La crisis*, then, was also a powerful state of exception (or "emergency") that rendered austerity and *apertura* culturally and ideologically normal and allowed for the dismantling of the welfare state and the implementation of neoliberal policies that dispossessed large segments of the middle classes without provoking widespread protest.[24]

At the heart of this shift in worldviews lay a debate about the role of the state in the economy. The de la Madrid administration set out to curtail state participation, congruent with the emerging IMF view that the role of the state should be limited and that the market, not the state, could best manage the economy.[25] During his presidency, for example, the government sold or liquidated 766 of more than a thousand state companies, beginning the wave of state divestiture, deregulation, and trade liberalization that occurred in the 1990s.[26]

Rebellion versus Obedience

Miguel de la Madrid did not have to embrace the IMF structural adjustment program; he decided to. Many economists, though, even those skeptical of the reforms, argue that the de la Madrid administration did not really have a choice. Nora Lustig and Jaime Ros insist that "after the 1982 debt crisis, the state redefined its role in the economy partly *because it could not do otherwise.*"[27] Certainly, de la Madrid faced real constraints on his autonomy; at the same time, however, Mexico's disadvantageous position in the world system did not strip him of his agency. Indeed, in late 1982 rumors circulated in the banking centers of New York and London as to whether or not Mexico would pay. In pubs after work, bankers speculated whether Mexico would form a debtors' cartel with Argentina and Brazil.[28] Bankers might well have been thinking about the Latin American debt crises of the 1930s and regretting having taken the risk of lending to Mexico. Instead of stopping payment—which would have forced banks and other credit-granting institutions to absorb the risk they had taken—de la Madrid "excessively" enforced the IMF austerity measures.[29] When the austerity measures went into effect, the Mexican population, and especially the middle classes, assumed the burden of the risks taken by foreign lenders.

Nonpayment was plausible—perhaps even a real option. This becomes clear by considering the case of Peru. In his July 1985 inaugural speech, Peruvian president Alan García (whose first term in office was from 1985 to 1990) declared that Peru would limit its debt payments to a maximum of 10 percent of its export earnings. Instead of kowtowing to the IMF, as de la Madrid had done three years earlier in his inaugural speech,

García politicized the foreign debt issue, and his strategy met with popular enthusiasm.[30] Over the summer of 1985, García's denunciations of the IMF became increasingly radical, and in August he described the IMF as "the sinister and dark figure of the twentieth century . . . the executor of exploitation and dominion."[31] García posed a political threat to the IMF, as sociologist Teivo Teivainen argues, because he would make only small payments when the Peruvian economy could have managed larger payments.[32] García challenged the agency's claim that it was politically neutral, which was based on the assumption that economic issues, such as foreign debt, are apolitical. Instead, the Peruvian president exposed the conditionality principle of the IMF, which made debt rescheduling conditional upon acceptance of structural adjustment programs, as a political policy and a political strategy.[33] And García was not the only head of state to call for rebellion against the emerging IMF hegemony. In September 1985, Cuba hosted an international conference on foreign debt, and Fidel Castro called upon Latin American countries to go on strike against payment.[34]

Activists in Mexico responded to calls for a debt rebellion. By 18 September 1985, Mexico had failed to meet the agreed-upon targets, and the IMF announced that it would withhold financing. One day later, a massive earthquake struck Mexico City. In the weeks and months after the natural disaster, the PRI's mismanagement of rescue and reconstruction galvanized tens of thousands of residents into a major protest movement. Residents demanded immediate shelter and a say in how the city would be rebuilt. They also called for a moratorium on debt repayment. (The earthquake and its aftermath are the subject of Chapter 6.)

Leftist activists referred to the example of Managua, Nicaragua, where an earthquake played a role in the triumph of the Sandinista revolution. Activists argued that, should the government not address their demands, they might organize on all levels and spark a social revolution similar to Nicaragua's.[35] Anger boiled up against groups of industrialists who worked against any possibility of a moratorium. "Wouldn't it be better," asked one activist, "if these industrialists—servants and representatives of foreign capital—stopped thinking of their foreign masters and instead thought for a moment of their brothers and joined the widespread demand for a one-year moratorium?"[36]

The Mexico City earthquake allowed activists to draw connections across Latin America, just when Peruvian president Alan García's debt rebellion was gaining momentum and debates over foreign debt raged across the continent. On 23 October 1985, the earthquake victims led a march of ten thousand residents to the president's home in Los Pinos. They left a petition at Los Pinos demanding, among other things, a moratorium on

Mexico's foreign debt payments. The placards and banners carried in the march included:

First Nicaragua, then El Salvador, Liberation for Latin America!

Moratorium on debt payment!

Miguel de la Madrid, you don't have the pants to make decisions![37]

García needed at least one of the big Latin American debtor nations (Argentina, Brazil, and Mexico) to join his rebellion to establish an alternative to the IMF program. But even if they had felt drawn to García's anti-imperialist argument, the other leaders worried that their relationship with creditors might be damaged if they appeared too sympathetic to García's rebellion. Mexico, in particular, was of almost no help, as it had already become, in the words of one expert, "an example of the rationality of obedient behavior [to the IMF]."[38] When García suggested, at a February 1986 meeting of Latin American leaders on the issue of foreign debt, that debt payments be linked to export capacity, the Mexican representative walked out of the meeting.[39] In March 1986 the IMF sent a mission to Lima to negotiate a debt-repayment schedule; García denounced it as a "colonial mission," calling the IMF letters of intent "letters of colonial concessions," and asked the IMF representative to leave the country.[40] The situation climaxed in September 1986, when the IMF declared Peru ineligible for further credit.[41]

Alan García's attempted debt rebellion puts Miguel de la Madrid's obedience into relief. In many ways, the Mexican president might have been better positioned to lead the kind of debt rebellion García later attempted. In 1982, Mexico inaugurated the debt crisis, and its behavior set the stage for the continent. By the time García began his rebellion, the large Latin American debtor nations had already struck deals with García's sinister foe; it was too late to form a debtors' cartel. De la Madrid had been uniquely positioned to challenge the IMF structural adjustment programs. Although neoliberal policy had been attempted in Latin America earlier, it had been under the military dictatorship of Augusto Pinochet in Chile (from 1973 to 1990). The Mexican debt crisis in 1982 was the first attempt to implement neoliberal changes outside a dictatorship; Mexico became a laboratory for the legal and nonviolent enforcement of neoliberal policy.[42]

Mexico, however, might have been able to shape an entirely different world. Mexico's debt crisis occurred as neoliberal economists began to consolidate their position within the IMF and the World Bank, whereupon they immediately "invented" structural adjustment.[43] Geographer David Harvey describes how, in the early 1980s, "the capitalist world stumbled towards neoliberalization" as the answer to the economic crises of the 1970s.[44] The neoliberal orthodoxy would be definitively established in the

1990s, when it became known as the "Washington Consensus." Structural adjustment had not been tried and tested in 1982, and the negotiation of Mexico's debt crisis was an experiment.

Thus, the significance of de la Madrid's obedience should not be underestimated; he had been positioned to forge a different relationship between international debtors and creditors. Instead, however, he stumbled toward obedience and in doing so provided the model that other countries, such as Peru, were supposed to emulate. Why Miguel de la Madrid and his top advisors embraced the IMF program, and neoliberalism more generally, remains an unanswered question. One possibility is that de la Madrid embodied the emerging neoliberal orthodoxy in Mexico. He was part of a new generation of politicians who had studied in the United States, having earned a master's degree in public administration from Harvard University; many of his top advisors had also been trained in American universities where neoliberalism was an influential ideology.[45] But arguments about education and ideology are only part of the explanation. One might ask: Had oil prices not collapsed and had interest rates not increased (had the oil boom continued), would the de la Madrid administration have pushed for a neoliberal reordering of the Mexican economy? Whatever the explanation for his acquiescence, as a result of de la Madrid's actions the Mexican cases mentioned earlier met their fates: Carmen gave up her independence and moved in with her children; Hermenegildo was forced out of retirement and into underemployment; Pilar and María Veronica ended their studies early; and Fernando suffered from headaches.

Miguel de la Madrid's priorities sparked controversy. As early as his presidential campaign, a politically charged dichotomy emerged between "technocrats" (like de la Madrid) and "politicians." Mexican newspapers characterized technocrats as overly rational actors who privileged economic efficiency over moral, human, and ethical considerations.[46] Many journalists connected de la Madrid and other technocrats to the Porfirian *científicos* and the Bourbon *ilustrados* and alluded to early twentieth-century fears of totalitarianism, casting technocrats as an unfortunate by-product of modernity.[47] In the face of coldly rational approaches to society, some writers emphasized the importance of considering the human dimension of Mexico's foreign debt and general economy. These writers worried that technocrats appeared to be neutral when, in fact, they were supported by the political Right and "Big Capital." Prominent PRI theoreticians, such as Mario Ezcurdia, accused technocrats of supporting IMF policies that most Mexicans paid dearly for.[48] (Such early fissures within the PRI would deepen over the course of the lost decade.)

Although many condemned the technocrats, some sectors of the middle classes found de la Madrid's style and policies appealing; they were drawn to the notion that technocrats might counteract the corruption that plagued state enterprises and the inefficiency of public bureaucracies. Indeed, technocrats impressed some members of the middle classes with their efficient, utopian, pseudoscientific meritocracy. This appeal likely diminished, though, as problems associated with the privatization of state enterprises became clearer: the fast pace and the lack of a regulatory framework concentrated wealth further and created oligopolies.[49]

This debate tended to juxtapose number-crunching technocrats and populist politicians. Those skeptical of neoliberal technocrats believed that populist economic planners sympathized more with the most vulnerable Mexican citizens. Those who supported neoliberal technocrats saw populist politicians as wasteful and inefficient. In this debate, the elastic term "populism" was associated with state-led development and technocracy with neoliberalism. But this schema of populist politicians versus market-driven technocrats is too neat; certainly, most of Mexico's leading decision makers were both technocrats and politicians, as some journalists pointed out at the time.[50] After all, when it suited their interests, neoliberal technocrats such as de la Madrid and his successor, Carlos Salinas, were just as capable of populist policy and style. Populism and technocracy are perhaps best described as political styles, unconnected to specific economic models.[51] What is important here is that de la Madrid's austerity program and neoliberal economic restructuring appeared cold-hearted on the heels of the economic policies, programs, and pronouncements of his two predecessors.

In his inaugural speech, de la Madrid explicitly distanced himself from populism: "I reject populism which yields to mere expediency and causes society to regress. . . . We shall strengthen the weakest sectors by providing training, without false paternalism or demagoguery."[52] In stark contrast to the discourse of López Portillo, de la Madrid declared that there was no "magic solution" to the economic problems; he would "govern with imagination but avoid fantasy."[53] Even de la Madrid's reserved personal style stood in contrast to López Portillo's exuberance. De la Madrid spoke in a measured tone without using his hands and avoided the jokes, plays on words, and intellectual turns of phrase that his predecessor had so enjoyed.[54] As López Portillo's discursive populism yielded to de la Madrid's discursive austerity, policy, ideology, and style all shifted.

La crisis was a balance-of-payments and socioeconomic crisis; it also captured the mood of the lost decade. The ISI model had, over several decades, generated hopes for greater production, upward mobility, and a brighter future, but these expectations came under threat in the 1970s. Although the oil boom resuscitated these hopes, however briefly and unsatisfactorily, they were dashed by the ensuing debt crisis.

Anatomy of a Crisis

The impact of the crisis varied considerably. Within the middle classes, some families at the lower end of the income spectrum curtailed their consumption of meat, while some in the upper echelons cut back on vacations or private school tuition.[55] Some of their experiences were captured by several surveys from the 1980s.

Between June 1985 and February 1988, the National Institute for the Consumer (Inco) undertook a series of surveys on consumption patterns.[56] While the surveys concentrated on the poor and the impoverished working classes, they included the "formal middle class" and the "informal middle class." According to Inco, the former consisted of families with heads of households who were employed by a third person, had health care as part of their benefits, and earned between 2.5 and 3.5 times the minimum wage; the latter was made up of families with self-employed heads of households without health care who earned between 1.5 and 3.5 times the minimum wage.[57] These families might best be described as the bottom range of the middle classes. The survey found that, among families in the formal middle class, the real income of heads of households fell by 33 percent, that of housewives by 45 percent, and that of children by nearly 3 percent. As families struggled to find additional sources of income, more members joined the workforce (children often leaving school), some members took on additional work, and the family began to engage in informal domestic production for sale. In the informal middle class, the decline was not as steep, perhaps because of increased flexibility. Heads of households saw their real income fall by 20 percent, and children's income declined by 1.5 percent. Housewives, however, experienced an increase of over 56 percent, suggesting that many women took on extra work.[58] Inco also traced a decline in meat purchases among the middle classes as families began to consume more vegetables and basic staple goods such as tortillas and beans.[59] The survey, which was presented at a 1987 academic conference on the middle classes, reveals some of the everyday ways in which families stopped being middle class. The boundary between the lower classes and bottom range of the middle classes was porous, especially during these times of economic instability.

A study by the National Minimum Wage Commission (Comisión Nacional de Salarios Mínimos) found that salaried middle-class families adjusted to falling wages by switching to public services. For instance, although families might have had access to public health care as part of their employment benefits, before the 1980s they often preferred to pay for private health care. The study found that, even though the number of members in public health programs declined during the 1980s (likely as the result of layoffs in the public sector), the use of public health services rose exponentially. The commission noted a similar trend from private to public education.[60] Of course, these budget-maximizing strategies were more common among the lower-paid strata of the middle classes.

The Minimum Wage Commission found that those at the upper end of the middle classes often received remuneration in kind to offset the loss of real income due to inflation. Such benefits typically included gasoline quotas, tuition payment for their children, private medical care, sports club memberships, and so on.[61] Economist Nora Lustig argues that the more affluent middle classes saw a disproportionate decline in their standard of living: "These are the families who were used to buying imported goods, traveling abroad, making extensive use of credit cards. And they had purchased durable goods (houses and cars, for example) on credit with floating interest rates."[62] However, as the National Minimum Wage Commission survey found, a few fortunate members of the middle classes benefited from the situation, especially those who had acquired assets by means of fixed-rate loans taken before the devaluation.[63]

The impact of *la crisis* on the middle classes was a major topic of discussion in Mexico's public sphere, in newspapers, academic conferences, and public forums. Many experts wondered if the middle classes would survive the turmoil; others worried about how the middle classes would react to the instability. The economic troubles of the middle classes generated both sympathy and sarcasm in Mexico's major newspapers. Journalists outlined the humiliating everyday impact of the crisis on middle-class lifestyles: people were forced to rent apartments instead of buying; many sold their summer homes; they canceled their trips abroad; families stopped eating out and going to shopping malls; adults quit their sports clubs; couples sold one of their two cars; and heads of tables switched from whiskey and French wine to tequila and Mexican wine.[64] Airlines reported a decline in flights abroad, movie theatres reported dwindling attendance, and it became chic to buy used clothing.[65] Some newspaper articles reporting the changes were sympathetic, while others criticized the consumption-driven middle classes as materialistic and superficial.

Between December 1984 and February 1985, journalist Raúl Olmedo published a series of articles titled "The Crisis and the Middle Classes" in *Excélsior*, one of Mexico's leading newspapers.[66] This series of forty articles plausibly represents a dominant perspective on the middle classes during the lost decade, given its length and the prominence of its publication in *Excélsior*. Its narrative of boom and bust reflects a standard interpretation of the 1980s that was told and retold in the public sphere.

In Olmeda's series, the generation born in 1940 epitomized the history of the middle classes in postrevolutionary Mexico.[67] These were the children of radio technicians and homemakers, and they grew up in small but comfortable apartments in Mexico's main cities. During their childhoods, they went to the movies frequently, visited their relatives in other parts of the country often, and even vacationed in Acapulco a few times. They studied in public schools and were often the first people in their families to attend university. By the mid-1960s, they had established themselves. They were married with their own families and lived comfortably in high-rise apartment complexes or suburban subdivisions that were much more modern than the older buildings they had grown up in (such as *vecindades*). When they watched television, they could see themselves in the *telenovelas*, whose main characters belonged to the middle classes.[68] Influenced by the images on television, they aspired to dress better, drive more expensive cars, and drink foreign liquor, just as the middle-class characters on television did.[69] They generated their identity through performance, by ways of thinking, living, and dressing, all of which were available for purchase.

These middle classes began to lose confidence during the late 1960s, in the context of economic instability. In Olmeda's historical narrative, the dentists and teachers of the boom generation would have been almost thirty years old. Their purchasing power declined just as their expectations peaked (vacations in Acapulco had been replaced by trips to Disneyland). Although they could comfortably provide shelter, food, and clothing for their families, their way of life had come under threat. As they experienced growing economic instability in the 1970s, they were drawn to political opposition on both the left and the right. By 1984 (when the newspaper series was published) their quest for status, prestige, and the esteem of others had become untenable. Olmeda's middle classes found recourse in alcohol and, at their lowest moments, thought about suicide.

So, too, did the typical small business owner. In its January 1983 cover story, the Mexican business magazine *Expansión* nominated the small business owner as its "Man of the Year."[70] According to the editorial staff, the business owner had stubbornly survived despite all odds: he could not get credit from the bank; the price of the imported parts he needed had increased; he was heavily indebted in American dollars; he worried that he might be forced to stop production; in an effort to cut costs, he canceled the staff Christmas party; he suffered from chronic gastritis; and his psychologist had diagnosed him as experiencing incredulity and fear. Although *Expansión* celebrated the business owner's uncanny ability to survive, the story also exposed the darker moments he experienced, including his thoughts of suicide. The businessman depicted in Figure 9, shopping for nooses, was perhaps a dubious choice for "Man of the Year."

When members of the middle classes considered suicide in *Excélsior* and *Expansión*, the political and existential crises that accompanied the

FIGURE 9. A businessman browses a catalogue of nooses. From "El empresario mexicano: Un terco sobreviviente," *Expansión*, 12 January 1983.

economic turmoil became the standard narrative of the time. In 1983 and 1984, Mexico's mainstream public sphere contained dark representations of the middle classes that call to mind the noir fiction of the 1970s.

In November 1985, the National Institute of Historical Studies of the Mexican Revolution, an institute dedicated to academic and popular history, held a public discussion about the middle classes. The invited guests—Juan Sánchez Navarro, José Cueli, and Javier Beristáin—joined commentator Manuel Camacho in a discussion of the past, present, and future of this group. In the context of ongoing economic instability, Camacho asked the discussants: "What hope do the middle classes have?"[71] Cueli responded that the economic crisis forced the middle classes to grapple with their own identity, their value system, and their role in Mexican history. Cueli described how they oscillated between alienation and socialization. He suggested that, if they were to survive the turmoil, it was of the utmost importance for them to continue to "feel" middle-class.[72] They urgently needed to feel middle class just when the structural basis for their class position—the state-led development of the Mexican Miracle—was being dismantled.

The economic crisis thus raised profound questions for teachers, pathologists, and airline pilots struggling to maintain their class status. At a 1987 academic conference about the middle classes, psychoanalyst Agustín Palacios argued that they were the social class least equipped to weather instability. He argued that the poor and the wealthy tend to suffer from chronic depression caused by frustration and feelings of abandonment by their absent or otherwise-occupied parents. In contrast, the middle classes are more likely to create stable homes. Even in the event of divorce, fathers are more psychologically available to their children; mothers have more time. Accordingly, they generally display greater emotional strength.[73] Palacios emphasized, however, that a middle-class individual depended upon a stable environment: "In moments of crisis like the present . . . this person experiences the losses with a frank expressiveness not shared by those who are accustomed to loss or those who can insulate themselves from it with their wealth. Every decline in his purchasing power represents a painful loss. A series of repeated losses in a short period of time results in depression and anxiety about the future."[74]

Physical insecurity further contributed to the material and emotional instability of the middle classes. Each crisis, it seems, has its symbolic crime. If whispers of a coup d'état (possible treason) represented the 1973–1976 crisis, robbery became the quintessential crime of the 1980s.[75] Between 1982 and 1983, crime increased by nearly 50 percent in Mexico City, with the greatest increase in robbery. In 1985, one crime analyst described how "a ghost roamed the city streets: it was the specter of assault. We are all afraid of being assaulted."[76]

In addition to the increase in actual crime, a wave of rumors spread in Mexico's main cities about assaults, vandalism, robberies, and kidnappings.[77] These rumors differed from the destabilizing rumors at the end of Echeverría's administration. The cast of characters—the perpetrators, their victims, and the spectators—had changed. In the 1970s, the middle classes did not usually have direct acquaintance with the feared stranglers or the kidnapped victims. In the 1980s, the fear was closer to home. Shopkeepers, doctors, and teachers now personally knew the victims. Furthermore, evidence of fear was hard to ignore, because—as one contemporary analyst noted—"merchants have shortened their schedules and in some stores you have to purchase goods through security bars; because in some neighborhoods residents have closed access to residential streets and monitor the comings and goings of people and vehicles; because in some areas of the city, like San Jerónimo or Las Lomas, residents have hired private, armed security."[78] Whereas the 1970s rumor mill was often believed to be the result of business leaders plotting to undermine Echeverría, the 1980s rumors were rooted in everyday encounters with crime.

The middle classes, then, experienced the economic instability in socio-economic, existential, psychological, and physical terms. Their ways of being middle class had been forged according to the model of midcentury state-led development. The Mexican middle classes, and many others in the developing world, had taken midcentury development theories as promises of modernity, modernization, and upward mobility.[79] They had pinned their hopes on those promises. When the midcentury model failed in the 1970s, and when it began to be dismantled in the 1980s, their way of life came under threat.

Many members of the middle classes no longer looked to the future with hope. Anthropologist Claudio Lomnitz analyzes this sentiment of hopelessness—a crisis of historicity, in his words—in the jokes of the early and mid-1980s.[80] In these jokes, middle-class aspirations became an embarrassment. But that did not mean that the desire for upward mobility and conspicuous consumption had vanished; instead it had become unspoken. As Lomnitz explains, "The tension between what is desired and the embarrassment of confessing one's inability to obtain it was expressed in a number of jokes that circulated at the time, such as the one where a man says to his friend: 'I want to go to Europe again this year.' And the friend responds, 'You mean you went last year?' The man answers, 'No, last year I wanted to go, too.'"[81]

Other jokes captured a feeling of having been betrayed. For example, when the López Portillo administration refused to honor dollar accounts and converted them into their peso equivalents at below-market rates, jokes spread about these new *pendólares*, a word that is a composite of dollar and *pendejo* (idiot). Lomnitz analyzes the significance of this play on words: "Giving credit to the government and, by extension, to the nation had turned depositors into so many *pendejos*—the sort of cuckolded husband who deposits his wife in the hands of a lover thinking that he is really a protector."[82] Likewise, when López Portillo declared that he would "defend the peso like a dog" and then the value of the peso plunged shortly afterward, it became difficult for him to enter restaurants or theatres without the crowd bursting into bouts of barking. Jokes circulated about the new pesos that would bear the inscription "In Dog We Trust."[83]

It is telling to compare these jokes with the humor of the mid-1970s. In the 1970s the jokes and gossip were political, often exhorting action, often connected to rumors of a coup d'état. In contrast, these jokes are cynical and make reference to failure. These jokes also seem wiser than the naïve and hopeful 1970s equivalents. After all, the jokes that circulated in the 1980s emerged during the triumph of the technocrats, the increasing normative power of neoliberalism, and the depoliticization of economic problems. In 1986, Enrique Semo, a prominent leftist economist decried,

"The economic crisis has remained unpoliticized. . . . It has stimulated no significant popular response."[84] Cynicism, perhaps, characterized the political culture of the middle classes during the lost decade.

Fighting for a Future

Why did the middle classes allow de la Madrid to continue with an economic plan that was so disadvantageous to them? Some had reasons for supporting him. For starters, they feared class violence and were loath to jeopardize their already precarious privilege. A prominent argument during the 1980s was that the middle classes were concerned that the economic turmoil would provoke poor and working-class mobilization.[85] Accordingly, they would not want to weaken the government's capacity to control or repress any protest from the poor, and so they were wary of expressing open political discontent even though they suffered from the austerity measures, and they gave their "resigned support" to de la Madrid.[86] Throughout the 1980s, analysts speculated about potential political upheaval among the middle classes, but no widespread anti-austerity movement emerged.[87]

In fact, several attempts to mount protest, from the left, ended in failure.[88] Internally, the Left was overwhelmed by divisions: should they cooperate with the austerity program and seek redress within the framework of austerity and *apertura*, or should they reject the new economic model wholeheartedly?[89] And, when anti-austerity protest movements did emerge from rank-and-file workers, these were beset by corrupt union leaders. For example, de la Madrid's decision to reduce the size of the public administration most directly affected civil servants. Public employees had been a traditional source of support for the PRI's system; nevertheless, labor historians point out that the early 1980s witnessed incipient political protest across government bureaucracies.[90] Civil servants demanded salary increases, continued access to credit, and greater union democracy. In August 1985, a group of civil servants formed the Intersecretarial Front for the Defense of Employment and Salaries, in reaction to a readjustment of the public budget and the dismissal of thousands of public employees. These civil servants were middle-class professionals in eleven different government ministries who described themselves as a group "on the margin" of the public employees union (the Federación de Sindicatos de Trabajadores al Servicio del Estado, or FSTSE). They claimed that their union leaders had betrayed them. Throughout the month of August, they organized protests in Mexico City's Zócalo, demanding a general salary hike for all bureaucrats and asking that those fired be reinstated. They complained that, for several months, their social security institute (the Instituto de Seguridad y Servicios Sociales de los Trabajadores del Estado, or ISSSTE) had denied all requests for individual loans and demanded that this access to credit be reinstated.[91] These workers met with resistance from their own union leaders, who had struck a political deal with the PRI. Union leaders could—and did—gut protests from above. One expert observed that labor leaders preferred "intra-élite" bargaining (between them and the PRI) to more radical action.[92] As a result, an unfavorable combination of government repression, corrupt unions, and internal divisions curtailed the possibility of a sustained anti-austerity labor movement.[93] Figure 10 sardonically illustrates the plight of middle-class workers during these years.

LOS EXCOMULGADOS

FIGURE 10. The excommunicated. A pilot offers his services on the informal labor market. His sign reads "I fly DC-10 and Boeing 757." By Leonardo Martínez Aguayo, reprinted in Galico, *Los 80's*, 50.

Airline pilots, who had embodied midcentury ideas about modernity and prosperity, were "excommunicated"; like many professionals, they found themselves in danger of falling into the working classes and poor.

The most notable middle-class protest against the austerity measures emerged when hundreds of thousands of university students demonstrated in the streets of Mexico City. The 1986 UNAM student movement constituted a significant, organized, and mass movement against technocratic, neoliberal worldviews.[94] In September 1986 University Rector Jorge Carpizo pushed through a series of reforms during the fall break. When students returned to classes and discovered the rector's stratagem, they launched the biggest student movement since 1968.[95] The most contentious reforms included plans to raise fees, to limit flexibility of time-to-degree, and to alter the policy that guaranteed automatic admission for students in the UNAM-affiliated *preparatorias*.[96]

Although Carpizo outlined many real problems at the UNAM—including low graduation rates, the declining quality of student work, and a labyrinthine bureaucracy—critics charged that, with these reforms, the rector had unfairly placed the blame on students.[97] One prominent political activist replied to Carpizo in the news magazine *Siempre!*: "The low rate of graduation is due to the deterioration of students' living and working conditions, not to negligence or irresponsibility."[98] Students contended that these reforms signaled a shift from the UNAM as a university of the masses toward an "elitist and efficient" university project in line with the government's austerity program.[99] The elimination of automatic admission to the UNAM from specific *preparatorias* was particularly symbolic, as public intellectual Carlos Monsiváis wrote at the time: "For hundreds of thousands of young people, the automatic admission is, in essence, *the right to the University*. . . . This *right to the University* is part of the imagined and real patrimony of the middle classes, and of a good part of the popular classes. It is a patrimony that provides cultural and psychological compensation in face of the harsh realities [of the present]."[100]

Students reacted to defend this patrimony, demanding complete annulment of Carpizo's reforms. The protest movement began with casual meetings; by October 1986 students from different university faculties and the *preparatorias* had formed the University Student Council (Consejo Estudiantil Universitario, or CEU). In late October the CEU organized a march of fifteen thousand; in early November a twenty-four-hour strike paralyzed the university; and in mid-November the Rector's Office opened talks with the student council. These proved ineffective as Carpizo remained inflexible. Over the next several months, the magnitude of the protest increased. A student strike was declared on 3 February 1987, and on 9 February, approximately four hundred thousand students and professors marched from Tlatelolco to the Zócalo. In these protests, hundreds of thousands of students attempted to call attention to the impact of the austerity program on the UNAM.[101] The day after the 9 February protest, the Rector's Office conceded several points. The students had won the right for a more democratic debate of university policy and blocked the most contentious reforms.[102] Their success, though, was limited to the UNAM; the student movement did not effectively challenge policies outside the realm of the university.

The conflict between the rector and the CEU encapsulated a broader conflict over competing visions for Mexico's future. Technocrats in the de la Madrid administration compared the UNAM to a wasteful and inefficient state enterprise. In doing so, they attacked one of the most valued institutions of the postrevolutionary middle classes: the public university system. In their protest, students struggled to protect their privileged position and to guarantee the possibility of upward mobility for future generations of students. When the university of the masses came under threat, they took to the streets to protest their right to a future.[103]

New Temples to the (New) Bourgeoisie

If UNAM students and civil servants suffered the effects of the lost decade, others thrived. A new type of middle-class citizen emerged during the 1980s crisis: yuppies, who defied the standard narrative of boom and bust. These young professionals between twenty and thirty-nine years old came of age professionally during economic uncertainty: "For us, it's common to consider variables such as 'crisis' or 'inflation' that, until recently, were unknown. We were born with these variables, professionally speaking. . . . Older people are waiting until things return to normal before they act economically. This might be to our advantage, because there are opportunities today," explained one young engineer.[104] These self-identified risk takers rejected the old dependence on the state. A young executive derided his father's career: "Dad lived off the fat of *Papa Gobierno* [Daddy Government]."[105] Instead, the yuppies embraced a "you-make-your-own-destiny" ethos. As the owner of a movie production company said: "There are no good times and bad times. . . . For capable people, there are a lot of opportunities for growth."[106]

These confident, risk-taking professionals embraced de la Madrid's economic policies. In contrast to individuals employed by state agencies, they did not suffer the effects of austerity. They worked as entrepreneurs or were employed by private businesses. But unlike those private business owners who depended on the government for subsidized services or for protection from foreign competition through high tariffs, this new generation of entrepreneurs embraced de la Madrid's economic liberalization. They did not fear the international competition that would come with Mexico's entry into GATT; instead, they eagerly anticipated entering foreign markets.[107] For these young professionals, economic liberalization—neoliberalism—promised new opportunities.

Perhaps more of an attitude than a social group—after all, those described as yuppies ranged from technical workers such as engineers to cultural workers in show business to entrepreneurs—to be a yuppie meant to have confidence. Newspaper accounts of this phenomenon described how yuppies believed in themselves under almost any circumstances.[108] And for Carlos Monsiváis, the yuppies embodied "the remains of the society of the bellicose vanguard."[109] In the context of the lost decade, the yuppies, it seemed, were the only ones who still dreamt of greatness.[110]

Their energetic confidence provided a welcome break from the economic desolation and despair that had come to dominate narratives of *la crisis*. The yuppies emerged in Mexico's social imaginary in 1985 and 1986, when a series of newspaper and magazine articles described this new social actor. There is a sense of exuberance, mixed with relief, in discussions of the yuppies in Mexico's public sphere, as though journalists and analysts hoped that this new social actor might lead Mexico (and especially the middle classes) out of crisis. The yuppies represented something new and vital—an optimistic spirit—connected with the economic liberalization. Focus on the yuppies offered an alternative to ongoing analysis of the apparent end of state-led development and the social devastation that accompanied it. In a refreshing change from its 1983 cover story about suicidal businessmen, the business magazine *Expansión* devoted its October 1985 cover story (see Figure 11) to the confident and stylish young professionals who were "born to win."

Despite the enthusiasm, the yuppies heralded a worrying trend within the middle classes: increasing inequality. Although the data are incomplete, early findings indicate that inequality increased within the middle classes.[111] For example, economists Diana Alarcón and Terry McKinley found that in 1984, 1989, and 1992 (years when household surveys were conducted), income inequality rose among urban wage earners with some tertiary education: simply put, university education became less of a social equalizer, as individuals who had studied at the undergraduate level earned increasingly disparate salaries. Likewise, there was growing income inequality within middle-class occupations. Alarcón and Terry found that people working in "élite occupations" such as professionals, public officials and private sector administrators, managers and supervisors, as well as "employees with technical or specialized training" such as teachers, technicians, and equipment operators, earned increasingly polarized salaries—some made a

FIGURE II. "Born to win" yuppy on the cover of the magazine *Expansión*. From "Nacidos para ganar: Los jóvenes empresarios y ejecutivos," *Expansión*, 30 October 1985.

lot more money, while others made a lot less. While income inequality, of course, had always existed among university graduates and within certain careers, it increased during the lost decade.[112]

De la Madrid's economic policies reconfigured patterns of class domination. Some members of the middle classes, such as the public employees who had benefited from state-led development, struggled to maintain their class status. The yuppies represented a new kind of middle class that prospered in a neoliberal economy. Monsiváis wrote sardonically about the new temples to a renewed faith in the bourgeoisie: expensive restaurants, boutiques, and clubs in upscale neighborhoods such as San Jerónimo in Mexico City, and posh American-style shopping malls on the suburban outskirts of the capital and other major cities.[113]

The Santa Fe megaproject in Mexico City is perhaps the most illustrative of these new temples to a neoliberal middle-class.[114] The brainchild of Carlos Hank González, mayor of Mexico City from 1976 to 1982, the megaproject was born in the optimism of the oil boom: "Where can I build my Manhattan?" González is rumored to have asked.[115] The answer was found in the sprawling Santa Fe garbage dump and its surrounding sand mines. Through fraud, violence, and expropriation, the city government acquired approximately nine square kilometers of land in the early 1980s.[116] González gifted López Portillo a large piece of this land so the president could build a personal mansion that would ultimately overlook the megaproject; López Portillo in turn donated twenty hectares for the construction of a new campus for the exclusive, private Ibero-Americana University (where his daughter studied).[117] With the onset of the debt crisis the project languished until 1987, when the vision of a Mexican Manhattan coincided with economic liberalization. The neoliberal technocrats saw a different kind of potential in the megaproject. Instead of building a symbol of Mexico's oil wealth and the power of the petro-state, they envisioned Santa Fe as a beacon of neoliberalism that would help to attract foreign investment and confirm Mexico's new economic role in the global economy following its entry into GATT.[118]

The garbage dump was transformed into one of the premier sites of neoliberal global capitalism, not only in Mexico but also in Latin America. Santa Fe became home to transnational and national companies (such as DaimlerChrysler, Citibank-Banamex, IBM, Televisa, and José Cuervo), a shopping mall, private schools and universities, and gated subdivisions and apartment buildings. All public space was controlled by private interests, multinational corporations, and neighborhood associations.[119] According to urban studies expert María Moreno Carranco, the street plan was designed to limit access to the area and create an exclusive enclave for the national and international middle and upper-middle classes.[120]

Santa Fe was a temple to a new sort of middle class. The older middle class, who had thrived in the era of state-led development, had also reconfigured the built environment. Large-scale public projects such as the Tlatelolco housing complex, built in the 1960s, or the cultural center of the UNAM, built in the 1970s, represented a different middle-class aesthetic—these were public spaces connected to state-led development. The new temples were more upscale, often private developments that promised "a new concept of living," as marketing campaigns for Santa Fe condominiums proclaimed, often in English.[121] Analyzing sales brochures, Moreno Carranco describes how the publicity emphasized a fantasy of tranquility (a "harmonious space" away from the "daily chaos" of Mexico City); elegance ("resort living"); convenience (ballet classes, salons, cafés, and a sky lounge in your building); connectivity ("live here, work here . . . a superconnected universe with high speed Internet"); and, most fundamentally, security ("only residents and their guests will circulate. . . . You can live in a totally walled city").[122] This was a world for the upper-middle classes and the wealthy, very far from the world of the hard-hit middle classes described by the Inco survey on household income and consumption. The "new concept of living" exemplified the increasingly segregated residential, work, and leisure worlds of the middle classes.[123]

The Ibero-Americana University campus, the first completed project in Santa Fe, is an example of another fracturing of the middle classes, caused by the rise of private education. Enrollment in private postsecondary institutions increased 92 percent between 1980 and 1990; in comparison, enrollment in public institutions increased 40 percent.[124] As those in the modest middle classes struggled to defend the right to public education (and could no longer afford to send their children to private schools), many at the other end of the income spectrum turned to private universities. Echeverría's education reform had produced a "massification" of the UNAM and rapid growth of other public universities during the 1970s; by the 1980s there was a devaluation of public degrees. As growing numbers of citizens earned degrees, public university education no longer carried the same cachet.[125] For those who could afford it, the stylish luxury of the Ibero and other institutions became an important marker of privilege and a new kind of middle-class status.[126]

La crisis may have created new forms of stratification among the middle classes, but both ends of the income spectrum were condemned to the insecurity of the present. For example, a 1987 Expansión exposé concluded that the vast majority of Mexican executives and business owners belonged to the middle classes. The majority were the sons of merchants, professionals, and white-collar employees; "only a minority had inherited their careers."[127] Expansión surveyed over two thousand executives and business owners; of these, 9.2 percent self-identified as lower-middle class, 42.2 percent as middle class, 37.2 percent as upper-middle class, and 9.2 percent as upper class.[128] While those surveyed were likely more privileged than the civil servants facing salary cuts and unemployment and might have been earning significantly more than a teacher or doctor working in a public school or hospital, the exposé reveals how members of the upper-middle classes struggled to maintain their status. They suffered from a structural instability similar to that which plagued the lower-middle classes. They did not belong to the independently wealthy minority (those who had enough wealth to sustain several generations), and they experienced their own economic booms and busts.

The first neoliberal boom and bust came with the stock market crash of 1987. Executives, business owners, housewives, and university students, among others, had invested in a bullish stock market in 1985 and 1986. In the aftermath of the bank nationalization, the Mexican Stock Exchange (Bolsa Mexicana de Valores, or BMV) assumed a more prominent role in the financial system.[129] The de la Madrid administration supported the stock exchange by permitting a growing number of companies and financial instruments to be traded. The stock market became an important, if unofficial, component of his economic liberalization program.[130] As a result, the stock market saw robust growth in the mid-1980s.

The boom captured the attention of the upper-middle classes. Although small, the number of investors increased over threefold during *la crisis*: in the early 1980s brokerage houses catered to approximately 50,000 clients; by 1986 they had more than 185,000.[131] Different types of investors joined this onrush to the stock market. Investors consisted of corporatist groups and big capitalists, to be sure, but also small business owners, housewives, and elderly citizens. Universities began to offer certificates and specializations in stock market studies, and books such as Timothy Hayman's *Invest against Inflation* flew off the shelves.[132] With a diverse array of eager investors, the BMV created an educational institute, the Mexican Institute of Capital Markets (Instituto Mexicano del Mercado de Capitales, or Immec). Its mission was to promote stock market culture (*cultura bursátil*).[133] Seminars such as "Stock Market School" were offered for high school and university students. "Stock Market for Women" catered to housewives, businesswomen, and professionals who, according to the director of the Institute, "have their little savings (*ahorritos*) in piggy banks, under the mattress, or in the bank, and who want to participate in the stock market but are frightened by something that they perceive as distant and mysterious."[134] He intended to assuage their fears.

The stock market "superboom" of 1987 suggests that the Institute of Capital Markets succeeded. Members of the upper-middle classes formed investment clubs and societies. The business magazine *Expansión* offered advice: "Are you anxious to enter the stock market and enjoy the attractive returns in this *superboom*? Yes?" *Expansión* advised the interested reader to join an investment society, in order to maximize profit by pooling resources.[135] Alternatively, investment clubs offered investors the opportunity to maximize their profits as well as learn about how the stock market worked; they were both financial and educational organizations. *Expansión* compared these investment clubs to aerobics clubs or movie clubs and urged its readers to "participate in the stock market bonanza!"[136] Figure 12 captures the feverish excitement that accompanied *Expansión*'s advice to its readers, as newcomers rushed to invest in the stock market.

The *superboom* became the *supercrack* (it went bust) on 19 October 1987, largely related to the crash of the American stock market.[137] In Mexico, experts blamed "immature and inexperienced" small investors. One investment analyst argued that the minimum investment of 500,000 pesos had admitted too many investors to the "fiesta."[138] A deputy for the Mexican Socialist Party and former employee of the investment division of the National Bank of Mexico (Banamex) put part of the responsibility for the *crack* on the "young graduates of the ITAM [Autonomous Institute of Technology of Mexico, a private university] who overnight became investment executives and mechanically applied the theories taught to them by their professors, without further reflection. Even worse, they quickly forgot these theories and played the stock market as if it were a game."[139]

FIGURE 12. A woman invests her savings in the stock market. From "¿Qué son las sociedades de inversión?," *Expansión*, 30 September 1987.

Despite the setback in October 1987, the stock exchange recovered slowly during 1988 and entered a prolonged period of growth in the early 1990s.[140] Enthusiasm for the stock market remained, though tempered. In its advice columns, for example, *Expansión* no longer urged countless small investors to form investment clubs with their friends, modeled on their aerobics clubs, but rather recommended that would-be investors seek professional advice. The woman depicted above, running to the stock exchange with her piggy bank, was shown, in 1988, investing her savings in her house or sitting in a financial consultant's waiting room.

The stock exchange and Santa Fe became temples par excellence to a new sort of middle class. The Mexican yuppies, among others, filled the pews to worship themselves and what they represented.

A New Current

In many ways, the yuppies and the technocrats both came to represent the neoliberal transition, the former predominantly in the economic arena and the latter principally in the political realm. Both pushed for a neoliberal economic opening; neither felt bound to the old model of state-led development. These new, or newly visible, social actors had little in common with others in the middle classes who had more invested in the older economic strategies of the Miracle years. During the lost decade they existed uneasily alongside teachers, civil servants, and dentists in the élite realm of the middle classes and the PRI.

This élite realm split; it could no longer contain the increasingly opposed interests of the middle classes. In the summer of 1986 an oppositionist tendency, known as the Democratic Current (Corriente Democrática), emerged within the PRI. De la Madrid's economic policies had alienated many left-wing PRI politicians. Many had objected to the austerity program from the outset, but ideological conflict reached new levels in 1985 when de la Madrid announced that Mexico would enter GATT. Entry into GATT represented a decisive move toward neoliberalism, from austerity measures to a combination of austerity and trade liberalization (*apertura*). Leading PRI politicians Cuauhtémoc Cárdenas Solórzano (governor of Michoacán and son of Lázaro Cárdenas), Porfirio Muñoz Ledo (former secretary general of the PRI), and Rodolfo González Guevara (a prominent political intellectual) formed the Democratic Current.[141] They voiced concern about the PRI's rightward turn, with the goal of fostering discussion within the party and refocusing policy toward the interests of the majority of Mexican citizens.

After several months of internal struggles and increasing rancour between the Democratic Current and Miguel de la Madrid's allies, in 1987 some members of the Democratic Current abandoned the PRI while others were expelled.[142] They then mounted a direct electoral challenge to the neoliberal technocrats by organizing an independent electoral campaign for the 1988 presidential elections. Cárdenas ran as candidate for a loose alliance of opposition parties that came together under the National Democratic Front (Frente Democrático Nacional, or FDN).[143] Cárdenas called for a complete rejection of de la Madrid's economic restructuring program and proposed a return to the populist redistribution of wealth, a suspension of foreign debt payments, and a reversal of the privatization of state enterprises.[144]

Campesinos from across the country, especially from the southern states, supported Cárdenas's campaign. Many of them had not benefited from the midcentury boom and instead looked back to a different golden age: the 1934–1940 presidency of General Lázaro Cárdenas.[145] The urban poor and middle classes who had suffered the effects of the economic instability and who felt threatened by neoliberal restructuring also swelled the ranks of the opposition movement. This population resented the decline in living standards, which they associated with economic liberalization.[146] These middle classes included residents in the Tlatelolco apartment complex, that outdated temple to an older middle class. The 1985 earthquake shook loose the discontent of Tlatelolco residents, and they joined forces with Cárdenas's electoral campaign. Drawing from the urban and rural poor, as well as the struggling middle classes, the opposition campaign gained ground. By the July 1988 elections, Cárdenas, fighting for economic justice and political democracy, presented a serious challenge to the PRI candidate, Carlos Salinas de Gortari. On election day, 6 July 1988, the de la Madrid government resorted to fraud (the computers "went down") to ensure Salinas's victory.[147]

Although a version of the PRI survived the electoral challenge, the political and economic landscape had changed profoundly. *La crisis* undermined patterns of class politics that had been established over several decades. Increasingly at odds, some segments of the middle classes suddenly experienced—or at least glimpsed—the structural violence of poverty, while others experienced "a new concept of living." As these two extremes became increasingly polarized, the élite realm of the PRI and the middle classes no longer constituted a cohesive dominant class. It ruptured along the line dividing neoliberalism and state-led development.

Requiem for a Model

When President Miguel de la Madrid embraced the IMF austerity measures and the structural readjustment of Mexico's economy, he began to dismantle a venerable economic model. But he altered much more than the degree of state participation in the economy. He altered a mode of being middle class. The middle classes experienced the crisis not just as a tangible material crisis but as something more profound.

The president, in his inaugural address, announced that Mexico was closing one chapter in its history and opening another: "We shall not overcome the crisis by aspiring to return to the conditions that preceded it. . . . We are going to create a different and better chapter in our history. . . . We will overcome the crisis by doing away with the causes that produced it, by making the qualitative changes that will lead us to a new society."[148] Instead of trying to return to the Miracle, de la Madrid and his top advisors were ready to craft a different vision for a prosperous and stable Mexico.

The demise of the Miracle began in the late 1960s, and the protests of the late 1960s and early 1970s were, in some sense, early transition pains. But these protests had been hopeful protests. With *la crisis*, any hope for a return to the Miracle vanished. By the 1980s, the midcentury modernization narrative of state-led development had collapsed, replaced by a new, neoliberal script.[149] Its collapse shook the middle classes, who had been the heroes of the midcentury narrative.

One expert, in 1982, called for a requiem for the old economic model.[150] Such a requiem would mourn the past and lament the future of the middle classes. This requiem might also ask why the middle classes did not effectively protest the economic restructuring. In contrast to their political turbulence in the late 1960s and early 1970s, the middle classes did not rise up when they saw their prospects dwindling. Even the 1986 UNAM strike did not alter the political system or challenge the economic reforms.

Analysis of middle-class political culture during the lost decade suggests that the magnitude of the changes underway provoked a form of political paralysis among the middle classes. It might even be anachronistic to ask why they allowed de la Madrid to forsake their future. Expecting them to react politically, on either the left or the right, to the lost decade might be expecting them to be the middle classes of 1968, 1971, 1973, or 1976. Those years had been infused with expectations of change. In the 1980s, the middle classes felt they were living in a historic moment, but it was not a hopeful one. Instead, it was the end of their world. From the dismantling of state enterprises to the reforms of the UNAM, the midcentury "miraculous" world was coming to a close.

In this process, many members of the middle classes were jettisoned from the modernization narrative that had organized their lives. What happens to the protagonist when the plotline is hijacked? When an earthquake struck the heart of Mexico City, new middle-class narratives and actors emerged.

6 Earthquake

CIVIL SOCIETY IN THE RUBBLE OF TLATELOLCO,
1985–1988

Early in the morning of 19 September 1985, an earthquake hit Mexico City. The next evening, a second earthquake rocked the capital. The first earthquake measured 8.1 on the Richter scale, the second registered at 7.3. Together, they left approximately 10,000 dead, 50,000 injured and 250,000 homeless. For many, it began as a bombardment of sounds: the shrill shattering of glass; the rumble of crumbling cement as it hit the ground; the deep groan, "a sort of *boooooo*"[1] of the earth moving; then, a moment—seconds or minutes, no one is sure—of surreal silence, soon filled by the muffled voices of those trapped beneath the rubble and desperate screams for help.[2] On the first day, in less than three minutes, the city center fractured into disarray. Thousands of buildings had fallen or been torn into; the pavement had cracked open; the water distribution system had ruptured; live electrical lines had been pulled from their posts and were left dangling.[3] Doomsayers appeared in the city's streets and meeting places, proclaiming the end of the world.[4]

The government desperately needed to make contact with residents. Radios broadcast information and instructions; pamphlets circulated throughout the city urging residents to stay in their homes: "Citizen: The priority is to save lives. . . . Allow the rescue workers to do their jobs. Stay at home. . . . Your solidarity is valiant. Read this and pass it along."[5] Official rescue workers did not appear, though, and it fell upon residents to dig through the rubble for their loved ones and neighbors. Public intellectual Elena Poniatowska chronicled the aftermath of the scene: "Around the ruins, enormous chains of people of all ages begin to form. The debris and broken concrete are passed from hand to hand in buckets, pots and pans, all sorts of kitchenware, any container at all. The spectacle of a single arm stretching for air among the masonry and iron rods seems intolerable."[6]

That first night, without electricity, darkness fell upon the downtown, and danger lurked. Ravaged buildings teetered, threatening to fall with the smallest aftershock. Bands of looters roamed the streets, and relief workers distributing blankets and milk armed themselves.[7]

Tens of thousands of victims (*damnificados*) soon organized a social movement of unprecedented scale in Mexico City's history.[8] They demanded help with the rescue work and a say in how the city would be rebuilt. Middle-class residents occupied key leadership positions in the victims movement, and they filled the rank and file, alongside the working classes and the urban poor. Cross-class mobilization was a defining element of the movement, but class tensions and competing interests nonetheless generated conflict. Where there had existed a vibrant political culture of protest in the working-class and poor neighborhoods before the disaster, middle-class protest after the earthquake marked a significant shift. For the first time since the late 1960s, large numbers of middle-class residents took to the streets to demand change.

The politicization of middle-class residents after the earthquake was connected to the wider economic crisis of the 1980s. Among the many issues that emerged, debates over urban property rights were center stage for the middle classes. Middle-class homeowners struggled to defend their access to housing as the government attempted to dismantle the midcentury public-housing apparatus and restructure the urban housing market along neoliberal lines. The earthquake acted as a catalyst for middle-class discontent—it provoked, increased, and sped it up.

Economic models shape the built environment, and midcentury state-led development had left its mark on the capital city in the form of large-scale public housing projects, public hospitals, and public schools. One of the most emblematic of such projects was the Tlatelolco apartment complex. Often referred to as a city within the city, on the eve of the earthquake the complex consisted of 102 buildings, with over 12,000 apartments housing approximately 100,000 residents—the largest of its kind in Latin America. It had its own commercial venues, schools, sporting centers, cultural centers, and medical clinics. In total, it covered over 750,000 square meters. Built by the government between 1962 and 1965 to house the middle classes, these apartment high-rises symbolized the growth of this class in postrevolutionary Mexico. Many of its residents were government bureaucrats, lawyers, university professors, and other professionals.[9] But Tatelolco was one of the areas hardest hit by the earthquake. And soon it became a nucleus of political activism.

When Tlatelolco residents took to the streets after the earthquake, they were struggling to protect a middle-class world that had already come under threat from the austerity measures and the broader shift from state-led development to neoliberalism. The administration of Miguel de la

Madrid kept a close eye on the protest in Tlatelolco; government spies reported copiously on activities there, using informants and through direct eavesdropping, and internal government discussions after the earthquake focused disproportionately on Tlatelolco. From the perspective of the de la Madrid administration, throngs of middle-class residents protesting in the city streets threatened the government's legitimacy and its ability to continue to restructure the economy. While the 1986 UNAM student movement did not significantly alter the administration's economic plans, the earthquake and its aftermath galvanized middle-class residents, turning them into a formidable force in urban politics. The victims movement demanded, and received, a seat at the political decision-making table. *Damnificados* gained an unprecedented say in how the city would be rebuilt. In unexpected ways, however, middle-class and working-class victims both facilitated and blocked neoliberal restructuring of the urban economy.

Tlatelolco, Mexico City, 19 September 1985

Tlatelolco quickly emerged as a symbol—to the country and the world—of the devastation. The Nuevo León building, fifteen stories tall, had toppled and lay on its side (see Figure 13). Within half an hour, hundreds of survivors in the apartment complex organized a rescue effort. Thin young men squeezed through narrow passages, following voices to enclaves of open space; many lost their lives trying to save others. Doctors and nurses who lived in the complex set up makeshift medical stations. In the first hours of the disaster, residents asked one another if the emergency services had been called, because they did not hear the wail of ambulance sirens. There were no signs of official rescue workers as residents dug through the rubble, directed traffic, organized food distribution, made lists of the survivors, and counted the dead. As the day progressed, residents from other areas of the city sent food and blankets. Volunteers worked for hours—ten, twelve, or more—without food or rest.

Signs and hand-written notes appeared on buildings that were still standing; some were personal messages left by family and friends desperate to locate their loved ones; others called upon residents to organize and demand a more systematic rescue effort. Many residents accused the government of shirking its responsibility. In the days after the earthquake, they took to the streets to demand that the government help those still alive under the debris. Men, women, and children wore placards:

"Mr. President and functionaries of [Mexico City], help us"

"Our parents are trapped"

"My wife is trapped, I need help"[10]

FIGURE 13. The fallen Nuevo León building. From Image 21, Mexico City, 1985, US Geological Survey Photographic Library.

Rescue workers in Tlatelolco complained that the government was actually impeding their work. They told NBC news that they could hear voices calling from under the fallen buildings, but that the machinery sent from the United States was sitting in a customs warehouse.[11] The government's handling of the disaster frustrated foreign rescue brigades. An Israeli team complained: "Up to now we haven't had a chance to use our air cushion that can lift up to 50 tons of concrete. . . . We're waiting to be coordinated. We're under the authority of Dr Aries, but we haven't seen her. Do you know who Dr Aries is?"[12]

Little organization and a lack of information characterized the work: the city did not provide rescuers with blueprints of the buildings or maps of the area. While initial chaos might be expected in such an event, the incapacity of the government to organize the workers likely cost countless lives. A professor of architecture and a volunteer described the situation:

Even after two or three days everyone was working chaotically, without any system. The desperation to save loved ones led to great inefficiency. I believe that the lack of coordination and organization made it impossible to save a great many people. There was even a lack of communication between soldiers and their captains. It's not for nothing that most countries have offices to deal with emergencies and people trained for such events.[13]

The Prevention of Disasters Office had been closed the year before, in a round of budget cuts related to the austerity measures agreed upon by the government and the IMF. In 1981 this office, as part of the Ministry of Human Settlements and Public Works (Secretaría de Astentamientos Humanos y Obras Públicas, or SAHOP), had published a short document on the impact of strong earthquakes on Mexico City. It anticipated, nearly point by point, what actually happened on 19 September. It also offered recommendations for avoiding such a tragedy—none had been followed. Instead, the government liquidated the office in 1984. As this became known after the earthquake, indignation erupted.[14]

The official emergency plan, "DN-3," became an infamously well-kept secret. No one knew what it contained or what the plans were for a disaster of this magnitude. Residents, political parties, and leftist organizations demanded that the government make public the plan, so that they might have a document against which to evaluate the actions of the military and police.[15] While soldiers had flooded into the capital city only hours after the disaster, they arrived bearing weapons instead of shovels and picks; instead of helping dig for survivors, they cordoned off the area and tried to prevent residents and volunteers from continuing their work.[16] At best, residents regarded the police, military, and state officials as onlookers; at worst, they viewed them as bullies and thieves who sought to benefit from the tragedy.[17] Residents in the Colima building in Tlatelolco, for example, reported soldiers stealing valuable goods from abandoned apartments.[18] At certain points, city officials tried to force eviction of residents in Tlatelolco, stealing electronics and threatening them with physical disappearance (*desaparición física*).[19]

Scandals surrounded the government's initial handling of the disaster. Rumors spread that President Miguel de la Madrid had refused to accept foreign aid in an attempt to present a "good image of the state" to the international community, an illusory vision of a self-sufficient Mexican state able to handle the disaster.[20] Making matters worse, when they did accept aid, authorities initially used some of it to make its foreign debt payments.[21] Victims resented the government's preoccupation with its international image; but with Mexico scheduled to host the 1986 World Cup, the government needed to assure the international community and FIFA (International Federation of Association Football) that the event would proceed as planned. Indeed, it was rumored that one of de la Madrid's first telephone calls on the morning of 19 September was to the football association. Victims complained that state officials worried more about the World Cup than it did about them: "Bravo Mr. President, we have the World Cup, but no housing for the victims!" proclaimed one handmade sign at a sit-in in front of Televisa headquarters (Mexico's largest television network).[22] An expression of their anger and frustration is shown in Figure 14.

As national and international aid poured into Mexico, victims accused the government of corruption and demanded more transparent distribution of the donations. They claimed that the government was siphoning the aid to PRI sycophants and members of the élite. It was reported that cheese sent by the Swiss government as part of an aid package—the highly coveted Swiss cheese—was being sold in Polanco, one of Mexico City's most exclusive neighborhoods, which was not located in the disaster

FIGURE 14. We don't want goals, we want beans! From Promotora Democrática de Comunicadores Gráficos, "¡No queremos goles, queremos frijoles!," *Calaveras*, November 1985, DFS, 009-031-003, legajo 20, AGN.

zone.[23] Messages on banners at a protest on 27 September capture victims' gratitude to those who helped, coupled with fury at the government:

"Mexican brothers, thank you"

"The children demand the foreign aid"

"Where is the national and international aid?"

"The national and international aid is for the victims, not for government offices"[24]

The rage of victims was not, then, limited to the turmoil that a natural disaster of such a scale would be expected to cause. Governments are frequently taken by surprise by disasters, which inevitably generates frustration. In the first few days following the Mexico City earthquake, however, residents expressed fury at the corruption of the state apparatus and the disrespect they accused the president of showing them. The wells of discontent went deep, and one of the victims' oft-repeated demands was for an intangible dignity (*dignidad*). Any nostalgia residents of Tlatelolco might have felt for the golden era of the Mexican Miracle disappeared as the corruption of the old model lay exposed on the city's streets.

The Nuevo León building was but one symbol of the corruption that had underlain the Mexican Miracle.[25] The physical manifestation of the Miracle—the housing, schools, and hospitals built by the state—had collapsed. Several other failures became evident in the rubble. The PRI's mismanagement of the rescue effort demonstrated the incapacity of the party to respond to the needs of its citizens. And the lack of respect with which the president and other leading politicians treated the victims was a moral failure that would have deep reverberations in the city's political landscape.

"To the Chamber of Deputies!"

Faced with official recalcitrance, residents decided to take action. Hundreds gathered in Tlatelolco's Plaza de las Tres Culturas to analyze the situation, and leaders argued that it was imperative to put pressure on the authorities.[26] Banners went up around the city. At first, they simply begged for help digging and asked for shelter; quickly, though, the extent of their demands grew. Residents organized protests, calling upon citizens to come together: "Once again they want to stain Tlatelolco with blood; those who speak of reconstruction have their hands and pockets full! Thursday the 26th, 11:00: To the Chamber of Deputies!"[27] Four days after the earthquake, the residents organizations wrote a letter to architect Enrique Ortiz Flores, the head of the National Fund for Popular Housing (Fondo Nacional de Habitación Popular, or Fonhapo), one of the principal government agencies responsible for the complex:

We write to you with strong feelings of pain, rage, impotence and uncertainty. Pain for our dead brothers; rage because this tragedy could have been avoided if the necessary preventative measures had been taken; impotence for not being able to rescue more survivors buried in the rubble; and uncertainty for the present and the future of our housing complex.

We are Tlatelolcas [residents of Tlatelolco]. We are proud to be Tlatelolcas and we will fight for our patrimony and our dignity, with the pain of our dead and the courage it inspires in us to move forward.[28]

They spoke of Tlatelolco as a site of blood and fire, from the conquest of Mexico in 1521 to the massacre of students on 2 October 1968. Once again, Tlatelolcas were witnessing pain and death.

Three primary demands emerged: first, punishment of those responsible for the shoddy construction and maintenance of the buildings, especially the Nuevo León; second, reconstruction in Tlatelolco, not another part of the city; and third, indefinite suspension of the plan to change the property rights pertaining to the complex.[29] The earthquake hit after years of struggle between residents and the state agencies responsible for the complex. Residents had written letters to these agencies, detailing the poor maintenance of many buildings and requesting repairs. This history of struggle in Tlatelolco would prove fundamental to shaping the social movement that emerged after the earthquake.

To begin with, residents demanded an investigation into the collapse of the Nuevo León building. Since at least 1983 the government agencies had refused to repair the building or, when pressured, undertook only the most superficial repairs. "How much," residents asked, "is the cost of re-cementing the foundation of a building, compared to the lives of those who live in it?"[30] For example, by 1979 the Nuevo León building was leaning seventy centimeters. This exceeded the maximum allowed by city safety regulations: for a building of its height, the maximum horizontal inclination ought to have been thirty-two centimeters. By early 1982, the inclination was over one hundred centimeters. In March of 1982 repair work reduced the inclination to eighty centimeters.[31] One activist recalled that, at one point during the bureaucratic back-and-forth regarding the safety of the Nuevo León building, authorities had "displayed blueprints and sketches, using technical terms far beyond the reach of our understanding, telling us in sum that 'the Nuevo León is the safest building not [only] in Tlatelolco, but in Mexico City.'"[32]

The attitude of government functionaries exacerbated the frustration of residents. For example, after the earthquake, on 9 October, Guillermo Carrillo Arena, who was minister of urban development and ecology (Secretaría de Desarrollo Urbano y Ecología, or SEDUE) until February 1986, claimed: "We still don't know why the Nuevo León fell. We must consider that many people modified their apartments and this could have altered the structural integrity of the building. We know who they are and we will proceed against them."[33] His insinuation that residents who might have taken down a wall in their apartment could have altered the structural integrity of the building fueled the anger of Tlatelolcas. Residents appeared on television and described a "collective psychosis of terror"; only a trustworthy inspection of the entire complex—by foreign technicians—could begin to calm the fear of further buildings collapsing.[34] Their insistence on foreign technicians demonstrates their profound distrust of the government.

Survivors accused city functionaries of criminal negligence in the construction of many of the fallen buildings. The majority were schools, hospitals, and housing units built by or for the state between 1950 and 1970.[35] Corruption in the construction industry had been an open secret. Before a project began, the contractor had to apply for a license and submit the architectural and structural plans. City authorities then filed these but rarely followed up to confirm that specifications had been followed; often contractors used lower-grade materials than those originally proposed. The seven-story Ministry of Labor building that collapsed during the earthquake offers one example of the disregard for safety standards: it had been built on a concrete base designed to hold only three stories.[36] Residents complained that no system was in place to check this corruption and that without democratically elected officials, the system was riddled with nepotism and incompetence.[37] Until 1997, it was the president who named the mayor of Mexico City, who in turn nominated the local city representatives (*delgados*) for presidential confirmation.[38] These were the public officials responsible for approving building licenses and performing inspections. Residents demanded to know who would be held responsible for the fallen buildings: "If the government itself built many of these buildings, who would judge it?"[39]

In the weeks following the disaster, residents organized massive protests against the construction industry and the corruption in these government contracts; meanwhile, the government, engineers, and developers closed ranks, claiming that it was impossible to assign blame because so many parties were involved in any given project. A lawyer from one of the hardest-hit neighborhoods complained that the rubble had been removed too quickly: "When should we assign blame? After the rubble has been removed? How can we look for proof of poor construction when there is a garden growing in every vacant lot?"[40] Indeed, lucrative demolition contracts had been awarded to powerful building-industry consortiums; these in turn pressured for the demolitions to begin before proper surveys could be performed to evaluate whether demolition was even necessary. Residents in Tlatelolco filed a complaint with the Federal Attorney General's Office (Procuraduría General de la República), and an official investigation into the Nuevo León building was opened. However, many of the very men responsible for the construction were charged with spearheading the investigation.[41]

The second major demand concerned reconstruction. Residents in Tlatelolco—and in many of the affected neighborhoods—insisted that their neighborhood be rebuilt on the same site. Rumors flew around the city about the government's intentions for the affected areas. Plans to create more green spaces met with anger from residents: "Mr. Mayor, it was a brilliant idea to build gardens in the Roma; how about we build houses in your garden?"[42] In Tlatelolco, organizers complained that residents were being pressured to move and that the PRI intended to use the buildings for its own offices. Residents worried that the area would be converted into a center for tourism, complete with casinos, and demanded immediate reconstruction of residential housing.[43] Residents did not want to leave; their attachment was emotional and their protests express a strong sense of place: "We are Tlatelolcas, we are proud to be Tlatelolcas, and we want to stay in Tlatelolco."[44] They also had economic motivation to stay, because Tlatelolco was centrally located and well connected to the city's public transportation. Had residents been forced to move—likely to the outskirts—their cost of living would have increased.[45] Residents sent telegrams to the president, trying to move him with personal pleas: "I am a pensioner. Minimal resources. Supporting my family. Asking you respectfully for your intervention. Rebuild Tlatelolco on the same site."[46]

The third demand involved a debate over property rights (*régimen de propiedad*) in the complex. The earthquake occurred in the context of a prolonged battle between residents and the National Fund for Popular Housing (Fonhapo). For several years, Fonhapo had been trying to convert the buildings into condominiums. This violated the spirit of the original contracts, which were meant to be nontransferable and nonnegotiable for ninety-nine years.[47] Under these contracts, residents did not own the apartments; they owned certificates of real estate participation with an array of government agencies.[48] These agencies were responsible for the maintenance and upkeep of the buildings. The proposed shift to condominiums would place the burden of maintenance upon residents.

Although faced with intimidation, campaigns of misinformation, and sometimes blackmail, many residents refused to consider the proposal until Fonhapo undertook the needed repairs. The agency delayed, trying to predicate the repairs on the change in property rights. This bureaucratic wrangling went on for years. In July 1985, only two months before the earthquake, residents of the Nuevo León building had hung a large banner on an outside wall of their building, calling upon Fonhapo to comply with the minimum safety requirements: "Residents of the Nuevo León building are in danger because Fonhapo is not maintaining the control panels."[49] Immediately before the earthquake, the director of Fonhapo had promised concrete replies to residents' demands by 15 September 1985. On the eighteenth, residents were still awaiting his reply.[50] When the earthquake struck on the morning of the nineteenth, it became evident why the agency wanted out.

Tlatelolcas recalled this history with bitterness and wrote in their political newsletters that even if earthquakes were not predictable, it could certainly be predicted that buildings with poor foundations would not fare well in such an event. One resident of the Nuevo León building, Jorge Coo, commented: "In total, FONHAPO saved—*saved?*—21 million pesos. 472 residents died and over 156 disappeared [their bodies were not found in the debris], who for us are also dead."[51] In the aftermath of the disaster, when the government tried to enforce the shift to condominium status as a condition of reconstruction, rage exploded in Tlatelolco.[52] With their letters unanswered and their demands unmet, the nature of the protest changed and Tlatelolcas took to the streets.

All of these demands—punishment for those responsible for the shoddy construction, reconstruction on the same site, and suspension of the plan to change property rights—demonstrate how the government had failed residents. Before the earthquake, government agencies had mismanaged the housing complex. And after the earthquake, it became clear that the complex web of customs, norms of communication, and channels of negotiation between the PRI and the middle classes had broken down; in Tlatelolco (once again) the system that governed the élite realm of the PRI and the middle classes had failed. But Tlatelolco residents resisted the shift to a new system: many rejected the proposal to withdraw government responsibility for the complex. Although they been unsatisfied for years and now faced devastation, residents fought to maintain a welfare state. In fact, they wanted to address the corruption and ineptitude in the PRI's welfare state, holding it accountable rather than jettisoning it.

In this process, a fourth demand emerged: residents called for a more transparent and democratic mode of politics for the reconstruction process and for urban politics in general. The demands discussed above were, in many ways, about redressing the failures of the past. The insistence upon participation in the decision-making process was a radical proposal for change. Residents wanted to be consulted on every decision regarding reconstruction. They did not channel their demands through the PRI's standard procedures; instead, they formed organizations outside the party to negotiate the terms of reconstruction directly with city officials. This was a powerful challenge to the PRI's political structure and legitimacy, and many scholars have described how these residents organizations ushered in a new mode of urban politics.[53]

Building a Protest Movement

There were several layers of organization within the victims movement. In Tlatelolco most buildings had committees, and there were several complexwide groups, joined together as the Tlatelolco Residents Front (Frente de Residentes de Tlatelolco). At first, residents argued that the tragedy offered the PRI an opportunity to recoup the legitimacy it had lost following the student massacres, economic crises, and corruption scandals that marked the 1970s and early 1980s. Residents worried that opposition political parties would infiltrate their organizations; they asserted that they could express their own demands, without the help of any intermediary.[54] However, instead of taking advantage of this opportunity, the PRI mismanaged the disaster. Organizers from an array of political parties appeared on the ground in Tlatelolco in the first few hours after the earthquake, helping with the rescue work. This earned them respect in the eyes of many residents; indeed, some of these political leaders were themselves residents of the complex. On-the-ground legitimacy, combined with their experience in political organizing and access to the necessary equipment (most residents did not own mimeographs or loudspeakers), brought many opposition parties into the protest movement. The parties active in Tlatelolco ranged from the Popular Socialist Party (Partido Popular Socialista, or PPS), which worked within the electoral arena determined by the PRI, to more radical parties such as the Unified Socialist Party of Mexico (Partido Socialista Unificado de México, or PSUM).[55]

Many of the activist leaders in Tlatelolco were members of these parties and had worked with them on urban issues before the earthquake. Often from the middle classes themselves (many had a degree from the UNAM or the National Polytechnic Institute), leaders of the victims movement were veterans of urban protest. Many of them had participated in the student movement of the 1960s, and after the 1968 massacre some ex–student leaders started organizing in poor and working-class neighborhoods.[56] During the 1970s and early 1980s, they had fought increases in rents and evictions. Their tactics included taking buildings by force, illegally occupying them, and sometimes even collecting rent for the landlords. They did this, for example, on the rooftops of Tlatelolco. They also organized homeowners to mobilize for urban services, as well as for education and health care. In the years before the earthquake, they fought the rising cost of living due to inflation and economic instability.[57] After the earthquake, these leaders joined forces with those in Tlatelolco who had been involved in the bureaucratic back-and-forth with government agencies; they helped shape a powerful protest culture and transformed the victims movement into an organized force in urban politics.

Their tactics included making banners, printing newsletters, circulating flyers, holding open-air meetings, marching to the presidential residence of Los Pinos, and organizing demonstrations that reclaimed historic sites such as the Angel of Independence monument. They also showed up in the Chamber of Deputies.[58] Figure 15 depicts a common political gathering in Tlatelolco. Local artists proposed street theatre and artistic festivals, and though initially received with skepticism by activists, these events became an important channel for protest and release.[59] As the weeks passed and their demands were still not addressed, residents' ideas for protest became more radical, such as a possible hunger strike by housewives, with leftist political parties as observers.[60]

The PRI claimed that activists did not enjoy majority support in the complex and accused leaders of agitating among residents. It is difficult to determine the degree of support for activist groups in Tlatelolco; they themselves admitted they did not have "overwhelming" support, and they described an ongoing battle against apathy and conformist tendencies.[61] Indeed, the fight was scattered and complicated. Many buildings had not been damaged and their residents resisted joining the protests; some building leaders signed agreements with government agencies agreeing to the change to condominium status, only to have these agreements challenged by residents. Accusations of intimidation abounded.[62]

In mid-October, these Tlatelolco groups united with other organizations to form the Overall Coordinating Committee of Disaster Victims (Coor-

FIGURE 15. Political meeting in Tlatelolco. From "Aspecto de los asistentes," 24 September 1985, DFS, 009-031-003, legajo 7, AGN.

dinadora Única de Damnificados, or CUD). Based in Tlatelolco, many residents from the complex held prominent positions in this umbrella organization that incorporated other neighborhood organizations as well as specific groups, such as garment and hospital workers, whose workplaces had been destroyed.[63] Each group continued to work toward its particular goals. The garment workers successfully organized for recognition of their union. And the poorer neighborhoods won a historical expropriation decree in which the government took control of thousands of abandoned or empty lots in the interests of public housing. These groups coordinated their efforts not only to express solidarity with one another but also to apply maximum pressure on government officials.[64]

Although residents from all of the affected areas worked together, class tensions emerged between different groups of victims. One leader from Tlatelolco described how the Overall Coordinating Committee had emerged because the media-savvy leaders in Tlatelolco had harnessed the national and international press to further the cause; this leader believed that the mobilization in Tlatelolco had impressed the victims organizations in other neighborhoods.[65] In contrast, residents of the poor and working-class Tepito and Morelos neighborhoods resented the media coverage of the disaster, which focused almost exclusively on the luxury Regis Hotel and the middle-class neighborhoods of Roma and Tlatelolco. They claimed the media had forgotten the victims from the marginal classes.[66]

Cross-class alliances in the Coordinating Committee were often difficult. Some residents of Tlatelolco considered themselves not just middle class but upper-middle class, and they disdained the notion of working alongside residents from lower classes. Residents who lived (as either sublessors or squatters) in the service rooms on the rooftops of the buildings fought to be considered victims and Tlatelolcas.[67] Many of the poorer neighborhoods had strong traditions of urban protest that pre-dated the earthquake, which compounded their resentment of Tlatelolco's emergence as a national and international symbol of the devastation. In turn, Tlatelolcas claimed that their case was unique, owing to its long-documented, bureaucratic history. This distinguished them from the extensive history of urban protest in working-class and poor neighborhoods, and they often identified as middle class with a sense of pride and entitlement.

The initial participation of middle-class residents in the protest movement may be largely attributed to the vehemence with which the earthquake devastated the neighborhood. But as demands expanded from immediate concerns to long-term economic reforms, it became clear that residents worried about Mexico's changing political economy. The public employees, university professors, and doctors living in Tlatelolco had been among the primary beneficiaries of Mexico's "miraculous" economic growth at midcentury; they were also the ones threatened with the onset of economic crisis. In her celebrated account of the tremors' immediate aftermath, Elena Poniatowska calls the Plaza de las Tres Culturas in Tlatelolco a battlefield (yet again): "As it was seventeen years before, the Plaza de las Tres Culturas is a battlefield; camping tents have been rigged up where incomplete families share their misfortune with their neighbors. Broken television sets, sewing machines, typewriters, canned goods, tablecloths, sheets, and mattresses form small pyramids."[68] If the pyramids of Giza represent an ancient Egyptian culture of power and glory, these small pyramids of middle-class material goods represented decades of small-scale dreams—to have a modest job, a safe home, and a modicum of prosperity.

One of the Worst Social Situations

The PRI understood that there was much at stake and monitored the protests closely, desperate to counteract any support the natural disaster might have generated for opposition political parties.[69] In a meeting with the president, Manuel Camacho Solís, who replaced Carillo Arena as minister of urban development and ecology in February 1986, acknowledged that activists had successfully generated an image of political incapacity, authoritarianism, and abuse on the part of the state, an image linked to symbols such as the 1968 student massacre.[70] Nearly six months after the earthquake, he remained worried about the political ramifications in Tlatelolco.

Camacho Solís perceived three main areas of contention: first, the accusations that building representatives had signed illegal contracts with the government regarding the shift to condominium status; second, disagreement over inspections; and third, the attorney general's investigation into responsibility for the collapse of the Nuevo León building. De la Madrid and Camacho Solís hoped to address the first two issues with a program of democratic reconstruction. This involved defining reconstruction as a service to the community, counteracting the rumors that the government had other uses for the buildings and land, and urging residents to participate in and supervise the program. Camacho Solís also created a high-level technical committee to address disagreements over the inspections, including members of the faculties of architecture and engineering at the UNAM, representatives from the construction industry, and internationally renowned leftist urbanists.[71]

Regarding the official investigation into responsibility for the Nuevo León building, the president and his top advisors wanted to do the minimum, as quietly as possible, to comply with their duty. In the attorney general's investigation, they would admit to civil responsibility but not to crime. Camacho Solís and the president worried about political fallout upon the release of the attorney general's report in May 1986, fearing that activists, especially women, would succeed in converting the issue into a referendum on the PRI's legitimacy—a referendum they feared they would lose. They sought to prevent the Nuevo León building from becoming a symbol of official corruption and ineptitude. In their internal memos, Camacho Solís suggested to the president that they scapegoat one of the engineers who had made technical mistakes in the repairs to the building's cement foundations. Beyond that, the official position should be that there were too many entities and people involved to assign blame, including residents who had been unwilling to pay a minimal amount to maintain the foundations.[72]

The PRI reached out to residents to reestablish on-the-ground legitimacy. Camacho Solís and de la Madrid considered which residents of Tlatelolco would be best suited to represent the government within the complex. Their criteria included neighbors who were generally regarded as honest, without close ties to the government, and who did not look down upon people of lower intellect.[73] Their desire for such representatives suggests that they were aware that residents commonly encountered corrupt and arrogant party cronies in their day-to-day dealings with the state. In a similar fashion, PRI functionaries attempted to control the victims movement. One of the reconstruction subcommittees proposed a program called "organized civil solidarity" to give coherent form and content to all levels of social mobilization, to be run through neighborhood and building committees, the city's boroughs (*delegaciones*), schools, unions, political parties, universities, businesses, and religious organizations.[74] Their vision was bureaucratic, top down and antidemocratic, as illustrated by the organizational charts they conceived—a vision at odds with the grassroots victims movement, which the PRI did not succeed in co-opting.[75] The desire of government functionaries to control "civil solidarity" indicates that, from their perspective, they had already lost control of it.

The PRI also used intimidation and repression with the victims movement. Leaders were kidnapped. Tlatelolco was under surveillance, with unmarked Dodge Darts driving through the complex at all hours. And the intelligence agents attempted to discredit leaders by accusing them of drinking and taking drugs in the complex's parking lots. Leaders were also accused of dealing in arms, thereby laying the groundwork to justify a more widespread, violent repression by the PRI. Indeed, before the movement's protest marches, government agents routinely spread rumors that the activists were armed.[76]

Why did Tlatelolco worry the PRI so much? For starters, the government worried about the shift in middle-class protest from writing letters to marching in the streets. In a group interview two months after the earthquake, prominent political organizers in Tlatelolco told how, for the first time since the late 1960s, wide sectors of the middle classes were suffering the government's policy of coercion. For middle-class residents, the mobilization became, in the words of one activist, "a political school of the highest order."[77] While members of the middle classes might have been involved in urban social movements before the earthquake, it was often as organizers. After the earthquake, throngs of middle-class residents formed the rank and file of a new kind of urban protest movement. Speaking with activists, Camacho Solís admitted that Tlatelolco was the PRI's priority because of the "escandalosa" middle classes—noisy and troublemaking.[78] Residents still penned bureaucratic letters to government agencies, but now they were also marching in the streets and contemplating hunger strikes.

The PRI feared that the economic crisis had generated an explosive atmosphere in which it would be easy to spark what one anonymous government analyst described as "one of the worst social situations."[79] Less than a year after the earthquake, the PRI developed Project "Middle Classes" (Proyecto de "Clases Medias"), designed to regain their support. PRI officials believed the middle classes were demonstrating their "repudiation" of the political system. In the project's founding document, PRI officials asked themselves: "What is their [the middle classes'] attitude toward the Mexican Revolution, the government, and the PRI?"[80]

The PRI fretted that the political straying of the middle classes was connected to the economic crisis. Project "Middle Classes" depicts them as particularly sensitive to any changes in their upward mobility or lifestyle. In conditions of economic uncertainty, the document argues, the middle classes are the ones who most quickly and acutely suffer insecurity and anguish, which aggravates levels of "malaise, irritation, [and] social inconformity, and leads to authoritarian attitudes."[81] These "pessimistic" attitudes produce a lack of confidence, indifference, or even frank rejection of official policies and programs. In this context, the PRI considered it of the utmost importance to acquire information on the socioeconomic changes that affect the middle classes:

> To what extent has the real quality of life of the middle classes deteriorated? . . . Are they becoming proletarianized? . . . How intense is their malaise in any given moment? What do they perceive to be the causes of their discontent? What are their expectations and fears? . . . And, more than anything: WHAT WILL BE THE LONG TERM EFFECTS OF THESE PHENOMENA ON THE SOCIAL DYNAMICS OF THE MIDDLE CLASSES?[82]

Project "Middle Classes" would provide a profound diagnostic of the middle classes, but it may have been a case of the serpent eating its own tail: a group of (most likely middle-class) PRI functionaries developed it to identify and better understand the middle classes. The project thus reveals either deep self-understanding—or a deep lack of it. The project would serve as the basis for a series of political, economic, and social actions. As the founding document asked, "What should be their link to the Party in power? What should a government policy for them look like? How could the social communication with the middle classes be improved? What alternatives can be offered them that would change their view of the economic crisis?"[83] According to the authors of this document, the rapidly changing economic structure provided the imperative for the project. The PRI foresaw that its economic readjustment program would continue at a rapid pace through the end of the de la Madrid presidency in 1988—and indeed through the end of the century—and anticipated that the accompanying changes in social and political structures would generate "dangerous tensions" among the middle classes.[84]

The PRI was right to worry. As the victims movement became stronger and better organized, it participated in public discussion about Mexico's political economy. Demands moved beyond immediate concerns such as rescue work and shelter and beyond urban issues such as housing, property rights, and indemnification payments. Residents clamored for a say in the country's political economy. As discussed in Chapter 5, residents' demands included a moratorium on Mexico's foreign debt payments. Reconstruction raised questions about Mexico's economic development model, especially as the estimated cost reached $US4 billion, equivalent to 11 percent of the government's spending budget for 1985.[85] With regard to economic planning, a flyer issued by the Mexican Labor Party (Partido Laboral Mexicano, or PLM) argued that "if we do not have the capacity to change while facing a catastrophe of this magnitude, then we do not have the moral capacity to survive as a nation."[86]

Competing visions for the future emerged, spawned by a natural disaster and a major economic crisis. After several months of protest, the victims movement successfully altered the established political culture in the capital city: victims won a seat at the negotiating table, where they hammered out, with city and federal politicians, the Pact of Democratic Agreement on Reconstruction (Convenio de Concertación Democrática para la Reconstrucción).

Rebuilding the Nation's Capital

On 13 May 1986, after escalating confrontation as well as strained negotiations, the PRI and the victims organizations signed the official reconstruction plan. The minister of urban development and ecology, the city government, and the official reconstruction organization, Popular Housing Renovation (Renovación Habitacional Popular), represented the government. The Overall Coordinating Committee of Disaster Victims (CUD) and many of the major victims organizations—but not all—signed the pact. University institutes, technical groups, various business chambers, and an array of foundations and civil associations, all involved in reconstruction, also signed the accord. It was announced to great fanfare at a press conference at which representatives of these diverse organizations pledged their support. At its core, the pact gave victims organizations a say in the reconstruction process, and victims participated in the decision making. It emphasized transparency in the distribution of funds, the need for victims to have safe and affordable shelter, and the importance of maintaining urban cultures and lifestyles. One expert argued that the process of negotiation and consensus building that led to the pact had ushered in a new type of conflict resolution in Mexico, one that emanated from below as well as above.[87]

What was won and what was lost? In some ways, everyone won something. The pact complemented other agreements between government agencies and specific neighborhoods or groups, and there was a separate decree for reconstruction in Tlatelolco. In Tlatelolco, residents and the government agencies agreed upon which buildings would be demolished and which needed repairs. They set a schedule for reconstruction and established that the government would bear all costs. Agreeing to a new condominium ownership scheme would not be a precondition for reconstruction.[88]

The PRI, however, also emerged victorious. With the exception of certain buildings in Tlatelolco, most of the housing built in the reconstruction program fell under a new condominium ownership program. Residents would be responsible for all maintenance. After a six-month guarantee against structural deficiencies, tenants—and not government agencies—would be responsible for structural defects.[89] The extension of these new terms of ownership to most of the new housing was a major victory for the government; only the most politically mobilized residents in Tlatelolco succeeded in resisting this change. The new terms would be implemented in all other buildings in the complex, and residents received information manuals that purported to teach them how to live under the Regime of Property in Condominium (Régimen de Propiedad en Condomino). These didactic manuals explained how to properly maintain and manage the units. One illustrated manual emphasized that Tlatelolco residents should be respectful of neighbors and not make too much noise. As depicted in Figure 16, it was perfectly clear that in these buildings, residents would be responsible for all maintenance and that everyone would have to pay a monthly fee for upkeep.

It is telling to compare the struggles over property rights in Tlatelolco with a decree in poorer neighborhoods, in which, only weeks after the

FIGURE 16. Learning how the maintenance fees work. In this cartoon, a resident of Tlatelolco speaks to the building administrator: "I did not use my apartment for four months." He replies: "Even still, you must pay the maintenance fees." From "Manual de organización y mantenimiento: Conjunto urbano 'Presidente Adolfo López Mateos' Nonoalco-Tlatelolco," July 1987, MMH, 20.01.00.00, c. 5, exp. 10, AGN.

earthquake, the government expropriated thousands of buildings and empty lots. Buildings would be converted into social housing—renters could purchase their apartments at affordable rates—and the empty lots would be used to construct affordable housing.[90] On the surface, the decree seemed to be a major concession by President de la Madrid. De la Madrid seemed to be backsliding on the austerity measures he had committed to with the IMF: the government was getting back into the business of providing housing.

The decree sparked outrage among the conservative opposition and many middle-class property owners. Gerardo Garza Sada, president of the Monterrey Chamber of Commerce, roundly condemned the expropriation decree as "vulgar populism and socialism [*populachera y estatizante*]" and asked the IMF to investigate de la Madrid's decision.[91] Middle-class property owners lined up for days to challenge the expropriation of their lots. They claimed that the government was appropriating their children's patrimony; they also complained about inaccuracy and randomness in the list of expropriated properties. (Some of the properties on the list were single-family homes where the owners lived; others were empty lots of uncertain ownership.)[92]

In the weeks after the decree, government spies attempted to verify the properties on the list and found a chaos of property arrangements, and no uniform reaction to the decree. One typical building on the expropriation list consisted of twenty-two apartments that were rented by tenants who included a taco vendor, several mechanics, a *lonchería* (snack bar) owner, a few decorators and painters, a federal employee who worked in the penal system, a chauffeur, an optometrist's assistant, several secretaries, a pensioner, a carpenter, a plumber, and a few white-collar employees. Although most of the women were housewives, some worked outside of the home; many of the children were university students. The tenants in this building earned various incomes and paid different rents. (In a single building, rents could range from 500 to 15,000 pesos per month, depending on whether some of the apartments were under rent control.)[93]

Unsurprisingly, there was no consensus on the expropriation decree. In some buildings, after the decree, landlords had moved into a unit in order to establish residence and fight the expropriation; in other buildings, powerful landlords tore down the expropriation notice and declared they would fight the government, threatening renters with eviction if they spoke with government agents. One landlord asked her tenants to sign a document stating that they were not renters but rather that she had "loaned" them use of an apartment (this landlord also moved into her building to establish residence).[94] Although many tenants supported expropriation, others preferred to remain tenants in rent-controlled apartments. Likewise, while some property owners rejected the decree, others saw it as an opportunity to get out of a difficult relationship with tenants who had paid the same rent for over fifty years or who claimed ownership of the property through occupation.[95]

Despite the disparate interests of tenants and landlords, the expropriation decree was generally regarded as a triumph for earthquake victims, and tens of thousands of residents marched in the streets to thank the president. Former tenants became property owners. Many of their subsequent demands centered on questions raised by the decree, including its possible amplification, the bureaucratic process of this transition, and the pace of reconstruction. At the signing of the pact, one activist described how "those of us who had been condemned to real estate slavery could now own our own homes."[96]

Several urban studies experts, however, point to negative long-term implications of the expropriation victory, which exposed tenants of previously
rent-controlled units to the open real estate market. Sociologist Diane Davis
describes how, when they acquired property titles, tenants lost the protection of rent control, which had kept the rent artificially low for several
decades. In this way, the seemingly populist concession to poorer residents
in the city center allowed the de la Madrid administration to break the grip
of rent control and probably paved the way for other uses of downtown
property, a goal previous administrations had worked toward without success.[97] Real estate developers had pushed for this shift in land tenure, which
they hoped would start a gradual process of boosting land values in the city
center.[98] Some developers also considered alternatives that might have been
worse—at least for them. One developer, interviewed by *Expansión* shortly
after the expropriation decree, argued that losing rental property in the city
center was better than expanding rent control there.[99] Thus, the expropriation became a medium-term victory for private real estate developers.[100]

At the heart of these debates over reconstruction lay competing visions
for urban life and, more broadly, for the future of Mexico's political economy. Miguel de la Madrid's expropriation decree may have seemed like a
populist, "big state" idea, but it actually expressed a neoliberal desire to
reorder the urban property market. Yet tenants celebrated the decree as
a shift back toward the PRI's populism. At the same time, middle-class
residents fought the privatization of their condominiums and the loss of a
social safety net they had grown accustomed to during the boom decades.
No doubt, they did not want the corrupt and inadequate welfare state that
had failed to maintain their apartments buildings, schools, and hospitals.
But they did want a democratic welfare state that would be responsible for
their day-to-day shelter and safety, one that was accountable to its citizens.
The everyday battle lines of broader economic change, then, were not always clear. As a moment of disaster capitalism, the earthquake catalyzed
competing visions for Mexico's future and encouraged all sides to fortify
their positions.[101]

What was lost? Residents mobilized successfully for housing, reconstruction, and urban services, and the victims movement raised questions
about urban democracy and economic planning. Nevertheless, instead of
granting Mexico City's residents the right to elect their mayor, the government established an elected Representative Assembly (Asamblea de
Representantes) that had no legislative power. And on the economic front,
Mexico did not lead Latin America to defy international creditors.

But just as some victories might have been illusory, it would be rash to
say that the call for greater democracy and a different political economy
failed. The most profound reverberation of the earthquake may be that it

created opportunities. Residents used the natural disaster to debate political economic questions, and they brought a wider array of citizens into the discussion.

A Middle-Class Civil Society?

Taking stock of these political successes and failures also involves reckoning with the legacy of the earthquake victims movement. One common interpretation credits the movement with the beginnings of democracy in Mexico. As discussed in the previous chapter, de la Madrid's economic policies had alienated many populist-leaning PRI politicians, and by 1986 populist PRI politicians had been expelled from the party. The booted populists mounted an independent electoral campaign for the 1988 presidential elections, with Cuahtémoc Cárdenas as their candidate.[102] Popular interpretations of the earthquake and its aftermath draw direct lines between the earthquake victims movement and this electoral challenge, by which the movement began to channel its influence into the Cárdenas campaign.

While there is no precise date on which the Overall Coordinating Committee of Disaster Victims dissolved, it had largely achieved its goal when earthquake victims began to receive their new homes and the reconstruction programs neared completion.[103] However, as earthquake victims gained their housing, others in need emerged. Some were earthquake victims who had fled the city, but many were urban residents who had needed housing before the earthquake—who were, in a sense, permanent victims. They approached the committee and neighborhood organizations for help. Just when some organizers thought they had won the battle, another fight began.[104] After much deliberation, in 1987 a group of organizers from the Coordinating Committee formed the Assembly of Barrios (Asamblea de Barrios) to address the concerns of the urban poor and the general problem of housing in Mexico City.

The Coordinating Committee and the Assembly of Barrios threw their support behind Cárdenas's presidential campaign: "*The narrative that we began to invent* was that 1985 was the outburst of citizen participation, the breaking of all the mechanisms of control in the city, and that 1988 was its political expression," explained activist Marco Rascón. "You could not explain 1988 without 1985."[105] The activists in the Coordinating Committee and Assembly of Barrios embraced this interpretation ("Nos abrogamos esa representación," in Rascón's words) and brought it to the Cardenista movement.[106] Because the Cárdenas campaign and the controversial 1988 elections are generally regarded as the beginnings of Mexico's transition to democracy, these activists created an influential origins story for electoral democracy in Mexico.

When the PRI's candidate, Carlos Salinas de Gortari, successfully claimed the presidency, he initiated a series of electoral reforms to gain credibility after the fraudulent 1988 elections. Perhaps most significantly, in 1990 Salinas created the Federal Electoral Institute (Instituto Federal Electoral, or IFE), a permanent body to oversee elections. The IFE was initially under the control of the Ministry of the Interior, but several political crises in 1994 sparked further reform. The outbreak of the Zapatista rebellion in the state of Chiapas in January, followed by the assassination of the PRI's presidential candidate, Luis Donaldo Colosio Murrieta, in March, led to another electoral reform: the IFE was granted an important degree of autonomy, with six "citizen councilors" elected by the Chamber of Deputies (although the minister of the interior still served as president of IFE).[107] Confronted with a broad threat to the PRI's legitimacy from the Zapatistas and dealing with discord and disarray within the party following the assassination—as well as widespread speculation that high-level PRI politicians had ordered the hit—the Salinas administration likely implemented the further electoral reform to assuage detractors and ensure stable elections and peaceful transfer of power for the 1994 presidential elections.[108]

Electoral reform gathered momentum under Ernesto Zedillo Ponce de León, Salinas's successor and the last president of the PRI dynasty (from 1994 to 2000). Zedillo passed an election law in 1996 that gave the IFE more meaningful autonomy—it was no longer under the control of the Ministry of the Interior. And the Federal District's electoral law was reformed so that residents of Mexico City gained the right to elect their mayor.[109] These reforms led to a growing confidence in the electoral system among Mexican voters, and the results were dramatic.[110] In 1997 there were mayoral elections in Mexico City; residents elected Cuauhtémoc Cárdenas. Also in 1997, the PRI lost its majority in the Chamber of Deputies. And, for the first time in many decades, the 2000 presidential elections were meaningfully contested: the middle classes, and many others, went to the booths to vote against the PRI.[111] The candidate of the conservative National Action Party (Partido Acción Nacional, or PAN), Vicente Fox, won approximately 43 percent of the vote; 37 percent went to the PRI; and the Party of the Democratic Revolution (Partido de la Revolución Democrática, or PRD), which had emerged from the coalition group that sponsored Cárdenas's 1988 campaign, came in third with 17 percent.[112] Zedillo quickly acknowledged Fox's victory, ending the PRI's long rule. Although the PAN became the first opposition party to benefit from the electoral reforms at the presidential level, much of the grassroots impetus for change came from the political left, from Cárdenas's 1988 campaign, and from the earthquake victims movement—in broad terms, from a dynamic civil society.[113]

The concept of civil society is crucial to the origins story of Mexican democracy. The narrative is not only about top-down electoral reform but also about political pressure emanating from diffuse sources below. Writing in the immediate aftermath of the shocks, some of Mexico's most prominent public intellectuals described the earthquake victims movement as nothing less that the spontaneous "birth of civil society." Carlos Monsiváis, perhaps the best-known proponent of this interpretation, articulated a few weeks after the earthquake: "What was most alive in Mexico City was the presence of a new social actor whose more appropriate name is 'civil society.'"[114] In Monsiváis's analysis, the term "civil society" signaled autonomous (from the one-party state), day-to-day participation in urban politics and political discourse.[115] Individuals, groups, and communities engaged in new political practices, what Monsiváis described as a learning process for "citizens in the making."[116]

Civil society became a popular concept among other scholars and activists working in Mexico and Latin America in the years after the earthquake.[117] Definitions vary, and the concept has been embraced by both the political Left and Right, but some consensus exists among social scientists that "civil society" refers to a terrain and a target of politics with a degree of autonomy from the state and the market.[118] Tentatively defined and not idealized, civil society became a central concept in the literature on democratization in Latin America.[119]

Yet, oddly, the middle classes are virtually absent from narratives about civil society, which focus almost exclusively on the poor and working classes. For example, while mobilization of Tlatelolco residents after the earthquake was center stage for the PRI, it is sidelined in analyses of the victims movement. In sociologist Susan Eckstein's study of the earthquake in the Centro neighborhood, for example, the middle-class participants and leaders of the CUD function as a foil for the poor and working-class residents of the Centro. Poor residents, Eckstein argues, saw the committee "as primarily a middle-class organization whose concerns differed from theirs."[120] While this may well have been the case, and helps to tease out nuances in the political strategies of poorer residents, the interpretation leads to a one-dimensional vision of middle-class political culture, as Eckstein describes it: "The middle-class *damnificados* [victims] who dominated the CUD lived in high-rise condominium apartments. Many of them had property title problems and no strong commitment to their place of residence. By contrast, the people of El Centro were tenants in rent-controlled buildings and had strong ties to their community."[121] However, the repeated invocations of Tlatelolco as an emotional and historically charged site ("we are Tlatelolcas, we are proud to be Tlatelolcas and we want to stay in Tlatelolco") underscore the strong sense of place that pervaded middle-class demands.

Although the middle classes are absent from narratives about civil society, Tlatelolco residents and others were very present in the social movement. This raises a deceptively simple question: Why have scholars avoided
serious consideration of the role of the middle classes in the victims movement? The answer may lie in two related phenomena: the people whom
scholars want to study and the stories that scholars want to tell. These
phenomena are dangerously close to what one academic referred to as "the
shadowy area of speculation about the psychological predispositions of
scholars."[122] Some scholars, however, explicitly discuss the personal and
political motivations that influence their work—and admit they sometimes
study poor people's social movements in search of an inspiring movement
for social change.[123] Certainly, the victims movement is inspiring, and it
did mark a new form of politics and political negotiation in Mexico City.
Residents altered power relations in the capital city; many previously excluded residents—poor and middle class—became important participants
in the political negotiations over reconstruction. But emphasizing the political successes of the poor and marginalized can distort our understanding
of recent history. It can overstate their power.[124] And it flattens the historical experiences of the nurses, dentists, university professors, shopkeepers,
and office workers who lived in Tlatelolco.

This contradictory presence and absence of the middle classes has
shaped the history of the earthquake. In fact, this contradiction is at the
center of postrevolutionary Mexican history and historiography. The middle classes are not only present but they constitute the premier vantage
point from which to examine the economic and political turmoil of the
late twentieth century. Although they are conspicuously absent from the
scholarly and popular writing about this history, their experiences are key
to understanding the transition from state-led development and one-party
rule to neoliberalism and electoral democracy. Tlatelolco residents, small
business owners, stock market investors, real estate developers, indebted
consumers, unemployed airline pilots, conservative parents, and radical
students were all protagonists in Mexico's recent history of economic and
political change.

Blasting Open the Continuum of History

Natural disasters are much more than physical events that suddenly erupt,
wreak havoc, and recede. They are historical events in which scientific,
religious, and political forces etch meaning into society's imaginary. Earthquakes happen, and they have real consequences for real people. Then they
are studied by seismologists, managed by governments, defined by intel-

lectuals, remarked upon by religious leaders, narrated by writers, and invoked by different social groups to advance an agenda.[125]

The Mexico City earthquake offers a glimpse into historical processes. When it sheared open the fault lines of the city, it threw a system into shock and exposed intricate power relations; it was, to borrow Walter Benjamin's words, "enough to blast open the continuum of history."[126] From the debris, the history of the disaster—the discursive event, the story we remember—emerged. Members of poor and working-class neighborhood organizations, together with scholars interested in the history of these movements, cast the earthquake as catalyst in poor and working-class political mobilization. For others, it signified the birth of a Mexican civil society or became the start of an origins story about democracy. As the earthquake has been invoked to tell particular stories—to transform the natural disaster into a discursive event—one story, about the rising fury and newfound force of the middle classes, has been largely overlooked.

This middle-class story, though, is lodged in both the Ministry of the Interior intelligence reports and the presidential archives. In these documents another story of the earthquake, another discursive event emerges. Residents of Tlatelolco experienced the incapacity, and even unwillingness, of the PRI to resolve their problems. The PRI perceived the antipathy of the middle classes with anxiety and dread. In fact, the party saw the unraveling of its official Institutional Revolutionary project within its archetypal social group, the middle classes.

The earthquake proved a formidable test for the one-party state and its institutions. The PRI had failed specific groups many times before, but on 19 September 1985, its failure lay exposed on the streets of the nation's capital, undeniable to even the most casual observer. What might have remained, on the eve of the earthquake, of the midcentury alliance between the PRI and the middle classes had vanished. In June 1986, at the opening ceremonies of the World Cup in Mexico City's Azteca Stadium, as President Miguel de la Madrid stepped out to greet the crowd, the entire stadium—over 110,000 middle- and upper-class fans—lustily booed their president in front of the whole world.[127]

Conclusion

THE DEBRIS OF A MIRACLE

In the twenty-first century, the long rule of the PRI seems almost unreal. After faltering but surviving for over seven decades, the one-party state came to an end with seemingly spectacular speed. But tensions had been simmering for decades, and they had been simmering especially among the middle classes. During the midcentury Miracle, doctors, office workers, and shopkeepers had represented a coveted (and seemingly plausible) ideal of how people could live, the promise of an era. When economic crisis took hold in the 1970s and 1980s, expectations for prosperity and upward mobility ruptured. A new mode of being middle class emerged, one that was grounded in economic instability.

In the denouement of the Miracle, the contradictions within both the PRI and the middle classes became clear, as students, yuppies, radio technicians, and business owners both rejected and sought refuge in the one-party state. At some moments, the middle classes denounced the state from the left and the right, such as during the guerrilla insurgency and *cacerolazo* protests of the 1970s. At other times, they fought to keep the state in their lives as an employer or as the caretaker of their schools and homes, as they did in the 1986 UNAM strike and following the 1985 earthquake. High- and midlevel PRI functionaries, for their part, looked to the middle classes (to whom they often belonged) with a mixture of hope and dread, alternately condemning them and courting them. The PRI and the middle classes, together, constituted an élite realm in turmoil, struggling for and against change.

That history exploded in 1994. On the first of January, the North American Free Trade Agreement (NAFTA) between Mexico, Canada, and the United States went into effect. The agreement consolidated Mexico's transition to neoliberal capitalism, especially in terms of trade liberalization, a process that had begun in the 1980s.[1] Between 1988 and 1994, President Carlos Salinas de Gortari expanded the neoliberal reforms introduced by Miguel de la Madrid, with NAFTA the culmination of this process. The Salinas administration dramatically reduced the role of the state in the economy through divestiture and privatization of state-owned enterprises, deregulation of key economic areas, elimination of many guaranteed prices, reduction of the public deficit through cutbacks in expenditure, and a constitutional change that allowed for the privatization of communal lands and the end of the process of land redistribution that had begun with the Mexican Revolution.[2]

Also on the first of January, the Zapatista Army of National Liberation (Ejército Zapatista de Liberación Nacional, or EZLN) declared war on the Mexican state. This, too, was a culmination of Mexico's transition to neoliberalism—of a different sort. These late twentieth-century Zapatistas in the state of Chiapas rebelled against the injustice and uneven development inherent in Mexico's capitalist economic growth.[3] The Zapatistas protested against the "New World Order" heralded by NAFTA, a neoliberal world predicated on the end of the land redistribution that had been, for many, one of the most meaningful legacies of the Revolution.[4] One of the Zapatistas' protest cries was: "NAFTA is death!"[5] The most prominent spokesperson for the EZLN, Subcomandante Marcos, belonged to the 1968 generation of middle-class leftists. He was one of the radicals who left Mexico City to work with peasants, and part of his trajectory must be explained as a middle-class story.[6]

Although NAFTA promised prosperity, the Mexican peso collapsed in late 1994 and the middle classes suffered yet another economic crisis—*el crack*. Their survival strategies included selling assets, borrowing money, giving up mistresses, taking in Spanish language students, canceling auto insurance, and reducing consumption by resoling shoes, eating out less, and buying cheaper clothes.[7] In his study of the middle classes in the 1990s, sociologist Dennis Gilbert argues that the 1994 crisis marked a major change in politics and political culture. But there was more continuity: the crisis mode had been forged during the 1970s and 1980s.[8] Gilbert's interviewees had much in common with their counterparts in the two previous decades, as they themselves described it: "We were going to become part of the First World . . . no longer the Third World. . . . Echeverría had done it to us. López Portillo had done it, and now Salinas. Once again, we Mexicans had been *engañados* [betrayed] by the PRI."[9]

Some of these *engañados* joined the Barzón, a debtors movement in which middle-class farmers and urban residents refused to pay their personal and small business debts whose value had been distorted by the plummeting peso. In Mexico City, women threw their credit cards (now worthless) and car keys (car loan payments had ballooned beyond budgets) at the presidential palace.[10] Even Sofía, the protagonist of Guadalupe Loaeza's novels—who, despite belonging to the upper echelons of the middle classes, awaited her monthly American Express bill with great anxiety—confessed to her fiancé, "I wanted to join the *barzón*."[11] The debt economy that emerged in the 1970s had boomed in the early 1990s during the optimism of the Salinas administration; its instability became undeniable by 1994.

The dramatic events of 1994 expressed historical processes that had been decades in the making. The debris left by the end of the Miracle had been accumulating. The wreckage of progress (to borrow philosopher Walter Benjamin's words) wrought social, political, and cultural turmoil among the middle classes and the PRI.[12] Ultimately, their élite realm collapsed. The dynamism of the PRI's corporatist system, which had once provided it with remarkable institutional flexibility, was insufficient in the face of the transformations underway since the 1970s. And the protean nature of the middle classes was stretched to its limits during the intervening decades—Hermenegildo, the seventy-five-year-old man forced out of retirement and into underemployment as a photographer, had little in common with the optimistic yuppies living in Santa Fe. The center could not hold.

This history of economic and political change, which is only now being written, is one of surprising turns, a multitude of experiences, and a considerable amount of happenstance. And as the Mexican Miracle and the PRI's one-party state become part of an increasingly distant past, it is urgent to remember the everyday complexity of this history. One expert has warned of a concrete-block effect, whereby the PRI period might be rendered an opaque inanimate object, as though it had not been real.[13] There is a danger that this history could become an ideological commodity (as tends to happen), its complexity turned into pat narratives used to advance political arguments.[14] Already, some look back on the PRI's rule with longing, others with incredulity. Interpretations have taken on urgency with the drug violence of the twenty-first century, and many citizens, politicians, and analysts have begun to base their visions for Mexico's future on how they understand the history of the PRI's one-party state. With the victory of the PRI's candidate, Enrique Peña Nieto, in the 2012 presidential elections, citizens are debating whether Peña Nieto represents a "new" PRI. The answer depends on what they mean by the "old" PRI. And as academic and cultural élites try to make sense of the recent past, preoccupation with the middle classes is once again appearing in the cultural and political imaginary.[15] Octavio Paz, writing in 1970, correctly predicted that the middle classes would lead "great political battles" in the near future.[16] These battles, perhaps more like guerrilla warfare than a traditional conflict, determined the end of the Miracle, the shift from state-led development to neoliberalism, and the emergence of electoral democracy.

The middle classes were the protagonists of this history. Studying them requires analysis of political, economic, and cultural change, to understand their political protests, their budget calculations, and what it meant to them to be middle class. This methodology offers an opportunity to bring together narratives and tools for doing history that are often separate. It also allows for a fuller understanding of Mexico's recent past and of crisis in the late twentieth-century capitalist world more generally. And if the diversity of middle-class experiences might be frustrating for anyone looking for clear categories or neat narratives, that discomfort is an achievement: studying the middle classes forces us to grapple with the contingency of history.

The past struggles of dentists, housewives, teachers, and airline pilots still matter; their political and economic longings still linger. Although they seem to belong to a world that has passed—after all, with the PRI reduced to one party among others that may or may not win electoral contests in the future, hasn't everything changed?—their struggles also belong in the present. From the students who gathered in Tlatelolco in 1968 to protest the PRI's authoritarianism, to the residents of that same neighborhood who, almost two decades later, held the party accountable for its systemic corruption, they fought against the end of midcentury aspirations. And they fought against an emerging middle-class reality that was rooted in instability. No doubt, the leftist students, enraged car owners, indebted consumer-citizens, hard-boiled detectives, suicidal small business owners, and protesting homeowners who appear in this book represented the limits of the midcentury boom. But they also embodied its successes. In the twenty-first century, their economic uncertainty seems anticlimactic after the struggles to preserve midcentury realities and dreams.

Many of the people in this book fought for what might be called a transparent and democratic welfare state. They fought for this in different ways. Although some wholeheartedly rejected the PRI, most sought to reform the system. Indeed, only the urban guerrillas truly belong to the first group; even leaders of the private sector, for all their denunciations, benefited greatly from the PRI's system. With the onset of economic crisis in the 1960s, different groups within the middle classes jockeyed for a place at the PRI's negotiation table, struggling to defend their shaky privileges. Many sought to defend these privileges for themselves and all those other Mexicans who aspired to social mobility. They wanted to improve and expand the welfare state and to participate in decision making, especially in times of crisis. This political project is as urgent today as it was during the 1970s and 1980s.

The creative, sometimes accidental politics of the middle classes generated a constellation of alternatives, full of possibility. Some of their successes, failures, and thwarted alternatives may offer ideas for anyone looking to create a better world.

Appendix

Social scientists have analyzed class stratification in Mexico, and their quantitative studies delimit the socioeconomic reality of the middle classes. Their discussion of their methods (whom they count as middle class and whom they do not, for example) and the different conclusions they reach also help to determine the relative size of this group.[1] Two groups of studies—the *Statistical Abstract of Latin America* project, which draws upon census data, and studies that use household surveys—are especially useful in quantifying the middle classes.[2]

In their pioneering study "Quantifying the Class Structure of Mexico, 1895–1970," James Wilkie and Paul Wilkins developed a new data series on Mexican class structure from 1895 to 1970.[3] The Wilkie and Wilkins series served as the basis for later studies, one by Stephanie Granato and Aída Mostkoff, the other by David Lorey and Aída Mostkoff Linares, who extended the series to 1980 and 1990, respectively.[4] All three studies are part of the *Statistical Abstract of Latin America* project. Wilkie and Wilkins defined classes by a combination of income and occupation, and they based their 1895 and 1940 estimates on two earlier studies, conducted by José Iturriaga and Howard Cline, respectively.[5] They reinterpret the Iturriaga and Cline data, creating new categories and eliminating others (for instance, they eliminate Cline's category of a "transitional class"). They then draw upon census data for their estimates for 1950, 1960, and 1970. Wilkie and Wilkins found evidence of considerable class mobility in Mexico, with the middle classes growing as a percentage of the national population from over 20 percent in 1950 to almost 30 percent in 1970. Their estimates of the middle classes (and the extension of their series to 1990 by Lorey and Mostkoff Linares) are reproduced in Table A.1 at the end of the Appendix.

Wilkie and Wilkins also analyze—and debunk—the data on class stratification presented by several scholars. They argue that, contrary to their own findings of a growing middle class, by the 1960s it was widely believed that Mexico's class structure was becoming increasingly polarized: "Many Mexican and foreign observers [came to] believe that Mexico's rich were getting richer and the poor were getting poorer."[6] This belief, according to Wilkie and Wilkins, stemmed from two oft-cited studies, *La distribución del ingreso y el desarollo económico de México*, by Ifigenia M. de Navarrete, and "Clases y estratos sociales," by Arturo González Cosío. Both of these works presented data that indicated increased class polarization in postrevolutionary Mexico (Navarrete focused on the 1950s, while González Cosío's analysis extended to 1960). Wilkie and Wilkins reanalyze Navarrete's and González Cosío's data and conclude that the former's are "incomplete" and the latter's "unusable." With regard to Navarrete's data, one reason for concern is that she did not take the necessary last step of calculating the average percentage distribution of income by class (which diminishes the degree of class polarization). Wilkie and Wilkins argue that the incomplete Navarrete data were "misinterpreted" by others to advance specific political agendas.[7] With regard to González Cosío's data, Wilkie and Wilkins conclude that he "might just as well have pulled his figures out of thin air."[8]

In Wilkie and Wilkins's view, the incomplete Navarrete data and the unusable González Cosío data constituted, in the 1960s, the basis of an argument by the political Left that the Mexican Revolution had failed the Mexican poor. Scholars and analysts on the left, according to Wilkie and Wilkins, uncritically accepted these data as evidence for their political argument. Consequently, Mexican and foreign scholars and commentators underestimated the growth of the middle classes in the postrevolutionary period. In contrast, the Wilkie and Wilkins series indicates impressive social mobility.[9]

While the *Statistical Abstract of Latin America* studies rely on census data, other scholars have made use of household surveys. In 1984, Mexico's National Institute of Statistics, Geography, and Information (Instituto Nacional de Estadística, Geografía e Informática, or INEGI) began a nationwide survey of household finances that collects detailed information on household demographics, income, and occupation. Using these surveys, Dennis Gilbert has put forth an alternative to the *Statistical Abstract of Latin America* estimates regarding the growth of the middle classes. Gilbert's figures are more modest, though they do support an overall trend of a growing middle class. For example, when they extended the Wilkie and Wilkins series to 1990, Lorey and Mostkoff Linares found that the middle classes made up 33 percent of the population in 1980 and 38 percent in 1990 (see Table A.1). In contrast, Gilbert estimates that in 1984, the middle classes made up 16 percent of the population, and 18 percent in 1992 (see Table A.1). These differences are remarkable, approaching 20 percent in the early 1990s.

The gulf between these estimates is, in part, a function of two important methodological differences between the *Statistical Abstract of Latin America* project and Gilbert's study. First, the *Statistical Abstract of Latin America* studies combine income and occupational criteria to define the middle class. In their original essay, Wilkie and Wilkins rely on a base estimate of 300 pesos per month as a middle-class income in 1950.[10] From this base, they extrapolated middle-class incomes for later decades, with adjustments only for inflation. As Gilbert argues: "The implicit, though perhaps unintended, assumption is that a middle-class or lower-class standard of living was the same in 2000 as it had been in 1950."[11] One flaw of this assumption for the purposes of quantifying class is that a television might have been a marker of middle-class status in 1950 but not necessarily in 1990. Further, when one follows Wilkie and Wilkins's footnote for the 300 pesos per month estimate, it becomes clear that they got this figure from Cline, who writes that "most students agree that an income of 300 pesos per month is the minimum for a reasonably secure but marginal living in Mexico."[12] Cline does not provide a source for this statement—to what students does he refer? Wilkie and Wilkins quote Cline's statement in their footnote but do not comment on the lack of rigor; surely, Cline could here be accused of having "pulled his figures out of thin air" in the style of González Cosío. Wilkie and Wilkins's silence on this matter, combined with their use of the 300 pesos monthly income in 1950 as the basis for middle-class incomes in later decades, may well have led them to overestimate the size of the middle classes.

Second, Gilbert has a narrower occupational definition of middle class. He does not, for example, count white-collar workers at the lower end of the income spectrum as middle class. These workers, such as office clerks and salespeople, are included in the *Statistical Abstract of Latin America* category of middle class.[13] Thus, Gilbert's estimates rely on stricter income and occupational criteria than the *Statistical Abstract of Latin America* estimates.

Another study, by Mexico's National Minimum Wage Commission, also uses household survey data (a 1977 precursor to the INEGI surveys that Gilbert uses). Samaniego de Villarreal concludes that, in 1977, the middle classes made up 25 percent of the national population (see Table A.1). She defines the middle classes by income deciles (eight, ninth, and first half of the tenth deciles) and reaches an estimate that falls between the *Statistical Abstract of Latin America* and the Gilbert estimates.[14]

All of this suggests that even the most rigorous quantitative and statistical estimates are partly subjective. They depend on evaluations of who counts as middle class and decisions as to what data to accept. Further, some data that might appear reliable are in fact highly impressionistic. None of these scholars purport to offer a definitive picture of class stratification in Mexico. Indeed, the authors explicitly discuss the limitations of their data and their methodologies. Wilkie and Wilkins, for instance, point out that while a scholar might categorize a Mexican worker as working class based upon income and occupation, that same worker might self-identify as middle class. They cite the results of several surveys on class and self-identification as evidence of this sort of discrepancy. For example, when Joseph Kahl interviewed white- and blue-collar workers in Mexico City and some small towns in the state of Hidalgo during 1965 and 1968, he found that almost 70 percent of blue-collar workers with some secondary education self-identified as middle or upper class.[15] Statistical estimates, then, do not offer objective, definitive answers to such questions as: Who counts as middle class? How big are the middle classes? Instead, the different estimates corroborate an overall pattern: the middle classes grew during the postrevolutionary period and constituted, from the midcentury decades on, an important sector of the population.

Another challenge for quantifying the middle classes (and other social classes) is the nature of the data available on income and wages. The estimates discussed above rely, principally, on a combination of income and occupation criteria. The sources and methods used by economic historians with regard to employment, wages, and income have advanced considerably in the past few decades, but, as Jeffrey Bortz argues, we are still missing important parts of the puzzle. For instance, much of our data on wages is related to the legal minimum wage and thus limited because of regional variation and because the legal minimum wage does not constitute an actual wage for most workers.[16] We still need more data on real wages, especially data culled from nonofficial sources, such as through research in business archives.[17] Synthesizing the extensive literature on wages, Bortz and Marcos Aguila outline some broad trends in real wages during the mid-twentieth century. Simply put, real wages rose during the 1930s and declined in the 1940s. In 1954, a peso devaluation helped curb inflation and triggered a long upswing through the late 1960s. During the 1970s there was some irregular movement but a general increase until the 1982 oil crisis. The 1982 oil crisis "shattered" real wages, and they have not recovered since then.[18]

Bortz and Aguila's overview of real wages, though, does not speak directly to middle-class wages. Most studies of employment, wages, and income focus on industrial workers by sector, which does not always provide clear categories for extrapolating the data into larger social classes. For example, Bortz and Aguila cite the example of railroad workers in the 1930s, whose consumption patterns indicate that they enjoyed a standard of living that was closer to the middle classes than that of other industrial workers.[19] Should these workers therefore be deemed middle class?

A basic question remains: What constitutes a real middle-class wage range, over time? This information would help sharpen the criteria for who counts as middle class; it would help us, for example, decide whether or not to count the 1990s clerks included by the *Statistical Abstract of Latin America* studies but excluded by Gilbert. Constructing this wage range would require original research in business archives and labor contracts, taking into account salaries, benefits, and other sources of remuneration, as well as a middle-class price index updated to reflect changing lifestyles. It is beyond the purview of this book to construct this sort of time series. Instead, Table A.2 contains various estimates of middle-class income that appear in scholarly studies of class stratification in Mexico. If and when a middle-class wage-range time series is developed, these estimates might prove bang-on or dead wrong, which in itself would reveal quite a bit about how scholars and analysts imagine the middle classes.

TABLE A.I. Middle-class households as a percentage of all households, 1895–2000 (estimates from various studies)

Study	Wilkie and Wilkins[1]					Lorey and Mostkoff Linares[2]		Samaniego de Villarreal[3]	Gilbert[4]					
Year	1895	1940	1950	1960	1970	1980	1990	1977	1984	1989	1992	1994	1996	2000
Middle class % of total households	7.8	15.8	20.1	21.8	29.1	33.0	38.2	25	16.2	16.1	18.3	19.4	14.7	19.5
Further specification of middle-class households	M, S	M, S	M, S	M, S	M, S	M, S	M, S	L, H	AA	AA	AA	AA	AA	AA
% of total households	1.7, 6.1	3.7, 12.1	6.0, 14.1	6.9, 14.9	9.2, 19.9	12.0, 21.0	12.6, 25.7	20.0, 5.0	13.5	16.0	18.3	19.4	14.7	19.5

Base: national.

AA = Alternative absolute standard

H = High

L = Low

M = Marginal middle class

S = Stable middle class

[1] Wilkie and Wilkins, "Quantifying the Class Structure of Mexico," 585; 1895 and 1940 based on Iturriaga's numbers; 1950, 1960, and 1970 based on income and occupation from census data. Criteria: income and occupation.

[2] Lorey and Mostkoff Linares, "Mexico's 'Lost Decade,'" 1345; based on SPP household survey data. Criteria: Income and occupation.

[3] Samaniego de Villarreal, "Algunas Reflexiones," 59; based on INEGI household survey data (precursor to surveys used by Gilbert). Criteria: income deciles.

[4] Gilbert, *Mexico's Middle Class*, 95; based on INEGI household survey data. Criteria: Relative standard ("upper-white-collar households with incomes over 1.5 times current household median"). Gilbert's alternative absolute standard consists of "upper-white-collar households with real incomes over 1.5 times the 2000 median."

TABLE A.2. Monthly middle-class salaries, 1932–2000

(Note that studies rely on different data and employ different methods.)

Author	Iturriaga (numbers in brackets represent real wages in 1932 pesos)		Cline[1]			González Cosío		Enriqueta Cepeda	Samaniego de Villarreal				
Year	1932	1950	1950			1960	1974	1970	1977				
Class	M	M	Middle			Middle	Middle	Middle				Middle	U
			Min	S	Max				VL	L	L	L	U	
Nominal monthly income (not in constant pesos, not adjusted for inflation)	100 (100)	297 (50)	300	600	9,999	2,693	2,742	2,000–5,000	1,196	3,500	6,991	11,787	22,137
In historical US dollars[2]	32	34	35	69	1,157	216	219	160–400	53	155	309	521	979
Equivalent in year 2000 US dollars[3]	970	346	356	702	11,800	1,460	821	719–1,800	156	455	907	1,530	2,870

Author	Gilbert (A): Real middle-class median household income (in 2000 pesos)					Gilbert (B): Spectrum of middle-class household income		
Year	1984	1989	1994	1996	2000	2000		
						Middle		
Class	M	M	M	M	M	Min	C	H
Nominal monthly income (not in constant pesos, not adjusted for inflation)	8,450	10,250	13,700	8,400	12,300	6,000	15,000	30,000–40,000
In historical US dollars[2]	893	1,084	1,448	888	1,300	634	1,586	
Equivalent in year 2000 US dollars[3]	1,550	1,480	1,740	1,000	1,300			3,172–4,229

Sources: Iturriaga, *Estructura social y cultural de México*, 79; based on Oficina Técnica del Presupuesto de la Secretaría de Hacienda data. Cline, *Mexico: Revolution to Evolution*, 116; based on 1956 Secretaría de Economía household survey data. González Cosío, "Clases y estrados sociales, 62, 64; based on Departamento de Muestreo of the SIC household survey data. Enriquieta Cepeda, "Papel del crédito," 3; based on Banco de México and Universidad Autónoma de Nuevo León household survey data from the city of Monterrey. Samaniego de Villarreal, "Algunas reflexiones," 59; based on SPP household survey data (precursor to INEGI data used by Gilbert). Gilbert, *Mexico's Middle Class*, 95–96 (A), 13(B); the former based on INEGI household surveys, the latter on INEGI household surveys and interviews.

C = Comfortable middle-class income
H = High middle-class income
L = Low
M = Middle
Max = Maximum middle-class income
Min = Minimum middle-class income
S = Stable middle-class income
U = Upper
VL = Very low

[1] Wilkie and Wilkins based their series on Cline's minimum of 300 pesos, but note Cline's further elaboration.

[2] Using "Measuring Worth" historical exchange rate calculator to ascertain the historical US dollar equivalent of the Mexican pesos; www.measuringwealth.org/exchangeglobal (May 2010).

[3] Using "Measuring Worth" consumer price index to compute the relative value of the historical US dollar amount in year 2000 US dollars; www.measuringworth.com/uscompare (May 2010).

Notes

1. The PRI's belief that, during the midcentury boom, the middle classes represented prosperity and stability is evident in a 1988 document in which party functionaries discuss the past, present, and future of the Mexican middle classes. See "Proyecto de 'Clases Medias,'" August 1986, MMH, c. 215, exp. 5, AGN. This document is analyzed in Chapter 6.

2. For helpful biographical sketches of the Mexican middle classes, see Gilbert, *Mexico's Middle Class*, and Gilbert, "Magicians."

3. Here I am drawing on Emilio Coral's work on the middle classes at midcentury; see Coral, "Clase media mexicana."

4. See Whiteford, *Two Cities*, 98–106.

5. Numbers are rounded. These figures are from Wilkie and Wilkens, "Quantifying the Class Structure of Mexico"; and Lorey and Mostkoff Linares, "Mexico's 'Lost Decade,'" which are part of the *Statistical Abstract of Latin America* project. See the Appendix for more on quantifying the middle classes.

6. See Claudio Stern's overview of several estimates, "Notas para la delimitación," 21–25.

7. The statistical estimates raise as many questions as they answer: Who is counted as middle class, and why? How reliable are the data? Does the label "middle class" correspond with how different people identify themselves? Such questions are addressed in the Appendix.

8. See the Appendix for the politics of quantifying social differentiation.

9. Samaniego de Villarreal, "Algunas reflexiones," 59.

10. For analysis of the theoretical overlap of and differences between "middle class," "bourgeois," and "petit bourgeois," see Wallerstein, "Bourgeois(ie)"; Williams, *Keywords*, 45–48, 60–68. For analysis of the function of "small" and "medium" descriptors in postrevolutionary Mexico, see Schers, *Popular Sector*, 65. Of course, a comparable multiplicity of terms exists to describe the poor and the wealthy: working classes, lower classes, lumpen, peasants; and aristocrats, capitalists, upper classes, among others.

11. I am drawing on Thompson, *Making of the English Working Class*, 9–13; Williams, *Keywords*, 61. I avoid the terms "bourgeoisie" and "petite bourgeoisie" except when referencing their use by historical actors or scholars in primary and secondary sources.

12. Most scholars of the middle classes in twentieth-century Mexico and elsewhere agree that these groups must be studied using a creative combination of analytical categories. My approach is inspired by Robert Johnston, historian of the United States, who calls for an "anti-definition" of the middle classes. Johnston

emphasizes the need to move away from strict delineations of who is "in" and who is "out": "To examine middling folks as they have constituted (or not constituted) a class *over time* requires giving up the illusion that sociological abstraction can aid us much beyond providing interesting ideas to reflect upon and use in a highly flexible manner. We must therefore blend together an eclectic mix of occupation and ideology, gender and culture, property and politics, in order to bring out a middle class—really, middle class*es*—with any significant complexity and historical meaning." Johnston, *Radical Middle Class*, 12 (emphasis in original).

13. Here I am drawing on Holloway, "Red Rose." See also Roux and Ávalos Tenorio, "Rupturas," who use Holloway's argument for analysis of the 1980s crisis (12).

14. To borrow the words of Corrigan and Sayer, "Capitalism is not just an economy, it is a regulated set of social forms of life" (*Great Arch*, 188).

15. Combining these methods allows historians to study the economy in Latin America in its many dimensions; separate cultural, economic, and political approaches to studying the economy (and other topics) risks reductionism. In this endeavor, I am responding to calls to integrate economic, political, and cultural approaches to Mexican history. After a generation of productive polemics, it is time to experiment with fusion. See, for example, Van Young, "New Cultural History"; Van Young, "Lugar de encuentro." On reductionism in political economy and cultural history, see Viotti da Costa, "New Publics." On the reductionism of the dependency theory approach, see Haber, "Economic Growth." Ironically, in his critique of dependency theory, Haber demonstrates a reductionist view of new economic history; on this, see Knight, "Export-Led Growth," 137–141.

16. In this regard, this book is part of a growing body of scholarship committed to explicit, sustained examination of the middle classes in Mexico, Latin America, and beyond. But it also departs from these studies. Most of these studies examine specific groups (such as professional agronomists or white-collar bureaucrats) in order to speak of the middle classes. Or they analyze the middle classes principally through one category of analysis (such as gender or education) to discuss the contested nature of class formation. Soledad Loaeza's *Clases medias y política en México*, which analyzes the middle classes through the lens of education, serves as an anchor for studies of the middle classes in twentieth-century Mexico. Her research focuses on the midcentury, but she offers a helpful overview of the earlier period. Work by Emilio Coral on American cultural influence, Susanne Eineigel on urban politics, Michael Ervin on agronomists, Dennis Gilbert on household consumption, and Susie Porter on female civil servants—all analyze the middle classes. See Coral, "Clase media mexicana"; Eineigel, "Revolutionary Promises"; Ervin, "1930 Agrarian Census"; Gilbert, *Mexico's Middle Class*; and Porter "Espacios burocráticos." For studies on other parts of Latin America, see, for example, Adamovsky, *Historia de la clase media argentina*; López, "Beautiful Class"; López and Weinstein, *Making of the Middle Class*; O'Dougherty, *Consumption Intensified*; Owensby, *Intimate Ironies*; Parker, *Idea of the Middle Class*; Parker and Walker, *Latin America's Middle Class*; Silva, "Origins of White-Collar Privilege"; and Visacovsky and Garguin, *Moralidades, economías e identidades de clase media*.

17. I am following E. P. Thompson's approach to class as a historical experience and relationship rather than a thing. Thompson, *Making of the English Working Class*, 9–13.

18. Womack, "Spoils of the Mexican Revolution," 677. The Mexican Revolution was a tumultuous process that involved different driving thrusts, which are often identified as (a) Emiliano Zapata's campesino army and Pancho Villa's northern army, both of which fought for autonomy, land rights, and social betterment; (b) liberals such as Francisco Madero, who fought for greater political representation; and (c) the more socially committed constitutionalist liberals and nationalist entrepreneurs, such as Álvaro Obregón. Crudely put, of all the revolutionary factions, it was the last group who came to dominate the postrevolutionary state during the period of political consolidation of the 1920s and 1930s and afterward. This is necessarily a very general sketch of the various revolutionary factions. The Mexican Revolution and its political consolidation in the 1920s and 1930s have been the focus of extensive historical study. See, for example, González y González, *San José de Gracia*; Joseph, *Revolution from Without*; Katz, *Life and Times*; Knight, *Mexican Revolution*; and Womack, *Zapata*.

19. Vargas Llosa, "Mexico: The Perfect Dictatorship," 23. I am indebted to Ingrid Bleynat for our conversations about the workings of the PRI's system and the midcentury boom; the following analysis has benefited immeasurably from her insight and critical readings.

20. No doubt, this summary does not do justice to the politics of the 1920s, 1930s, and 1940s, from which the PRI eventually emerged in 1946 (and in which the middle classes played a central role). For more information, see, for example, Bertaccini, *Régimen priísta*; Carr, *Marxism and Communism*; Hamilton, *Limits of State Autonomy*; Hernández Chávez, *Mecánica cardenista*; Knight, "Rise and Fall of Cardenismo"; Meyer, "Revolution and Reconstruction"; and Niblo, *Mexico in the 1940s*.

21. The National Revolutionary Party (Partido Nacional Revolucionario, or PNR) governed Mexico from 1929 to 1938, and the Mexican Revolutionary Party (Partido Revolucionario Mexicano, or PRM) from 1938 to 1946. The PRI was founded in 1946 and ruled until its defeat in the 2000 presidential elections. Although the transitions from PNR to PRM to PRI represented tensions within the political élite and were more than mere name changes, the 1929–2000 period can be conceptualized as an extended political dynasty, fraught with internal divisions but durable.

22. For more on the PRI's structure, see Garrido, *Partido de la Revolución*.

23. This general sketch of the PRI's midcentury rule will likely be challenged and complicated by an emerging literature on this period. See Alegre, "Contesting the 'Mexican Miracle'"; Bachelor, "Edge of Miracles"; Gillingham, "Force and Consent"; McCormick, "Political Economy of Desire"; Navarro, *Political Intelligence*; Padilla, *Rural Resistance*; and Smith, *Pistoleros*.

24. See, for example, Octavio Paz's description of the PRI's system in "The Other Mexico."

25. The term "Mexican Miracle" is a play on the German economic "Miracle" that followed the Second World War. In 1970, economist Clark Winton Reynolds

described the "widely heralded 'Mexican Miracle' of today," referring to Mexico's 1940–1970 economic growth. Likewise, in an influential textbook, historians Aguilar Camín and Meyer describe how, after 1940, "observers and analysts started to talk unblushingly about 'the Mexican Miracle.'" While I have been unable to pinpoint the first use of the term "Mexican Miracle," it appears in numerous other textbooks and scholarly monographs as a shorthand reference to the 1940–1970 period. Reynolds, *Mexican Economy*, 1–3; Aguilar Camín and Meyer, *In the Shadow of the Mexican Revolution*, 162. For a discussion of how analysts embraced the idea of a miracle, even though the reality of underdevelopment belied such optimism, see Carmona et al., *Milagro mexicano*.

26. Stephen Niblo argued this almost twenty years ago, but we still need more studies of the midcentury economy that examine some widely assumed historical categories, such as "miracle" and an "ISI model." Julio Moreno's analysis of Sears in Mexico and economic nationalism represents one exciting move in this direction, although focused on a slightly earlier period. Stephen Haber et al. have questioned just how miraculous the "Miracle" really was, at least in comparison with Spain, Portugal, and Greece; since it is not the main focus of their work, this argument could be taken up by other historians. While the midcentury decades are not the subject of this book, the messy history of economic policy in the 1970s and 1980s suggests that projecting an organizing logic onto the earlier period could be wishful thinking and a tautological trap. Haber et al., *Mexico since 1980*, 55–57; Moreno, *Yankee Don't Go Home!*; Niblo, *War, Diplomacy, and Development*.

27. My description of the middle classes and the PRI from the 1920s to the 1960s is influenced by Soledad Loaeza's work, especially *Clases medias y política en México*. We still need more studies of the middle classes during these decades. The history of the Mexican middle classes, of course, begins before the postrevolutionary period. Many scholars date the emergence of the modern middle classes with the professionals of the nineteenth-century dictatorship of Porfirio Díaz. These new middle classes (see discussion below on "old" versus "new" middle classes) played an important role in the Porfiriato and the Revolution and then thrived in the postrevolutionary period. Coral, "La clase media mexicana"; Loaeza, *Clases medias y política*, 42–46. For studies of the middle classes in earlier periods, see the essays in Mentz, *Movilidad social de sectores medios*.

28. Michael Jiménez discusses the growth of the middle classes in Latin America more generally. He describes how the middle classes benefited from the growth of leviathan states—large and formidable states—across Latin America in the twentieth century, in the form of direct employment and in the networks of loyalty they generated. The middle classes often looked to the state to protect their interests from the conflicts between workers and capital and from the ravages of an open market. In doing so, they, in turn, helped to propagate and legitimate the state. The Latin American middle classes, were, in Jiménez's words, "Leviathan's children." Jiménez, "Elision of the Middle Classes," 218–219.

29. Numbers are rounded. Coplamar, *Necesidades esenciales en México: Educación*, 54–58, esp. table 3.22. See also Loaeza, "Clases medias mexicanas," 225–227.

30. Loaeza, *Clases medias y política*, 129–130.

31. Ibid., 130.

32. Peter Smith argues that "the Revolution redistributed political power among relatively dispossessed segments of the nation's middle class." Smith, *Labyrinths of Power*, 102.

33. The CNOP emerged, in part, as a response to political mobilization by the middle classes in the late 1930s. Alarmed by the leftward turn of the party during the presidency of Lázaro Cárdenas, several independent groups formed to influence the 1940 elections, in order to thwart any further move to the left. In this context, politicians began the process of bringing the diffuse middle classes into the Mexican Revolutionary Party (PRM)'s corporatist structures. In 1938, public bureaucrats were the first middle-class group to be incorporated, with the creation of the Federation of Unions of Government Workers (Federación de Sindicatos de Trabajadores al Servicio del Estado, or FSTSE). This was a response to both middle-class discontent and grassroots activity, as well as an extension of the general policy to organize politically as many social groups as possible. Bertaccini, *Régimen priísta*, 224–235; Schers, *Popular Sector*, 13–15.

34. Schers, *Popular Sector*, 18–19. See also Smith, *Labyrinths of Power*, 218.

35. For a list of the CNOP's different branches and member organizations, see Schers, *Popular Sector*, 18–19, 161–162. On institutional flexibility, see ibid., 65.

36. Ibid., 73–75. Importantly, Schers argues, public employees were in the popular sector, not the worker sector; this prevented what might have been a powerful alliance between working-class and middle-class workers. Ibid., 16.

37. Soledad Loaeza argues that, after the creation of the CNOP, the middle classes held the Mexican state "hostage." Accordingly, the influence of workers and campesinos on the state diminished. Loaeza, "Clases medias mexicanas," 230.

38. This sketch of the relationship between the middle classes, the PRI, and the state raises questions about the makeup of the PRI and the nature of the state. These questions are complicated by the one-party PRI system, for a commonsensical description could hold that the PRI was the state and the state was the PRI. In this analysis, the state is both a set of ideas and a set of practices. It is the organization and apparatus of government, with a monopoly over the legitimate use of force (dominated by the PRI from 1946 to 2000). It is also the PRI's ideational construct of the Institutional Revolution: a stable, prosperous, middle-class Mexico. This may have been a fantasy, but it was a powerful one that the PRI sought to realize; it was a "way the world was made sense of." Corrigan and Sayer, *Great Arch*, 1–2.

39. In this way, the growth of the middle classes profoundly altered the built environment of the capital and other cities. See Garay Arellano, *Modernidad habitada*; Ballent, "El arte de saber vivir"; and Noelle, *Mario Pani*.

40. Coral, "La clase media mexicana," 107–116. Julio Moreno's work on the Sears department store in Mexico details the complicated process by which American brands, products, and lifestyles entered Mexico. Moreno, *Yankee Don't Go Home!*

41. Almond and Verba, *Civic Culture*, 423.

42. Ibid., 420–423. See also Dennis Gilbert's analysis of this survey, *Mexico's Middle Class*, 64–66. Citing the survey, Gilbert writes: "The middle class 'wor-

shipped' education, and to those on the lower margins of the middle class education was 'a magic passport for social mobility'" (27).

43. González Casanova, "México: El ciclo de una revolución agraria," 27; González Casanova, *Democracy in Mexico*, 109–119.

44. González Casanova, *Democracy in Mexico*, 114.

45. Contending interpretations of Mexico's so-called Miracle—how miraculous was it? for whom was it miraculous?—represent different historical and ethical analyses of progress. Some analysts choose to emphasize Mexico's economic and political advances during the midcentury decades; others focus on inequality and violence. González Casanova describes how conservatives, establishment politicians, impatient radicals, old revolutionaries, party functionaries, and business executives put forth different arguments about the so-called Miracle, often related to their distinct political agendas. Ibid., 110.

46. These examples illustrate both the strength and the weakness of the PRI: the state had access to violence but was forced to use it. Padilla, *Rural Resistance*; Alegre, "Contesting the 'Mexican Miracle.'"

47. New historical studies on this period, which directly address the nature of the PRI's hegemony, are being published at an exciting rate. Synthetic and paradigmatic analysis promises to soon be a productive enterprise. See note 23 above. Until then, Alan Knight's metaphor of a "Swiss cheese PRI" (full of holes) is helpful. Knight characterizes the midcentury PRI state as "chronically faltering but remarkably durable." Knight, "Historical Continuities," 93–95.

48. Almond and Verba, *Civic Culture*, 422. Dennis Gilbert also analyzes Almond and Verba's Civic Culture survey and concludes that the midcentury middle classes were "loyal, passive, and cynical." Gilbert, *Mexico's Middle Class*, 64–68 (quote from 64).

49. For more on the contradiction between the folk archetype in official rhetoric and the PRI's goals, see Zolov, "Discovering a Land."

50. Soledad Loaeza describes how, after 1940, the PRI adopted middle-class values without publicly renouncing the ideology of the earlier postrevolutionary years that had upheld the interests of workers and campesinos. In his analysis of how ruling classes rule, Göran Therborn argues that bourgeois ruling classes depend upon the reproduction of representations that conflate the bourgeoisie and the nation-state: "In the general bourgeois format representation of the ruling class has to be expressed as *national representation*." Loaeza, *Clases medias y política*, 124; Therborn, *What Does the Ruling Class Do When It Rules?*, 183.

51. While this book is national in scope, Mexico City is intentionally overrepresented in the analysis, especially in Chapters 1 and 6. The capital city dominated midcentury fantasies about a modern, middle-class Mexico; studying the end of these fantasies necessitates an emphasis on Mexico City.

52. Carey, *Plaza of Sacrifices*, 49–50; Rodríguez Kuri, "Los primeros días." The students came from a broad spectrum of middle-class families. Those at the IPN tended to come from the emerging and lower-middle classes, while students at the UNAM generally belonged to the higher echelons of the middle classes and the élite. For analysis of the different student populations at the two institutions, see Pensado, "Political Violence and Student Culture," 24–84.

53. Poniatowska, *Massacre in Mexico*, 53; Zolov, *Refried Elvis*, 120–123.

54. Carey, *Plaza of Sacrifices*, 51–54.

55. Ibid., 82–83.

56. Poniatowska, *Massacre in Mexico*, 5–6, 17.

57. Carey, *Plaza of Sacrifices*, 122–133.

58. Womack, "The Spoils," 683.

59. For more on the Olympics, see Rodríguez Kuri, "Hacia México 68"; and Zolov, "Showcasing the 'Land of Tomorrow.'"

60. For analysis of the events of 2 October 1968, see Carey, *Plaza of Sacrifices*, 134–151; and Poniatowska, *Massacre in Mexico*, 169–323.

61. Paz, "The Other Mexico," 235.

62. See influential textbooks such as Aguilar Camín and Meyer's *In the Shadow of the Mexican Revolution* and Meyer, Sherman, and Deed's *The Course of Mexican History*. This analysis also appears in books that consciously avoid emphasis on 1968, such as Dawson's *First World Dreams: Mexico since 1989*.

63. See Foweraker and Craig, *Popular Movements and Political Change*; and Semo, *Transición interrumpida: México 1968–1988*. These origin stories were prominent themes in the fortieth anniversary commemoration events in the summer and fall of 2008 (field notes and recordings in possession of author). In contrast, some scholars emphasize continuity rather than disruption or inception, analyzing the students' political protest and the PRI's violence in a longer history of resistance and repression. Jaime Pensado argues that the 1968 movement did not constitute a major break with previous student politics but instead belonged to a longer history of student political culture that emerged as early as the mid-1950s. Pensado, "Political Violence and Student Culture."

64. Agustín; *Tragicomedia mexicana 2*, 7.

65. Paz, "The Other Mexico," 260, 271. The social reality outside the middle classes was dismal. As Jeffrey Bortz characterizes the boom years: "The highly successful industrialization after 1940 modernized the country without lifting it from underdevelopment." Bortz, "Effects of Mexico's Postwar Industrialization," 229.

66. For analysis of the exhaustion of ISI, see Moreno-Bird and Ros, *Development and Growth in the Mexican Economy*, 115–123, 140–142. One of the first analyses of this phenomenon appeared in 1963 with Raymond Vernon's *Dilemma of Mexico's Development*, esp. 182–183. It is important to note that there exists no consensus on whether or to what degree the Mexican economy was in trouble. For different arguments about the economic problems of the late 1960s, especially in terms of underemployment and anemic public revenue, for example, see Reynolds, "Why Mexico's 'Stabilizing Development' Was Actually Destabilizing," 1005–1006; Looney, "Mexican Economic Performance," 61–65; and Buffie and Krause, "Mexico: 1958–86," 141–145. I do not advance a new argument about structural economic problems in the 1960s; instead, I follow Hirschman's diagnosis that a combination of slowdown and the perception of crisis can lead to crisis. Doubts about economic crisis, however, were dispelled by the early 1970s, when the inflation rate began to rise significantly and the peso was devalued for the first time since 1954. Hirschman, "Political Economy of Import-Substituting Industrialization"; Hirschman, "Search for Paradigms," 336–338.

67. Hirschman, "Political Economy of Import-Substituting Industrialization," 3.

68. Ibid., 12. Indeed, taking the example of Brazil, Hirschman suggests that the perceived ISI exhaustion was the result of political rather than economic crisis. Likewise, Jeremy Adelman has posited that the "exhaustion thesis" was an inaccurate interpretation of Latin American economies, especially with regard to South American economies. Adelman argues that in the early 1970s the exhaustion thesis became a popular deus ex machina used to explain conflicts that were primarily political rather than economic in nature. Adelman, "International Finance and Political Legitimacy," 119–121; Hirschman, "Political Economy of Import-Substituting Industrialization," 9.

69. Hirschman, "Search for Paradigms," 336–337.

70. Pozas Horcasitas, "Democracia en blanco"; Soto Laveaga, "The 'Emperor' Has a New Lab Coat."

71. Soto Laveaga, "The 'Emperor' Has a New Lab Coat."

72. Ibid.

73. López Cámara, *El desafío*, 92. López Cámara, a social scientist and author of several books on the middle classes, was a member of the MLN (Movimiento de Liberación Nacional) in the 1960s and later became an official in the CNOP. He consulted with the Echeverría and López Portillo administrations on how to incorporate the middle classes back into the PRI. These biographical details come from Schmidt, *Deterioration of the Mexican Presidency*, 89. On economic crisis and job prospects for university students at the end of the 1960s, see also ibid., 20–21, 55.

74. Cuevas Díaz, *Partido Comunista Mexicano*, 44–48.

75. López Cámara, *El desafío*, 100.

76. "[The middle class] is a diffuse and national force, active and critical. Because it sows nonconformity and rebelliousness, it is destined to awaken and inspire the other groups and classes to the extent that, in the near future, the persistence of the crisis aggravates the political struggles. These are certain to come, and it is not worth asking whether or not there will be great political battles in Mexico but rather whether they will be public or clandestine, pacific or violent." Paz, "The Other Mexico," 268.

77. López Cámara, *El desafío*, 57.

78. Wallerstein examines the "new" salaried middle classes, who are middle class in terms of consumption habits and lifestyle but less so in terms of the criteria of capital and property ownership; thus they are not classically bourgeois. According to Wallerstein, the classic bourgeois dreamed of becoming an aristocrat and living off rent. In twentieth-century Mexico, this would be equivalent to a member of the middle classes aspiring to join the wealthy upper-class minority. In his analysis: "[The new middle classes] live off their advantages attained in the present, and not off privileges they have inherited from the past. Furthermore, they cannot translate present income (profit) into future income (rent). That is to say, they cannot one day represent the past off which their children will live. Not only do they live in the present, but also so must their children and their children's children. This is what bourgeoisification is all about—the end of the possibility of aristocratisation (that fondest dream of every classical propertied bourgeois), the end of constructing a past for the future, a condemnation of living in the present." Wallerstein, "Bourgeois(ie)," 340.

79. Paz, "The Other Mexico," 267. The relatively small size of the Mexican middle classes underlined their precarious privilege and accentuated their fears of class conflict and the threat of falling into the lower classes. These fears were an essential aspect of the reciprocal relationship between the middle classes and the PRI. Political stability was paramount to their self-preservation and reproduction, especially in the context of increasing inequality during the Mexican Miracle.

80. Alan Knight describes how, prior to the 1970s, crises in Mexico tended to be political in nature; starting in the 1970s, economic crises became more common. Likewise, Jonathan Heath describes a "crisis generation" of Mexicans born in the 1970s, 1980s, and 1990s, who never experienced a continuous economic boom or even an extended period of low inflation and a stable exchange rate. Knight, "Mexico and Latin America in Comparative Perspective," 77; Heath, *Mexico and the Sexenio Curse*, 1–3.

81. Agustín, *Tragicomedia mexicana 2*, 7.

82. The literature on the role of crisis in capitalist accumulation is abundant. For an analysis of crisis and the shift from postwar Fordist accumulation to what he terms "flexible accumulation" (or neoliberalism), see David Harvey's *Condition of Postmodernity*, 119–197. Naomi Klein has argued that the shift to neoliberalism (or free-market fundamentalism, in her words) required more severe crises than earlier shifts between other modes of accumulation. She terms this need for severe crisis the "shock doctrine." Klein, *Shock Doctrine*, 25.

83. Gramsci, *Prison Notebooks*, 2:32–33.

84. There are not many scholarly analyses of the CNOP, and what exists is uneven in quality. David Schers's 1972 doctoral dissertation on the popular sector remains unsurpassed. Diane Davis's *Urban Leviathan* adds to Schers's work, analyzing the history of the CNOP in the context of Mexico City's urban politics and extending the period under study through the late 1980s. Tiziana Bertaccini's *Régimen priísta frente a las clases medias* is a promising attempt, with a new focus on public discourse, but it is limited by the undigested presentation of interview material. We need more analysis of this crucial organization, especially during its midcentury heyday. Such an endeavor must confront a major methodological challenge: to date, there is no available archive of the CNOP. Given this, creative research strategies are needed that move beyond analysis of speeches and interviews. Speeches and other published primary sources are collected in Instituto de Capacitación Política (Partido Revolucionario Institucional), *Historia documental de la CNOP*; Osorio Marbán, *Sector popular del PRI*.

85. See, for example, Brunk, "Remembering Emiliano Zapata"; and Middlebrook, *Paradox of Revolution*.

86. Johnston, *Radical Middle Class*, 3–10.

87. Gilbert Joseph discusses a similar tendency in the study of bandits in Latin American history, and Mark Berger analyzes how different international intellectuals see what they want to see in the 1994 Zapatista rebellion. Joseph, "On the Trail"; Berger, "Romancing the Zapatistas."

88. Eric Van Young uses the expression "to see someone not seeing" to describe the difficulties of writing about the poor, marginalized, or subaltern, who do not often appear in the historical record. Recently, though, scholars seem unwilling to ana-

lyze those historical actors who are squarely at the forefront of the extant historical record. Ironically, one of the proposals of the subaltern studies school was to recover precisely this cadre of actors (the lower-level colonial administrators, for example). Somewhere, somehow, we have lost sight of them. Van Young, "To See Someone."

89. Wallerstein points out that there is remarkable similarity among most theorists, whether liberal, conservative, or Marxist, vis-à-vis the middle classes, the bourgeoisie, or the petite bourgeoisie. According to Wallerstein, theorists who diverge radically in most other respects share many of the same stereotypes and myths about the middle classes. They concur that the middle classes appear to be growing (from the eighteenth century, and perhaps earlier) and that they are drawn to a wide array of political ideologies. Theorists also generally agree on a historical distinction between the "old" middle classes (such as small producers, artisans, independent professionals, farmers, and yeomen peasants) and the "new" middle classes (such as clerical and technical workers, education workers, civil servants, and so forth). But beyond this, the middle classes have been undertheorized. Wallerstein, "Bourgeois(ie)," 326–334.

90. Dirección Federal de Seguridad (or DFS) and Dirección General de Investigaciones Políticas y Sociales (or DGIPS) collections. These two collections are the Ministry of the Interior (Gobernación) secret police archive, which was opened to the public in 2002.

91. Aguayo, *La charola*, 40, 76.

92. Ibid., 124. My analysis of this archive draws on Aguayo's research. For a political history of the intelligence agencies, see Navarro, *Political Intelligence*, 150–186. For historical analysis of specific spy reports, as well as a consideration of the methodological challenges and historiographical impact of this archive, see Padilla and Walker, "Spy Reports."

93. Quoted in Aguayo, *La charola*, 230.

94. Quoted in ibid.

95. Ibid., 36.

96. Ibid., 38, 68, 124.

97. Ibid., 124.

98. Ibid., 50, 68, 110–115.

99. Ibid., 17–38.

CHAPTER 1

1. "Visita que realiza el día de hoy . . . ," 14 March 1975, DGIPS, c. 1161B, exp. 3, AGN.

2. On the *porra*, see Pensado, "Political Violence and Student Culture."

3. "Visita que realiza el día de hoy . . . ," 14 March 1975, DGIPS, c. 1161B, exp. 3, AGN.

4. Ibid.

5. Ibid.

6. "Diversas opiniones que se han . . . ," 17 March 1975, DGIPS, c. 1161B, exp. 3, AGN.

7. Sociedad Nacional de Periodistas y Escritores, *Boletín Semanal*, 1 April 1975, DGIPS, c. 1101B, exp. 4, AGN.

8. I use the term "rebel generation" somewhat ironically, because the term "generation" risks eliding differences within a group, thus making critical analysis more difficult. I discuss some of the challenges of writing a critical history of the rebel generation at the end of this chapter.

9. López Cámara, *El desafío*, 47, 89. See also Octavio Paz's predictions of upheaval among the middle classes, discussed in the Introduction.

10. Davis, *Urban Leviathan*, 193–194.

11. Bertaccini suggests that the CNOP and PRI began declining in the 1970s, because of the bureaucratization of political posts, wherein administrative qualifications replaced political ones. This claim, however, is not sufficiently developed. Davis provides a more rigorous explanation for the slow erosion of the CNOP's influence in the 1970s and 1980s. Focusing on the capital city, Davis argues that one of the CNOP's principal functions—to represent the interests of urban residents—was challenged by two factors: First, the massive urbanization of Mexico City made resolution of urban issues increasingly difficult and thus diminished the appeal of the CNOP. Second, recurrent ideas about (and tentative steps toward) urban democracy threatened the CNOP's monopoly on political representation. Both factors encouraged urban residents to turn increasingly to new social movements. Finally, although Schers does not point to a decline, he suggests that the CNOP faced several challenges in the early 1970s: a generalized crisis of legitimacy after the 1968 massacre, internal tensions among different groups under the umbrella of the CNOP, and threats from new organizations, especially the Congress of Labor (Congreso de Trabajo), which was created in 1966. Bertaccini, *Régimen priísta*, 375–376; Davis, *Urban Leviathan*, 236–237, 252–253, 272; Schers, *Popular Sector*, 24–25, 137–146.

12. Davis, *Urban Leviathan*, 189–197.

13. Mendoza Rojas, *Conflictos de la UNAM*, 146–152. As Mendoza Rojas notes (146), the UNAM's budget increased by 1,688 percent between 1968 and 1978. The education reform also included a controversial textbook, discussed in the next chapter.

14. Despite these reforms, the education system remained vertical, paternalistic, and at heart elitist. Teachers unions continued to be riddled with corruption. And, alongside the education reform, Echeverría fostered (and subsidized) a campaign of ongoing *porra* violence within the schools to terrorize the students. That said, programs such as Echeverría's democratic opening and the education reform—combined with the continued violence—did succeed in placating much leftist discontent. As José Agustín writes, "By the end of the 1970s the students in Mexico City, as [Echeverría] wanted, had become depoliticized and wouldn't mobilize again until 1986." The 1986 student movement is discussed in Chapter 5. Agustín, *Tragicomedia mexicana 2*, 54.

15. Ibid., 15. Echeverría's use of indigenous tropes harked back to President Lázaro Cárdenas and thus served a double political function. They also had symbolic value in the provinces, especially in indigenous rural areas.

16. "Momentos antes de iniciarse . . . ," 17 May 1972, DGIPS, c. 659, exp. 5, AGN.

17. "Ho Ho Ho Chimin, LEA LEA LEA a la chingada, Lucio Lucio al gobierno

dale duro, venceremos." "De la Escuela Superior de Economía . . . ," 8 May 1973, DGIPS, c. 705, exp. 2, AGN.

18. Quoted in Hellman, *Mexico in Crisis*, 187–189.

19. Davis, *Urban Leviathan*, 197–202. As Davis argues, these reforms often lacked "teeth" and so they failed to satisfy the middle and popular classes. In Mexico City, for example, reforms also confused the channels of urban politics—the urban poor used the new agencies, the traditional middle classes went to the mayor, and the bureaucrats were left with little to do.

20. "En la preparatoria no. 6 . . . ," 7 June 1971, DGIPS, c. 625, exp. 2, AGN.

21. The narrative of the events of 10 June is reconstructed from a long Ministry of the Interior report on the event and confirmed by testimonies and secondary sources. "Sucesos relacionados con la anunciada . . . ," 10 June 1971, DGIPS, c. 625, exp. 2, AGN.

22. Ibid.

23. The workings of this group are gleaned from the testimonies of former Halcones, told to Ministry of the Interior agents, following their arrests for bank robberies. After the dissolution of the group, many former Halcones lived together and formed bands of armed robbers. They targeted banks and often shouted radical, revolutionary slogans such as: "Viva Genaro Vázquez!" (referring to a rural guerrilla leader in Mexico) to confuse the police and cause them to attribute the robberies to radical guerrilla groups. "En declaraciones . . . ," 26 June 1971, DFS, 21-438-71, legajo 1, h. 1, AGN; "Comisión de estudiantes . . . ," 28 August 1971, DFS, 11-4-71, legajo 143, h. 230–237, AGN; and [no title], 7 January 1972, DFS, 35-24-72, legajo 1, h. 1, AGN. To be sure, this sort of extralegal organization was not new in Mexico. See, for instance, Aguayo, *La charola*; and Pensado, "Political Violence and Student Culture."

24. "Sucesos relacionados con la anunciada . . . ," 10 June 1971, DGIPS, c. 625, exp. 2, AGN.

25. "Los familiares del estudiante . . . ," 11 June 1971, DGIPS, c. 625, exp. 2, AGN.

26. Agustín, *Tragicomedia mexicana 2*, 26.

27. Diane Davis argues that "by staging repression in the name of Echeverría, Alonso Martínez Domínguez sought to remind students of Echeverría's role in the 1968 Tlatelolco student massacre and thereby resuscitate a repressive and antidemocratic image of the president." Davis, *Urban Leviathan*, 201.

28. "En el periódico 'Universidad' . . . ," 25 June 1971, DGIPS, c. 619, exp. 3, AGN.

29. Agustín, *Tragicomedia mexicana 2*, 7.

30. The repression of urban guerrilla groups, despite the president's statements, increased throughout Echeverría's administration. It must also be emphasized that while massacres of students in the main cities ceased, the state engaged in a low-intensity war against campesino activists in many rural areas. See Aviña, "Seizing Hold of Memories in Moments of Danger"; Aviña, "'We Have Returned to Porfirian Times'"; and Blacker-Hanson, "¡La Lucha Sigue!"

31. "En el periódico 'Universidad' . . . ," 25 June 1971, DGIPS, c. 619, exp. 3, AGN.

32. "En las diversas escuelas . . . ," 7 June 1971, DGIPS, c. 625, exp. 2, AGN.

33. "Consecuencias y repercusiones . . . ," 13 June 1971, DGIPS, c. 625, exp. 2, AGN.

34. The student movement was never monolithic, and divisions could be discerned among the radical students in the Committees of Struggle. Rumors about specific leaders abounded and sometimes crystallized in accusations that they were government spies and worked against the movement. Grievances, personal attacks, and ideological differences were often mixed in with specific accusations. For instance, rumors circulated about one student leader who had been spotted with large amounts of cash; he was accused of being in the pocket of the powerful bankers and the private sector. One persistent rumor among the student population held that the private sector had partially financed the student movement to create problems for Echeverría. While specific rumors may have had a basis in fact, as rumors they demonstrate what both students and government spies considered *plausible* at the time; they show how the power nexus was perceived. "En un mitin . . . ," 4 October 1972, DGIPS, c. 665, exp. 1, AGN.

35. "En la Escuela Superior de Economía . . . ," 28 February 1973, DGIPS, c. 711, exp. 1, AGN.

36. No doubt, intelligence reports on these classes could have been exaggerated by Ministry of the Interior intelligence agents in order to create an atmosphere of crisis. "En las diversas clases . . . ," 22 September 1971, DGIPS, c. 620, exp. 3, AGN.

37. "En la Escuela Superior de Economía . . . ," 28 February 1973, DGIPS, c. 711, exp. 1, AGN.

38. "Asuntos universitarios . . . ," 8 July 1971, DFS, 11-4-71, legajo 138, h. 88, AGN.

39. On the liberal-democratic nature of student demands, see Carr, *Marxism and Communism*, 257.

40. "Por medio de la circular . . . ," 14 April 1972, DGIPS, c. 660, exp. 1, AGN.

41. Braun, "Protests of Engagement," 540.

42. The literature on state formation during the early years after the Mexican Revolution details the day-to-day tensions and consensus between the PRI (and its precursors) and a variety of social sectors. This scholarship offers a helpful framework for interpreting the negotiated hegemony that generated common ground between reformist students and the state in the 1970s. See, for example, Joseph and Nugent, eds., *Everyday Forms of State Formation*.

43. Ignacio Salas Obregón, "Acerca del movimiento revolucionario del proletariado estudiantil." I am grateful to Alexander Aviña for sharing this document.

44. Rapprochement between the PRI and moderate students has been little studied. Likewise, scholarly understanding of the post-1968 period has relied upon too-sharp dichotomies between the PRI and its critics, in which students are cast against the state. Interestingly, while many scholars point to the inaccuracy of portraying the early postrevolutionary state as a Leviathan, they do not always shy away from characterizing the Mexican state of the 1970s and 1980s that way. For example, Alan Knight has warned of conflating several decades under the rubric of

"Postrevolutionary Mexico," as this could overstate the power of the pre-1940s state. Knight nevertheless characterizes the Mexican state in the mid-1980s as "today's Leviathan." Why is the post-1968 state not afforded the same degree of complexity? Knight, "Mexican Revolution: Bourgeois?," 26–27, 12.

45. Quoted in Zolov, *Refried Elvis*, 132.

46. Ibid., 132–133.

47. "Mitin efectuado hoy . . . ," 29 November 1973, DGIPS, c. 709, exp. 2, AGN.

48. Agustín, *Tragicomedia mexicana* 2, 30–35. In contrast, Eric Zolov argues that the countercultural movement challenged forms of authoritarianism: "politically conscious students from the middle classes [began] to defy societal norms of fashion as a vehicle for self-expression and criticism." Without denying the significance of these cultural politics, it is important to examine how the hippies were perceived by more activist peers; the tensions the emerged often turned on the class status of many hippies. Zolov, *Refried Elvis*, 9, 104.

49. "Como un experimento social . . . ," 14 September 1971, DGIPS, c. 620, exp. 3, AGN. This accusation was leveled following a controversial music festival; for more on the Avándaro rock festival, see Zolov, *Refried Elvis*, 201–233.

50. Quoted in Zolov, *Refried Elvis*, 111.

51. Zolov, "Expanding Our Conceptual Horizons."

52. "Inspección ocular . . . ," 12 June 1971, DGIPS, c. 625, exp. 2, AGN.

53. Exploring the tensions between students and workers—or students and shantytown residents—does not diminish the value of the work that they accomplished together, nor does it take away from the satisfaction many experienced when working together. Analysis of class tensions adds to our understanding of this collaboration. For a study of the positive aspects of student-resident collaboration in shantytowns, see Massolo, *Por amor y coraje*.

54. The politics of economics education is discussed in greater depth in Chapter 5.

55. Chabal, *Amílcar Cabral*, 174–182 (quote from 174).

56. For more on conditions in these neighborhoods, see Adler de Lomnitz, *Cómo sobreviven los marginados*.

57. "Al estar repartiendo ropa . . . ," 7 November 1971, DGIPS, c. 624, exp. 3, AGN; "Brigadas de ayuda estudiantil . . . ," 31 October 1971, DGIPS, c. 624, exp. 3, AGN; "El comité de lucha . . . ," 28 October 1971, DGIPS, c. 624, exp. 3, AGN; "Alumnos de las preparatorias . . . ," 26 September 1973, DGIPS, c. 707, exp. 1, AGN.

58. This definition of students as middle class is also consistent with analysis in the Ministry of the Interior spy reports, with the testimonies of political actors, and with the works of prominent public intellectuals. In these sources, the categories of student, youth, and middle class are alternatively invoked to describe these historical protagonists. In her study of morality campaigns in 1960s Buenos Aires, Valeria Manzano argues that the category of "youth" often refers to middle-class youths. She argues that the campaigns to defend "youth" from sexual immorality, communism, and the effects of the Cuban Revolution were specifically aimed at middle-class youths: "Not all teenagers and young women and men constituted

'the youth' that the police, the family leagues, the experts, and the new media constructed. Rather, both liberal and conservative actors were interested, fundamentally, in middle-class youths, who allegedly embodied the promises and fears of modernization." Manzano, "Sexualizing Youth," 436.

59. Bourdieu, *The State Nobility*; Bourdieu, *Distinction: A Social Critique*.

60. "Francisco de la Cruz Velazco . . . ," 1 June 1973, DGIPS, c. 705, exp. 3, AGN.

61. Ibid.

62. Members of this group debated the sincerity of Echeverría's democratic opening but decided to take advantage of it and, if it proved insufficient, to take it over (*conquistarla*). Among their concrete ideas, they considered advocating for the nationalization of basic industry and the private banks and fighting against corruption in public administration. Most of these platforms would resonate fairly well with Echeverría's policies. This party might have been a significant intellectual-leftist alliance and a political force to be reckoned with, but in the end, Paz and Fuentes abandoned this project. Heberto Castillo and Demetrio Vallejo formed the Mexican Workers Party (Partido Mexicano de los Trabajadores, or PMT). Echeverría tried to bring the PMT under the PRI umbrella, but when its members resisted, the president directed some of his allies to form the Socialist Workers Party (Partido Socialista de los Trabajadores, or PST), which successfully confused many with its similar name. Agustín, *Tragicomedia mexicana 2*, 106.

63. "Se llevó a cabo el final . . . ," 13 November 1971, DGIPS, c. 625, exp. 3, AGN; "A las 10.45 horas . . . ," 14 November 1971, DGIPS, c. 625, exp. 3, AGN.

64. Ulloa Bornemann, *Surviving Mexico's Dirty War*, 113.

65. Ibid., 54.

66. Ibid., 49. This example calls to mind Mao's refusal to engage in the "bourgeois" practice of brushing his teeth (he preferred to rinse with tea), or his description of barbershops as the "bourgeois stink" of Chiang Kai-shek's ghost. Indeed, Ulloa Bornemann admired Mao (ibid., 50). See MacFarquhar, Wu, and Cheek, *Secret Speeches of Chairman Mao*, 417; and Li, *Private Life of Chairman Mao*, 99.

67. Ulloa Bornemann, *Surviving Mexico's Dirty War*, 47–49.

68. Poniatowska, *Fuerte es el silencio*, 201.

69. "Explosión de un artefacto . . . ," 20 July 1974, DFS, 38-0-74, legajo 2, h. 20–27, AGN; "Llamada anónima . . . ," 11 October 1974, DFS, 11-235-74, legajo 22, h. 268, AGN; "Asalto a una caseta . . . ," 26 June 1973, DFS, 34-9-73, legajo 2, h. 45, AGN; "Comandos armados 'Lacandones' . . . ," 1 March 1973, DFS, 28-15-1-73, legajo 4, h. 30, AGN; "Liga Comunista 23 de Septiembre . . . ," 14 November 1975, DFS, 11-235-75, legajo 34, h. 7, AGN; [no title], 5 September 1975, DFS, 11-235-75, legajo 32, h. 117, AGN.

70. Debray, *Revolution in the Revolution?* Herbert Braun describes middle-class radicals as "members of a generation of politicized young Latin Americans brought up in the wake of the Cuban Revolution who were convinced that a dependent form of capitalism was about to come to an end, [and] felt that they were at the forefront of world historical changes." Braun, "Protests of Engagement," 519–520.

71. Jean Franco describes how "the 'liberated territory' was a power fantasy of

the period of the Cold War, a hope of liberation that would turn first Cuba, then Nicaragua, and finally Chile into political and cultural showcases that bore the burden of high expectations." Franco, *Decline and Fall*, 86. Franco emphasizes middle-class angst: "The guerrilla movements drew the intelligentsia and the middle class into their ranks. . . . [Many] of those who died as a result of the counter-insurgency repression were intellectual workers, many of whom must have been students who wanted to purge themselves of the original sin of being middle-class intellectuals" (88). Franco, however, does not analyze how middle-class angst played out on the ground.

72. The university-factory thesis is formulated, in extensive detail, in Ignacio Salas Obregón, "Acerca del movimiento revolucionario del proletariado estudiantil." See also Castellanos and Jiménez, *México armado*, 206; and Tecla Jiménez, *Universidad, burguesía y proletariado*.

73. Ignacio Salas Obregón, "Acerca del movimiento revolucionario del proletariado estudiantil," 3–4.

74. Ibid., 22.

75. Ibid., 3.

76. "Liga Comunista 23 de Septiembre," 8 January 1974, DFS, 11-235-74, legajo 5, h. 1, AGN.

77. Esteban's perception of Mexico from abroad speaks to the success of the PRI's international leftist rhetoric. For example, the party had defended the Cuban Revolution and later spoke out against the Contra War in Nicaragua.

78. "Liga Comunista 23 de Septiembre," 8 January 1974, DFS, 11-235-74, legajo 5, h. 1, AGN.

79. Ibid.

80. This raises serious methodological questions. These reports may tell us more about the state than about the guerrilla movement. It is likely that agents either over- or underestimated the threat, depending on the political expediency. I am not advancing an argument regarding the size or threat of the movement; rather, I am analyzing these documents for the middle-class background of the guerrilla fighters. As with other studies using police, secret police, or inquisition records, the information gleaned from them is corroborated in a variety of ways. Published, unpublished, and Internet testimonies, along with scholarship on this subject, help round out the information in these intelligence reports. The Ulloa Bornemann and Reyes Peláez memoirs discussed in this chapter are examples of such testimonies.

81. Some groups fought for specific marginalized groups in Mexico. Ordinary citizens sometimes came into contact with these activities. One man testified that members of another group, the Lacandones, kidnapped him and forced him to drive them in their car as they ran errands around the UNAM campus. They told him they were trying to change the destitute conditions of the Indians who lived in the Lacandón forest. "Secuestro de . . . ," 17 January 1973, DFS, 28-15-1-73, legajo 2, h. 215, AGN.

82. "Boletín de prensa . . . ," 15 March 1971, DGIPS, c. 626, exp. 2, AGN.

83. Reyes Peláez, "Al cielo por asalto."

84. "Al parecer, con el fin de crear . . . ," 28 February 1975, DGIPS, c. 1161A, exp. 2, AGN.

85. "Liga Comunista 23 de Septiembre," 13 March 1977, DFS, 11-235-77, legajo 43, h. 105.

86. Ibid.

87. "Grupo afín a Genaro Vázquez Rojas," 21 April 1971, DFS, 100-10-16-2, legajo 3, h. 35–55, AGN. I am grateful to Alexander Aviña for this citation and for his suggestions regarding the tensions between the urban and rural guerrillas.

88. In some ways, the romanticizing of the rural guerrillas is similar to how some of the Mexican hippies abandoned the capital city to "discover" the indigenous, rural Mexico. Zolov, *Refried Elvis*, 138.

89. For work in this direction, see Aviña, "Insurgent Guerrero"; Aviña, "'We Have Returned to Porfirian Times'"; Calderón and Cedillo, *Challenging Authoritarianism in Mexico*; Calderón, "Contesting the State from the Ivory Tower"; Castellanos and Jiménez, *México armado*.

90. "En el centro de la ciudad . . . ," 17 November 1973, DGIPS, c. 709, exp. 2, AGN.

91. Poniatowska, *Massacre in Mexico*, 34.

92. Ibid.

93. Ibid., 79.

94. Ibid., 81.

95. Ibid., 47.

96. A complete bibliography cannot be listed here, but early influential texts include: García Cantú and Barros Sierra, *Javier Barros Sierra*; González de Alba, *Los días y los años*; Monsiváis, *Días de guardar*; Paz, *Posdata*; Poniatowska, *Noche de Tlatelolco*; and Revueltas, *México 68*. For analyses of the 1968 canon, see Braun, "Protests of Engagement"; Frazier and Cohen, "Defining the Space"; and Markarian, "Movimiento estudiantil."

97. While the books, films, and essays that tell and retell the story of 1968 often fall outside the domain of scholarly history (defined as works that cite all references and sources and provide a full bibliography), the heroic narrative has also been reproduced in academic accounts, even by scholars who aim to nuance our understanding of the events. For example, although Elaine Carey advances an analysis of gender politics and chauvinism in the Mexican student movement, she largely replicates the heroic narrative by relying extensively on interviews with the official custodians of the movement. Diana Sorensen also studies gender politics in 1960s Latin America, but she focuses on the most prominent writers of the Boom generation, which produces a celebratory and nostalgic interpretation. This phenomenon is not unique to Mexico or Latin America. For example, Kristin Ross analyzes the "afterlives" of May 1968 in France and argues that the French event has been "overtaken by its subsequent representations." Ross charts how a specific narrative of May '68 emerged that purged the roles of workers, the Old Left, and anticolonial fighters. She argues that May '68 has become a disembodied, vague, and discursive phenomenon, marshalled to serve particular interests. Carey, *Plaza of Sacrifices*; Sorensen, *A Turbulent Decade Remembered*; Ross, *May '68*.

98. Field notes and recordings in possession of author. I attended over fifty commemoration events in Mexico City in the summer and fall of 2008. There were

remarkably few exceptions to this trend, among them talks by Soledad Loaeza, Ariel Rodríguez Kuri, Ilán Semo, Sergio Zermeño, and Eric Zolov.

99. At "A 40 años del 68," a colloquium at the Centro Cultural Universitario UNAM, 2 October 2008. Field notes and recordings in possession of author.

100. With the declassification of Mexican intelligence archives and declassified American intelligence reports, we are getting a fuller picture of the radicalism of the 1960s and 1970s. If a critical history of this radicalism involves moving beyond a heroic narrative, it also involves moving beyond a condemnation of the 1960s and 1970s radicals, especially of the urban guerrillas who turned to violence. The most troubling manifestation of this tendency blames the guerrillas for provoking the state-sponsored torture, murder, and disappearance of tens of thousands of citizens in Latin America. This analysis comes out most clearly in Paul Lewis's *Guerrillas and Generals*, 51–69. Lewis condemns the middle-class guerrillas for suffering existential angst and provoking the military coup in Argentina. For an analysis of the politics of violence, see Alexander Aviña's study of guerrilla movements in 1960s and 1970s Mexico. Aviña challenges scholars who portray the turn to guerrilla violence in Latin America as a deluded imitation of the Cuban Revolution. In contrast, Aviña documents the process of political radicalization as a response to state-sponsored repression and the closing down of legal channels of reform. According to this view, state-sponsored terrorism provoked some to take up arms, not vice versa. Aviña, "Insurgent Guerrero," 26–28, 209–210. For reconstruction and analysis of the events of 1968 based on newly available Mexican intelligence reports, see Aguayo, *1968: Los archivos de la violencia*; Jardón, *El espionaje contra el movimiento estudiantil*; Rodríguez Munguía, *1968: Todos los culpables*. On declassified American intelligence reports, see the National Security Archive's Mexico Project at the George Washington University website.

CHAPTER 2

1. I began my review of the DGIPS intelligence reports with the 1969 reports. The first reports on anonymous, casual conversations appeared among those for 1973. Of course, the secret police had reported gossip beforehand—often indiscriminately mixing rumor and reality; what changed in 1973 was that gossip was reported as gossip. On the confusion between rumor and reality, see Aguayo, *La charola*, 51.

2. Margaret Power has suggested that the scholarly focus on the Left reflects the left-leaning politics of many historians of Latin America, who prefer to study those with whom they agree or sympathize. There is, however, a growing scholarship on the Right in Latin America. Power, *Right-Wing Women in Chile*, 2–4. See also Deutsch, *"Las Derechas"*; Finchelstein, *Transatlantic Fascism*; and González and Kampwirth, *Radical Women in Latin America*. For Mexico, see Pani, *Conservadurismo y derechas*; and Lucas, *Rightward Drift*.

3. On consumption and the middle classes see Davidoff and Hall, *Family Fortunes*; Moreno, *Yankee Don't Go Home!*; and Veblen, *Theory of the Leisure Class*.

4. We should not underestimate the zeal with which the middle classes will defend their class position; however, this force has received little scholarly attention.

Indeed, in a study of various egalitarian movements in the late twentieth century, D. A. Low concludes that the resistance of small landholding peasants to agricultural reform ultimately confounded a variety of attempts to implement egalitarian reform. He stresses the need to understand these middling historical actors: "Whilst the world had come to have a fairly good idea about how to curtail the power of those who lived in big houses at the end of driveways . . . it was still very much at a loss to know how to go about curbing the power of those who lived in the better houses in the village." Low, *Egalitarian Moment*, 126.

5. Soledad Loaeza cautions against assuming the formula "middle classes–inflation–proletarianization–fascism," which posits a clear alliance among the private sector, ecclesiastical élites, and middle classes against the state. Instead, she describes a more ambiguous relationship among these groups. The middle classes, she argues, are indecisive about aligning themselves with the national capitalists and the clergy; for them, the most powerful draw of any such compact stems from their desire for internal order and stability. Loaeza, "Clases medias mexicanas," 235.

6. Agustín, *Tragicomedia mexicana 2*, 90.

7. José Campillo Sainz, 25 July 1973, LEA, c. 814, 714/22, AGN.

8. "Encuesta sobre el precio . . . ," February 1973, DGIPS, c. 704, exp. 1, AGN. While various government agencies had compiled data on urban prices and consumer mood since at least the 1930s, in my review of the DGIPS archive from 1969 on, the first of these reports appeared in 1973, possibly reflecting a growing concern over the economic situation. See Ochoa, *Feeding Mexico*, 32.

9. Reynolds, "Why Mexico's 'Stabilizing Development' Was Actually Destabilizing," 1005–1006. See also Buffie, "Shared Development," 417–418; Looney, "Mexican Economic Performance," 61–65; and Solís, *Economic Policy Reform*, 105–108.

10. Cornelius "Political Economy of Mexico," 87.

11. Echeverría, *Mexico: 1970–1976*, 7; also cited in Basurto, "Late Populism of Luis Echeverría," 97.

12. For more detail on the aims of shared development, see Buffie, "Shared Development," 417–418; Looney, "Mexican Economic Performance," 57; Santacruz, "Algunas apreciaciones," 1; and Solís, *Economic Policy Reform*, 107.

13. For detailed analysis of Echeverría's policies, see Schmidt, *Deterioration of the Mexican Presidency*, 37–69.

14. Ibid., 50.

15. Hellman, *Mexico in Crisis*, 200. These enterprises provided employment for the discontented students of Chapter 1, and in this regard, Echeverría's strategy is often analyzed as a populist episode in Mexican history, one that attempted to tap into the nostalgia for Lázaro Cárdenas's populism. Basurto, "Late Populism of Luis Echeverría," 93–94.

16. Buffie, "Economic Policy and Foreign Debt," 418–419; Elizondo Mayer-Serra, "In Search of Revenue," 165–171; Solís, *Economic Policy Reform*, 67–77.

17. Buffie, "Economic Policy and Foreign Debt," 426; see also Looney, "Mexican Economic Performance," 58–59.

18. Buffie, "Economic Policy and Foreign Debt," 420–421; Looney, "Mexican Economic Performance," 59.

19. Historian Roderic Camp underscores the irony of the tension between

Echeverría and the private sector, because it was mostly based upon the president's rhetoric. According to Camp, Echeverría's reforms did not seriously weaken the private sector. Camp, *Entrepreneurs and Politics*, 25–26. Echeverría's abandonment of progressive tax reform is one example of how he often lacked the ability (and to a certain degree, the will) to follow through on his progressive rhetoric.

20. And then, in order to placate those who opposed more metro construction, Echeverría ordered additional metro cars but held back on building too much new track. This contradictory approach to urban planning, which oscillated between supporting the pro- and antigrowth interests, functioned as a sort of compromise that allowed him to balance these different forces until late 1975 and early 1976. Still, the results were costly. Diane Davis characterizes the end result of Echeverría's oscillation as "urban and national fiscal insolvency" and his urban policies as "inherently inconsistent." Davis, *Urban Leviathan*, 221–225.

21. Camp, *Entrepreneurs and Politics*, 25–26.

22. While Canacintra was technically just one of sixty-two industrial chambers, political scientist Dale Story argues that its membership (some sixty thousand members from the leading industries in the early 1980s) transformed it into a major political and economic force that rivaled Concamin. Story, "Industrial Elites in Mexico," 354–357.

23. Ibid.

24. In 1990, the CCE created the Coordinator of Foreign Trade Businesses (Coordinadora de Organismos Empresariales de Comercio Exterior) to represent the private sector in NAFTA negotiations. According to Ben Schneider, these voluntary associations make the Mexican private sector distinct from other private sectors in Latin America. Schneider, "Why Is Mexican Business So Organized?," 85–100. For a history of the private sector in the early postrevolutionary years, see Gauss, *Made in Mexico*.

25. Camp, *Entrepreneurs and Politics*, 44–46.

26. Agustín, *Tragicomedia mexicana 2*, 37–44.

27. I have taken some liberties when translating the jokes, in an effort to convey the humor to English readers; as Spanish readers will note, the originals include many rich plays on words. "En relación al aumento del presupuesto para el DDF, se dice que obedece a los gastos que tendrá que efectuar para la ampliación de Los Pinos y el Palacio Nacional para que se construyan sendos conventos para guardar todas las madres que se le echan a Echeverría." "En los cafés de Sanborns . . . ," 26 December 1973, DGIPS, c. 710, exp. 3, AGN.

28. Ibid.

29. In his studies of Mexican political humor, Samuel Schmidt points to the Echeverría period as a moment when jokes and rumors acquired significant political importance. Likewise, Soledad Loaeza argues that rumor functions both as a barometer of social tension and, on some occasions, as a catalyst for panic and rebellion, as was the case with the proliferation of rumors toward the end of the Echeverría administration. The analysis in this book adds to these studies in two ways. First, it contributes more jokes and rumors to the archive, with specific information about where they were told and by whom and as part of a broader argu-

ment about middle-class political culture. Second, because these jokes and rumors were culled from the Ministry of the Interior intelligence reports, this material illuminates on-the-ground political culture and the concern this political culture caused among state officials. Schmidt, *Deterioration of the Mexican Presidency*, 9, 110–117, 179–180; Loaeza, "Política del rumor," 575–581.

30. On the value of rumor and gossip as historical sources, Luise White argues: "It was a world we couldn't see if we labeled accounts true or false and stopped there. . . . The power and importance of the made-up and the make-believe are precisely that they are made-up and make-believe: they have to be constituted by what is credible. The imaginary and the fantastic must be constructed out of what is socially conceivable." White, "Telling More," 13–14.

31. "En la taquería . . . ," 2 December 1973, DGIPS, c. 1050, exp. 1, AGN. Note that this document contains reports from the taco shop and the Sanborns café. These documents often include reports from several locations. The titles given are abbreviations of rather long summaries at the top of each report.

32. Ibid. For more on conspicuous consumption, see Chapter 4.

33. "Diariamente en el café . . . ," 18 December 1973, DGIPS, c. 710, exp. 3, AGN.

34. "Preguntó a los parroquianos que si estaban enterados de que en la noche anterior habían querido asesinar a Echeverría, respondiendo algunos que no, replicándoles que le habían echado sal en su cama y que de todos es sabido que solo así matan a los 'babosos.'" "En la taquería . . . ," 2 December 1973, DGIPS, c. 1050, exp. 1, AGN.

35. "Volvió a interrogar a los clientes, si estaban enterados que el presidente había ordenado cerrar todas las taquerias, porque quiere que nuestro país sea un país 'des . . . tacado.'" Ibid.

36. "Para conocer los comentarios . . . ," 8 December 1973, DGIPS, c. 710, exp. 1, AGN.

37. "Existe temor entre cuentahabientes . . . ," 23 October 1973, DGIPS, c. 708, exp. 3, AGN.

38. Sociedad Nacional de Periodistas y Escritores Mexicanos, *Boletín Semanal*, 18 June 1975, DGIPS, c. 1163A, exp. 1, AGN.

39. "Expresiones y aspectos de diversos . . . ," 21 November 1974, DGIPS, c. 1057, exp. 2, AGN.

40. "Hoy se presentaron . . . ," 2 October 1974, DGIPS, c. 1055, exp. 2, AGN.

41. Quoted in Agustín, *Tragicomedia mexicana 2*, 59 (source of citation not given).

42. A comparison with Chilean events must be limited because the army was not a central actor in Mexico, whereas the Chilean army led the September 1973 coup d'état in that country. I do not compare the Chilean and Mexican *cacerolazos*; instead, I argue that the events in Chile inspired emulation, fear, and condemnation among historical actors in Mexico. On the army in Mexico, see Rath, "'Que el cielo.'"

43. Agustín, *Tragicomedia mexicana 2*, 59, 123.

44. Power, *Right-Wing Women in Chile*, 5.

45. Ibid., 193–216.

46. Ibid., 186–188.

47. Power addresses the possibility of a transnational history of these destabilization strategies, especially between Brazil and Chile, but documents are scarce. Power, *Right-Wing Women in Chile*, 161. However, that Chile appeared so often in the speeches, conversations, threats, and pamphlets of both the Left and the Right would seem to indicate that many in Mexico were looking to Santiago de Chile for precedents.

48. "Texto del volante . . . ," 19 November 1973, DGIPS, c. 709, exp. 2, AGN.

49. "Diversas críticas . . . ," 12 October 1973, DGIPS, c. 709, exp. 1, AGN.

50. "Varias amas de casa . . . ," 10 December 1973, DGIPS, c. 710, exp. 1, AGN.

51. "Al parecer el PAN . . . ," 13 November 1974, DGIPS, c. 1057, exp. 1, AGN.

52. "Opiniones que se escuchan . . . ," 18 October 1973, DGIPS, c. 708, exp. 2, AGN.

53. "Estado de Nuevo León," 22 September 1973, DFS, 11-219-73, legajo 4, h. 19–22, AGN.

54. "En Monterrey, Guadalajara, León . . . ," 17 December 1973, DGIPS, c. 710, exp. 3, AGN. Cívico Nacional was purportedly formed by the Unión Nacional de Padres de Familia (National Union of Parents), an organization discussed below. It is unclear whether Solidaridad Orden Libertad existed, but the description of it is similar to other pro-Pinochet groups, such as the Movimiento Unidad Nacional. See "Movimiento de Unidad Nacional apoyará la acción del Gobierno," *La Tercera de la Hora* (Santiago de Chile), 28 April 1975; and "León Vilarín: El MUN no tiene fines políticos," *La Tercera de la Hora* (Santiago de Chile), 28 April 1975. Both are located in the Hemeroteca, Biblioteca Nacional, Santiago de Chile. I am grateful to Alison Bruey for these citations and for her help with the Chilean context.

55. Middlebrook, "Party Politics and Democratization," 7, 19, 24, 28. This is necessarily a brief sketch of the PAN, as in-depth analysis is beyond the scope of this chapter. See, for example, Loaeza, *Partido Acción Nacional*; and Middlebrook, *Party Politics and the Struggle for Democracy*.

56. "El Lic. José Ángel Conchello . . . ," 3 October 1973, DGIPS, c. 708, exp. 1, AGN.

57. "Al parecer el PAN . . . ," 13 November 1974, DGIPS, c. 1057, exp. 1, AGN.

58. In her study of the middle classes, economic crisis, and hyperinflation in Brazil during the 1990s, Maureen O'Dougherty analyzes the feelings of urgency that invaded the "mundane routines of everyday life" (53). According to O'Dougherty, the threats to consumption during the economic crisis undermined the "basis and purpose of their [the middle classes'] social existence" (22–23). She describes how interviewees experienced crisis on two levels, one related to day-to-day consumption, another related to their dreams of being modern and first world: "Looking at the procurement of goods and experiences in unremarkable sites (supermarkets, banks) and the means employed (comparison shopping, stockpiling), as well as at remarkable sites (Disney) and means (e.g., contraband of microwaves), I also draw atten-

tion to the ways that desire and value, and frustration and politics, were developing together, creating a dual vision—of the immediate reality of crisis and the desired reality of the First World" (15).

59. For more on the education reform program, see Chapter 1.

60. Torres Septién, *Educación privada*, 196–201. For more on the 1958–1963 protests, see Loaeza, *Clases medias y política*.

61. Torres Septién, *Educación privada*, 21. For more on the Union of Parents, see Delgado, *El Yunque*; and Loaeza, *Clases medias y política*.

62. Torres Septién, *Educación privada*, 218.

63. Ibid., 222–223.

64. Ibid., 232–241; Villa Lever, *Libros de texto gratuitos*, 169–200.

65. "El mitin programado contra . . . ," 22 June 1975, DGIPS, c. 1163A, exp. 1, AGN.

66. Rodríguez Kuri, "Secretos de la idiosincracia," 35.

67. Ibid., 44–47. Results of the 1966 survey are published in Elu de Leñero, *¿Hacia dónde va la mujer mexicana?*; and Leñero Otero, *Investigación de la familia en México*; and Maldonado, *Los cátolicos y la planeación familiar*. Results of the 1969 survey can be found in Brito Velázquez, *¿Quién escucha al Papa?* For analysis of the two surveys, see Rodríguez Kuri, "Secretos de la idiosincracia," 34–48.

68. Gutmann, *Fixing Men*, 101–102.

69. Quoted in ibid., 106–107.

70. Ibid., 107–108.

71. Ibid., 101–102.

72. Ibid., 11. See also Langland, "Birth Control Pills and Molotov Cocktails"; Necochea López, "Priests and Pills"; and Soto Laveaga, "'Let's Become Fewer.'"

73. "Por medio de pegas . . . ," 19 June 1975, DGIPS, c. 1163A, exp. 1, AGN. In this regard, the textbook controversy could also be analyzed as an episode in the history of secularization and its limitations in modern Mexico. See Rodríguez Kuri, "Urbanización y secularización"; and Rodríguez Kuri, "Proscripción del aura."

74. "El mitin programado contra . . . ," 22 June 1975, DGIPS, c. 1163A, exp. 1, AGN. See also Unión Nacional de Padres de Familia, "Síntesis del memo-randum . . . ," 4 January 1975, DGIPS, c. 1160B, exp. 4, AGN. For more on the Cristero War, see Meyer, *Cristero Rebellion*.

75. "Conferencia de prensa . . . ," 12 February 1975, DGIPS, c. 1161A, exp. 1, AGN.

76. "CNOP," 12 May 1971, DFS, 30-24-71, legajo 8, h. 1–8, AGN.

77. "Hoy se llevó a cabo . . . ," 28 July 1973, DGIPS, c. 707, exp. 2, AGN; "El MRM pretende intervenir . . . ," 6 April 1973, DGIPS, c. 704, exp. 3, AGN.

78. In addition to the 1958–1963 protests described above, even earlier, in the 1930s, President Cárdenas's "socialist education" policy provoked vast protests. See Vaughan, *Cultural Politics in Revolution*. For an overview of textbook controversies from the 1970s through the 1990s, see Mabire, *Políticas culturales y educativas*. For an analysis of controversies over the historical role of the United States in Mexican textbooks, see Tenorio-Trillo, "Riddle of a Common History."

79. "La clase media mexicana es una fuerza que actúa . . . ," *El Nacional*, 5 March 1975.

80. "Fascismos en Latinoamérica," *El Nacional,* 14 February 1975.

81. "La CNOP reprueba al nuevo fascismo . . ." *El Nacional,* 13 February 1975.

82. "CNOP," 4 January 1974, DFS, 30-24-74, legajo 9, h. 78, AGN.

83. López Cámara, *Clase media en la era del populismo,* 52. Similar accusations of fascism appear in other Latin American countries. Margaret Power describes how Allende decried the *cacerolazo* protest as a "fascist upsurge," but she does not analyze the meaning of fascism. Power, *Right-Wing Women in Chile,* 158.

84. As Robert O. Paxton details, the term "fascist" has suffered from overuse. Indeed, in Paxton's "anatomy of fascism" there is little that resembles the campaign of destabilizing rumors, gossip, and jokes that percolated among Mexico's conservative middle classes. Paxton describes five historical stages of fascism: "(1) the initial creation of fascist movements; (2) their rooting as parties in a political system; (3) the acquisition of power; (4) the exercise of power; and finally, in the longer term, (5) radicalization or entropy." By any measure, even Paxton's initial stage of fascism, the conservative middle classes in Mexico were not fascist. Paxton, "Five Stages," 11. In his study of fascism in 1930s and 1940s Argentina, Federico Finchelstein explores its connections with nationalism and anti-Semitism. He describes how fascism and nationalism were often used interchangeably by the historical actors he studies. Finchelstein, "Anti-Freudian Politics," 77 n.2. Although their usage of the term might be inconsistent, inaccurate, or merely vague—in 1970s Mexico and elsewhere—historical actors invoke "fascism" to convey a specific set of images and historical references. PRI leaders, for instance, might have hoped such an insult would spur more generalized resentment, fear, and protest against the Mexican private sector.

85. "Empresarios contra el estado," October 1974, LEA, c. 708, AGN.

86. "En el número 4 del periódico . . . ," 6 May 1974, DGIPS, c. 1052, exp. 3, AGN.

87. The 1970s *cacerolazo* rumors were part of a diffuse conspiracy. On the other end of the spectrum, a network called the Yunque (the Anvil) was a more organized and lasting conspiracy, from the 1950s through at least the early twenty-first century. Indeed, the Yunque is perhaps the most notorious conspiracy of the Right: a network of ultra-Catholics, including members of the National Union of Parents, the PAN, and conservative student organizations, founded during the anticommunist hysteria of the Cold War and oriented toward establishing the City of God in Mexico. See Delgado, *El Yunque;* and the Ministry of the Interior intelligence file on the Yunque.

88. This description draws on Aaronovitch, *Voodoo Histories,* 5–6.

89. Jameson, *Postmodernism,* 38.

90. "En una asamblea informativa . . . ," 28 September 1972, DGIPS, c. 665, exp. 1, AGN; "Aproximadamente mil personas . . . ," 1 October 1973, DGIPS, c. 707, exp. 1, AGN.

91. "El PST emitió . . . ," 29 November 1976, DGIPS, c. 2226B, exp. 2, AGN.

92. "Boletín de prensa del PPS . . . ," 4 October 1973, DGIPS, c. 708, exp. 1, AGN.

93. "Estado de Chihuahua," 27 September 1974, DFS, 100-5-1-74, legajo 49, h. 243, AGN.

94. "Conferencia telefónica . . . ," 7 September 1976, DFS, 9-236-76, legajo 2, h. 199, AGN.

95. "Estado de Guerrero," 20 August 1976, DFS, 9-236-76, legajo 2, h. 93, AGN.

96. "Actividades de Carlos Sparrow Sada," 15 September 1976, DFS, 9-236-76, legajo 2, h. 207, AGN.

97. "La serie de rumores . . . ," 19 November 1976, DGIPS, c. 2226B, exp. 2, AGN.

98. "Nueva solidaridad: La guerra y el genocidio," November 1976, DFS, 65-221-76, legajo 7, h. 5, AGN.

99. "En las diferentes instituciones bancarias . . . ," 17 September 1976, DGIPS, c. 2225C, exp. 4, AGN; "Hoy en algunos bancos . . . ," 21 September 1976, DGIPS, c. 2225C, exp. 4, AGN; "Debido a que en el banco . . . ," 20 September 1976, DGIPS, c. 2225C, exp. 4, AGN; "En completa normalidad . . . ," 23 September 1976, DGIPS, 2225B, exp. 1, AGN.

100. "Las gasolineras que se encuentran . . . ," 21 September 1976, DGIPS, c. 2225B, exp. 1, AGN; "De 18 estaciones de gasolina . . . ," 28 September 1976, DGIPS, c. 2225B, exp. 1, AGN.

101. "Al darse a conocer . . . ," 27 October 1976, DGIPS, c. 2225B, exp. 3, AGN.

102. "Hoy en la Cámara de Diputados . . . ," 25 November 1976, DGIPS, c. 2226B, exp. 2, AGN.

103. "Panorama de la iniciativa privada," 23 August 1976, DFS, 9-236-76, legajo 2, h. 113, AGN.

104. Agustín, *Tragicomedia mexicana* 2, 96–100; Schmidt, *Deterioration of the Mexican Presidency*, 97–102. Judith Hellman describes the irony of the situation by pointing out that this land redistribution did little to alter inequality in the country; the campesinos took mostly bad land. Hellman, *Mexico in Crisis*, 199.

105. "Apoyo de la iniciativa privada," 25 November 1976, DFS, 9-236-76, legajo 3, h. 289, AGN.

106. [No title], 18 September 1976, DFS, 9-236-76, legajo 2, h. 235, AGN.

107. "Cámara de Senadores," 25 November 1976, DFS, 44-10-76, legajo 59, h. 144–146, AGN.

108. "A través de un panfleto . . . ," 23 August 1976, DGIPS, c. 2225C, exp. 2, AGN.

CHAPTER 3

1. There are six episodes: "La clase media en México"; "La enajenación de la clase media"; "Ideas políticas de la clase media"; "Ideología y clase media"; "La mujer de la clase media"; "El típico joven de la clase media." See Salgado et al. in the Bibliography under "Primary Sources" for further information.

2. Speech delivered to the National Executive Council of the CNOP on 1 October 1975. Instituto de Capacitación Política (of the PRI), *Historia documental de la CNOP: 1970–1984*, 225.

3. Speech delivered to members of the CTM (Confederation of Mexican Workers) in Mexico City on 9 January 1980. López Portillo, *Consolidación de la economía*, 25.

4. Salgado et al., "Ideas políticas de la clase media."

5. For historical analysis of the discourse about (or idea or imagining of) "middle class" in other places and times, see Parker, *Idea of the Middle Class*; and Wahrman, *Imagining the Middle Class*.

6. "Discourse" may be understood as a practice that systematically forms the object it talks about. The consistency in ways of talking about the middle class could be an example of what Michel Foucault describes as the sort of discursive similarity that generates a system of thought, or *episteme*. Foucault, *Archaeology of Knowledge*, 189–192. See also Hall, "Foucault"; and Hall, "Work of Representation."

7. I am drawing on Jürgen Habermas's image of the public sphere as a battleground in which bourgeois actors produce and consume political discourse. In Habermas's formulation, private citizens gather in public places to reach agreements, using persuasion and reason, on what constitutes the public good. The physical spaces of these meetings, such as salons, cafés, or newspapers, and the intellectual and political production together constitute the public sphere. Habermas is ultimately concerned with the emergence of a public sphere and its implications for the meanings and possibilities of democracy. He examines eighteenth-century bourgeois protests against the absolutist state, especially in terms of its bureaucratic structure and the arbitrary nature of justice. He argues that rational law and order characterized the emergence of the bourgeois public sphere. Habermas and Foucault advance competing versions of the history of modernity and the liberal state: a Habermasian fantasy of law and order competes with a Foucauldian nightmare of the repressive apparatus of law and order. These are not mutually exclusive narratives but rather two sides of the same coin. One emphasizes the ideal and the other the dark side. This chapter studies some of the ways in which these two narratives of modern history depend on ideas about the historical role of the middle class. Habermas, *Structural Transformation*; Foucault, *Discipline and Punish*.

8. And it is perhaps more difficult to evaluate the impact of the public sphere on the opinions of the urban and rural poor. Although Habermas's formulation has been criticized for focusing too narrowly on élite, male political production, that very elitism offers an analytical framework for teasing out middle-class public opinion. Narratives about the middle class were produced by middle-class writers, politicians, and academics. And while political speeches targeted wide audiences, it is likely that the middle classes constituted the main audience for Televisa educational programming, as well as the principal readership for novels and newspapers. Thus, while Habermas's conceptualization might be limited as a tool for studying the public opinion of the poor and marginalized, it does shed light on middle-class political persuasion and public opinion. For historical studies of the public sphere in Mexico, see the essays in Piccato and Sacristán, *Actores, espacios y debates*, which illuminate both the participatory nature and the elitism of urban political discourse in late nineteenth and early twentieth-century Mexico.

9. Remarks made at a press conference in Mexico City on 3 December 1979. López Portillo, *Política petrolera*, 11.

10. State of the Union address, 1 September 1977. López Portillo, *Política petrolera*, 9.

11. On the Cárdenas period, see Santiago, *Ecology of Oil*; and Brown, *Oil and Revolution*.

12. State of the Union address, 1 September 1979. López Portillo, *Política petrolera*, 11.

13. Elsa Gracida charts this transformation through analysis of presidential rhetoric about oil from the 1930s through the 1970s. Gracida, "Retórica petrolera," 12.

14. Lustig, *Remaking of an Economy*, 151 nn.21, 22.

15. Ibid., 20.

16. Ibid., 22, 32.

17. Ibid., 23.

18. Karl, *Paradox of Plenty*, 3. Karl does not analyze Mexico as one of her case studies, but her conclusions are illustrative and Mexico is included in her data.

19. Ibid., 16.

20. Ibid., 67.

21. Speech delivered at a conference on science and world affairs in Mexico City on 18 July 1979. López Portillo, *New International Energy Order*, 21–22.

22. Speech to the National Convention of Bankers in Acapulco on 23 May 23 1979. Díaz Serrano, *Política petrolera*, 42.

23. "El progreso financiero de México durante 1978 'estará escrito con petróleo': Lloyds," *El Universal*, 10 February 1978.

24. Speech to the Administrative Council of PEMEX in Mexico City on 2 August 1977. López Portillo, *Política petrolera*, 35–36.

25. State of the Union address, 1 September 1980. López Portillo, *Control de la inflación*, 10–11.

26. Speech to the Rotary Club in Mexico City on 17 June 1980. Díaz Serrano, *Política petrolera*, 22–23.

27. Remarks made at a press conference in Mexico City on 4 January 1979. López Portillo, *Financiamiento para el desarrollo*, 17.

28. Remarks made at a televised press conference on 5 December 1977. Ibid., 18.

29. Speech delivered in Hermosillo on 5 February 1981. López Portillo, *Consolidación de la economía*, 34.

30. Speech delivered to members of the CTM in Mexico City on 9 January 1980. Ibid., 25.

31. Guillermo Tardiff, "La riqueza petrolera y la realidad económica," *El Heraldo de México*, 4 December 1978.

32. Ángel Escalante Baranda, "Los hombres del petróleo," *Novedades*, 27 November 1980.

33. Remarks made at an archaeological convention in Mexico City on 10 February 1978. Díaz Serrano, *Política petrolera*, 90.

34. Speech delivered in Mexicali, Baja California, 1 October 1979. Ibid., 98.

35. Speech delivered to PEMEX workers on 9 January 1978. Ibid., 10.
36. Speech delivered to the National Executive Council of the CNOP on 1 October 1975. Instituto de Capacitación Política (of the PRI), *Historia documental de la CNOP 1970–1984*, 225–228. See also López Cámara, *Clase media en la era del populismo*, 119–120.
37. Speech delivered to the National Executive Council of the CNOP on 1 October 1975. Instituto de Capacitación Política (of the PRI), *Historia documental de la CNOP 1970–1984*, 227.
38. For more detail concerning economic programs during these years, see "Impacto económico de las divisas," 6 September 1979, JLP, c. 2307, exp. 1863, AGN; Mirón and Pérez Fernández del Castillo, *López Portillo*, 77–86. On the Cultural Center, see Artigas, *UNAM*, 109–175.
39. Gavin, "Mexican Oil Boom," 185.
40. Trejo Reyes, "Notas sobre el seminario," 103.
41. Loaeza makes this argument about middle-class prosperity for the entire 1970s. Indeed, in several separate publications both Loaeza and Gilbert argue for the 1970s as a generalized boom for the middle class. Though the middle class no doubt benefited from Echeverría's education and political reforms, such a generalization of the 1970s underestimates the crises during Echeverría's presidency. Loaeza, "Clases medias mexicanas," 232; Gilbert, *Mexico's Middle Class*, 21.
42. López Cámara, *Clase media en la era del populismo*, 12.
43. It is unclear whether the decline in public protest is related to the economic boom, to the relatively successful counterinsurgency campaign, or to the 1977–78 amnesty program for ex-guerrillas and jailed social activists. Agitation for union democracy—such as the electrical workers' movement for union democracy—declined in the late 1970s. Notwithstanding the reasons for diminished protest (and notwithstanding the continued public dissent among some sectors), during the oil boom there was a noted decline in public struggles between the PRI and its opponents on both the right and the left. Monsiváis describes the oil boom as the moment when "civil society was at its weakest" (Scherer and Monsiváis, *Tiempo de saber*, 221). On labor struggles, see La Botz, *Mask of Democracy*, 72–74. Importantly, rural protests increased during the 1970s and 1980s. See Bartra, *Los herederos de Zapata*.
44. Karl, *Paradox of Plenty*, 16. Karl's study offers a helpful comparison of this process across several petro-states. Fernando Coronil analyzes how the corruption associated with petrolization manifested in Venezuela, where he argues that the modern state had been founded, both materially and discursively, upon the "magical" powers of oil. Through detailed case studies of several development projects and a political murder, Coronil examines the lived experience of the state's corruption. He focuses on the mundane, everyday level of this corruption among public employees, the midlevel functionaries who profited from the oil wealth. Coronil's analysis of the effects of oil on Venezuela is instructive for Mexico, because in both countries oil is a state-run industry and profits from the boom were often channeled through government bureaucracies. Civil servants, then, were well positioned to benefit from the newfound lucre. Coronil, *Magical State*.
45. Jesús Guisa y Azevedo, "En lo económico somos países de petróleo, y de

qué más?," *El Universal*, 12 May 1979. This refers to a section of Ramón López Velarde's "La suave patria":

LA SUAVE PATRIA	SWEET LAND
Patria: tu superficie es el maíz	*Patria*: your surface is the gold of maize,
tus minas el palacio del Rey de Oros,	below, the palace of gold medallion kings,
y tu cielo, las garzas en desliz	your sky is filled with the heron's flight
y el relámpago verde de los loros.	and green lightning of parrots' wings.
El Niño Dios te escrituró un establo	God the Child deeded you a stable,
y los veneros del petróleo el diablo.	lust for oil was the gift of the devil.

Translation from López Velarde, *Song of the Heart*, 78–79.

46. Jorge Eugenio Ortiz, "Los empleos del gobierno," *El Universal*, 14 April 1978.

47. Ana Mairena, "La clase ridícula," *El Día*, 20 January 1978.

48. José J. Castellanos, "La gran esperanza económica de México," *El Heraldo de México*, 11 August 1978.

49. "Sí se está petrolizando la economía de nuestro país," *Novedades*, 22 April 1981.

50. Jorge Eugenio Ortiz, "Los empleos del gobierno," *El Universal*, 14 April 1978.

51. My research suggests that we need more nuanced evaluations of the Mexican press. For an unfavorable overview of the press, see Scherer and Monsiváis, *Tiempo de saber*.

52. Ana Mairena, "La clase ridícula," *El Día*, 20 January 1978.

53. Horacio Quiñónez, "La tiranía burocrática," *El Día*, 4 February 1977; José Vitelio García, "Burocracia," *El Sol de México*, 13 September 1977.

54. Paco Ignacio Taibo, "El burocratón astuto," *El Universal*, 1 August 1978. It seems that this article was written by Paco Ignacio Taibo senior, but it is possible that it was authored by Paco Ignacio Taibo II, his son and the author of the detective fiction analyzed later in this chapter.

55. Eduardo Orvañanos, "Una nueva casta de privilegiados en México," *Heraldo de México*, 18 September 1981.

56. Mario Sepúlveda Garza, "El discreto encanto de la burocracia," *Avances: Diario de la Capital*, 16 December 1981.

57. Sergio Sánchez Franco, "La burocracia al ataque," *El Nacional*, 12 January 1980.

58. Salgado et al., "Enajenación de la clase media."

59. For example, the development studies paradigm sought to analyze (and promote) democracy in Latin America in the context of the Cold War. Based largely in the disciplines of political science, sociology, and anthropology, this school identified the middle class as the foundation for stable, constitutional democracies. Policymakers in the United States looked for a democratic and reform-minded middle class in Latin America's most industrialized countries—an ideal of North American and Latin American policymakers in their quest to rid the continent of "communism" (a catchall term that, for many, included social movements to oust

dictators, to reduce inequalities, or to enforce constitutional rights). Many scholars, intentionally or inadvertently responding to the political question, advanced analyses about the function of the Latin American middle class at midcentury. A six-volume landmark study by the Social Sciences Section of the Pan-American Union, published in 1948, came to no definitive conclusion on the historical role of the Latin American middle class; indeed, the volume highlighted the diversity of the "middle class" in the region and the contradictions within it (with some scholars questioning the usefulness of the term "middle class" itself). In 1958, historian John J. Johnson published the watershed English-language analysis; he concluded that the Latin American middle class was engaged in modernizing reform (such as industrialization, worker protection legislation, and the expansion of public education). In contrast, other scholars argued that the Latin American middle class lacked a capitalist, entrepreneurial, and modernizing drive that could create wealth in their various countries. In this line of analysis, the middle class emerges as a conservative defender of its shaky privilege, at the expense of the public good. Johnson, *Political Change in Latin America*; Crevenna, *Materiales para el estudio de la clase media*. For negative appraisals of the Latin American middle class, see Hoselitz, "Economic Growth in Latin America"; Nun, "Middle-Class Military Coup in Latin America"; Petras, *Politics and Social Structure in Latin America*, 37–53; Pike, "Aspects of Class Relations in Chile, 1850–1960"; and Zeitlin, *Civil Wars in Chile*. For analysis of this literature, see Jiménez, "Elision of the Middle Classes and Beyond." In my understanding of the midcentury social science literature, I have benefited tremendously from collaboration with David Parker. In particular, see Parker, "Making and Endless Remaking of the Middle Class"; and Parker and Walker, *Latin America's Middle Class*, especially the essays in part 1.

60. The following discussion of representations of the middle class is based upon periodicals research in the newspaper archive Fondos Económicos at the Miguel Lerdo de Tejada library in Mexico City. I researched categories such as "middle class," "public employees," and "CNOP." I analyzed hundreds of articles that discussed the middle class from the early postrevolutionary years through the late 1980s. Details in the following discussion are representative of these articles in general and, for example, appear in: "La clase media despierta," *El Día*, 15 August 1935; "Para la historia," *El Nacional*, 10 October 1941; "La clase media," *La Prensa*, 9 October 1941; "Sección editorial: Puente al futuro," *El Universal*, 10 September 1962; "Sección editorial: Izquierda y derecha," *El Universal*, 11 June 1963; and Carlos Denegri, "Buenos días: Guzmán Orozco," *Excélsior*, 1 March 1965.

61. Unlike the classic European bourgeoisies, the Latin American middle class did not appear inclined to lead the region's (implicitly hoped for) transition to capitalist modernity. Jiménez, "Elision of the Middle Classes and Beyond," 217. Parker discusses the irony of this "failure" narrative, as British and French historiography has questioned the historical role of the bourgeois subject in the French Revolution and British Industrial Revolution. Parker, "Making and Endless Remaking of the Middle Class."

62. The following discussion draws from "The Pitfalls of National Consciousness," chapter 3 of Fanon's *Wretched of the Earth*. I am grateful to Jon Soske for

our discussions of Fanon and other points of comparison between Africa and Latin America.

63. Fanon, *Wretched of the Earth*, 175.

64. Ibid., 170.

65. Ibid., 172.

66. Ibid., 149.

67. In Fanon's view, the bourgeoisie in the developed world have successfully created bourgeois states and established a certain amount of legitimacy. Ibid., 175.

68. Ibid., 165.

69. Salgado et al., "Clase media en México."

70. Salgado et al., "Ideología y clase media."

71. "Impacto económico de las divisas," 6 September 1979, JLP, c. 2307, exp. 1863, AGN, 17–24; Mirón and Pérez Fernández del Castillo, *López Portillo*, 77–86; Street, "Can Mexico Break the Vicious Cycle?," 603–604.

72. Solís M., *Economic Policy Reform in Mexico*, 104. For more on the problems associated with imported consumer goods, see DICMAC, *Investigación cuantitativa*, 1–9.

73. On the meaning of hard-boiled, or noir, see Mandel, *Delightful Murder*, 30–39.

74. Taibo himself described his protagonist as a refugee from the middle class. Stavans, "A Brief Talk with Paco Ignacio Taibo II."

75. Mandel, *Delightful Murder*, 10.

76. Ibid., 122.

77. As literary scholar Sean McCann argues in his analysis of the hard-boiled detective in the context of New Deal American liberalism, "the detective story had always been a liberal genre, centrally concerned with a fundamental premise of liberal theory—the rule of law—and with the tensions fundamental to democratic societies that constantly threw that principle into doubt." McCann, *Gumshoe America*, 6.

78. Braham, *Crimes against the State*, xiii.

79. Martín-Cabrera, *Radical Justice*, 23–24.

80. This intellectual production generated some of the most important essays of the postrevolutionary period. However, the endeavor to define a national culture has been criticized for being overly general and for reducing Mexico's diverse peoples to a few essential qualities. The essays discussed in the following paragraphs are, in part, attempts to psychoanalyze a national identity, or a people; Claudio Lomnitz describes this methodology as turning history into a "psychodrama." For example, both Samuel Ramos and Octavio Paz avail themselves of the analytical categories and tools of psychoanalysis and, at the same time, rely on psychoanalysis as an excuse to avoid "proof." Octavio Paz declared, "The example of psychoanalysis saves me from wasting time on boring proof"; and Samuel Ramos wrote, "It seems unnecessary to base this conclusion on an accumulation of documents." Moreover, cultural critic Roger Bartra has criticized the "lo mexicano" literature for producing an identity (Mexican-ness) that could be manipulated by the one-party state and other interests. The focus here is not on an analysis of these essays on epistemological or political grounds but rather on an examination of the historical role that the authors assigned to the Mexican middle class. Lomnitz, *Exits*

from the Labyrinth, 2; Paz, *Labyrinth of Solitude,* 253; Ramos, *Profile of Man and Culture,* 56; Bartra, *Jaula de la melancolía.*

81. Ramos, *Profile of Man and Culture,* 75–76.

82. Ibid., 69.

83. Ibid., 95–96, 129.

84. Paz, *Labyrinth of Solitude,* 124.

85. This is not to suggest that Paz desired capitalist modernity and electoral democracy; he decried the effects of the so-called European bourgeois revolutions, which turned people, in his words, into "mere phantoms." The focus here is Paz's conceptualization of the historical role of the bourgeoisie. Ibid., 176–177.

86. "Despite the predictions of the clearest thinkers, the liberal revolution did not bring about the birth of that strong bourgeoisie which everyone, even Justo Sierra, saw as the only hope for Mexico." Ibid., 128–129.

87. Ibid., 130–131, 176–177.

88. Ibid., 146. Here, Paz ironically invokes the "historical normality" of the so-called classic European bourgeois revolutions. On the debated role of the bourgeois in the European revolutions, see note 61 above.

89. Ibid., 146.

90. Ibid., 177.

91. At this point in his essay, Paz uses the terms "middle class" and "bourgeois" interchangeably. Ibid., 179–182.

92. Ibid., 194, 212.

93. Alegre, "Contesting the 'Mexican Miracle'"; Aviña, "Insurgent Guerrero"; Padilla, *Rural Resistance*; Poniatowska, *Massacre in Mexico*; Soto Laveaga, "The 'Emperor' Has a New Lab Coat."

94. Monsiváis, "Notas sobre la cultura mexicana en el siglo XX," 419. Monsiváis's essay, published in 1976 as part of the Colegio de México's series *Historia General de México,* advances an influential argument about the history of Mexican culture, especially literature, from the mid-nineteenth century through the early 1970s. As such, it provides a sort of "current state of affairs" on the eve of Paco Ignacio Taibo II's publication of the first Belascoarán novel (also 1976).

95. Ibid., 419–422. For an overview of this period in Mexico and Latin America more generally, see Sorensen, *Turbulent Decade.*

96. This is necessarily a narrow and brief summary of these two novels, which could be considered Fuentes's magnum opus and have been celebrated for their technical innovation. The focus here is on his critique of the midcentury Mexican middle-class world.

97. Monsiváis, "Notas sobre la cultura mexicana," 407–417. A close reading of Monsiváis's essay suggests that the "years of confidence" generation belonged to a long tradition of Mexican writers preoccupied with the historical role of the middle class, including nineteenth-century liberals such as Justo Sierra; members of the Ateneo de la Juventud; the proponents of cultural nationalism from the Generation of 1915, such as Vasconcelos; the authors of the novels of the Revolution; the essayists of "lo mexicano" (discussed above); and the early critics, such as Rulfo, Yáñez, and Revueltas, of the "profound desperation" caused by the postwar capitalist boom. Indeed, Monsiváis's essay can be read as a history of literary production

about the middle class. To the above, I would add the social realism literature on the middle class, such as Usigli's *Medio tono* (1938) and Sodi's *Clase media* (1948), together with the sociological realism of the 1970s such as Careaga's *Biografía de un joven de la clase media* (1977). A fascinating counterpoint to Monsiváis's essay can be found in Marcelo Pogolotti's collection *Clase media en México* (1972), in which Pogolotti compiles short excerpts by writers as diverse as J. J. Fernandez de Lizardi and Gustavo Sainz.

98. Monsiváis, "Notas sobre la cultura mexicana," 430.

99. Monsiváis's exceptions included Poniatowska's *La noche de Tlatelolco* (1971); Manjarrez's *Lapsus* (1971); Aguilar Mora's *Cadáver lleno de mundo* (1971); and Agustín's *Se está haciendo tarde* (1973). Monsiváis, "Notas sobre la cultura mexicana," 431.

100. Taibo's innovation was unexpected. When Monsiváis had asked, in his 1976 overview of Mexican culture, "Can we speak of culture before and after Tlatelolco?" he had not anticipated that hard-boiled detective fiction would emerge in the post-Tlatelolco cultural landscape. In fact, in a 1973 article, Monsiváis had argued that Mexico did not have—and likely would not develop—a significant detective novel genre. Monsiváis, "Notas sobre la cultura mexicana," 43; Monsiváis, "Ustedes que jamás han sido asesinados"; Close, *Contemporary Hispanic Crime Fiction*, 28–29.

101. In doing so, Taibo combines Mexican literary representations of the middle class (see note 97 above) with a literary tradition of hard-boiled detective fiction. Regarding the latter, Taibo builds on an earlier tradition of detective fiction in Mexico, such as Usigli's *Ensayo de un crimen* (1944), which itself offers a portrait of the bourgeoisie, and an emergent noir tradition that might be dated from Rafael Bernal's *El complot mongol* (1969). By combining these different literary traditions, Taibo effectively explores the inner turmoil of the middle class, which sets him apart from the "years of confidence" generation. In this regard, the Belascoarán series has more in common with Pacheco's *Batallas en el desierto* (1981) than the boom authors (even the inner turmoil of Artemio Cruz serves as a foil for Fuentes's "total novel" depiction of postrevolutionary failure).

102. For example, see Braham, *Crimes against the State*; and Sánchez, "El asesinato como un arte."

103. At present, there are ten novels in the series (the last one cowritten with Subcomandante Marcos). *Algunas nubes* falls in the narrative between *Cosa fácil* and *No habrá final feliz*. It should be noted that the protagonist, Héctor, dies at the end of *No habrá final feliz* but is resurrected to continue the series in *Regreso a la misma ciudad y bajo la lluvia* (1989).

104. Taibo, *No habrá final feliz*, 128.

105. Ibid., 224–225.

106. Ibid., 222.

107. Taibo, *Días de combate*, 222–223.

108. Taibo, *Algunas nubes*, 49–53.

109. Ibid., 72.

110. Taibo, *Días de combate*, 15–16.

111. Ibid., 39.

112. Ibid., 41–42.
113. Ibid., 43.
114. Taibo, *Cosa fácil*, 19.
115. Taibo, *Días de combate*, 35.
116. Ibid., 87–92.
117. Ibid., 149–170.
118. Taibo, *Cosa fácil*, 100.
119. Ibid., 59–60.
120. Ibid., 60.
121. Ibid., 64.
122. Taibo, *Días de combate*, 20.
123. Taibo, *Cosa fácil*, 68.
124. Ibid., 25. In her analysis of the Belascoarán series, Braham also refers to this passage but cites a different portion of it, using it to argue: "Belascoarán's personal identity as a Mexican of the masses—a victim who complains about the price of tortillas and the corruption of the transit police—is the source of his energy and diligence as a detective." I would argue, however, that the passage illustrates his struggle with his middle-class identity vis-à-vis the masses: he complains about the price of Pepsi to feel more Mexican, not because he cannot afford it. Likewise, Glen Close presents Belascoarán as an economically marginal character, stressing that he cannot afford a private office or a secretary; like Braham, Close avoids analysis of Belascoarán's class position, accepting at face value the character's denial of his middle-class status. Braham, *Crimes against the State*, 92; Close, *Contemporary Hispanic Crime Fiction*, 35.
125. Taibo, *Días de combate*, 118.
126. Taibo, *Cosa fácil*, 77.
127. Taibo, *Algunas nubes*, 103–104.
128. Ibid., 133–134.
129. Ibid., 103–105.
130. Taibo, *Cosa fácil*, 100.
131. Ibid., 173, 205.
132. Ibid., 219.
133. Ibid., 222.
134. Taibo, *No habrá final feliz*, 240–245.
135. Pérez Alfonso, *Hundiéndonos en el excremento del diablo*; Coronil, *Magical State*, 353.
136. This possible alternative to petrolization is outlined by Karl, *Paradox of Plenty*, 66.
137. This argument draws upon Fernando Coronil's analysis of the magic of oil in Venezuela. See Coronil, *Magical State*; and note 44 above.
138. Galeano, *Open Veins*.

CHAPTER 4

1. The rate varied regionally (6 percent in the northern states), and in the 1980s variation increased with lower rates for goods that were deemed more necessary (but not exempt).

2. In his study of the Sears department store, business culture, and consumer culture, Julio Moreno discusses earlier associations of consumption with democracy. No doubt, before the 1970s consumers were both political and politicized. However, with the creation of Fonacot and the new law, consumers acquired an institutionalized (within the PRI's Institutional Revolution) political identity. See Moreno, *Yankee Don't Go Home!*

3. By studying the emergence of the consumer-citizen in Mexico, this chapter responds to Néstor García Canclini's call to update our understanding of citizenship in the context of rising consumerism. García Canclini calls attention to the twenty-first-century incongruity whereby consumers and citizens in Mexico (and elsewhere) are "21st-century consumers; 18th-century citizens" (15). Writing in the mid-1990s, García Canclini analyzes cultural globalization and the privatization of the public sphere—when individuals are "brought together as consumers even when we are being addressed as citizens" (29). I would argue that the twenty-first-century conflation of consumers and citizens was institutionalized in the PRI's system during the 1970s. It should be noted that my term "consumer-citizen" is different in meaning from the term "citizen consumer" in Lizabeth Cohen's history of consumption in the postwar United States. Whereas Cohen refers to an activist consumer protecting his or her rights, in my analysis consumers become consumer-citizens when their relationship with the state changes. See Cohen, *A Consumers' Republic*, 18–61; García Canclini, *Consumers and Citizens*.

4. Bortz and Aguila, "Earning a Living," 127–128.

5. Mexico's increased inflation during the 1970s and 1980s was part of both a Latin American and a global trend. For a discussion of inflation elsewhere during the 1970s, see De Long, *America's Only Peacetime Inflation*.

6. The scholarly literature, both historical and theoretical, on consumption and conspicuous consumption is extensive. The foundational text is Veblen, *Theory of the Leisure Class*. For an anthropological analysis of this phenomenon in recent Brazilian history, see O'Dougherty, *Consumption Intensified*. No doubt, irresponsible conspicuous consumption is not exclusively a middle-class phenomenon, but this chapter focuses on the increased use of consumer credit to fund conspicuous consumption, and in 1970s Mexico the availability of consumer credit was largely limited to the middle classes.

7. On the impact of large-scale apartment complexes on urban middle-class lives, see Ballent, "El arte de saber vivir"; Garay Arellano, *Modernidad habitada*; and Garay Arellano, *Rumores y retratos*. On the culture and business of American department stores, see Moreno, *Yankee Don't Go Home!* On the importance of essential consumer goods, see DICMAC, *Investigación cuantitativa*. See also the material culture in Oscar Lewis's anthropological study *Five Families* (and in particular a comparison between the Sánchez family, on the line between the working and middle classes, and the Castro family, on the line between the middle and upper classes).

8. Fonacot and the consumer-rights law were part of an ambitious program to protect worker salaries developed by the PRI in 1973. The Chamber of Deputies also recommended continuing with minimum wage and price control policies. And it underscored the need to fortify the existing network of worker stores, where

workers of a specific company, industry, or union could purchase goods at lower prices. Among these measures, Fonacot and the new law represented innovative new directions in salary protection policies. It was hoped that these measures, along with more standard strategies, would help mitigate the effects of escalating inflation. FONACOT, *Esto es FONACOT*, 10. Although I will discuss wages and prices in the pages that follow, I concentrate on credit, consumer rights, and taxation, which are more specifically related to middle-class consumption. There exists an extensive literature on minimum wages and prices in Mexico. For an overview of the scholarship, see Bortz and Aguila, "Earning a Living." For contemporary analysis, see Comisión Nacional de los Salarios Mínimos, "Los salarios mínimos legales en México." For analysis of salary protection policy under Echeverría, see Bortz and Sánchez, "Salarios y crisis económica en México"; Reyes Heroles, *Política macroeconómica y bienestar en México*, 296–335; and Schmidt, *Deterioration of the Mexican Presidency*.

9. There exist few studies of Fonacot. For a synthesis of Fonacot's activities from 1975 to 1980, published by the Ministry of Labor and Social Security (Secretaría del Trabajo y Previsión Social), see Núñez Birrueta and Lavalle Montalvo, *Análisis de los medios de protección*, esp. 81–105. The scholarship on nonagricultural credit in twentieth-century Mexico has itself been relatively underdeveloped until recently. See Ángel Mobarak and Marichal, "Poder y crisis."

10. Secretaría del Trabajo y Previsión Social, "Fondo de Fomento y Garantía para el Consumo de los Trabajadores, Memoria Institucional 1983–1988," MMH, 14.10.01.20, c. 1, exp. 8, pg. 6, AGN.

11. Rodolfo Stavenhagen, "Inflación, crédito y salarios: Explotación de los trabajadores," *Excélsior*, 12 March 1974.

12. Gustavo Salinas Iñiguez, "Alianza nacional en defensa del salario," *El Universal*, 11 April 1974.

13. Reyes Heroles González Garza defines middle-class families as those who earn one to nine times the minimum wage. Although housing is not a consumer commodity, homeownership might be conceptualized as such. See Reyes Heroles González Garza, *Financial Policies and Income Distribution*, 20–23; and Garza and Schteingart, *Acción habitacional del estado*.

14. "FONACOT: Protección al consumo," *Novedades*, 2 May 1974.

15. FONACOT, *Esto es FONACOT*, 28. Fonacot also extended credit to institutions, such as worker stores that supported worker consumption. In this chapter, I focus on credit given directly by Fonacot. "Memoria Sexenal FONACOT 1976–1982," MMH, 14.10.01.20, c. 1, exp. 4, pg. 10, AGN.

16. My argument that Fonacot targeted the middle classes runs counter to traditional interpretations of Fonacot and of salary protection more generally. Government propaganda and newspaper coverage from the 1970s and 1980s almost invariably describe Fonacot recipients as workers, as low income, and as economically weak (all of which, no doubt, theoretically could include significant portions of the middle classes, but that is likely not the intended meaning). But journalists and politicians frequently used the term "salaried worker" (*asalariado*), a term that was also used in official Fonacot publications. To earn a salary, rather than a wage, has been a standard measure of middle-class status; it suggests formal employment,

fixed residence, and predictable income. It should be mentioned that, on occasions, journalists did refer to the middle- or lower-middle-class status of Fonacot recipients. Perhaps the most helpful term from the time is "salaried class."

17. FONACOT, *Esto es FONACOT*, 12.

18. Samaniego de Villarreal, "Algunas reflexiones sobre el impacto económico," 59.

19. In his study of the middle class in the mid-1990s, Gilbert suggests that a middle-class income is more than five times the minimum wage. I should note, however, that Gilbert relies on other income measures, not only multiples of the minimum wage, to round out his definition of the middle class. His reference to the minimum wage serves as context for the expansion of the Fonacot requirements to one to ten times the minimum wage in 1993: Fonacot was still targeting middle-class consumers. Gilbert, "Magicians," 129; "Sólo 30% de trabajadores del país utiliza los beneficios de FONACOT," *El Nacional*, 8 May 1993; "Amplía FONACOT créditos a trabajadores que ganen hasta 10 salarios mínimos vigentes," *Uno más Uno*, 8 May 1993.

20. Secretaría del Trabajo y Previsión Social, "Fondo de Fomento y Garantía para el Consumo de los Trabajadores, Memoria Institucional 1983–1988," MMH, 14.10.01.20, c. 1, exp. 8, pgs. 118–123, AGN.

21. Ibid.

22. "Incidencia del FONACOT en la producción nacional," *El Universal* 5 May 1976.

23. In this case, the ministry was trying to list which goods would be subjected to a higher, "luxury" consumer tax. Luis E. Mercado, "Sólo a 13 productos 20% de IVA," *El Universal*, 10 December 1982.

24. This is not unique to Mexico; geographer Mike Davis describes a global phenomenon in which the middle classes are the beneficiaries of social policy designed for the poor. See Davis, *Planet of Slums*.

25. Santacruz (pseud.), "Algunas apreciaciones," 2.

26. FONACOT, *Esto es FONACOT*, 24.

27. We still need research on commercial and bank interest rates for loans to private citizens. It appears that neither the Bank of Mexico nor the Ministry of the Treasury collected this data, and research might involve consulting individual banks and other institutions that offered such credit. Until we have the data, a comparison with the CPP buttresses Fonacot's claim that it charged lower interest rates than other credit providers. While the Fonacot records provide some data on the commercial and bank interest rates, there is no long time series available for rate comparison.

28. Secretaría del Trabajo y Previsión Social, "Fondo de Fomento y Garantía para el Consumo de los Trabajadores, Memoria Institucional 1983–1988," MMH, 14.10.01.20, c. 1, exp. 8, pg. 113, AGN (underlining in original).

29. Ibid., pg. 114; "Ayuda al trabajador," *El Universal*, 30 April 1984; "Bajan 9 puntos tasas de interés en FONACOT," *Novedades*, 30 April 1984; "Redujo FONACOT de 42 a 33 por ciento los intereses para los trabajadores," *Uno más Uno*, 30 April 1984; "FONACOT: A la mitad, intereses para adquirir útiles y uniformes," *El Universal*, 3 August 1987.

30. Secretaría del Trabajo y Previsión Social, "Fondo de Fomento y Garantía para el Consumo de los Trabajadores, Memoria Institucional 1983–1988," MMH, 14.10.01.20, c. 1, exp. 8, AGN; "La tasa de intereses con que el FONACOT otorga crédito a los obreros se mantendrá inalterable," *El Universal*, 25 February 1982; "Los trabajadores podrán seguir disfrutando del crédito de FONACOT a intereses muy bajos," *El Nacional*, 5 January 1982.

31. Luzmaría Mejia Morales, "Da prioridad FONACOT a personas con menos recursos económicos," *El Día*, 3 February 1983.

32. Mary Poovey describes how the collective faith in the fiction of paper money (and the credit economy) can lead to a "problematic of representation"— and political, social, economic, and legal crisis—when authorities refuse to redeem paper money as promised, as happened with the 1797 British Restriction Act. See Poovey, *Genres of the Credit Economy*, 57–83, 171–283.

33. Jean-Joseph Goux argues that the historical shift from cash to checks as a method of payment—the "dematerialization of money"—may be analyzed in conjunction with the twentieth-century philosophical concern with representation, the nature of signs, and language. In his analysis, credit (especially the credit card) is a rupture from concrete conditions of commercial exchange. He argues that, in the late twentieth century, money (in the form of checks and, especially, credit) is an "inconvertible signifier that circulates . . . that floats, that always postpones its 'realization,' guarantees the monetary function in the realm of pure symbolicity, but only by mourning the loss of the unlocatable (or floating) standard and the uncertain reserve value, secured by nothing." Goux, "Cash, Check, or Charge?," 115.

34. Luzmaría Mejia Morales, "Da prioridad FONACOT a personas con menos recursos económicos," *El Día*, 3 February 1983.

35. Margarita Hurtado, "Refuerza FONACOT su apoyo a los asalariados con mayor número de créditos en 82," *El Día*, 8 June 1982; "FONACOT firmó un convenio con el gobernador para otorgar créditos a burócratas y maestros," *El Universal*, 25 March 1982.

36. Though much discussed, cars were never included on Fonacot's list of approved items; motorcycles and car repairs were. "En casi dos meses de operaciones el FONACOT ha otorgado créditos por más de 50 millones de pesos," *El Nacional*, 12 February 1975; Georgina Howard, "Cupones FONACOT para que los trabajadores adquieran víveres," *El Día*, 21 July 1985; "Créditos de FONACOT para comprar alimentos," *El Día*, 27 July 1985; Enrique Sánchez Márquez, "De $10,000 a $70,000, créditos FONACOT para adquirir víveres," *El Universal*, 28 November 1985; "Crédito para comida darán al trabajador," *Excélsior*, 16 January 1986; Aurelio Ramos M., "Una vergüenza, el plan de créditos del FONACOT para adquirir víveres," *Excélsior*, 17 January 1986; Alejandro Tello Macías, "Un salario de marginación," *Uno más Uno*, 20 January 1986.

37. Expansion of credit and improved repayment rates might also indicate Fonacot's increased internal sophistication. Secretaría del Trabajo y Previsión Social, "Fondo de Fomento y Garantía para el Consumo de los Trabajadores, Memoria Institucional 1983–1988," MMH, 14.10.01.20, c. 1, exp. 8, pg. 38, AGN.

38. On earlier department store credit, see Moreno, *Yankee Don't Go Home!*, 190–197. On credit as a salary benefit, see Israel Núñez's "Prestaciones sociales,"

which focuses on the 1950 to 1975 period. Commentators have suggested that, during the crisis of the 1980s, the middle classes increasingly relied on payment in benefits. But to my knowledge there is no analytical synthesis of changes in benefits during the 1970s and 1980s. Such a study could draw upon original research in labor contracts, household surveys, and possibly interviews. On credit available to lower-income groups, see Francois, *Culture of Everyday Credit*; Karon, "Law and Popular Credit in Mexico"; Lustig, "La paradoja en un mercado informal de crédito"; and Mansell Carstens, *Las finanzas populares en México*.

39. Sánchez Herrero, *Mexican Experience with Bank Credit Cards*, 3.

40. Ibid., 10.

41. Ángel Mobarak, "Computerization," 92–99.

42. Fregoso Saucedo, "Efectos de las tarjetas," 99.

43. Fonacot, "Memoria Sexenal FONACOT 1976–1982," MMH, 14.10.01.20, c. 1, exp. 4, pg. 29, AGN.

44. FONACOT, *Esto es FONACOT*, 19.

45. The three students studied at the University of Nuevo León, where researchers at the Center for Economic Investigations (Centro de Investigaciones Económicas) had completed, in 1968, a survey of household finances in the city of Monterrey (in conjunction with the Bank of Mexico). This Monterrey survey was one of the pilot surveys for what would become a national survey of household finances. The undergraduate students used the data from the survey. Each student focused on household consumption in different social strata (low, middle, and high). They complemented the survey data with questionnaires and interviews. These three theses are part of a broader effort to analyze household finance data in Monterrey, albeit at the undergraduate level. To my knowledge, there are no advanced (doctoral or postdoctoral) studies that deal with the use and perceptions of consumer credit in 1970s Mexico. These undergraduate theses are thus useful because they offer a comparative view of household finances in different social classes, using a similar methodology and the same principal data source (with different, creative additional information). The Faculty of Economics approved the three theses in August 1970. Cepeda, "Papel del crédito en la compra"; Gutiérrez Rocha, "Papel del crédito en las compras"; Ibarra Vargas, "El crédito como variable explicativa."

46. Gutiérrez Rocha, "Papel del crédito en las compras," graph 2. This upper-middle-class category is also more consistent with the middle-class income estimates outlined in the Appendix.

47. Ibarra Vargas, "El crédito como variable explicativa."

48. Gutiérrez Rocha, "Papel del crédito en las compras," 21.

49. Cepeda, "Papel del crédito en la compra"; Gutiérrez Rocha, "Papel del crédito en las compras."

50. Peebles, "Anthropology of Credit and Debt," 226.

51. Cepeda, "Papel del crédito en la compra," 19.

52. Whereas the three theses on credit and household finances in Monterrey were based on analysis of data collected by researchers at the University of Nuevo León and the Bank of Mexico, supplemented with questionnaires and interviews conducted by the undergraduate students, it is unclear what sources the author

of the fourth thesis, José Alberto Fregoso Saucedo, drew upon to substantiate his conclusions about credit cards. But this does not invalidate the study for our purposes, as it speaks to how credit was perceived (95–106). Fregoso Saucedo's categorization of social classes roughly corresponds with the other estimates in this chapter and in the Appendix to this book. For Fregoso Saucedo, lower-class or "clase popular" families earn less than 3,000 pesos per month; lower-middle-class families earn between 3,000 and 6,000 pesos; upper-middle-class families earn between 8,000 and 25,000 pesos; and wealthy families have a monthly income above 25,000 pesos. The 2,000-peso gap between the lower-middle class and the upper-middle class was likely meant to indicate the fuzziness of the dividing lines; indeed, Fregoso Saucedo goes to great length to discuss the variables that complicate any categorization based solely upon income, such as regional variation or the role of race in social differentiation. Fregoso Saucedo, "Efectos de las tarjetas," 63–93.

53. Ibid., 96.

54. Ibid., 102.

55. Ibid.

56. Fonacot, "Memoria Sexenal FONACOT 1976–1982," MMH, 14.10.01.20, c. 1, exp. 4, pgs. 44–53, AGN; "Concurso mobiliario de interés social: Una respuesta extraordinaria," *Excélsior*, 27 May 1978.

57. Fonacot. "Memoria Sexenal FONACOT 1976–1982." MMH, 14.10.01.20, c. 1, exp. 4, pg. 21, AGN. This formula is by no means a truism—indeed, spending-led economic stimulus has been hotly debated whenever it has been proposed (inside and outside Mexico). For example, one concern is that inflation might increase with subsidized spending; as one journalist asked, "Is it useful, in times of inflation, to spend many millions of pesos to increase the purchasing power of the middle and lower-middle class?" José Dudet, "Original mecánica de operación del 'FONACOT,'" *Excélsior*, 10 March 1974.

58. Secretaría de Industria y Comercio (hereafter SIC), *Ley Federal de Protección al Consumidor*, 16.

59. Ibid.

60. The full text of the 1976 law, along with Campillo Sainz's speech including the question and answer period, is published in ibid. There is a significant body of scholarship on this law and the institutions it created, but to my knowledge none of it studies the law as political or cultural history nor as a window onto the relationship between citizens and the state. Instead, scholars have paid close attention to the legal ramifications of, juridical problems with, and legislative changes to the law, and other studies have focused on consumption patterns. See, for example, Lares Romero, *El derecho de protección a los consumidores*; Ovalle Favela, *Comentarios a la Ley Federal de Protección al Consumidor*; Ovalle Favela, *Derechos del consumidor*; Sánchez-Cordero Dávila, *La protección del consumidor*; and Solórzano Peña and Contreras Acevedo, *Derecho de consumo en México*.

61. SIC, *Ley Federal de Protección al Consumidor*, 19.

62. Since the early colonial period, La Malinche has been a controversial figure in Mexican history—some argue that she betrayed her people, while others commend her political savvy. See Messinger Cypess, *La Malinche in Mexican Literature*.

63. SIC, *Ley Federal de Protección al Consumidor*, 28.

64. The Mexican legislation was part of an international trend in consumer protection and was noteworthy for its focus on credit arrangements. The trend was sparked by President John F. Kennedy's 1962 speech to the American Congress on consumer rights. In 1973 the European Commission created the Consumer Consultative Committee. Maier, "Institutional Consumer Representation," 355–356.

65. According to the new law, the SIC would determine the maximum interest rate allowed in the marketplace. If an individual or an entity charged above this rate, it would be guilty of usury. Until 1976, a maximum interest rate had not been established, so the usury law was not put into practice. Banks were exempted from these regulations. SIC, *Ley Federal de Protección al Consumidor*, 78.

66. Ibid., 14.

67. Ibid., 12.

68. Ibid., 26.

69. Ibid., 29.

70. M. A. Carballo, "Fueron instalados la Procuraduría y el Instituto del Consumidor," *Excélsior*, 6 February 1976.

71. SIC, *Ley Federal de Protección al Consumidor*, 69.

72. Ibid., 15.

73. Ibid., 60–61, 66; "La Ley de Protección al Consumidor," *Excélsior*, 10 January 1976; "Habrá sanciones para proteger al consumidor," *El Universal*, 10 January 1976.

74. See Chapter 2 for analysis of rumors in dry cleaning shops and other places frequented by the middle classes.

75. SIC, *Ley Federal de Protección al Consumidor*, 26–27.

76. M. A. Carballo, "Innecesario, fijar precios tope a más artículos," *Excélsior*, 20 January 1976; "Inversiones y producción," *El Sol de México*, 21 January 1976.

77. Neftali Celis, "La ley del consumidor puede dar paso a excesivo aparato burocrático," *Novedades*, 20 January 1976.

78. "Aplicando efectivamente la Ley Federal del Consumidor se eliminará al comerciante venal," *El Nacional*, 25 July 1976.

79. Neftali Celis, "Difundir la Ley de Protección al Consumidor será misión primordial que realice el INC," *Novedades*, 24 February 1976.

80. SIC, *Ley Federal de Protección al Consumidor*, 22.

81. Ibid., 21.

82. "Con nuevos artículos se manipula al consumidor, dice Campillo Sainz," *Excélsior*, 21 January 1976.

83. "Usuarios defraudados presentaron ayer las primeras denuncias a la Procuraduría Federal del Consumidor," *El Nacional*, 7 February 1976.

84. "Justificada energía en defensa del consumidor," *El Nacional*, 16 February 1976; Javier López Moren, "Ley para impulsar a la revolución," *El Día*, 23 February 1976.

85. Profeco's archive has information about denunciations and investigations, but its fifty-nine boxes only have files from 1981 (with the exception of a single case from 1976). Newspaper coverage of Profeco is more helpful for tracking change over time. However, press accounts and archival documents both indicate the same trends in denunciations.

86. Based on review of several hundred articles about Profeco catalogued in the Archivos Económicos collection of the Miguel Lerdo de Tejada library, Mexico City. See, for example, "Freno a los abusos en colegios particulares," *El Nacional*, 12 August 1976; Guillermo Pacheco, "Las cuotas de las escuelas particulares no deben lesionar el gasto familiar," *El Nacional*, 11 August 1976; "Eliminarán las agencias de viajes cláusulas lesivas a los usuarios de sus operaciones," *El Nacional*, 20 June 1978; "Por defraudar a clientes, la PFC multó con medio millón de pesos a una agencia de viaje," *El Nacional*, 18 March 1981; "Ha recibido la PFC 80 mil denuncias contra empresas de 'Tiempos Compartidos' en centros vacacionales," *El Nacional*, 22 April 1981; "Son un fraude los tratamientos de rejuvenecimiento," *El Nacional*, 9 April 1981; "Condominios, viajes, tarjetas, etc.: Iniciativa de ley para frenar abusos en 'ofertas' comerciales," *El Sol de México*, 28 May 1981; Octavio Medal, "Mano dura a tintorerías y lavanderías," *El Nacional*, 27 July 1982.

87. Profeco 1981, c. 9, exp. 2240, AGN; Profeco 1981, c. 11, exp. 2719, AGN; Profeco 1981, c. 48, exp. 22722, AGN. The names of individuals have been changed to protect their privacy.

88. This is clearly the case in the 1981 files in Profeco's archive and appears to be a trend in press coverage of the agency from 1976 through 1985. After these types of complaints, the second most common set of complaints concern prices of basic goods, from illegal or unposted prices to fiddling with measurements. The concentration of denunciations at two extremes of the income spectrum, from the cost of luxury apartments to the cost of beans, illustrates the array of consumers who sought recourse with the agency.

89. For example, in Lomas de San Mateo in the State of Mexico suburbs of Mexico City, consumers filed complaints about high interest rates and hidden fees. Another common complaint concerned price speculation on the part of "social interest" housing developers; this type of housing targeted lower-income families, but these practices often put it out of their price range. "Medidas contra fraccionadoras que actúen en forma impropia," *El Nacional*, 22 April 1976; "A 20 millones de pesos asciende el fraude en Cuautitlán Izcalli," *El Día*, 16 March 1976; Octavio Medal, "'Constructora Arga' defraudó con enganches de casas a 30 personas de escasos recursos," *El Nacional*, 10 March 1976. Worldwide, "social interest" housing has often been of more benefit to the middle classes; see Davis, *Planet of Slums*.

90. José Rosso L., "El 'Consumerismo' arriba a México," *El Nacional*, 24 May 1976; José Rosso L., "Condominios hechos con pura publicidad," *El Nacional*, 14 April 1976.

91. "La Procuraduría Federal del Consumidor alerta a la ciudadanía sobre la compra de condominios," *El Nacional*, 13 April 1976; "Miles de quejas ha recibido la PFC en contra de inmobiliarias," *El Heraldo de México*, 28 April 1981; "Implica adquirir un condominio riesgos y molestias imprevistas," *El Día*, 13 October 1983.

92. Profeco 1981, c. 15, exp. 3930, AGN. Names of individuals have been changed.

93. Carolina Navarrete, "Advierte la PFC: Epidemia de fraudes en bienes raíces," *El Sol de México*, 24 April 1982.

94. Profeco 1981, c. 17, exp. 4430, AGN; Profeco 1981, c. 50, exp. 24660, AGN. Names of individuals have been changed.

95. Profeco 1981, c. 44, exp. 19673, AGN. Individual's name has been changed.

96. Nidia Marín, "Al que cobre en dólares, multa, arresto y clausura," *El Universal*, 1 October 1976; Antonio Lara Barragán, "Quieren cobrar miles de créditos, en dólares," *El Universal*, 4 October 1976.

97. Gonzalo Martre, "Contra el consumidor," *Excélsior*, 8 November 1976.

98. The text of Mexico's monetary law is available at the Bank of Mexico website.

99. "El consumidor sin procuraduría," *El Sol de México*, 19 November 1976.

100. Juan Ignacio Vigueras, "84 mil 500 mexicanos adeudan 40 millones de dólares a comercios de El Paso, Texas," *El Día*, 25 January 1983.

101. Alfredo Jiménez, "No hay por qué dolarizarnos," *Excélsior*, 15 March 1977; "Las faccionadoras se rebelan contra la PFC," *El Día*, 14 May 1978; "Si las inmobiliarias no ceden, se llegará a los tribunales," *El Día*, 15 December 1976; Triunfo A. Elizalde, "No prosperan en México los contratos en dólares: PFC," *Novedades*, 4 February 1982.

102. "A no aceptar deudas en dólares llama la PFC," *Novedades*, 11 March 1982.

103. Víctor Manuel Juárez, "Se ha agudizado la anarquía en la comercialización de básicos: PFC," *Uno más Uno*, 6 October 1982.

104. "A no aceptar deudas en dólares llama la PFC," *Novedades*, 11 March 1982; Manuel Mejido, "Alto poder: Advertencia de la PFC: Colegiaturas elevadas," *El Universal*, 4 June 1982; Octavio Medal, "Actuará con energía la Profeco en contra de los abusos en escuelas particulares: Algunos propietarios han tenido el cinismo de cobrar colegiaturas y uniformes ¡en dólares!," *El Nacional*, 24 August 1982; Jamie Contreras Salcedo, "No podrán alterarse contratos de compraventa firmados antes del 6 de Agosto: Profeco," *Excélsior*, 11 August 1982; "Fraguaban varias inmobiliarias un multimillonario fraude: Efectuaron miles de contratos en dólares," *El Nacional*, 11 July 1982; Fernando Aranzábal, "Improcedente la actitud de las aerolíneas al cobrar los incrementos: Pliego Montes," *Excélsior*, 13 July 1985.

105. Octavio Medal, "Actuará con energía la Profeco en contra de los abusos en escuelas particulares: Algunos propietarios han tenido el cinismo de cobrar colegiaturas y uniformes ¡en dólares!," *El Nacional*, 24 August 1982.

106. SIC, *Ley Federal de Protección al Consumidor*, 33.

107. Ibid., 34.

108. Ibid., 33–34, 69.

109. The Books for the Consumer series published novels and essays by some of Mexico's most prominent writers. In addition to Loaeza's two novels, its list includes Cristina Pacheco's *La rueda de la fortuna* (The wheel of fortune; 1993), Carlos Monsiváis's *Los rituales del caos* (Rituals of chaos; 1995), and several studies of patterns of consumption, especially as related to health and medicine. I focus on Loaeza's *Compro, luego existo* because it is closest to the time period under study; to round out the story, I also include an analysis of the sequel. Note that

Inco dissolved in 1992 and Profeco took over its functions. Loaeza's first book and Pacheco's book were published by Inco, while Monsiváis's essay and Loaeza's sequel were published by Profeco.

110. Both *Compro, luego existo* and *Debo, luego sufro* are part of Loaeza's opus of novels and essays that sardonically chronicle the trials and tribulations (or, better said, the discreet pleasures?) of this social stratum. See also Loaeza, *Las reinas de Polanco* and *Las niñas bien*.

111. Loaeza, *Compro, luego existo*, 16.

112. Loaeza, *Debo, luego sufro*, 25.

113. Ibid., 27–28.

114. Ibid., 28.

115. Ibid., 101–104. I discuss the 1994 devaluation in the Conclusion.

116. Ibid., 261–271.

117. Ibid., 108.

118. Loaeza, *Compro, luego existo*, 68–75.

119. Ibid., 112, 123.

120. Loaeza, *Debo, luego sufro*, 273–276.

121. Ibid., 44.

122. Ibid., 51.

123. There is an abundant literature on the value-added tax in Mexico. Most of these books are guides for accountants and businesses on how to comply with the tax. There is a surprisingly scant amount of scholarly interest in the IVA and taxation more generally, especially from the analytical perspectives of political and cultural history. This seems to be changing, however. An article by Carlos Elizondo has opened the study of tax reform to political (and, to a lesser extent, cultural) analysis. Further, a team of researchers at the CIDE (Centro de Investigación y Docencia Económicas) have started ongoing research on taxation in Mexico. The fruits of these efforts can already be seen in working papers and student theses. Elizondo, "In Search of Revenue"; Elizondo Mayer-Serra and Pérez de Acha, "Separación de poderes y garantías individuales."

124. If these goods were consumed in the place of sale, as in a restaurant, however, they would be considered a service, and consumers would have to pay the IVA. All books, magazines, and newspapers were exempt. Professional and independent services, such as a lawyer, were likewise exempt, as were private schools and other educational services. Secretaría de Hacienda y Crédito Público (hereafter SHCP), *Preguntas y respuestas en torno del Impuesto al Valor Agregado: Reforma fiscal; Viva el cambio*; SHCP, *El ABC del IVA*.

125. SHCP, *Régimen fiscal de los causantes menores en el I.V.A.: Viva el cambio; Reforma fiscal*; SHCP, *Preguntas y respuestas en torno del Impuesto al Valor Agregado: Reforma fiscal; Viva el cambio*; SHCP, *El ABC del IVA*, 1979.

126. Note that the IVA rate was 6 percent in the border areas and free trade zones. SHCP, "Tasa 6% 1980," 1979, JLP, c. 1897, exp. 4, AGN.

127. David Ibarra Muñoz, remarks made at a seminar on the IVA in Mexico City on 14 December 1979. Ibarra Muñoz, *Hacienda y crédito público*, 16–17.

128. David Ibarra Muñoz, remarks made at a convention of finance executives in Guadalajara on 19 November 1970. Ibid., 18–19.

129. SHCP, *Régimen fiscal de los causantes menores en el I.V.A.: Viva el cambio; Reforma fiscal.*

130. Elizondo, "In Search of Revenue," 163, 171–173; Solís, *Economic Policy Reform in Mexico*, 67–77.

131. Carlos Elizondo makes a similar point about Salinas's successful income tax reform. In that instance, the political capacity to introduce an asset tax represented a greater victory than the meager revenue generated by the rather symbolic rate of 2 percent. Elizondo, "In Search of Revenue," 177–180.

132. Mo Lai-Lan, *Tax Avoidance and Anti-Avoidance Measures*, 123–131.

133. SHCP, *Las aventuras del Fideo: El caso del monstruo que resultó cuate*, 1979, JLP, c. 1897, exp. 7, AGN.

134. One journalist anticipated the confusion and controversies around application of the IVA, predicting that the new tax would worsen New Year's Day hangovers. Manuel Roberto Montenegro, "Y mañana . . . el IVA," *Excélsior*, 31 December 1979.

135. Elda Montiel Toral, "Mil 90 quejas ha recibido la PFC debido al Valor Agregado," *El Día*, 5 January 1980; "Cientos de denuncias por cobro indebido del IVA recibe la PFC," *Excélsior*, 11 January 1983.

136. SHCP, *Régimen fiscal de los causantes menores en el I.V.A: Viva el cambio; Reforma fiscal*, 1979, JLP, c. 1899, exp. 58, pg. 6, AGN.

137. "¿Qué onda con el IVA?," *Expansión* 6 February 1980.

138. Ibid.

139. J. Jesús Rangel M., "Injusto, no aplicar IVA en tiendas sindicales," *Excélsior*, 30 December 1979; "¿Hacía dónde quieren ir los empresarios?," *El Día*, 7 January 1980; "Presentarán un amparo por la exclusión del pago del IVA en tiendas sindicales," *Excélsior*, 8 January 1980; Neftali Celis, "No procede el amparo contra el IVA," *Novedades*, 13 February 1980.

140. Ignacio Moreno Tagle, "Justicia equitatIVA," *El Universal*, 19 January 1983; Luis E. Mercado, "Sólo a 13 productos 20% de IVA," *El Universal*, 10 December 1982; "Cientos de denuncias por cobro indebido del IVA recibe la PFC," *Excélsior*, 11 January 1983.

141. Carlos Velasco Molina, "Aprueba la Cámara la inclusión del IVA en el precio final," *Excélsior*, 21 December 1984.

142. Luis E. Mercado, "Noticias bursátiles," *El Universal*, 18 December 1984.

CHAPTER 5

1. The history of the lost decade, the debt crisis, and the emergence of neoliberalism is a Latin American one; the Mexican experiences described in this chapter are part of broader historical processes.

2. Amparo Espinosa de Serrano, "En época de austeridad se requiere credulidad," *Novedades*, 22 June 1982.

3. Here, I am drawing on David Harvey's definition of neoliberalism: "Neoliberalism is in the first instance a theory of political economic practices that proposes that human well-being can best be advanced by liberating individual entrepreneurial freedoms and skills within an institutional framework characterized by strong private property rights, free markets, and free trade. The role of the state is to create

and preserve an institutional framework appropriate to such practices. . . . State interventions in markets (once created) must be kept to a bare minimum. . . . It holds that the social good will be maximized by maximizing the reach and frequency of market transactions, and it seeks to bring all human action into the domain of the market." Harvey, *Brief History*, 2.

4. Lustig, *Remaking of an Economy*, 24.

5. For more on the nationalization of the Mexican banks, see Ángel Mobarak, Bazdresch Parada, and Suárez Dávila, *Cuando el estado se hizo banquero.*

6. Cornelius, "Political Economy of Mexico," 93. The letter of intent, together with its technical memorandum, was leaked to the Mexican press and published by the political magazine *Proceso* on 29 November 1982. An IMF publication describes the negotiations between the IMF and Mexican policymakers: Boughton, *Silent Revolution*, esp. chap. 7, "The Mexican Crisis: No Mountain Too High?"

7. Wayne Cornelius discusses both negative and positive evaluations of de la Madrid's enforcement of the IMF agreement during his first year in office. The point here is not whether de la Madrid's actions constituted sound economic policy but that the president was considered to have gone above and beyond the requirements of the IMF. Abel Beltrán del Río's negative appraisal described how Mexico "complied excessively" with the IMF; William Cline praised the "overkill." Cornelius, "Political Economy of Mexico," 97.

8. For analysis of increased income polarization within the middle classes, see Alarcón and McKinley, "Increasing Wage Inequality."

9. For more on private-sector organizations, see Chapter 2.

10. "Reunión de empresarios . . . ," 8 November 1982, DFS, 009-025-012, 8/11/82, AGN.

11. Ibid.

12. "Reunión de empresarios . . . ," 11 November 1982, DFS, 009-025-012, AGN.

13. In 1980, political scientist Dale Story surveyed leading industrialists in Mexico about their attitudes toward state intervention in the economy, among other topics. He found that 82 percent of the 109 respondents were critical of the state's intervention in the economy. From the 1940s through the early 1970s, industrialists supported state aid for industry, but by the mid-1970s they were uniting against further state "encroachment" into the economic sphere (365). In particular, they opposed nationalization of industries. With regard to six specific issues of state-industry relations—credit, prices, protectionism, labor, public spending, and taxes—the majority of industrialists surveyed believed that only two issues (credit and protectionism) were favorable to industry (371). Story concludes that "government intervention is seen as overly excessive in Mexico at the present time" (366). Story, "Industrial Elites in Mexico." For analysis of reactions from different private sector organizations to the bank nationalization, see Luna, Millán, and Tirado, "Empresarios en los inicios," 220–223.

14. De la Madrid, *Inaugural Address*, 29–30.

15. Massive public sector reform became the central feature of the president's worldview. Whereas Echeverría and López Portillo had increased the number and

size of the state-run enterprises, de la Madrid aimed to curtail or eliminate such enterprises. See Lustig and Ros, "Economic Reforms."

16. De la Madrid, *Inaugural Address*, 5–7.

17. Ibid., 8.

18. Ibid., 8, 9, 12.

19. In this regard, de la Madrid's economic plan can be understood as part of the global phenomenon of neoliberal structural adjustment as described by Harvey: "In return for debt rescheduling, indebted countries were required to implement institutional reforms, such as cuts in welfare expenditures, more flexible labor market laws, and privatization. Thus 'structural adjustment' was invented." Harvey, *Brief History*, 29.

20. Judith Teichman describes three overlapping periods in de la Madrid's economic policies: "(1) 1983–1984, economic stabilization and strict austerity, along with resistance to economic liberalization, (2) 1984–1986, economic reactivation combined with a clear commitment to economic liberalization, and (3) 1987–1988, a return to austerity and a continued commitment to economic liberalization." Teichman, "The Mexican State and the Political Implications of Economic Restructuring," 91.

21. Knight, "Populism and Neo-Populism," 244–248. See also Cornelius, Craig, and Fox, *Transforming State-Society Relations in Mexico*.

22. Thatcher's statement comes from a 1981 interview with the *Sunday Times*, in which she described her goal to emphasize individualism in her economic policy. For Thatcher, this was an important shift away from what she described as the "collectivist" approach of the 1950s–1970s. Her emphasis on individualism, or "personal society," was a quest to change "the heart and soul of the nation." Holmes, *First Thatcher Government*, 209. Also quoted in Harvey, *Brief History*, 22–23.

23. Williams, *Keywords*, 14.

24. States of exception, or states of emergency, have been extensively analyzed on theoretical and historical grounds, especially in relation to dictatorships and fascism. The most prominent scholars of these concepts include Carl Schmitt, Walter Benjamin, and Giorgio Agamben. Whereas Schmitt postulates that the power of a sovereign is the power to declare an exception, Agamben (following Benjamin) contends that that power acquired by a sovereign through declaring a state of exception is an aberration of law and abuse of power on part of the sovereign (as opposed to the legal and philosophical basis for sovereignty, à la Schmitt). Both Benjamin and Agamben emphasize the danger (fascism) inherent in states of exception/emergency, especially when the exception becomes the rule. Whereas Schmitt, Benjamin, and Agamben analyze states of exception/emergency as legal declarations by a sovereign or a government (and the implications of and actions following such declarations), in this chapter I consider a more diffuse state of exception/emergency, one created by a zeitgeist of crisis. While de la Madrid did not declare a legal state of exception/emergency (which might have included martial law and suspension of certain rights), I argue that, from the outset, he promoted a feeling of exception and emergency. This is best exemplified by his inaugural address, cited above. Agamben, *State of Exception*; Benjamin, "Theses on the Philosophy of History"; Schmitt, *Political Theology*.

25. We should, however, avoid too-extreme oppositions. In Mexico, the private sector did not necessarily represent a free market ideal. Instead, it largely comprised monopolistic family dynasties that depended upon state subsidies. Mexico's economy is best described as a mixed economy, under both ISI and neoliberalism, characterized by a mixture of state and private investment. Change occurred with regard to the ratio of state to private sector participation.

26. Teichman, "Neoliberalism and the Transformation of Mexican Authoritarianism," 3–5.

27. Lustig and Ros, "Economic Reforms, " 27 (italics added). Lustig and Ros continue: "Given its limited resources and the need to rely on external savings to restore and sustain growth, to have access to public credit the government had to introduce market-oriented reforms to please multilateral institutions and the U.S. government" (27).

28. Raúl Sohr, "Fuerte inflación augura a México: *The Economist*," *Novedades*, 15 August 1982.

29. See note 7 above.

30. Teivainen, *Enter Economism, Exit Politics*, 68. The following analysis of García's debt rebellion draws extensively from Teivainen's study.

31. Quoted in ibid., 73.

32. Ibid., 76.

33. Teivainen describes the view that economic issues are apolitical as "economism." And he argues that the conditionality principle became "one of the most effective mechanisms of global economic surveillance." Ibid., 1, 39–40.

34. "Situación que prevalece con motivo de los movimientos telúricos," 23 September 1985, DFS, 009-031-003, legajo 6, AGN.

35. DFS, "Información del Frente Nacional Contra la Represión," 25 September 1985, DFS, 009-031-003, legajo 7, AGN. For analyses of the political effects of earthquakes in Latin America, see Buchenau and Johnson, eds., *Aftershocks*.

36. Francisco Ortiz Mendoza, "Terremoto, industriales y deuda externa," *Combatiente*, 30 September 1985, MMH, 32.03.00.00, c. 2, exp. 4, AGN.

37. "Marcha plantón de la coordinadora única de damnificados," 26 October 1985, DFS, 009-031-003, legajo 20, AGN.

38. Teiveinen, *Enter Economism*, 84.

39. Ibid.

40. Ibid., 74–75.

41. Ibid., 75.

42. That said, many potential opponents of neoliberalism in Mexico had suffered repression or been killed in the state-sponsored violence, massacres, and dirty wars of the 1960s and 1970s. And throughout the 1980s, labor agitation against austerity measures was repressed. Further, in Mexico another form of coercion shaped the implementation of neoliberalism: it is conceivable that the debt crisis and the international credit system substituted, in part, for Pinochet's repressive apparatus and his University of Chicago economic advisors. Thus, Mexico's neoliberal transition was not without violence. It occurred, however, in a supposedly democratic country, unlike Pinochet's Chile. As such, the Mexican case stands as a partial exception to the argument that state-sponsored terror was necessary for the

implementation of neoliberalism in Latin America; see, for example, Grandin, *Last Colonial Massacre*.

43. In 1982 the United States forced the "purge" of Keynesian influence in the IMF, after which both the IMF and the World Bank became centers of neoliberal orthodoxy. Harvey, *Brief History*, 29. See also Stiglitz, *Globalization and Its Discontents*.

44. Harvey, *Brief History*, 13.

45. David Harvey describes how the spread of neoliberalism through an array of educational, cultural, corporate, state, and international institutions in the United States conferred on neoliberal thinking the illusion of common sense (e.g., by the end of the 1980s, most economics departments at research universities in the United States had fallen into line with neoliberalism). Sarah Babb argues that changes in economics education facilitated the shift to neoliberalism in Mexico. She charts how the UNAM economics faculty, influenced by the Cambridge Keynesian model, had been the center of academic power during the midcentury boom decades. Babb documents the rising importance of private universities from the 1960s on, which were oriented toward a finance theory economics convergent with academic trends in the United States. The gulf between the UNAM and the private universities widened in the 1970s as the former became more radical, embracing Marxist economics. Babb argues that the rise of private education in Mexico, and the ideological alignment of their economics departments with American institutions, altered how Mexican policymakers conceptualized the relationship between the economy and society. In this line of argument, de la Madrid represented "a group of technocrats whose training in mainstream neoclassical economics predisposed them to look favorably on the dismantling of the developmentalist state" (171). Babb, *Managing Mexico*, esp. 171–198; Harvey, *Brief History*, 3, 39; see also Carr, *Marxism and Communism*, 243–244.

46. Some journalists asked what would be sacrificed in the name of efficiency. Journalists reported fears that the new class of technocrats—a new governing class—would implement models of development that were out of step with Mexico's social reality. See the folder of newspaper clippings "Tecnoburocracia" in the Archivos Económicos collection of the Lerdo de Tejada library, including, for example, "¿Político o tecnócrata?," *El Día*, 4 July 1981; Alfredo Kawage Ramira, "¿Y cuándo las palabras pierden significado?," *Novedades*, 11 July 1981; Roberto Gómez Reyes, "Capacidad política no es tecnoburocracia," *El Sol de México*, 16 November 1981; Víctor Rodríguez Juárez, "Tecnocracia o política," *El Sol de México*, 9 July 1981; Javier Ibarrola, "La política de la tecnocracia," *El Universal*, 4 July 1981.

47. José Luis Mejías, "Tecnocracias," *Excélsior*, 8 July 1981.

48. Mario Ezcurdia, "Por qué un político y no un tecnócrata?," *El Día*, 1 July 1981; Luis Cervantes Jáuregui, "Límites del decisionismo," *Uno más Uno*, 18 December 1982. See also Ezcurdia, *Análisis teórico del Partido Revolucionario Institucional*.

49. On corruption in the privatization of public enterprises, see Lustig and Ros, "Economic Reforms," 32–33.

50. "¿Político o tecnócrata?," *El Día*, 4 July 1981; Alfredo Kawage Ramira,

"¿Y cuándo las palabras pierden significado?," *Novedades,* 11 July 1981. See also historian Roderic Camp's study of technocrats and politicians, "Political Technocrat in Mexico."

51. Alan Knight argues against a schematization that reflexively connects populism with ISI. In his analysis, populism is best defined loosely as a political style, not a set of policies connected to any specific mode of development. Knight, "Populism and Neo-Populism."

52. De la Madrid, *Inaugural Address,* 19–20.

53. Ibid., 32.

54. Poniatowska, *Domingo 7,* 156. See also Schmidt, "Mexican Foreign Debt," 242.

55. Dennis Gilbert, however, argues that the crisis of the 1980s did not have an overly adverse effect on the middle classes. He interviewed middle-class residents in Cuernavaca after the 1994–95 economic crisis and finds that the period from 1982 to 1994 was a "fondly remembered era of middle-class prosperity" that came to an end in 1994 (40). It is possible, though, that when asked about their memory of the 1980s so soon after the 1994 crisis, his interviewees' memories of the 1980s might have been rosier than what they experienced at the time. In addition to interviews, Gilbert uses income and consumption data for the 1984–1994 period, but he often takes the years between 1984 and 1994 as a single unit (37–41, 106). No doubt, the middle classes began to emerge from the crisis in the late 1980s and indeed did fairly well for a few years until 1994, but it is problematic to conflate the late 1980s with the early 1980s. Instead of a major change in 1994, I would emphasize greater continuity between the 1970s, 1980s, and 1990s. That said, Gilbert's argument about the 1980s serves as a helpful reminder that not all the middle classes suffered in the economic crisis. Gilbert, *Mexico's Middle Class.*

56. Contemporary analyses of these studies were published by experts at Inco: Manjarrez Medina, "Cambios en el consumo" and de Lara Rangel, "Impacto económico." The survey was called "Seguimiento de la situación [or gasto] alimentaria de la población de escasos recursos en el área metropolitana de la Ciudad de México." Escobar Latapí and Roberts also draw upon these surveys (versions of the surveys that were presented in a conference paper), alongside other sources, to chart decreased social mobility in Mexico during the 1980s. Escobar Latapí and Roberts, "Urban Stratification."

57. De Lara Rangel, "Impacto económico," 30–31.

58. Ibid., 32–33.

59. Ibid., 33–35.

60. Samaniego de Villarreal, "Algunas reflexiones," 56–57. Diane Davis notes that the cost of private education increased up to 100 percent during the 1980s crisis. Davis, *Urban Leviathan,* 278.

61. Samaniego de Villarreal, "Algunas reflexiones," 58.

62. Lustig, "1982 Debt Crisis," 158.

63. Samaniego de Villarreal, "Algunas reflexiones," 58.

64. Fernando Cantu Jauckens, "Tribulaciones de la clase media," *El Universal,* 3 January 1983.

65. Juan Rodríguez, "Sólo 1.5 millones de mexicanos viajarán al extranjero en 1983," 15 March 1983; Mario García Sordo, "Tres millones de capitalinos dejaron de ir al cinematógrafo; causa, la austeridad," *Uno más Uno*, 27 December 1982; Reynaldo González Santos, "La crisis borró los prejuicios; ahora demasiada gente 'prefiere' ponerse zapatos y ropa usada," *El Universal*, 16 October 1984.

66. Olmedo is a professor of political and social science at the UNAM. From 1976 to 1986 he was director of the financial section of *Excélsior*.

67. I have not included notes that link every point to a different article because there is significant repetition within this series. Interested readers should consult the entire forty articles, which appeared in *Excélsior* between 12 December 1984 and 2 February 1985.

68. This is Olmedo's argument, but many *telenovelas* featured the upper classes.

69. Here, Olmeda makes an important argument about reception and the power of the public sphere, that is, that the middle classes internalize images of "middle class"—representations have material force.

70. "El empresario mexicano: Un terco sobreviviente," *Expansión*, 12 January 1983.

71. Camacho et al., *Sociedad: Las clases medias*, 15.

72. Ibid., 14–15.

73. Palacios, "Efectos psicológicos," 111–112.

74. Ibid., 113.

75. Barreda Solórzano, "La crisis y la criminalidad," 120.

76. Ibid., 117.

77. Loaeza, "Clases medias mexicanas," 236.

78. Barreda Solórzano, "La crisis y la criminalidad," 117–118.

79. As James Ferguson argues, "The breakdown of certain teleological under-standings of modernity (on which much ink has lately been spilled in academia) has occurred not only in the world of theory, but in the lived understandings of those who received such myths as a kind of promise" (14). Ferguson charts the experience of economic decline among workers in the Zambian copper belt. He describes the feelings of abjection and disconnect among workers in this former boom area (236–238). Though focused on the other side of the world, Ferguson's study is illustrative for our purposes. Like the Mexican Miracle, the Zambian copper boom had been cast as a teleological narrative of modernization and prosperity; like Mexico, Zambia was portrayed as "entering" the developed world (2–6). Studying the social experience of economic decline, Ferguson describes how workers, "now in tattered clothes . . . could remember ordering tailored suits from London or owning a car." Following the crash in world copper prices, this material comfort was lost, and so was a set of intangible expectations that had accompanied these material goods: "A certain ethos of hopefulness, self-respect, and optimism that, many seemed sure, was now (like the cars) simply 'gone, gone never to return again'" (12). Ferguson, *Expectations of Modernity*.

80. Lomnitz, "Times of Crisis," 130–132.

81. Ibid., 139–140.

82. Ibid., 135.

83. Ibid., 136.

84. Semo, "The Left and the Crisis," 31.

85. Loaeza argues this point but does not document the middle classes' fear of class violence. Loaeza, "Clases medias mexicanas," 236.

86. Ibid., 236.

87. Speculation about how the middle classes would react to the economic crisis abounded. See, for example, a series of articles in the business magazine *Expansión*: "Ningún partido ha podido movilizar a la clase media," *Expansión*, 11 November 1981; "La agonía silenciosa de la clase media," *Expansión*, 11 May 1983; "La clase media Mexicana: Del éxtasis a la agonía," *Expansión*, 10 December 1986.

88. For a summary, see Carr, "The Mexican Left."

89. Ibid., 9–10.

90. Ibid., 3–8.

91. Georgina Howard, Armando Cruz, and Julio César Escobar, "Burócratas de confianza demandarán su reubicación y cese al despido masivo," *El Día*, 14 August 1985; "Crearán un frente intersecretarial para defensa del empleo y salario," *Excélsior*, 31 July 1985; Armando Cruz and Julio César Escobar, "El FIDE en sesión permanente; hará hoy una manifestación frente al Zócalo," *El Día*, 8 August 1985; "FIDE: Nos regresan el empleo o seguirán marchas y plantones," *El Universal*, 13 August 1985; "Para fines de año más de 100 mil burócratas estarán sin empleo," *El Día*, 11 August 1985; Georgina Howard and MPU, "Se ampliarán burócratas despedidos contra la supresión de oficinas," *El Día*, 17 August 1985.

92. Middlebrook, "Sounds of Silence," 208.

93. Ibid.

94. Prominent middle-class participation in the social movement that emerged after the September 1985 earthquake revealed another form of protest against the economic changes underway during the 1980s; this is the subject of Chapter 6. While the UNAM and earthquake protests could be analyzed together, I separate them because the former represented a localized mobilization and the latter represented more generalized discontent.

95. My discussion of the 1986 student movement draws extensively from Gutiérrez Garza, "Respuesta estudiantil," and Monsiváis, *Entrada libre*, which provide information about the motivation for and development of the protest movement. See also Casanova Cardiel, "UNAM entre 1970 y 2000," 298–305; Mendoza Rojas, *Conflictos de la UNAM*, 168–177; and Moreno, *Reforma universitaria*.

96. Gutiérrez Garza, "Respuesta estudiantil," 218–219.

97. Monsiváis, *Entrada libre*, 246–247.

98. Salvador Martínez Della Rocca, quoted in Monsiváis, *Entrada libre*, 247 (original citation information not given).

99. Gutiérrez Garza, "Respuesta estudiantil," 219.

100. Monsiváis, *Entrada libre*, 252 (italics in original).

101. Ibid., 232.

102. Ibid., 220–225.

103. Gutiérrez Garza, "Respuesta estudiantil," 234. Lomnitz argues, however, that the striking students engaged in a destructive self-sacrifice of their future. Accordingly, their fears about the present undermined their capacity to construct a future. In his account, the university student confronts the reality that his or her education will not lead to a job, then hijacks the university through a strike, which further undermines the value of the education. Lomnitz, "Times of Crisis," 132. These different interpretations of strikes—are they a form of self-sacrifice or an alternative vision of the future?—carry political implications. Because strikes and labor activism more generally can achieve significant victories for students and other university workers—at Yale University in the United States, for example—it is politically troubling to characterize student strikes as a form of self-sacrifice. There was a lot at stake in the struggles at the UNAM in 1986. These stakes are similar, if not higher, today as access to high-quality and affordable education becomes increasingly restricted in both Mexico and the United States. See the analysis of the union struggle at Yale, for example, "The Yale Strike Dossier," *Social Text*, no. 49 (Winter 1996). For analyses of labor and higher education, see various issues of *Workplace: A Journal for Academic Labor*.

104. "Nacidos para ganar: Los jóvenes empresarios y ejecutivos," *Expansión*, 30 October 1985.

105. Ibid.

106. Ibid.

107. Ibid. On the expectations for GATT, see also "La clase media mexicana: Del éxtasis a la agonía," *Expansión*, 10 December 1986.

108. Ricardo Medina Macías, "Ahí vienen los 'yuppies,'" *Expansión*, 16 October 1986.

109. Monsiváis, *Escenas de pudor y liviandad*, 347.

110. Not all portrayals of the yuppies were positive, however, and some journalists worried that a dark, perturbed reality might lie beneath their confidence. Ricardo Medina Macías, "Ahí vienen los 'yuppies,'" *Expansión*, 16 October 1986.

111. We know that inequality increased in general in Mexico during these years, especially from 1984 to 1994, but still need more studies on inequality within groups. For a big-picture analysis, see Lustig and Gasparini, "Rise and Fall of Income Inequality in Latin America," esp. 18–22; Scott, "Social Failure of the Mexican Revolution."

112. Alarcón and McKinley, "Increasing Wage Inequality."

113. Monsiváis, *Escenas de pudor y liviandad*, 345.

114. Scholarly analysis of the neoliberal built environment focuses heavily on Mexico City, although other megaprojects include residential and tourism developments in Baja California and the Yucatán, the Angelopolis project in Puebla, and the JVC project in Guadalajara. Likewise, neoliberalism produced new rural geographies, including massive agribusiness, poisonous pesticides, and migration. For the purposes of this analysis, Santa Fe is most relevant because its development connects the optimism of the oil boom with enthusiasm over economic liberalization. For analysis of other urban built environments, see Jones and Moreno-Carranco, "Megaprojects." For analysis of rural geographies, see Wright, *Death of Ramón González*.

115. Moreno Carranco, "Socio/Spatial Production of the Global," 52. My analysis of Santa Fe draws extensively from Moreno Carranco's dissertation.

116. Although these figures are disputed, it seems that the city government paid 3 centavos (considerably less than one American cent at the time) per square meter in the early 1980s, then sold the land in the late 1980s and early 1990s for nearly US$200 per square meter. In the early 2000s, land values range from US$800 to US$2000 per square meter. Moreno Carranco, "Socio/Spatial Production," 61–62.

117. Ibid., 65–66.

118. Ibid., 11, 42.

119. Ibid., 11, 28.

120. Ibid., 78, 232. See also Giglia, "Gated Communities."

121. Moreno Carranco, "Socio/Spatial Production," 232.

122. Ibid., 232–239. To be sure, advertising masked a different reality, as residents complained about deficiencies and failing services.

123. There is a growing interest in the social and cultural worlds of the middle classes and other social groups. In the 1990s, the National Institute of Statistics, Geography, and Information (Instituto Nacional de Estadística, Geografía e Informática, or INEGI) began to conduct surveys to collect information on cultural practices, providing researchers with valuable information for recent decades. Unfortunately, though, we do not have this sort of information for earlier decades. Also in the 1990s, anthropologists and other social scientists turned their attention to cultural consumption and everyday cultural practices in Mexico, with an important focus on the middle classes. See García Canclini, *Consumo cultural en México* (esp. the discussion of sources and methodology, 15–16).

124. Mendoza Rojas, "Educación superior privada," 336. For analysis of private education before 1970, see Torres Septién, *Educación privada en México*.

125. Babb, *Managing Mexico*, 155; Levy, *Higher Education*, 46–47. It is important to remember, however, that any kind of higher education remained a privilege, as explained in the Introduction. Loaeza, "Clases medias mexicanas," 227; Coplamar, *Necesidades esenciales en Mexico: Educación*, 54–58.

126. Education remained a fault line within the middle classes throughout the 1990s and 2000s. Legovini, Bouillón, and Lustig, "Can Education Explain"; Haber et al., *Mexico after 1980*, 175–176; Gilbert, *Mexico's Middle Class*, 48–50.

127. Carmen Aguilar and Gerardo Mendiola, "Perfil del ejecutivo en México," *Expansión*, 13 May 1987.

128. Ibid. Of those surveyed, 2.2 percent did not answer this question.

129. Minushkin, "Banqueros and Bolseros," 928–933.

130. Although the stock market had received some support from previous administrations, it had traditionally been a weak and secondary institution in the financial system as compared to the powerful banks. On the history of the stock market, see Minushkin, "Banqueros and Bolseros." Moreno Carranco connects the stock market to the neoliberal vision of Mexico City as a financial and commercial capital for the nation and the continent. Moreno Carranco, "Socio/Spatial Production," 39.

131. Ernesto Flores, "El bienestar de la cultura bursátil," *Expansión*, 15 April 1987.

132. Ibid.

133. Ibid.

134. Ibid.

135. "¿Qué son las sociedades de inversión?," *Expansión*, 30 September 1987.

136. "Métase a un *club*, pero de inversión," *Expansión*, 5 August 1987.

137. Ernesto Flores Vega, "El *supercrack* ¿presagia tormenta?," *Expansión* 25 November 1987.

138. Ibid.

139. Ibid.

140. Minushkin, "Banqueros and Bolseros," 933–938.

141. Bruhn, *Taking on Goliath*, 71–77. Bruhn describes the alliance: "If Cárdenas became the spiritual heart of the Corriente, and González Guevara its head, Porfirio Muñoz Ledo was its hands" (77). See Bruhn, *Taking on Goliath*; Carr, *Marxism and Communism*, 306–317; Gilly, *Cartas a Cuauhtémoc Cárdenas*; and Wuhs, *Savage Democracy*.

142. Bruhn, *Taking on Goliath*, 78–103.

143. Ibid., 103–115.

144. Teichman, "Mexican State and the Political Implications," 97–98.

145. On the diverse campesino support for Cuauhtémoc Cárdenas, see the letters sent to the candidate collected in Gilly, *Cartas a Cuauhtémoc Cárdenas*.

146. Teichman discusses this negative perception of neoliberalism in the public mind. Possibly, the decline in living standards might be attributed to the failure of state-led development (and the petro-state) and not to the emerging neoliberal paradigm, but what is important here is public perception. Teichman, "Mexican State and the Political Implications," 101.

147. For analysis of the campaign and the elections, see Bruhn, *Taking on Goliath*, 115–164.

148. De la Madrid, *Inaugural Address*, 29–30.

149. I am drawing upon James Ferguson's discussion of "scripts" of modernization and urbanization. By script of development, I envision an economic model, such as ISI or neoliberalism, as a script with a plotline and characters that advance toward a specific goal. Ferguson, *Expectations of Modernity*, 6.

150. Rolando Cordera Campos, "Requiem para un modelo," *Uno más Uno*, 14 November 1982.

CHAPTER 6

An earlier version of this chapter appeared in Jürgen Buchenau and Lyman L. Johnson, eds., *Aftershocks: Earthquakes and Popular Politics in Latin America* (Albuquerque: University of New Mexico Press, 2009). I am grateful to the University of New Mexico Press for permission to republish.

1. Serna and Coordinadora Única de Damnificados (henceforth CUD), *¡Aquí nos quedaremos!*, 33.

2. This description of the sounds draws from the testimonial literature and first-hand accounts of the event. See, for example, Aguilar Zinser, Morales, and Peña, *Aún tiembla*; Núñez de la Peña and Orozco, *El terremoto*; Poniatowska, *Nothing, Nobody*; Serna and CUD, *¡Aquí nos quedaremos!*

3. "Información del DDF [Departamento del Distrito Federal]," 19 September 1985, MMH, 30.00.00.00, c. 1, AGN.

4. Raúl Macín A., "Una lectura del apocalipsis," *Los Universitarios*, December 1985, MMH, 32.06.01.00, c. 7, exp. 11, AGN.

5. "Ciudadano," 22 September 1985, DFS, 009-031-003, legajo 6, AGN.

6. Poniatowska, *Nothing, Nobody*, 11.

7. "Situación que prevalece en la Col. Morelos y zonas aledañas, respecto al movimiento telúrico ocurrido hoy," 19 September 1985, DFS, 009-031-003, legajo 5, AGN; and "Situación que prevalece con motivo de los movimientos telúricos," 23 September 1985, DFS, 009-031-003, legajo 6, AGN.

8. "Victim" is a translation of the Spanish word *damnificado*, which is used to refer to the earthquake victims. But it is an imperfect translation, because the Spanish word does not imply victimization as its English equivalent does. Residents who joined the protest movement were not victimized but empowered.

9. Cantú Chapa, *Tlatelolco*.

10. "Por medio de la presente," 24 September 1985, DFS, 009-031-003, legajo 7, AGN.

11. "Entrevista realizada por el corresponsal en México," 25 September 1985, DFS, 009-031-003, legajo 7, AGN.

12. Quoted in Poniatowska, *Nothing, Nobody*, 73–77.

13. "Tras el porqué del por qué," *Obras*, November 1985, MMH, 32.05.00.00, c. 1, exp. 3, AGN.

14. "Ciudad de México: Vulnerabilidad y alto riesgo," *Punto Crítico*, December 1985, MMH, 32.05.00.00, c. 2, exp. 6, AGN.

15. "Información del frente nacional contra la represión," 25 September 1985, DFS, 009-031-003, legajo 7, AGN.

16. Gustavo Suárez, "Movimiento del sistema," *Insurgencia Popular*, October 1985, MMH, 32.03.00.00, c. 2, exp. 17, AGN.

17. "Información del Frente Nacional contra la Represión," 25 September 1985, DFS, 009-031-003, legajo 7, AGN.

18. "Actividades de militantes del PMT," 26 September 1985, DFS, 009-031-003, legajo 8, AGN.

19. "Arbitrario desalojo en el Churubusco," *El Tlatelolco*, 18 September 1986, MMH, 32.01.00.00, c. 4, exp. 11, AGN.

20. "Al pueblo de México," 1 October 1985, DFS, 009-031-003, legajo 10, AGN.

21. Davis, "Reverberations," 269.

22. "Situación que prevalece con motivo de los movimientos telúricos," 15 December 1985, DFS, 009-031-003, legajo 32, AGN.

23. Aguilar Zinser, Morales, and Peña, *Aún tiembla*, 33.

24. "Los manifestantes que se dirigen a la residencia oficial de los Pinos," 27 September 1985, DFS, 009-031-003, legajo 8, AGN.

25. In Tlatelolco alone, 43 of the 102 buildings were completely destroyed. Davis, "Reverberations," 268.

26. "Situación que prevalece con motivo de los movimientos telúricos," 23 September 1985, DFS, 009-031-003, legajo 6, AGN.

27. "¡De nuevo quieren manchar Tlatelolco!," 22 September 1985, DFS, 009-031-003, legajo 6, AGN.

28. "Al dirigirnos a usted," 23 September 1985, DFS, 009-031-003, legajo 8, AGN.

29. "Situación que prevalece con motivo de los movimientos telúricos," 23 September 1985, DFS, 009-031-003, legajo 6, AGN; "Al dirigirnos a usted," 23 September 1985, DFS, 009-031-003, legajo 8, AGN; Frente de Residentes de Tlatelolco, "Como es de su conocimiento," 7 October 1985, DFS, 009-031-003, legajo 11, AGN.

30. "Al dirigirnos a usted," 23 September 1985, DFS 009-031-003, legajo 8, AGN.

31. "Tlatelolco: A la hora de los sismos," *Punto Crítico*, December 1985, MMH, 32.05.00.00, c. 2, exp. 6, AGN.

32. Poniatowska, *Nothing, Nobody*, 255.

33. Coo, "Después de la caída," 43. Note that in 1983 the SAHOP was renamed SEDUE; these were the federal entities in charge of urban planning. On the politics of urban planning, see Garza, *Una década de planeación*; and Ward, *Mexico City*, esp. 159–186.

34. "Extracto de información," 22 September 1985, DFS, 009-031-003, legajo 6, AGN.

35. Davis, "Reverberations"; CEPAL, "Daños causados."

36. "El terremoto: Heroísmo y corrupción," *Contenido*, December 1985, MMH, 32.05.00.00, c. 1, exp. 7, AGN.

37. And this system persisted after the earthquake. For example, a journalist living in the disaster zone called authorities to schedule a structural inspection of his home to ascertain whether it needed repairs. When the inspector arrived, the journalist recognized him as one of the city's press liaison officials; the journalist had attended many press briefings delivered by this supposed technician. The technician / press liaison officer explained that there were not enough trained personnel to conduct the inspections. Countless such examples intensified the conflict between residents and the government, as residents realized that the government had not altered its ways even after the effects of corruption had made themselves so devastatingly manifest. "Se han detectado anomalías en las supervisiones de las construcciones afectadas por los sismos," 7 October 1985, DFS, 009-031-003, legajo 11, AGN.

38. On Mexico City's political structure, see Davis, *Urban Leviathan*; and Ward, *Mexico City*.

39. Gustavo Suárez, "Movimiento del sistema," *Insurgencia Popular*, October 1985, MMH, 32.03.00.00, c. 2, exp. 17, AGN.

40. "El terremoto: Heroísmo y corrupción," *Contenido*, December 1985, MMH, 32.05.00.00, c. 1, exp. 7, AGN.

41. Núñez de la Peña and Orozco, *El terremoto*, 124.

42. "Mitin-plantón silencioso de la unión de vecinos y damnificados '19 de septiembre,'" 8 October 1985, DFS, 009-031-003, legajo 12, AGN.

43. "Asamblea plenaria del PRS en el DF," 28 September 1985, DFS, 009-031-003, legajo 9, AGN.

44. Frente de Residentes de Tlatelolco, "Como es de su conocimiento," 7 October 1985, DFS, 009-031-003, legajo 11, AGN.

45. "Asamblea informativa en la Plaza de las Tres Culturas," 3 October 1985, DFS, 009-031-003, legajo 10, AGN.

46. "Textos de telegramas que se enviarán mañana," 23 October 1985, DFS, 009-031-003, legajo 19, AGN.

47. "Tlatelolco: A la hora de los sismos," *Punto Crítico*, December 1985, MMH, 32.05.00.00, c. 2, exp. 6.

48. For more on this, see Coo, "Después de la caída," 44–54.

49. *El Tlatelolco*, 6 October 1985, DFS, 009-031-003, legajo 11, AGN.

50. "Al dirigirnos a usted," 23 September 1985, DFS, 009-031-003, legajo 8, AGN.

51. Coo, "Después de la caída," 50 (italics added).

52. "Al dirigirnos a usted," 23 September 1985, DFS, 009-031-003, legajo 8, AGN.

53. See, for example, Eckstein, "Poor People versus the State and Capital," 345.

54. "Situación que prevalece en ayuda a los damnificados en Tlatelolco por parte del PSUM y el PRT," 26 September 1985, DFS, 009-031-003, legajo 8, AGN.

55. Frente de Residentes de Tlatelolco, "Como es de su conocimiento," 7 October 1985, DFS, 009-031-03, legajo 11, AGN; "Situación que prevalece con motivo de los movimientos telúricos," 23 September 1985, DFS, 009-031-003, legajo 6, AGN. Barry Carr describes the PPS as the "loyal left." For more on the history of leftist political parties in Mexico, see, for example, Carr, *Marxism and Communism*.

56. "A las 12:45 hs. del día de hoy," 24 September 1985, DFS, 009-031-003, legajo 7, AGN.

57. "Antecedentes de los principales líderes y militantes en las colonias populares," October 1985, DFS, 009-031-003, legajo 22, AGN.

58. "Frente de residentes de Tlatelolco," 18 October 1985, DFS, 009-031-003, legajo 17, AGN.

59. Serna and CUD, *¡Aquí nos quedaremos!*, 45.

60. "Frente de residentes de Tlatelolco," 18 October 1985, DFS, 009-031-003, legajo 17, AGN.

61. "Un año después, hay que reforzar el trabajo organizativo," *El Tlatelolco*, 18 September 1986, MMH, 32.01.00.00, c. 4, exp. 11, AGN.

62. "Situación que prevalece en la unidad Nonoalco-Tlatelolco," 18 October 1985, DFS, 009-031-003, legajo 17, AGN. This had also been a problem before the earthquake. An article in the July–August issue of a Tlatelolco newsletter, *Unidad Urbana*, reveals that many residents challenged the legality of the contracts switching the building to condominium status that the building leaders had signed with government agencies. *Unidad Urbana*, July–August 1985, DFS, 009-031-003, legajo 31, AGN.

63. Of the many instances of corruption exposed by the earthquake, the discovery of sweatshops of garment workers in the city center was among the most notorious. In the immediate aftermath, the police and military helped factory owners rescue the sewing machines, while seamstresses lay buried alive underneath the rubble. Davis, "Reverberations," 267–269.

64. The victims movement worked with other social organizations. While student groups from the city's universities and *preparatorias* participated in the rescue work and political mobilization, they were not a dominant force in the victims movement. One activist complained about how some student organizations had declared themselves leaders of the movement. See Serna and CUD, *¡Aquí nos quedaremos!*, 73. More commonly, the victims movement worked with religious organizations, which because of their international reach were well equipped to collect and distribute aid. In pamphlets distributed throughout the city, the archdiocese urged everyone to help in the rescue efforts. It supported the victims and their organizations and urged the authorities to respond quickly and competently to their demands. In Tlatelolco, many of the activists were atheists who had a casual, respectful relationship with the archdiocese, the Jesuits, and other prominent religious organizations. Priests inspired by liberation theology contributed to the grassroots movement, and religious organizations often provided meeting places. However, just as some activists expressed concern at working closely with the Catholic Church, it, too, was reticent to work with prominent members of the Communist Party. Further, the Church hesitated to enter into formal relations with the victims organizations because of a constitutional ban on its political activity. See Serna and CUD, *¡Aquí nos quedaremos!*, 48–50, 77–80; *Mensaje guadalupano a los damnificados del Valle de México*, December 1985, DFS, 009-031-003, legajo 32, AGN; and "Coordinadora única de damnificados," 23 December 1985, DFS, 009-031-003, legajo 33, AGN.

65. Serna and CUD, *¡Aquí nos quedaremos!*, 72–75. It also did not hurt that the world-renowned opera singer Plácido Domingo had family who lived in the Nuevo León building and was on the ground in Tlatelolco in the aftermath.

66. "Situación que prevalece con motivo de los movimientos telúricos," 23 September 1985, DFS, 009-031-003, legajo 6, AGN; "Asamblea informativa del STUNAM," 24 September 1985, DFS, 009-031-003, legajo 7, AGN.

67. Serna and CUD, *¡Aquí nos quedaremos!*, 49, 72–75.

68. Poniatowska, *Nothing, Nobody*, 11.

69. "Extracto de información," 22 September 1985, DFS, 009-031-003, legajo 6, AGN.

70. "Estrategia política en Tlatelolco," 5 March 1986, MMH, c. 161, exp. 5, AGN.

71. Ibid.

72. "Edificio Nuevo León," May 1986, MMH, c. 162, exp. 2, AGN; "Edificio Nuevo León," 9 September 1986, MMH, c. 162, exp. 4, AGN.

73. "Movimientos internos," 5 March 1986, MMH, c. 161, exp. 5, AGN.

74. Subcomité de movilización social para la defensa civil Comité de Reconstrucción del Área Metropolitana, "Conclusiones," 1986, MMH, 30.00.00.00, c. 4, exp. 5, AGN.

75. "¿Qué pueden hacer Las Brigadas Juveniles de Solidaridad Social?," October 1985, MMH, 30.00.00.00, c. 4, exp. 5, AGN.

76. "Coordinadora de Tlatelolco," 20 November 1985, DFS, 009-031-003, legajo 28, AGN; DFS, "Datos de los principales dirigentes," 25 October 1985, DFS, 009-031-003, legajo 20, AGN; "Conferencia de prensa del Dr. Cuauhtémoc Abarca Chávez," 16 November 1985, DFS, 009-0310-003, legajo 26, AGN.

77. "Entrevista con cinco dirigentes de Tlatelolco," *El Tlatelolco Semanal,* 18 December 1985, MMH, 32.01.00.00, c. 6, exp. 4, AGN.

78. Serna and CUD, *¡Aquí nos quedaremos!,* 95.

79. "Informe de la dinámica post-sísmica macrosismos del 19 y 20 septiembre 1985," MMH, 30.00.00.00, c. 5, exp. 4, DDF, AGN.

80. "Proyecto de 'Clases Medias,'" August 1986, MMH, c. 215, exp. 5, AGN.

81. Ibid.

82. Ibid. (capitalization in original).

83. Ibid.

84. Ibid.

85. CEPAL, "Daños causados."

86. Partido Laboral Mexicano, *Reconstruir y salvar vidas es la prioridad,* 1 October 1985, DFS, 009-031-003, legajo 11, AGN.

87. Eckstein, "Poor People versus the State," 343.

88. "¡Por fin!," *El Tlatelolco,* 13 March 1986, MMH, 32.01.00.00, c. 6, exp. 3, AGN.

89. "Hoy te cumple," [ca. 1986], MMH, 30.00.00.00, c. 9, exp. 3, DDF, AGN.

90. Although the cost of purchasing the new housing was pegged to the minimum wage, it did constitute a significant increase in monthly housing expenses for many families in the poorer neighborhoods. Eckstein, "Poor People versus the State," 339.

91. Quoted in Monsiváis, *Entrada libre,* 109 (no citation given).

92. "Expropiaciones," 17 October 1985, DFS, 009-031-003, legajo 16, AGN.

93. Ibid.; "Expropiaciones," 17 October 1985, DFS, 009-031-003, legajo 21, AGN.

94. These examples and many others can be found in the files "Expropiaciones," "Expropiación de predios," and "Predios que aparecen . . . ," all collected in 17 October 1985, DFS, 009-031-003, legajo 16, AGN.

95. "Expropiaciones," 17 October 1985, DFS, 009-031-003, legajo 16, AGN.

96. "Convenio de concertación democrática para la reconstrucción," 13 May 1986, MMH, 30.00.00.00, c. 5, exp. 11, AGN.

97. Davis, "Reverberations," 272.

98. Ibid.

99. "Ante la expropiación, ¿quién quiere construir?," *Expansión,* 11 December 1985.

100. Davis describes how the effects of this began to be seen twenty years after the earthquake. Davis, "Reverberations," 272.

101. For an analysis of how natural (and other) disasters have been manipulated to advance the interests of big capital, see Klein, *Shock Doctrine.*

102. Carr, *Marxism and Communism,* 302; Bruhn, *Taking on Goliath.*

103. Serna and CUD, *¡Aquí nos quedaremos!,* 150–153.

104. Ibid., 139.

105. Ibid., 147 (italics added).

106. Ibid.

107. Gómez Tagle, "Public Institutions and Electoral Transparency," 89–91. In-depth analysis of the electoral reforms is beyond scope of this book. See, for example, the essays in Middlebrook, *Dilemmas of Political Change in Mexico.*

108. Middlebrook, "Mexico's Democratic Transitions," 15–17. Julia Preston and Sam Dillon describe how speculation about Colosio's assassination harmed the PRI's public image: "To the public the assassination was a sign that the ruling party, consumed with ambitions and jealousies that Salinas had stirred, was destroying itself." Despite rumors about a plot, after a six-year investigation the special prosecutor concluded that the gunman had acted alone. Preston and Dillon, *Opening Mexico*, 231–232.

109. Gómez Tagle, "Public Institutions and Electoral Transparency," 91–95.

110. Buendía, "Changing Mexican Voter," 118–119, table 4.3.

111. Gilbert, *Mexico's Middle Class*, 84–92.

112. Crespo, "Party Competition in Mexico."

113. Middlebrook, "Mexico's Democratic Transistions," 11–13; Olvera, "Civil Society in Mexico," 412–19.

114. Carlos Monsiváis, "Organizaciones populares y resistencia a su acción," *Proceso*, 9 November 1985.

115. Monsiváis, *Entrada libre*, 11.

116. Ibid., 13. Monsiváis's interpretation was widely accepted; for example, Elena Poniatowska also referred to the birth of a civil society. However, many contested the supposed "newness" of civil society. After all, if civil society was "born" after the 1985 earthquake, the implication is that the PRI was an all-encompassing Leviathan before then; such a characterization would not only be ahistorical, as demonstrated by the political struggles analyzed in this book, but also politically troubling insofar as it erases the history of political struggle. Many scholars have traced links between the earthquake protests and previous forms of urban protest, demonstrating that the so-called civil society did not emerge phoenixlike from the rubble but instead drew upon a long history of urban protest. For example, Ligia Tavera-Fenollosa, among others, argues that civil society existed before the earthquake and that it was by drawing upon an established ideology of protest that the victims movement acquired its strength. While helpful in illuminating the history of urban protest in poor and working-class areas, these studies do not explain middle-class protest. Poniatowska, *Nothing, Nobody*, 310; Tavera Fenollosa, "Social Movements and Civil Society."

117. Jean Cohen and Andrew Arato, writing in the early 1990s, describe how "phrases involving the resurrection, reemergence, rebirth, reconstruction, or renaissance of civil society are heard repeatedly today." Cohen and Arato connect the popularity of the concept to, among other things, an antistatism that emerged at the beginning of the 1980s. Cohen and Arato, *Civil Society and Political Theory*, 29. Most scholarship on the Mexico City earthquake belongs to an abundant literature on civil society and social movements in Latin America during the 1980s and 1990s. Because there is little historical scholarship on the 1970s and 1980s, most of the scholarly analysis of the earthquake, and social movements more broadly, has been undertaken by sociologists, political scientists, and anthropologists. The body of literature that I refer to includes: Alvarez, Dagnino, and Escobar, *Cultures of Politics / Politics of Cultures*; Alvarez and Escobar, *The Making of Social Movements in Latin America*; Cohen and Arato, *Civil Society and Political Theory*; Eckstein, *Power and Popular Protest*; Foweraker and Craig, *Popular Movements*

and Political Change in Mexico; Haber, *Power from Experience*; Tavera-Fenollosa, "Social Movements and Civil Society"; and several contemporaneous publications by public intellectuals and activists in Mexico about the earthquake.

118. Cohen and Arato offer a working definition of the concept: "We understand 'civil society' as a sphere of social interaction between economy and state, composed above all of the intimate sphere (especially the family), the sphere of associations (especially voluntary associations), social movements, and forms of public communication. Modern civil society is created through forms of self-constitution and self-mobilization. It is institutionalized and generalized through laws, and especially subjective rights, that stabilize social differentiation. While the self-creative and institutionalized dimensions can exist separately, in the long term both independent action and institutionalization are necessary for the reproduction of civil society." Cohen and Arato, *Civil Society and Political Theory*, ix.

119. Alvarez, Dagnino, and Escobar, *Cultures of Politics / Politics of Cultures*, 17. Most scholars resist idealizing the term, emphasizing that civil society can be undemocratic, racist, sexist, and exclusionary, and that while autonomy is a central element, there are often important links between civil society, the state, and the market.

120. Eckstein, "Poor People versus the State and Capital," 338.

121. Ibid., 338 n.8.

122. Hellman, "The Study of New Social Movements," 56.

123. For example, Paul Haber describes his decision to study the urban poor and social movements in Mexico: "We want to live differently. For many of us, this has meant pursuing a socialist ideal, a democratic socialism. . . . Social movements are attractive in part because they very clearly proclaim that there is something terribly wrong about how we are living and that something can and should be done about it." Haber, *Power from Experience*, vii. Another reason for the lack of scholarly interest in the middle classes could be connected to the wariness which scholars, and in particular political philosophers, have expressed concerning the classical conflation of bourgeois political subjectivity and civil society. For instance, Cohen and Arato carefully disaggregate the bourgeois subject from philosophical definitions of both the public sphere and civil society. It seems that this disaggregation is necessary before any articulation of a contemporary theory of civil society can be outlined. The absence of the middle classes in analyses of recent Latin American political movements could be an unintended consequence of this discomfort with the bourgeois subject of classical political philosophy. Cohen and Arato, *Civil Society and Political Theory*, esp. chaps. 2 and 3.

124. In contrast to more positive accounts, Sergio Zermeño argues that the economic displacements of the 1970s and 1980s generated a proliferation of the excluded, without necessarily sparking the emergence of a popular subject. Instead, he suggests that the political mobilizations of these decades empowered—if they empowered any group—the middle classes, not the popular classes. Zermeño, "Crisis, Neoliberalism, and Disorder," 168–169. Notably, Zermeño, one of Mexico's leading sociologists, is one of very few skeptical voices. Indeed, in 2008 I attended a series of events at the UNAM commemorating the 1968 student movement; here, too, Zermeño stood almost alone in his skepticism about the legacy of 1968.

125. Here I am drawing on Grégory Quenet's history of earthquakes as historical events in ancien régime France. Discussing the 1 November 1755 earthquake in Lisbon, Quenet points out that while this was the first earthquake to have a Europe-wide effect, it was not the biggest or most damaging natural disaster in modern history. He suggests that it was Voltaire's subsequent writings that transformed the Lisbon earthquake into a European event. Quenet, *Tremblements de terre*, 9.

126. Benjamin, "Theses on the Philosophy of History," 262.

127. I did not set out to begin and end this book with sporting events. But the 1968 Olympic games and the 1986 World Cup serve as appropriate bookends, and the two events encapsulate some of the themes of this study. The PRI managed to pull off the Olympic spectacle without much controversy only weeks after massacring hundreds of students in the streets of the capital city. By contrast, in 1986 Miguel de la Madrid was rejected—condemned, even—by middle-class Mexicans at the opening ceremony of the World Cup. A lot had changed in the intervening eighteen years. Nearly two decades of widespread discontent, malaise, and mobilization had reconfigured the political culture of the middle classes and the PRI. Another contrast: at the opening ceremonies of the 1970 World Cup, also in Azteca Stadium, President Gustavo Díaz Ordaz was booed. The 1970 *chiflado* (booing) expressed the trauma of state-sponsored terror; the 1986 *chiflado* expressed the trauma of economic terror.

CONCLUSION

1. In other countries, especially in the southern cone, the transition to neoliberalism occurred through military dictatorship and state-sponsored terror. For Chile, economist Orlando Letelier connected state terror and the implementation of economic liberalism in a 1976 article in the *Nation*; he was assassinated a few weeks later. In a study on this topic across Latin America, Greg Grandin points to Mexico as an exception. I argue that the Mexican exception is explained, in part, because the history of neoliberalism is the history of the PRI and the middle classes. Orlando Letelier, "The Chicago Boys in Chile: Economic Freedom's Awful Toll," *Nation*, 28 August 1976; Grandin, *Last Colonial Massacre*, 14.

2. For more on these reforms and their impact, see Teichman, "Neoliberalism and the Transformation of Mexican Authoritarianism," esp. 3–8.

3. See Womack, "Chiapas, the Bishop of San Cristóbal, and the Zapatista Revolt."

4. Henck, *Subcommander Marcos*, 144–146.

5. Hayden, *Zapatista Reader*, 2. Further, in an interview Marcos described NAFTA as a death sentence. Henck, *Subcommander Marcos*, 414 n.73.

6. For analysis of Marcos's life as a student in Tampico and Mexico City, see Henck, *Subcommander Marcos*, 23–41.

7. Gilbert, *Mexico's Middle Class*, 40–56.

8. Certainly, notable differences emerge in the 1990s, such as the refusal of struggling middle-class families to give up private education; in contrast, in the 1980s studies found that middle-class families had been willing to cut spending on private education. This difference can be attributed to an erosion of quality in the public education system (or a perception thereof).

9. Gilbert, *Mexico's Middle Class*, 79.

10. Grammont, *El Barzón*; Williams, *Planting Trouble*; Williams, *Social Movements and Economic Transition*.

11. Loaeza, *Debo, luego sufro*, 53.

12. Benjamin, "Theses on the Philosophy of History," 257.

13. Lomnitz, Untitled presentation.

14. For example, the prominent Mexican author Jorge Volpi wrote a novel about the 1968 protests, in which he describes twentieth-century history as a giant deception: "Behind its well wishes, its anxiety to improve the world and its passion for utopia was always concealed a totalitarian temptation. *Always.*" This passage, and the novel itself, is nothing less than a rejection of the "ideological" generation of 1968; in another novel Volpi celebrates the end of ideologies with the collapse of the USSR in 1989. Volpi's aggressive cynicism about the political projects of the 1960s, 1970s, and 1980s seems specious given the intense and at times painful history of resistance, malaise, and negotiation documented in this book. *Muertos incómodos*, the most recent novel in the Belascoarán series, coauthored by Subcomandante Marcos and Paco Ignacio Taibo II, offers a counterpoint to Volpi's novels. Marcos and Taibo historicize neoliberalism by connecting the radicalism and repression of the 1970s with the neoliberal triumph of the 1990s. On the 1968 protests, see Volpi, *Fin de la locura*, 448–449; on the end of ideology, see Volpi, *Season of Ash*. See also Ehrenreich, "The Crack-Up"; Marcos and Taibo, *Muertos incómodos*.

15. Some commentators describe recent history as the triumph of the middle classes, while others underscore the continuing economic vulnerability of this group. For optimistic narratives, see Castañeda, *Mañana Forever?*, 34–67; and the debate sparked by Calle and Rubio, *Clasemediero*. Castañeda and Calle and Rubio point to the rise in private education, plasma televisions, and consumer credit since 1994, among other things, as indicators of the success of the middle classes in Mexico. In these narratives, the earlier history of the middle classes is something to be overcome—an important beginning to move away from. For more cautious appraisals, see OECD Development Centre, *Latin American Economic Outlook 2011*. This report underscores the economic vulnerability of the middle classes across Latin America. Hotel owners and communications engineers might own cell phones and have access to the Internet, but the poor condition of public services and social security, such as education and pensions, threatens to undermine their class status. The report emphasizes the need for a social contract between the middle classes and nation-states.

16. Paz, "The Other Mexico," 268.

APPENDIX

1. Before getting started, however, a caveat is in order: I do not analyze the data (most often drawn from census and household surveys). Instead, I analyze how different generations of scholars have delimited social classes.

2. No doubt, additional studies could be included. I have found the studies that rely extensively on the census or household data, however, to be the most thorough in terms of extended time series and discussion of their sources and methods. As

Wilkie and Wilkins point out, most studies of class structure in Mexico (and especially of the middle classes) avoid quantification. Wilkie and Wilkins, "Quantifying the Class Structure of Mexico," 578.

3. Ibid., 584.

4. Granato and Mostkoff, "The Class Structure of Mexico"; Lorey and Mostkoff Linares, "Mexico's 'Lost Decade.'"

5. Iturriaga, *La estructura social y cultural de México*; Cline, *Mexico: Revolution to Evolution*.

6. Wilkie and Wilkins, "Quantifying the Class Structure of Mexico," 587.

7. Ibid., 586.

8. Ibid., 587; González Cosío, "Clases y estratos sociales"; Navarrete, *Distribución del ingreso*.

9. Wilkie and Wilkins, "Quantifying the Class Structure of Mexico," 584–588.

10. Ibid., 581.

11. Gilbert, *Mexico's Middle Class*, 117.

12. Cline, *Mexico: Revolution to Evolution*, 116.

13. Gilbert, *Mexico's Middle Class*, 117.

14. Samaniego de Villarreal, "Algunas reflexiones."

15. Stern and Kahl, "Stratification since the Revolution," 25.

16. Bortz, "The Development of Quantitative History," 1119–1123.

17. In their literature review, Bortz and Aguila discuss some innovations in this direction; Bortz and Aguila, "Earning a Living," 132–134. See also Bortz, *Revolution within the Revolution*.

18. Bortz and Aguila, "Earning a Living," 126–127.

19. Ibid., 117–118.

Bibliography

ARCHIVES AND COLLECTIONS

Archivo General de la Nación (AGN)
    Ramo Dirección Federal de Seguridad (DFS)
    Ramo Dirección General de Investigaciones Políticas y Sociales (DGIPS)
    Ramo Presidentes
        José López Portillo (JLP)
        Luis Echeverría Álvarez (LEA)
        Miguel de la Madrid Huerta (MMH)
    Ramo Profeco
Banco de México, Biblioteca
Biblioteca Miguel Lerdo de Tejada, Archivos Económicos
Biblioteca Nacional
Hemeroteca Nacional

NEWSPAPERS AND MAGAZINES

Excélsior
Expansión
El Heraldo de México
La Jornada
El Nacional
Novedades
Proceso
Punto Crítico
Siempre!
El Universal
Uno más Uno

PRIMARY SOURCES

Banco de México. *Indicadores economicos* (vol. 3). Mexico City: Banco de México, 1994. Available at the Bank of Mexico library.

Camacho, Manuel, Juan Sánchez Navarro, José Cueli, and Javier Beristáin. *Sociedad: Las clases medias*. Mexico City: Instituto Nacional de Estudios Históricos de la Revolución Mexicana, 1986. Available at the National Library of Mexico.

Cepeda, María Enriqueta. "El papel del crédito en la compra de bienes de consumo durable y no durable de las familias de la Zona Metropolitana de Monterrey (estrato medio)." Undergraduate thesis, Universidad Autónoma de Nuevo León, 1970. Available at the Bank of Mexico library.

de la Madrid, Miguel. *Inaugural Address.* Mexico City: Dirección General de Comunicación Social de la Presidencia de la República, 1982.

Díaz Serrano, Jorge. *Política petrolera.* Mexico City: Secretaría de Programación y Presupuesto, 1981. Available at JLP, c. 2186, exp. 1141-I-14, AGN.

DICMAC (Desarrollo Industrial y Comercial Mexicano, A.C.). *Investigación cuantitativa del consumo de artículos extranjeros en México.* Mexico City: DICMAC, 1972. Available at the University of California–San Diego library.

Echeverría, Luis. *Mexico: 1970–1976; Presidential Inauguration.* Mexico City: Mexican Business Council, 1970.

FONACOT. *Esto es FONACOT.* Publication information unknown. Pamphlet available at the Bank of Mexico library.

Fregoso Saucedo, José Alberto. "Efectos de las tarjetas de crédito bancarias en México, en los diferentes niveles socio-económicos." Undergraduate thesis, UNAM, 1970. Available at the Bank of Mexico library.

Gutiérrez Rocha, Dora Elva. "El papel del crédito en las compras de bienes de consumo para las familias del estrato alto en la Zona Metropolitana de Monterrey." Undergraduate thesis, Universidad de Nuevo León, 1970. Available at the Bank of Mexico library.

Ibarra Muñoz, David. *Hacienda y crédito público.* Mexico City: Secretaría de Programación y Presupuesto, 1980. Available at JLP, c. 2186, exp. 1141-I-5, AGN.

Ibarra Vargas, Valentín. "El crédito como variable explicativa de la compra de bienes de consumo." Undergraduate thesis, Universidad de Nuevo León, 1970. Available at the Bank of Mexico library.

Instituto de Capacitación Política (of the PRI [Partido Revolucionario Institucional]). *Historia documental de la CNOP: 1970–1984.* Mexico City: Instituto de Capacitación Política, 1984.

López Portillo, José. *Consolidación de la economía.* Mexico City: Secretaría de Programación y Presupuesto, 1981. Available at JLP, c. 2214, exp. 1280, AGN.

———. *Control de la inflación.* Mexico City: Secretaría de Programación y Presupuesto, 1981. Available at JLP, c. 2214, exp. 1279, AGN.

———. *Financiamiento para el desarrollo.* Mexico City: Secretaría de Programación y Presupuesto, 1980. Available at JLP, c. 2213, exp. 1253, AGN.

———. *New International Energy Order.* Mexico City: Secretaría de Programación y Presupuesto, 1979. Available at JLP, c. 2213, exp. 1249, AGN.

———. *Política petrolera.* Mexico City: Secretaría de Programación y Presupuesto, 1980. Avaible at JLP, c. 2213, exp. 1233, AGN.

Osorio Marbán, Miguel. *El sector popular del PRI.* Mexico City: Coordinación Nacional de Estudios Históricos, Políticos y Sociales, PRI, 1994.

Reyes Peláez, Juan Fernando. "Al cielo por asalto: La Liga Comunista 23 de Septiembre." Unpublished paper, Center for U.S.-Mexican Studies, University of California–San Diego, 2000. In possession of author.

Salas Obregón, Ignacio. "Acerca del movimiento revolucionario del proletariado estudiantil," Liga Comunista 23 de Septiembre folder, digital archive (CD-ROM) compiled by José Luis Moreno Borbolla, Centro de Investigaciones Históricas de los Movimientos Sociales A.C., 1973. Document in possession of author. CD-ROM in possession of Alexander Aviña.

Salgado, Arturo, Jorge Rubí, Jorge Leegi, Rubén García, Ricardo Alvarez, Elisa Velázquez, and Mario Melgarejo. "El típico joven de la clase media mexicana." Mexico City: Dirección General de Divulgación Universitaria, UNAM, 1979. Available at the Videoteca of the National Library of Mexico, Mexico City.

———. "Ideas políticas de la clase media." Mexico City: Dirección General de Divulgación Universitaria, UNAM, 1979. Available at the Videoteca of the National Library of Mexico.

———. "Ideología y clase media." Mexico City: Dirección General de Divulgación Universitaria, UNAM, 1979. Available at the Videoteca of the National Library of Mexico, Mexico City.

———. "La clase media en México." Mexico City: Dirección General de Divulgación Universitaria, UNAM, 1979. Available at the Videoteca of the National Library of Mexico, Mexico City.

———. "La enajenación de la clase media en México." Mexico City: Dirección General de Divulgación Universitaria, UNAM, 1979. Available at the Videoteca of the National Library of Mexico, Mexico City.

———. "La mujer de la clase media mexicana." Mexico City: Dirección General de Divulgación Universitaria, UNAM, 1979. Available at the Videoteca of the National Library of Mexico, Mexico City.

Sánchez Herrero, Santiago. *The Mexican Experience with Bank Credit Cards.* Mexico City: Banco de México, 1971. Mimeo available at Bank of Mexico library.

Secretaría de Hacienda y Crédito Público. *El ABC del IVA.* Mexico City: Taller Gráfica de la Nación, 1979. Available at the University of Texas–Austin library.

———. *Preguntas y respuestas en torno del Impuesto al Valor Agregado: Reforma fiscal; Viva el cambio.* Mexico City: Taller Gráfica de la Nación, 1979. Available at JLP, c. 1899, exp. 49, AGN.

———. *Régimen fiscal de los causantes menores en el I.V.A.: Viva el cambio; Reforma fiscal.* Mexico City: Taller Gráfica de la Nación, 1979. Available at JLP, c. 1899, exp. 58, AGN.

Secretaría de Industria y Comercio. *Ley Federal de Protección al Consumidor: Precedida por la comparecencia del Srio. de Industria y Comercio Lic. José Campillo Sainz, ante la H. Cámara de Diputados, para explicar la iniciativa de la misma.* Mexico City: Ed. Solidaridad, 1976. Available at the Bank of Mexico library.

SHCP. *See* Secretaría de Hacienda y Crédito Público.

SECONDARY SOURCES

Aaronovitch, David. *Voodoo Histories: The Role of the Conspiracy Theory in Shaping Modern History.* New York: Riverhead Books, 2010.

Adamovsky, Ezequiel. *Historia de la clase media argentina: Apogeo y decadencia de una ilusión, 1919–2003.* Buenos Aires: Planeta, 2009.

Adelman, Jeremy. "International Finance and Political Legitimacy: A Latin American View of the Global Shock." In *The Shock of the Global: The 1970s in Perspective,* edited by Niall Ferguson, Charles S. Maier, Erez Manela, and Daniel J. Sargent, 113–127. Cambridge, MA: Harvard University Press, 2010.

Adler de Lomnitz, Larissa. *Cómo sobreviven los marginados.* Mexico City: Siglo Veintiuno, 1975.

Agamben, Giorgio. *State of Exception.* Chicago: University of Chicago Press, 2005.

Aguayo, Sergio. *1968: Los archivos de la violencia.* Mexico City: Grijalbo, 1998.

———. *La charola: Una historia de los servicios de inteligencia en México.* Mexico City: Grijalbo, 2001.

Aguilar Camín, Héctor, and Lorenzo Meyer. *In the Shadow of the Mexican Revolution: Contemporary Mexican History, 1910–1989.* Austin: University of Texas Press, 1993.

Aguilar Mora, Jorge. *Cádaver lleno de mundo.* Mexico City: J. Mortiz, 1971.

Aguilar Zinser, Adolfo, Cesáreo Morales, and Rodolfo F. Peña. *Aún tiembla: Sociedad política y cambio social; El terremoto del 19 de septiembre de 1985.* Mexico City: Grijalbo, 1987.

Agustín, José. *Tragicomedia mexicana 2: La vida en México de 1970 a 1988.* Mexico City: Planeta Mexicana, 1992.

Agustín Ramírez, José. *Se está haciendo tarde (final en laguna).* Mexico City: J. Mortiz, 1973.

Alarcón, Diana, and Terry McKinley. "Increasing Wage Inequality and Trade Liberalization in Mexico." In *Poverty, Economic Reform and Income Distribution in Latin America,* edited by Albert Berry, 137–153. Boulder, CO: Lynne Rienner, 1998.

Alegre, Robert. "Contesting the 'Mexican Miracle': Railway Men and Women Struggle for Democracy, 1943–1959." PhD diss., Rutgers University, 2007.

Almond, Gabriel, and Sidney Verba. *The Civic Culture: Political Attitudes and Democracy in Five Nations.* Princeton, NJ: Princeton University Press, 1963.

Alvarez, Sonia E., Evelina Dagnino, and Arturo Escobar. *Cultures of Politics / Politics of Cultures: Re-visioning Latin American Social Movements.* Boulder, CO: Westview Press, 1998.

Alvarez, Sonia, and Arturo Escobar, eds. *The Making of Social Movements in Latin America: Identity, Strategy and Democracy.* Boulder, CO: Westview Press, 1992.

Ángel Mobarak, Gustavo A. del. "Computerization of Commercial Banks and the Building of an Automated Payments System in Mexico, 1965–1990." In *Technological Innovation in Retail Finance: International Historical Perspectives,* edited by Bernardo Bátiz-Lazo, J. Carles Maixé-Altés, and Paul Thomes, 92–117. New York: Routledge, 2011.

Ángel Mobarak, Gustavo A. del, Carlos Bazdresch Parada, and Francisco Suárez Dávila, eds. *Cuando el estado se hizo banquero: Consecuencias de la nacionalización bancaria en México.* Mexico City: Fondo de Cultura Económica, 2005.

Ángel [Mobarak], Gustavo A. del, and Carlos Marichal. "Poder y crisis: Historiografía reciente del crédito y la banca en México, siglos XIX y XX." *Historia Mexicana* 52, no. 3 (2003): 677–724.

Anzaldúa Montoya, Ricardo, and Barry Carr, eds. *The Mexican Left: The Popular Movements and the Politics of Austerity.* San Diego: Center for U.S.-Mexican Studies, University of California–San Diego, 1986.

Artigas H., Juan B. *UNAM México: Guía de sitios y espacios.* Mexico City: UNAM, 2006.

Avella, I., and Ibarra, A. "Mesa redonda: Hacia una historia intelectual." Roundtable discussion, CLADHE-II/AMHE-IV, Centro Cultural Universitario Tlatelolco, Mexico, 4 February 2010.

Aviña, Alexander. "Insurgent Guerrero: Genaro Vázquez, Lucio Cabañas and the Guerrilla Challenge to the Postrevolutionary Mexican State, 1960–1996." PhD diss., University of Southern California, 2009.

———. "Seizing Hold of Memories in Moments of Danger: Guerrillas and Revolution in Guerrero, Mexico." In Calderón and Cedillo, *Challenging Authoritarianism in Mexico*, 40–59.

———. "'We Have Returned to Porfirian Times': Neo-populism, Counterinsurgency, and the Dirty War in Guerrero, Mexico 1969–1976." In *Populism in 20th Century Mexico: The Presidencies of Lázaro Cárdenas and Luis Echeverría*, edited by Amelia Kiddle and María L. O. Muñoz, 106–121. Tucson: University of Arizona Press, 2010.

Babb, Sarah. *Managing Mexico: Economists from Nationalism to Neoliberalism.* Princeton, NJ: Princeton University Press, 2001.

Bachelor, Steven J. "The Edge of Miracles: Postrevolutionary Mexico City and the Remaking of the Industrial Working Class, 1925–1982." PhD diss., Yale University, 2003.

———. "Toiling for the 'New Invaders': Autoworkers, Transnational Corporations, and Working-Class Culture in Mexico City, 1955–1968." In *Fragments of a Golden Age: The Politics of Culture in Mexico, 1940–2000*, edited by Gilbert M. Joseph, Ann Rubenstein, and Eric Zolov. Durham, NC: Duke University Press, 2001.

Ballent, Anahí. "El arte de saber vivir: Modernización del habitar doméstico y cambio urbano, 1940–1970." In *Cultura y comunicación en la Ciudad de México*, edited by Néstor García Canclini, 1:65–131. Mexico City: Grijalbo, 1998.

Barajas, Rafael [El Fisgón]. *Sobras escogidas.* Mexico City: Claves Latinoamericanas, 1986.

Barreda Solórzano, Luis de la. "La crisis y la criminalidad." In González Casanova and Camín, *México ante la crisis*, 2:117–126.

Barros, Rodolfo. *Fuimos: Aventuras y desaventuras de la clase media.* Buenos Aires: Aguilar, 2005.

Bartra, Armando. *Los herederos de Zapata: Movimientos campesinos posrevolucionarios en México, 1920–1980.* Mexico City: Ediciones Era, 1985.

Bartra, Roger. *Jaula de la melancolía.* Mexico City: Grijalbo, 1987.

Basurto, Jorge. "The Late Populism of Luis Echeverría." In *Latin American Populism in a Comparative Perspective*, edited by Michael L. Conniff, 93–111. Albuquerque: University of New Mexico Press, 1982.

Benjamin, Walter. "On the Concept of History." In *Selected Writings*, vol. 4: *1938–1940*, edited by Howard Eiland and Michael W. Jennings, 389–400. Cambridge, MA: Belknap Press of Harvard University Press, 2003.

———. "Theses on the Philosophy of History." In *Illuminations: Walter Benjamin,*

Essays and Reflections, edited by Hannah Arendt, 253–264. New York: Schocken Books, 1968.

Berger, Mark T. "Romancing the Zapatistas: International Intellectuals and the Chiapas Rebellion" *Latin American Perspectives* 117, no. 28 (2001): 149–170.

Bernal, Rafael. *El complot mongol*. Mexico City: J. Mortiz, 2008.

Bertaccini, Tiziana. *El régimen priísta frente a las clases medias, 1943–1964*. Mexico City: Consejo Nacional para la Cultura y las Artes, Dirección General de Publicaciones, 2009.

Bethell, Leslie, and Ian Roxborough. *Latin America between the Second World War and the Cold War, 1944–1948*. Cambridge: Cambridge University Press, 1992.

Blacker-Hanson, O'Neill. "La Lucha Sigue! ("The Struggle Continues!"): Teacher Activism in Guerrero and the Continuum of Democratic Struggle in Mexico." PhD diss., University of Washington, 2005.

Bortz, Jeffrey. "The Development of Quantitative History in Mexico since 1940: Socioeconomic Change, Income Distribution, and Wages." In *Statistical Abstract of Latin America*, 27:1107–1127. Los Angeles: UCLA Latin American Institute, 1989.

———. "The Effects of Mexico's Postwar Industrialization on the U.S.-Mexico Price and Wage Comparison." In *U.S.-Mexico Relations: Labor Market Interdependence*, edited by Jorge Bustamante, Clark W. Reynolds, and Raúl A. Hinojosa Ojeda, 214–234. Stanford, CA: Stanford University Press, 1992.

———. *Revolution within the Revolution: Cotton Textile Workers and the Mexican Labor Regime, 1910–1923*. Stanford, CA: Stanford University Press, 2008.

Bortz, Jeffrey, and Marcos Aguila. "Earning a Living: A History of Real Wage Studies in Twentieth-Century Mexico." *Latin American Research Review* 41, no. 2 (2006): 112–138.

Bortz, Jeffrey, and Rafael Sánchez. "Salarios y crisis económica en México." In *La estructura de salarios en México*, edited by Jeffrey Bortz. Mexico City: Universidad Autónoma Metropolitana-Azcapotzalco, 1985.

Boughton, James M. *Silent Revolution: The International Monetary Fund, 1979–1989*. Washington, DC: IMF, 2001.

Bourdieu, Pierre. *Distinction: A Social Critique of the Judgement of Taste*. Cambridge, MA: Harvard University Press, 1984.

———. *The State Nobility: Elite Schools in the Field of Power*. Oxford: Polity Press, 1996.

Braham, Persephone. *Crimes against the State, Crimes against Persons: Detective Fiction in Cuba and Mexico*. Minneapolis: University of Minnesota Press, 2004.

Braun, Herbert. "Protests of Engagement: Dignity, False Love, and Self-Love in Mexico during 1968." *Comparative Studies in Society and History* 39, no. 3 (1997): 511–549.

Brito Velázquez, Enrique. *¿Quién escucha al Papa? Sondeo efectuado sobre las actitudes ante la encíclica Humanae vitae*. Mexico City: Instituto Mexicano de Estudios Sociales, 1971.

Brown, Jonathan C. *Oil and Revolution in Mexico*. Berkeley: University of California Press, 1993.

Bruhn, Kathleen. *Taking on Goliath: The Emergence of a New Left Party and the*

Struggle for Democracy in Mexico. University Park: Penn State University Press, 1997.

Brunk, Samuel. "Remembering Emiliano Zapata: Three Moments in the Posthumous Career of the Martyr of Chinameca." *Hispanic American Historical Review* 78 (1998): 457–490.

Buchenau, Jürgen, and Lyman L. Johnson, eds. *Aftershocks: Earthquakes and Popular Politics in Latin America*. Albuquerque: University of New Mexico Press, 2009.

Buendía, Jorge. "The Changing Mexican Voter, 1991–2000." In Middlebrook, *Dilemmas of Political Change in Mexico*, 108–129.

Buffie, Edward F. "Economic Policy and Foreign Debt in Mexico." In *Developing Country Debt and Economic Performance. Country Studies: Argentina, Bolivia, Brazil and Mexico*, edited by Jeffrey D. Sachs, 394–551. Chicago: University of Chicago Press, 1990.

Buffie, Edward F., and Allen Sangines Krause. "Mexico 1958–86: From Stabilising Development to Debt Crisis." In *Developing Country Debt and the World Economy*, edited by Jeffrey D. Sachs, 141–168. Chicago: University of Chicago Press, 1989.

Calderón, Fernando Herrera. "Contesting the State from the Ivory Tower: Student Power, Dirty War and the Urban Guerrilla Experience in Mexico, 1965–1982." PhD diss., University of Minnesota, 2012.

Calderón, Fernando Herrera, and Adela Cedillo, eds. *Challenging Authoritarianism in Mexico: Revolutionary Strugges and the Dirty War, 1964–1982*. New York: Routledge, 2012.

Calle, Luis de la, and Luis F. Rubio. *Clasemediero: Pobre no más, desarrollado aún no*. Mexico City: Centro de Investigación para el Desarrollo, 2010.

Camp, Roderic A. *Entrepreneurs and Politics in Twentieth-Century Mexico*. New York: Oxford University Press, 1989.

———. "The Political Technocrat in Mexico and the Survival of the Political System." *Latin American Research Review* 20, no. 1 (1985): 97–118.

———. *Politics in Mexico: The Democratic Transformation*. New York: Oxford University Press, 2003.

Cantú Chapa, Rubén. *Tlatelolco: La autoadministración en unidades habitacionales gestión urbana y planificación*. Mexico City: Plaza y Valdés, 2001.

Careaga, Gabriel. *Biografía de un joven de la clase media*. Mexico City: J. Mortiz, 1978.

———. *Mitos y fantasías de la clase media en México*. Mexico City: J. Mortiz, 1974.

Carey, Elaine. *Plaza of Sacrifices: Gender, Power, and Terror in 1968 Mexico*. Albuquerque: University of New Mexico Press, 2005.

Carmona, Fernando, Guillermo Montaño, Jorge Carrión, and Alonso Aguilar M. *El milagro mexicano*. Mexico City: Editorial Nuestro Tiempo, 1970.

Carr, Barry. *Marxism and Communism in Twentieth-Century Mexico*. Lincoln: University of Nebraska Press, 1992.

———. "The Mexican Left, the Popular Movements and the Politics of Austerity 1982–1985." In Anzaldúa Montoya and Carr, *The Mexican Left*, 1–18.

Casanova Cardiel, Hugo. "La UNAM entre 1970 y 2000: Expansión y compleji-dad." In *La Universidad de México: Un recorrido histórico de la época colonial al presente*, edited by Renate Marsiske, 261–326. Mexico City: Centro de Estudios sobre la Universidad, UNAM, 2001.

Castañeda, Jorge G. *Mañana Forever? Mexico and the Mexicans*. New York: Alfred A. Knopf, 2011.

Castellanos, Laura, and Alejandro Jiménez. *México armado, 1943–1981*. Mexico City: Ediciones Era, 2007.

CEPAL (Comisión Económica Para América Latina). *Daños causados por el movimiento telúrico en México y sus repercusiones sobre la economía del país*. N.p.: CEPAL, 1985.

Chabal, Patrick. *Amílcar Cabral: Revolutionary Leadership and People's War*. New York: Cambridge University Press, 1983.

Cline, Howard F. *Mexico: Revolution to Evolution, 1940–1960*. London: Oxford University Press, 1962.

Close, Glen Steven. *Contemporary Hispanic Crime Fiction: A Transatlantic Discourse on Urban Violence*. New York: Palgrave Macmillan, 2008.

Cohen, Jean L., and Andrew Arato. *Civil Society and Political Theory*. Cambridge, MA: MIT Press, 1994.

Cohen, Lizabeth. *A Consumers' Republic: The Politics of Mass Consumption in Postwar America*. New York: Knopf, 2003.

Comisión Nacional de los Salarios Mínimos. "Los salarios mínimos legales en México." *Revista Mexicana de Sociología* 34, no. 2 (April–June 1972): 355–357.

Coo, Jorge. "Después de la caída." In Aguilar Zinser, Morales, and Peña, *Aún tiembla*, 39–54.

Coplamar (Coordinación General del Plan Nacional de Zonas Deprimidas y Grupos Marginados). *Necesidades esenciales en México: Educación*. Mexico City: Siglo Veintiuno, 1982.

Coral, Emilio. "La clase media mexicana, 1940–1970: Entre la tradición, la izquierda, el consumismo y la influencia cultural de los Estados Unidos." *Historias* 63 (2006): 103–125.

Cornelius, Wayne A. "The Political Economy of Mexico under de la Madrid: Austerity, Routinized Crisis, and Nascent Recovery." *Mexican Studies/Estudios Mexicanos* 1, no. 1 (1985): 83–124.

Cornelius, Wayne A., Ann L. Craig, and Jonathan Fox, eds. *Transforming State-Society Relations in Mexico: The National Solidarity Strategy*. San Diego: Center for U.S.-Mexican Studies, University of California–San Diego, 1994.

Coronil, Fernando. *The Magical State: Nature, Money, and Modernity in Venezuela*. Chicago: University of Chicago Press, 1997.

Corrigan, Philip, and Derek Sayer. *The Great Arch: English State Formation as Cultural Revolution*. New York: Blackwell, 1985.

Crespo, José Antonio. "Party Competition in Mexico: Evolution and Prospects." In Middlebrook, *Dilemmas of Political Change in Mexico*, 57–81.

Crevenna, Theo R., ed. *Materiales para el estudio de la clase media en América Latina*. Washington, DC: Unión Panamericana, Departamento de Asuntos Culturales, 1950.

Cuevas Díaz, J. Aurelio. *El Partido Comunista Mexicano: La ruptura entre las clases medias y el estado fuerte en México*. Mexico City: Editorial Línea, 1984.

Cypess, Sandra Messinger. *La Malinche in Mexican Literature from History to Myth*. Austin: University of Texas Press, 1991.

Davidoff, Leonore, and Catherine Hall. *Family Fortunes: Men and Women of the English Middle Class, 1780–1850*. Chicago: University of Chicago Press, 1991.

Davis, Diane E. "Reverberations: Mexico City's 1985 Earthquake and the Transformation of the Capital." In *The Resilient City: How Modern Cities Recover from Disaster*, edited by Lawrence J. Vale and Thomas J. Campanella, 255–279. Oxford: Oxford University Press, 2005.

———. *Urban Leviathan: Mexico City in the Twentieth Century*. Philadelphia: Temple University Press, 1994.

Davis, Mike. *Planet of Slums*. New York: Verso, 2006.

Dawson, Alexander S. *First World Dreams: Mexico since 1989*. New York: Zed Books, 2006.

Deans-Smith, Susan, and Gilbert M. Joseph, eds. "Mexico's New Cultural History: ¿Una Lucha Libre?" Special issue, *Hispanic American Historical Review* 79, no. 2 (1999).

Debray, Régis. *Revolution in the Revolution? Armed Struggle and Political Struggle in Latin America*. New York: Grove Press, 1967.

de Lara Rangel, Salvador. "El impacto económico de la crisis sobre la clase media." In Loaeza and Stern, *Las clases medias*, 29–49.

De Long, J. Bradford. *America's Only Peacetime Inflation: The 1970s*. Cambridge, MA: National Bureau of Economic Research, 1996.

Delgado, Álvaro. *El Yunque: La ultraderecha en el poder*. Mexico City: Plaza Janés, 2003.

Deutsch, Sandra McGee. *"Las Derechas": The Extreme Right in Argentina, Brazil, and Chile, 1890–1939*. Stanford, CA: Stanford University Press, 1999.

Eckstein, Susan. "Poor People versus the State and Capital: Anatomy of a Successful Community Mobilization for Housing in Mexico City." In *Power and Popular Protest: Latin American Social Movements*, 329–350.

———, ed. *Power and Popular Protest: Latin American Social Movements*. Berkeley: University of California Press, 2001.

Ehrenreich, Ben. "The Crack-Up." *Nation*, 12 April 2010.

Eineigel, Susanne. "Revolutionary Promises Encounter Urban Realities for Mexico City's Middle Class, 1915–1928." In López and Weinstein, *The Making of the Middle Class*, 253–266.

Elizondo, Carlos. "In Search of Revenue: Tax Reform in Mexico under the Administrations of Echeverría and Salinas." *Journal of Latin American Studies* 26, no. 1 (1994): 159–190.

Elizondo Mayer-Serra, Carlos, and Luis Manuel Pérez de Acha. "Separación de poderes y garantías individuales: La Corte Suprema y los derechos de los contribuyentes." *Cuestiones Constitucionales* 14 (2006): 91–130.

Elu de Leñero, María del Carmen. *¿Hacía donde va la mujer mexicana? Proyecciones a partir de los datos de una encuesta nacional*. Mexico City: Instituto Mexicano de Estudios Sociales, 1969.

Ervin, Michael. "The 1930 Agrarian Census in Mexico: Agronomists, Middle Politics, and the Negotiation of Data Collection." *Hispanic American Historical Review* 87, no. 3 (2007): 537–570.

Escobar Latapí, Agustín, and Bryan R. Roberts. "Urban Stratification, the Middle Classes, and Economic Change in Mexico." In *Social Responses to Mexico's Economic Crisis of the 1980s*, edited by Mercedes González de la Rocha and Agustín Escobar Latapí, 91–114. San Diego: Center for U.S.-Mexican Studies, University of California–San Diego, 1991.

Ezcurdia, Mario. *Análisis teórico del Partido Revolucionario Institutional*. Mexico City: B. Costa-Amic, 1968.

Fanon, Frantz. *The Wretched of the Earth*. New York: Grove Press, [1961] 1963.

Ferguson, James. *Expectations of Modernity: Myths and Meanings of Urban Life on the Zambian Copper Belt*. Berkeley: University of California Press, 1999.

Fernández Barraza, María de Lourdes. *Breve estudio del salario: Su protección y del Fondo de Fomento y Garantía para el Consumo de los Trabajadores*. Mexico City: Escuela Libre de Derecho, 1976.

Finchelstein, Federico. "The Anti-Freudian Politics of Argentine Fascism: Anti-Semitism, Catholicism, and the Internal Enemy, 1932–1945." *Hispanic American Historical Review* 87, no. 1 (2007): 77–110.

———. *Transatlantic Fascism: Ideology, Violence, and the Sacred in Argentina and Italy, 1919–1945*. Durham, NC: Duke University Press, 2010.

Foucault, Michel. *The Archaeology of Knowledge*. New York: Pantheon Books, 1972.

———. *Discipline and Punish: The Birth of the Prison*. New York: Pantheon Books, 1977.

Foweraker, Joe, and Ann L. Craig, eds. *Popular Movements and Political Change in Mexico*. Boulder, CO: Lynne Rienner, 1990.

Franco, Jean. *The Decline and Fall of the Lettered City: Latin America in the Cold War*. Cambridge, MA: Harvard University Press, 2002.

Francois, Marie Ellen. *A Culture of Everyday Credit: Housekeeping, Pawnbroking, and Governance in Mexico City, 1750–1920*. Lincoln: University of Nebraska Press, 2006.

Fraser, Nancy. "Rethinking the Public Sphere: A Contribution to the Critique of Actually Existing Democracy." *Social Text* 25/26 (1990): 56–80.

Frazier, Leslie Jo, and Deborah Cohen. "Defining the Space of Mexico '68: Heroic Masculinity in the Prison and 'Women' in the Streets." *Hispanic American Historical Review* 83, no. 4 (2003): 617–660.

French, John, and Daniel James. "The Travails of Doing Labor History: The Restless Wanderings of John Womack Jr." *Labor* 4 (2007): 95–116.

Fuentes, Carlos. *Las buenas conciencias*. Mexico City: Fondo de Cultura Económica, Ediciones Nuevo País, 1959.

———. *The Death of Artemio Cruz*. New York: Farrar, Straus & Giroux, 1964.

———. *Where the Air Is Clear*. New York: I. Obolensky, 1960.

Galeano, Eduardo. *Open Veins of Latin America: Five Centuries of the Pillage of a Continent*. New York: Monthly Review Press, 1973.

Galico, Salvador. *Los 80's: En pocas palabras*. Mexico City: Hersa, 1989.

Garay Arellano, Graciela de, ed. *Modernidad habitada: Multifamiliar Miguel Alemán, Ciudad de México, 1949–1999.* Mexico City: Instituto Mora, 2004.

———, ed. *Rumores y retratos de un lugar de la modernidad: Historia oral del Multifamiliar Miguel Alemán, 1949–1999.* Mexico City: Instituto Mora, 2002.

García Canclini, Néstor. *Consumers and Citizens: Globalization and Multicultural Conflicts.* Minneapolis: University of Minnesota Press, 2001.

———, ed. *El consumo cultural en México.* Mexico City: Consejo Nacional para la Cultura y las Artes, Dirección General de Publicaciones, 1993.

García Cantú, Gastón, and Javier Barros Sierra. *Javier Barros Sierra, 1968: Conversaciones con Gastón García Cantú.* Mexico City: Siglo Veintiuno, 1972.

Garrido, Luis Javier. *El Partido de la Revolución Institucionalizada: Medio siglo de poder político en México.* Mexico City: Siglo Veintiuno, 1982.

Garza, Gustavo. *Una década de planeación urbano-regional en México, 1978–1988.* Mexico City: Colegio de México, 1989.

———. *La urbanización de México en el siglo XX.* Mexico City: Colegio de México, 2003.

Garza, Gustavo, and Martha Schteingart. *La acción habitacional del estado en México.* Mexico City: Colegio de México, 1978.

Gauss, Susan M. *Made in Mexico: Regions, Nation, and the State in the Rise of Mexican Industrialism, 1920s–1940s.* University Park: Penn State University Press, 2010.

Gavin, Michael. "The Mexican Oil Boom, 1977–85." In *Trade Shocks in Developing Countries,* vol. 2: *Asia and Latin America,* edited by Paul Collier and Jan Willem Gunning, 164–200. Oxford: Oxford University Press, 2000.

Giglia, Angela. "Gated Communities in Mexico City." *Home Cultures* 5, no. 1 (March 2008): 65–84.

Gilbert, Dennis. "Magicians: The Response of Middle-Class Mexican Households to Economic Crisis." *Journal of Latin American Anthropology* 10, no. 1 (2005): 126–150.

———. *Mexico's Middle Class in the Neoliberal Era.* Tucson: University of Arizona Press, 2007.

Gillingham, Paul. "Force and Consent in Mexican Provincial Politics: Guerrero and Veracruz, 1945–1953." DPhil, University of Oxford, 2005.

———. "Fraud and Agency in Early PRIísta Electoral Practice." Paper presented at the annual meeting of the Latin American Studies Association, Montreal, 5–8 September 2007.

Gilly, Adolfo, and Rhina Roux. *Cartas a Cuauhtémoc Cárdenas.* Mexico City: Ediciones Era, 1989.

Gómez Tagle, Silvia. "Public Institutions and Electoral Transparency in Mexico." In Middlebrook, *Dilemmas of Political Change in Mexico,* 82–107.

González, Victoria, and Karen Kampwirth, eds. *Radical Women in Latin America: Left and Right.* University Park: Penn State University Press, 2001.

González Casanova, Pablo. *Democracy in Mexico.* New York: Oxford University Press, 1970.

———. "México: El ciclo de una revolución agraria." *Cuadernos Americanos* 120, no. 1 (January–February 1962): 7–29.

González Casanova, Pablo, and Héctor Aguilar Camín, eds. *México ante la crisis.* Vol. 2. Mexico City: Siglo Veintiuno, 1985.

González Cosío, Arturo. *Clases medias y movilidad social en México.* Mexico City: Editorial Extemporáneos, 1976.

———. "Clases y estratos sociales." In *México cincuenta años de revolución II: La vida social,* edited by Julio Durán Ochoa et al., 31–77. Mexico City: Fondo de Cultura Económica, 1961.

González de Alba, Luis. *Los días y los años.* Mexico City: Ediciones Era, 1971.

González González, José. *Lo negro del Negro Durazo.* Mexico City: Posada, 1983.

González y González, Luis. *San José de Gracia: Mexican Village in Transition.* Austin: University of Texas Press, 1974.

Goux, Jean-Joseph. "Cash, Check, or Charge?" In *The New Economic Criticism: Studies at the Intersection of Literature and Economics,* edited by Martha Woodmansee and Mark Osteen, 114–127. New York: Routledge, 1999.

Gracida, Elsa M. "Retórica petrolera: Nuevos fundamentos de la retórica y la política económica mexicanas durante el auge petrolero." Paper presented at the XIII Reunión de Historiadores de México, Estados Unidos y Canadá, Santiago de Querétaro, 26–30 October 2010.

Grammont, Hubert C. de [Hubert Carton]. *El Barzón: Clase media, ciudadanía y democracia.* Mexico City: Instituto de Investigaciones Sociales / Editorial Plaza y Valdés, 2001.

Gramsci, Antonio. *Prison Notebooks.* Vol. 2. New York: Columbia University Press, 1992.

Granato, Stephanie, and Aída Mostkoff. "The Class Structure of Mexico, 1895–1980." In *Society and Economy in Mexico,* edited by James W. Wilkie, 103–115. Los Angeles: UCLA Latin American Center Publications, 1990.

Grandin, Greg. *The Last Colonial Massacre: Latin America in the Cold War.* Chicago: University of Chicago Press, 2004.

Gutiérrez Garza, Esthela. "Respuesta estudiantil ante la austeridad." In *Testimonios de la crisis: Austeridad y reconversión,* vol. 3, edited by Esthela Gutiérrez Garza, 209–235. Mexico City: Siglo Veintiuno, 1988.

Gutmann, Matthew C. *Fixing Men: Sex, Birth Control, and Aids in Mexico.* Berkeley: University of California Press, 2007.

Haber, Paul. *Power from Experience: Urban Popular Movements in Late Twentieth-Century Mexico.* University Park: Penn State University Press, 2006.

Haber, Stephen H. "Economic Growth and Latin American Economic Historiography." In *How Latin America Fell Behind: Essays on the Economic Histories of Brazil and Mexico, 1800–1914,* 1–33. Stanford, CA: Stanford University Press, 1997.

Haber, Stephen H., Herbert S. Klein, Noel Maurer, and Kevin J. Middlebrook. *Mexico since 1980.* New York: Cambridge University Press, 2008.

Habermas, Jürgen. *The Structural Transformation of the Public Sphere: An Inquiry into a Category of Bourgeois Society.* Cambridge, MA: MIT Press, [1962] 1989.

Hall, Stuart. "Foucault: Power, Knowledge and Discourse." In *Discourse Theory and Practice: A Reader,* edited by Margaret Wetherell, Simeon Yates, and Stephanie Taylor, 72–81. London: Sage, 2001.

———. "The Work of Representation." In *Representation: Cultural Representations and Signifying Practices*. London: Sage, 1997.

Hamilton, Nora. *The Limits of State Autonomy: Post-Revolutionary Mexico*. Princeton, NJ: Princeton University Press, 1982.

Harvey, David. *A Brief History of Neo-Liberalism*. Oxford: Oxford University Press, 2005.

———. *The Condition of Postmodernity: An Enquiry into the Origins of Cultural Change*. Cambridge, MA: Blackwell, 1989.

Hayden, Tom. *The Zapatista Reader*. New York: Thunder's Mouth Press/Nation Books, 2002.

Heath, Jonathan. *Mexico and the Sexenio Curse: Presidential Successions and Economic Crises in Modern Mexico*. Washington, DC: Center for Strategic and International Studies, 1999.

Hellman, Judith. *Mexico in Crisis*. New York: Holmes & Meier, 1983.

———. "The Study of New Social Movements in Latin America and the Question of Autonomy." In Alvarez and Escobar, *The Making of Social Movements in Latin America*, 52–61.

Henck, Nick. *Subcommander Marcos: The Man and the Mask*. Durham, NC: Duke University Press, 2007.

Hernández, José. *The Gaucho Martín Fierro*. Translated by Frank G. Carrino, Alberto J. Carlos, and Norman Mangouni. Delmar, NY: Scholars' Facsimiles & Reprints, 1974.

———. *Martín Fierro*. Barcelona: Credsa, [1872] 1966.

Hernández Chávez, Alicia. *La mecánica cardenista*. Mexico City: Colegio de México, 1980.

Hinojosa, Iván. "On Poor Relations and the Nouveau Riche: Shining Path and the Radical Peruvian Left." In *Shining and Other Paths: War and Society in Peru, 1980–1995*, edited by Steve J. Stern, 60–83. Durham, NC: Duke University Press, 1998.

Hirschman, Albert O. "The Political Economy of Import-Substituting Industrialization in Latin America." *Quarterly Journal of Economics* 82, no. 1 (1968): 1–32.

———. "The Search for Paradigms as a Hindrance to Understanding." *World Politics* 22, no. 3 (April 1970): 329–343.

Hoffmann Calo, Juan. *Crónica política del Ayuntamiento de la Ciudad de México (1917–1928): Los partidos, las elecciones, los gobernantes*. Mexico City: Gobierno de la Ciudad de México, 2000.

Holloway, John. "The Red Rose of Nissan." *Capital & Class* 11, no. 2 (Summer 1987): 142–164.

Holmes, Martin. *The First Thatcher Government, 1979–1983: Contemporary Conservatism and Economic Change*. Sussex: Wheatsheaf Books, 1985.

Hoselitz, Bert F. "Economic Growth in Latin America." In *First International Conference of Economic History, Stockholm*, 87–101. Paris: Mouton & Co., 1960.

Hubbard, William H. "The New Inflation History." *Journal of Modern History* 62, no. 3 (September 1990): 552–569.

Iturriaga, José E. *La estructura social y cultural de México*. Mexico City: Instituto

Nacional de Estudios Históricos de la Revolución Mexicana and Secretario de Gobernación, [1951] 2003.

Jameson, Fredric. *Postmodernism, or, The Cultural Logic of Late Capitalism.* Durham, NC: Duke University Press, 1991.

Jardón, Raúl. *El espionaje contra el movimiento estudiantil: Los documentos de la Dirección Federal de Seguridad y las agencias de "inteligencia" estadounidenses en 1968.* Mexico City: Itaca, 2003.

Jiménez, Michael F. "The Elision of the Middle Classes and Beyond: History, Politics, and Development Studies in Latin America's 'Short Twentieth Century.'" In *Colonial Legacies: The Problem of Persistence in Latin American History,* edited by Jeremy Adelman, 207–228. New York: Routledge, 1999.

Johnson, John J. *Political Change in Latin America: The Emergence of the Middle Sectors.* Stanford, CA: Stanford University Press, 1958.

Johnston, Robert. *The Radical Middle Class: Populist Democracy and the Question of Capitalism in Progressive Era Portland, Oregon.* Princeton, NJ: Princeton University Press, 2003.

Jones, Gareth A., and Moreno-Carranco, Maria. "Megaprojects: Beneath the Pavement, Excess." *City: Analysis of Urban Trends, Culture, Theory, Policy, Action* 11, no. 2 (2007): 144–164.

Joseph, Gilbert M. "On the Trail of Latin American Bandits: A Reexamination of Peasant Resistance." *Latin American Research Review* 25, no. 3 (1990): 7–53.

———. *Revolution from Without: Yucatán, Mexico, and the United States, 1880–1924.* Cambridge: Cambridge University Press, 1982.

Joseph, Gilbert M., and Daniel Nugent, eds. *Everyday Forms of State Formation: Revolution and the Negotiation of Rule in Modern Mexico.* Durham, NC: Duke University Press, 1994.

Karl, Terry Lynn. *The Paradox of Plenty: Oil Booms and Petro-States.* Berkeley: University of California Press, 1997.

Karon, Paul. "Law and Popular Credit in Mexico." *Arizona Journal of International and Comparative Law* 1 (Winter 1982): 88–121.

Katz, Friedrich. *The Life and Times of Pancho Villa.* Stanford, CA: Stanford University Press, 1998.

Klein, Noami. *The Shock Doctrine: The Rise of Disaster Capitalism.* New York: Metropolitan Books, 2007.

Knight, Alan. "Export-Led Growth in Mexico, c. 1900–30." In *An Economic History of Twentieth-Century Latin America,* vol. 1, edited by Enrique Cárdenas, José Antonio Ocampo, and Rosemary Thorp, 119–151. New York: Palgrave, 2000.

———. "Historical and Theoretical Considerations." In *Elites, Crises, and the Origins of Regimes,* edited by Mattei Dogan and John Higley, 29–45. Oxford: Oxford University Press, 1998.

———. "Historical Continuities in Social Movements." In Foweraker and Craig, *Popular Movements and Political Change in Mexico,* 78–102.

———. *The Mexican Revolution.* 2 vols. Cambridge: Cambridge University Press, 1986.

———. "Mexican Revolution: Bourgeois? Nationalist? Or Just a 'Great Rebellion'?" *Bulletin of Latin American Research* 4, no. 2 (1985): 1–37.

———. "Mexico and Latin America in Comparative Perspective." In *Elites, Crises, and the Origins of Regimes*, edited by Mattei Dogan and John Higley, 71–91. Oxford: Oxford University Press, 1998.

———. "Populism and Neo-Populism in America Latina, Especially Mexico." *Journal of Latin American Studies* 30 (1998): 223–248.

———. "The Rise and Fall of Cardenismo, c. 1940–c. 1946." In *Mexico since Independence*, edited by Leslie Bethell, 241–320. Cambridge: Cambridge University Press, 1991.

La Botz, Dan. *Mask of Democracy: Labor Supression in Mexico Today.* Boston: South End Press, 1992.

Langland, Victoria. "Birth Control Pills and Molotov Cocktails: Reading Sex and Revolution in 1968 Brazil." In *In from the Cold: Latin America's New Encounter with the Cold War*, edited by Gilbert M. Joseph and Daniela Spenser. Durham, NC: Duke University Press, 2008.

Lares Romero, Víctor Hugo. *El derecho de protección a los consumidores en México.* Mexico City: Universidad Autónoma Metropolitana, 1991.

Legovini, Arianna, César Bouillón, and Nora Lustig. "Can Education Explain Changes in Income Inequality in Mexico?" In *The Microeconomics of Income Distribution Dynamics in East Asia and Latin America*, edited by François Bourguignon, Francisco H. G. Ferreira, and Nora Lustic, 275–312. New York: World Bank / Oxford University Press, 2005.

Leñero Otero, Luis. *Investigación de la familia en México: Presentación y avance de resultados de una encuesta nacional.* Mexico City: Instituto Mexicano de Estudios Sociales, 1971.

Levy, Daniel C. *Higher Education and the State in Latin America: Private Challenges to Public Dominance.* Chicago: University of Chicago Press, 1986.

Lewis, Oscar. *Five Families: Mexican Case Studies in the Culture of Poverty.* Foreword by Oliver La Farge. New York: Basic Books, 1959.

Lewis, Paul H. *Guerrillas and Generals: The "Dirty War" in Argentina.* Westport, CT: Praeger, 2002.

Li Zhisui. *Private Life of Chairman Mao: The Memoirs of Mao's Personal Physician.* New York: Random House, 1994.

Loaeza, Guadalupe. *Compro, luego existo.* Mexico City: Patria/Inco, 1992.

———. *Debo, luego sufro.* Mexico City: Océano/Profeco, 2000.

———. *Las niñas bien.* Mexico City: Océano, 1987.

———. *Las reinas de Polanco.* Mexico City: Cal y Arena, 1988.

Loaeza, Soledad. "Las clases medias mexicanas y la coyuntura económica actual." In González Casanova and Aguilar Camín, *México ante la crisis*, 2:221–237.

———. *Clases medias y política en México: La querella escolar, 1959–1963.* Mexico City: Colegio de México, 1988.

———. "El comportamiento político de las clases medias en la crisis." In Loaeza and Stern, *Las clases medias*, 69–75.

———. "México, 1968: Los orígenes de la transición." In Semo, *La transición interrumpida: México 1968–1988*, 15–48.

———. *El Partido Acción Nacional: La larga marcha, 1939–1994; Oposición leal y partido de protesta.* Mexico City: Fondo de Cultura Económica, 1999.

―――. "La política del rumor: México, noviembre–diciembre de 1976." *Foro Internacional* 17, no. 4 (April–June 1977): 557–586.

Loaeza, Soledad, and Claudio Stern, eds. *Las clases medias en la coyuntura actual: Seminario llevado a cabo en el Centro Tepoztlán, A.C., Tepoztlán, Mor., 26 de septiembre de 1987.* Mexico City: Colegio de México, 1990.

Lomnitz, Claudio. "The Depreciation of Life during Mexico City's Transition into 'the Crisis.'" In *Wounded Cities: Destruction and Reconstruction in a Globalized World,* edited by Jane Schneider and Ida Susser, 47–69. Oxford: Berg, 2003.

Lomnitz-Adler, Claudio. *Exits from the Labyrinth: Culture and Ideology in the Mexican National Space.* Berkeley: University of California Press, 1992.

―――. "Times of Crisis: Historicity, Sacrifice, and the Spectacle of Debacle in Mexico City." *Public Culture* 15, no. 1 (2003): 127–147.

―――. Untitled presentation. Workshop on Critical Approaches to Race and Ethnicity at the Center for the Study of Ethnicity and Race, Columbia University, New York, April 2011.

Looney, Robert E. "Mexican Economic Performance during the Echeverría Administration: Bad Luck or Poor Planning?" *Bulletin of Latin American Research* 2, no. 2 (May 1983): 57–68.

López, Abel Ricardo. "A Beautiful Class, an Irresistible Democracy." PhD diss., University of Maryland, 2008.

López, Abel Ricardo, and Barbara Weinstein, eds. *The Making of the Middle Class: Toward a Transnational History of the Middle Class.* Durham, NC: Duke University Press, 2012.

López Cámara, Francisco. *La clase media en la era del populismo.* Mexico City: Miguel Ángel Porrúa, 1988.

―――. *El desafío de la clase media.* Mexico City: J. Mortiz, 1971.

López Velarde, Ramón. *Song of the Heart: Selected Poems.* Translated by Margaret Sayers Peden. Austin: University of Texas Press, 1995.

―――. *La suave patria y otros poemas.* Mexico City: Fondo de Cultura Económica, 1987.

Lorey, David E., and Aída Mostkoff Linares. "Mexico's 'Lost Decade,' 1980–90: Evidence on Class Structure and Professional Employment from the 1990 Census." In *Statistical Abstract of Latin America* 30:2, 1340–1360. Los Angeles: UCLA Latin American Institute, 1993.

Low, D. A. *The Egalitarian Moment: Asia and Africa, 1950–1980.* Cambridge: Cambridge University Press, 1996.

Lucas, Jeffrey K. *The Rightward Drift of Mexico's Former Revolutionaries: The Case of Antonio Díaz Soto y Gama.* Lewiston, NY: Edwin Mellen Press, 2010.

Luna, Matilde, René Millán, and Ricardo Tirado. "Los empresarios en los inicios del gobierno de Miguel de la Madrid." *Revista Mexicana de Sociología* 47, no. 4 (October–December 1985): 215–257.

Lustig, Nora. "The 1982 Debt Crisis, Chiapas, NAFTA, and Mexico's Poor." In Randall, *Changing Structure of Mexico,* 157–168.

―――. "La paradoja en un mercado informal de crédito: El caso de las tandas en México." *Investigación Económica* 45, no. 178 (October–December 1986): 315–317.

———. *The Remaking of an Economy.* Washington, DC: Brookings Institute, 1992.
Lustig, Nora, and Leonardo Gasparini. "Rise and Fall of Income Inequality in Latin America." Tulane Economics Working Paper Series 1110, Tulane University, New Orleans, 2011. http://econ.tulane.edu/RePEc/pdf/tul1110.pdf.
Lustig, Nora, and Jaime Ros. "Economic Reforms, Stabilization Policies and the 'Mexican Disease.'" In *After Neoliberalism: What Next for Latin America?*, edited by Lance Taylor, 17–52. Ann Arbor: University of Michigan Press, 1999.
Mabire, Bernardo. *Políticas culturales y educativas del estado mexicano de 1970 a 1997.* Mexico City: Colegio de México, 2003.
MacFarquhar, Roderick, Eugene Wu, and Timothy Cheek, eds. *The Secret Speeches of Chairman Mao: From the Hundred Flowers to the Great Leap Forward.* Cambridge, MA: Council on East Asian Studies / Harvard University Press, 1989.
Maier, Lothar. "Institutional Consumer Representation in the European Community." *Journal of Consumer Policy* 16, no. 3–4 (December 1993): 355–374.
Maldonado, Oscar. *Los católicos y la planeación familiar: Resultados de una encuesta nacional.* Mexico City: Instituto Mexicano de Estudios Sociales, 1969.
Mandel, Ernesto. *Delightful Murder: A Social History of the Crime Story.* London: Pluto Press, 1984.
Manjarrez, Héctor. *Lapsus: Algunos actos fallidos.* Mexico City: J. Mortiz, 1971.
Manjarrez Medina, José. "Los cambios en el consumo alimentario por efecto de la crisis económica en la ciudad de México y área conurbana (1985–1988)." *Investigación Económica* 48, no. 190 (October–December 1989): 107–142.
Mansell Carstens, Catherine. *Las finanzas populares en México: El redescubrimiento de un sistema financiero olvidado.* Mexico City: CEMLA/Milenio/ ITAM, 1995.
Manzano, Valeria. "Sexualizing Youth: Morality Campaigns and Representations of Youth in Early 1960s Buenos Aires." *Journal of the History of Sexuality* 14, no. 4 (2005): 433–461.
Marcos, Subcomandante, and Paco Ignacio Taibo II. *Muertos incómodos: Falta lo que falta.* Mexico City: J. Mortiz, 2005.
Markarian, Vania. "El movimiento estudiantil mexicano del 1968: Treinta años de debates públicos." *Anuario de Espacios Urbanos* 46 (2001): 239–264.
Martín-Cabrera, Luis. *Radical Justice: Spain and the Southern Cone beyond Market and State.* Lewisburg, PA: Bucknell University Press, 2011.
Marx, Karl. *Critique of Hegel's "Philosophy of Right."* Cambridge: Cambridge University Press, [1843] 1972.
Massolo, Alejandra. *Por amor y coraje: Mujeres en movimientos urbanos de la Ciudad de México.* Mexico City: Colegio de México, 1992.
McCann, Sean. *Gumshoe America: Hard-Boiled Crime Fiction and the Rise and Fall of New Deal Liberalism.* Durham, NC: Duke University Press, 2000.
McCormick, Gladys. "The Political Economy of Desire in Rural Mexico: Revolutionary Change and the Making of a State, 1935–1965." PhD diss., University of Wisconsin–Madison, 2009.
Mendoza Rojas, Javier. *Los conflictos de la UNAM en el siglo XX.* Mexico City: UNAM, 2001.
———. "La educación superior privada." In *Un siglo de educación en México,*

vol. 2, edited by Pablo Latapí Sarre, 323–354. Mexico City: Consejo Nacional para la Cultura y las Artes, 1998.

Mentz, Brígida von. *Movilidad social de sectores medios en México: Una retrospectiva histórica (siglos XVII al XX)*. Mexico City: Centro de Investigaciones y Estudios Superiores en Antropología Social, 2003.

Messmacher, Miguel, and Alejandro Werner. "Inflación en México: 1950–2000." In "La inflación en México," special issue, *Gaceta de Economía* (2002): 19–60.

Meyer, Jean A. *The Cristero Rebellion: The Mexican People between Church and State, 1926–1920*. Cambridge: Cambridge University Press, 1976.

———. "Revolution and Reconstruction in the 1920s." In *Mexico since Independence*, edited by Leslie Bethell, 201–240. Cambridge: Cambridge University Press, 1991.

Meyer, Michael C., William L. Sherman, and Susan M. Deeds. *The Course of Mexican History*. New York: Oxford University Press, 1999.

Middlebrook, Kevin J., ed. *Dilemmas of Political Change in Mexico*. London: Institute of Latin American Studies, University of London, 2004.

———. "Mexico's Democratic Transitions: Dynamics and Prospects." In *Dilemmas of Political Change in Mexico*, 1–53.

———. *Paradox of Revolution: Labor, the State, and Authoritarianism in Mexico*. Baltimore: Johns Hopkins University Press, 1995.

———. "Party Politics and Democratization in Mexico: The Partido Acción Nacional in Comparative Perspective." In *Party Politics and the Struggle for Democracy in Mexico: National and State-Level Analyses of the Partido Acción Nacional*, 3–46. San Diego: Center for U.S.-Mexican Studies, University of California–San Diego, 2001.

———. "The Sounds of Silence: Organised Labour's Response to Economic Crisis in Mexico." *Journal of Latin American Studies* 21, no. 2 (May 1989): 195–220.

Minushkin, Susan. "Banqueros and Bolseros: Structural Change and Financial Market Liberalization in Mexico." *Journal of Latin American Studies* 34, no. 4 (November 2002): 915–944.

Mirón, Rosa Ma, and Germán Pérez Fernández del Castillo. *López Portillo: Auge y crisis de un sexenio*. Mexico City: Plaza y Valdés, 1988.

Mo Lai-Lan, Phyllis. *Tax Avoidance and Anti-Avoidance Measures in Major Developing Economies*. Westport, CT: Praeger, 2003.

Monsiváis, Carlos. *Días de guardar*. Mexico City: Ediciones Era, 1970.

———. *Entrada libre: Crónicas de la sociedad que se organiza*. Mexico City: Ediciones Era, 1987.

———. *Escenas de pudor y liviandad*. Mexico City: Grijalbo, 1988.

———. "Notas sobre la cultura mexicana en el siglo XX." In *Historia general de México*, vol. 4, edited by Daniel Cosío Villegas, 303–476. Mexico City: Colegio de México, 1976.

———. *Los rituales del caos*. Mexico City: Ediciones Era/Profeco, 1995.

———. "Ustedes que jamás han sido asesinados." *Revista de la Universidad de México* 27, no. 7 (1973): 1–11.

Montemayor, Carlos. *La guerrilla recurrente*. Juárez: Universidad Autónoma de Ciudad Juárez, 1999.

Moreno, Julio. *Yankee Don't Go Home! Mexican Nationalism, American Business Culture, and the Shaping of Modern Mexico, 1920–1950.* Chapel Hill: University of North Carolina Press, 2003.

Moreno, Rafael. *La reforma universitaria de Jorge Capizo y su proyección actual.* Mexico City: UNAM, 1990.

Moreno-Bird, Juan Carlos, and Jaime Ros. *Development and Growth in the Mexican Economy: A Historical Perspective.* New York: Oxford University Press, 2009.

Moreno Carranco, María del Carmen. "The Socio/Spatial Production of the Global: Mexico City Reinvented through the Santa Fe Urban Megaproject." PhD diss., University of California, Berkeley, 2008.

Navarrete, Ifigenia M. de. *La distribución del ingreso y el desarrollo económico de México.* Mexico City: Escuela Nacional de Economía, 1960.

Navarro, Aaron W. *Political Intelligence and the Creation of Modern Mexico, 1938–1954.* University Park: Penn State University Press, 2010.

Necochea López, Raúl. "Priests and Pills: Catholic Family Planning in Peru, 1967–1976." *Latin American Research Review* 43, no. 2 (2008): 34–56.

Nelson, Cary, ed. "The Yale Strike Dossier." Special issue, *Social Text* 49 (Winter 1996).

Niblo, Stephen. *Mexico in the 1940s: Modernity, Politics and Corruption.* Wilmington, DE: Scholarly Resources, 1999.

———. *War, Diplomacy, and Development: The United States and Mexico, 1938–1954.* Wilmington, DE: Scholarly Resources, 1995.

Noelle, Louise. *Mario Pani: Una visión moderna de la ciudad.* Mexico City: CONACULTA, 2000.

Nun, José. "The Middle-Class Military Coup in Latin America." In *Latin America: Reform or Revolution? A Reader,* edited by James Petras and Maurice Zeitlin, 145–185. Greenwich, CT: Fawcett, 1968.

Nuncio, Abraham. *El Grupo Monterrey.* Mexico City: Nueva Imagen, 1982.

Núñez, Israel. "Prestaciones sociales y estructura salarial en México." In *La estructura de salarios en México,* edited by Jeffrey Bortz, 315–368. Mexico City: Universidad Autónoma Metropolitana Azcapotzalco, 1984.

Núñez Birrueta, José Israel, and David Lavalle Montalvo. *Análisis de los medios de protección al salario de los trabajadores en el área del consumo.* Mexico City: Instituto Nacional de Estudios del Trabajo, Secretaría del Trabajo y Previsión Social, 1982.

Núñez de la Peña, Francisco J., and Jesús Orozco. *El terremoto: Una versión corregida.* Guadalajara: ITESO, 1988.

OECD (Organisation for Economic Co-operation and Development) Development Centre. *Latin American Economic Outlook 2011: How Middle-Class Is Latin America?* Paris: OECD Development Centre, 2010.

Ochoa, Enrique. *Feeding Mexico: The Political Uses of Food since 1910.* Wilmington, DE: Scholarly Resources, 2000.

O'Dougherty, Maureen. *Consumption Intensified: The Politics of Middle-Class Daily Life in Brazil.* Durham, NC: Duke University Press, 2002.

Olvera, Alberto J. "Civil Society in Mexico at Century's End." In Middlebrook, *Dilemmas of Political Change in Mexico,* 403–439.

Ovalle Favela, José. *Comentarios a la Ley Federal de Protección al Consumidor: Legislación, doctrina y jurisprudencia.* Mexico City: McGraw-Hill, 1995.

———. *Derechos del consumidor.* Mexico City: UNAM, 2001.

Owensby, Brian. *Intimate Ironies: Modernity and the Making of Middle-Class Lives in Brazil.* Stanford, CA: Stanford University Press, 1999.

Pacheco, Cristina. *La rueda de la fortuna.* Mexico City: Ediciones Era/Inco, 1993.

Pacheco, José Emilio. *Las batallas en el desierto.* Mexico City: Ediciones Era, 1981.

Padilla, Tanalís. "Crossing the Historical and National Divide: Post-1940 Social Movements, Some Comments on the State of the Historiography." Paper presented at the annual meeting of the Tepoztlán Institute for the Transnational History of the Americas, Tepoztlán, 1–8 August 2007.

———. *Rural Resistance in the Land of Zapata: The Jaramillista Movement and the Myth of the Pax Priísta, 1940–1962.* Durham, NC: Duke University Press, 2008.

Padilla, Tanalís, and Louise E. Walker, eds. "Spy Reports: Content, Methodology and Historiography in Mexico's Secret Police Archives." Special dossier, *Journal of Iberian and Latin American Research,* forthcoming.

Palacios, Agustín. "Efectos psicológicos de la crisis sobre las clases medias." In Loaeza and Stern, *Las clases medias,* 111–113.

Pani, Erika, ed. *Conservadurismo y derechas en la historia de México.* 2 vols. Mexico City: Fondo de Cultura Económica, 2009.

Parker, David S. *The Idea of the Middle Class: White-Collar Workers and Peruvian Society, 1900–1950.* University Park: Penn State University Press, 1998.

———. "The Making and Endless Remaking of the Middle Class." In Parker and Walker, *Latin America's Middle Class,* forthcoming.

Parker, David S., and Louise E. Walker, eds. *Latin America's Middle Class: Unsettled Debates and New Histories.* Lanham, MD: Lexington Books, forthcoming.

Paxton, Robert O. "The Five Stages of Fascism." *Journal of Modern History* 70, no. 1 (1998): 1–23.

Paz, Octavio. *The Labyrinth of Solitude and Other Writings.* New York: Grove Press, 1985.

———. "The Other Mexico." In *The Labyrinth of Solitude and Other Writings,* 213–325.

———. *Posdata.* Mexico City: Siglo Veintiuno, 1970.

Peebles, Gustav. "The Anthropology of Credit and Debt." *Annual Review of Anthropology* 39 (2010): 225–240.

Pensado, Jaime. "Political Violence and Student Culture in Mexico: The Consolidation of Porrismo during the 1950s and 1960s." PhD diss., University of Chicago, 2008.

Pérez Alfonzo, Juan Pablo. *Hundiéndonos en el excremento del diablo.* Caracas: Editorial Lisbona, 1976.

Petras, James. *Politics and Social Structure in Latin America.* New York: Monthly Review Press, 1970.

Piccato, Pablo. *City of Suspects: Crime in Mexico City, 1900–1931.* Durham, NC: Duke University Press, 2001.

———. "Conversación con los difuntos: Una perspectiva mexicana ante el debate sobre la historia cultural." *Signos históricos* 8 (2002): 13–41.

Piccato, Pablo, and Cristina Sacristán, eds. *Actores, espacios y debates en la historia de la esfera pública en la Ciudad de México.* Mexico City: Instituto Mora, 2005.

Pike, Frederick. "Aspects of Class Relations in Chile, 1850–1960." *Hispanic American Historical Review* 43, no. 1 (February 1963): 14–33.

Pilcher, Jeffrey M. *¡Que Vivan los Tamales! Food and the Making of Mexican Identity.* Albuquerque: University of New Mexico Press, 1998.

Pogolotti, Marcelo. *La clase media en México.* Mexico City: Editorial Diógenes, 1972.

Poniatowska, Elena. *Domingo 7.* Mexico City: Océano, 1983.

———. *Fuerte es el silencio.* Mexico City: Ediciones Era, 1980.

———. *Massacre in Mexico.* Columbia: University of Missouri Press, 1975.

———. *La noche de Tlatelolco: Testimonios de historia oral.* Mexico City: Ediciones Era, 1971.

———. *Nothing, Nobody: The Voices of the Mexico City Earthquake.* Philadelphia: Temple University Press, [1988] 1995.

Poovey, Mary. *Genres of the Credit Economy: Mediating Value in Eighteenth- and Nineteenth-Century Britain.* Chicago: University of Chicago Press, 2008.

Porter, Susie. "Espacios burocráticos, normas de feminidad e identidad de la clase media en México durante la década de 1930." In *Orden social e identidad de género: México siglos XIX y XX*, edited by María Teresa Fernández Aceves, Carmen Ramos Escandón, and Susie Porter. Guadalajara: CIESAS, 2006.

Power, Margaret. *Right-Wing Women in Chile: Feminine Power and the Struggle against Allende, 1964–1973.* University Park: Penn State University Press, 2002.

Pozas Horcasitas, Ricardo. *La democracia en blanco: El movimiento médico en México, 1964–1965.* Mexico City: Siglo Veintiuno, 1993.

Preston, Julia, and Samuel Dillon. *Opening Mexico: The Making of a Democracy.* New York: Farrar, Straus & Giroux, 2004.

Quenet, Grégory. *Les tremblements de terre aux XVIIe et XVIIIe siècles: La naissance d'un risque.* Seyssel: Champ Vallon, 2005.

Ramos, Samuel. *Profile of Man and Culture in Mexico.* Austin: University of Texas Press, [1934] 1969.

Randall, Laura, ed. *Changing Structure of Mexico: Political Social and Economic Prospects.* Armonk, NY: Sharpe, 1996.

Rath, Thomas. "'Que el cielo un soldado en cada hijo te dio . . .': Conscription, Recalcitrance and Resistance in Mexico in the 1940s." *Journal of Latin American Studies* 37 (2005): 507–531.

Revueltas, José. *México 68: Juventud y revolución.* Mexico City: Ediciones Era, 1978.

Reyes Heroles González Garza, Jesús. *Financial Policies and Income Distribution in Mexico.* Available through ILL from the Colegio de México library.

———. *Política macroeconómica y bienestar en México.* Mexico City: Fondo de Cultura Económica, 1983.

Reynolds, Clark W. *Mexican Economy: Twentieth-Century Structure and Growth.* New Haven, CT: Yale University Press, 1970.

———. "Why Mexico's 'Stabilizing Development' Was Actually Destabilizing (with Some Implications for the Future)." *World Development* 6, no. 7–8 (July–August 1978): 1005–1018.

Rodríguez Kuri, Ariel. "Hacia México 68: Pedro Ramírez Vázquez y el proyecto olímpico." *Secuencia* 56 (2003): 37–73.

———. "El lado oscuro de la luna: El momento conservador en 1968." In Pani, *Conservadurismo y derechas en la historia de México*, 2:512–559.

———. "Los primeros días: Una explicación de los orígenes inmediatos del movimiento estudiantil de 1968." *Historia Mexicana* 53, no. 1 (2003): 179–228.

———. "La proscripción del aura: Arquitectura y política en la restauración de la catedral de México, 1967–1971." *Historia Mexicana* 56, no. 4 (2007): 1309–1391.

———. "Secretos de la idiosincrasia: Urbanización y cambio cultural en México, 1950–1970." In *Ciudades mexicanas del siglo XX: Siete estudios históricos*, edited by Ariel Rodríguez Kuri and Carlos Lira Vásquez, 19–57. Mexico City: Colegio de México, 2009.

———. "Urbanización y secularización en México: Temas y problemas historiográficos, ca. 1960s–1970s." In *México en tres momentos: 1810–1910–2010. Hacia la conmemoración de la Independencia y del Centenario de la Revolución Mexicana. Retos y perspectivas*, vol. 1, edited by Alicia Mayer, 107–120. Mexico City: Universidad Nacional Autónoma de México, 2007.

Rodríguez Munguía, Jacinto. *1968: Todos los culpables*. Mexico City: Random House Mondadori, 2008.

Ros, Ana. "Inheritance: Living Memory, Leaving Countries. Uruguayan and Argentinean Fictionalization at the Turn of the Millennium." PhD diss., University of Michigan, 2008.

Ross, Kristin. *May '68 and Its Afterlives*. Chicago: University of Chicago Press, 2002.

Roux, Rhina, and Gerardo Ávalos Tenorio. "Rupturas." In Gilly and Roux, *Cartas a Cuauhtémoc Cárdenas*, 11–21.

Samaniego de Villarreal, Norma. "Algunas reflexiones sobre el impacto económico de la crisis en las clases medias." In Loaeza and Stern, *Las clases medias*, 51–67.

Sánchez, Fernando Fabio. "El asesinato como un arte (pos)nacional en el México moderno." PhD diss., University of Colorado, 2006.

Sánchez-Cordero Dávila, Jorge A. *La protección del consumidor*. Mexico City: Editorial Nueva Imagen, 1981.

Santacruz, Miguel [pseud.]. *Algunas apreciaciones sobre el desarrollo compartido durante el período de Luis Echeverría Álvarez: Ensayo*. Mexico: n.p., 1978.

Santiago, Myrna I. *The Ecology of Oil: Environment, Labor, and the Mexican Revolution, 1900–1938*. Cambridge: Cambridge University Press, 2006.

Scherer García, Julio, and Carlos Monsiváis. *Tiempo de saber: Prensa y poder en México*. Mexico City: Aguilar, 2003.

Schers, David. *The Popular Sector of the Partido Revolucionario Institucional in Mexico*. Tel Aviv: David Horowitz Institute for the Research of Developing Countries, Tel Aviv University, 1972.

Schmidt, Henry C. "The Mexican Foreign Debt and the Sexennial Transition from López Portillo to De la Madrid." *Mexican Studies / Estudios Mexicanos* 1, no. 2 (1985): 227–254.

Schmidt, Samuel. *The Deterioration of the Mexican Presidency: The Years of Luis Echeverría*. Tucson: University of Arizona Press, 1991.

Schmitt, Carl. *Political Theology: Four Chapters on the Concenpt of Sovereignty*. Cambridge, MA: MIT Press, 1985.

Schmuckler, Nathan, and Edward Marcus, eds. *Inflation through the Ages: Economic, Social, Psychological, and Historical Aspects*. New York: Columbia University Press, 1983.

Schneider, Ben Ross. "Why Is Mexican Business So Organized?" *Latin American Research Review* 37, no. 1 (2002): 77–118.

Scott, John. "The Social Failure of the Mexican Revolution: Redistributive Constraints under High Inequality." Paper presented at the UCLA conference Latin American Economies: History and Globalization, Los Angeles, April 2009.

Semo, Enrique. "The Left and the Crisis." In Anzaldúa Montoya and Carr, *The Mexican Left*, 19–32.

Semo, Ilán, ed. *La transición interrumpida: México 1968–1988*. Mexico City: Universidad Iberoamericana / Nueva Imagen, 1993.

Serna, Leslíe, and Coordinadora Unica de Damnificados. *¡Aquí nos quedaremos! Testimonios de la Coordinadora Unica de Damnificados: Entrevistas*. Mexico City: Universidad Iberoamericana, 1995.

Silva, Pablo. "The Origins of White-Collar Privilege in Chile: Arturo Alessandri, Law 6020, and the Pursuit of a Corporatist Consensus, 1933–1938." *Labor* 3, no. 1 (2006): 87–112.

Smith, Benjamin T. *Pistoleros and Popular Movements: The Politics of State Formation in Postrevolutionary Oaxaca*. Lincoln: University of Nebraska Press, 2009.

Smith, Peter. *Labyrinths of Power: Political Recruitment in Twentieth-Century Mexico*. Princeton, NJ: Princeton University Press, 1979.

Sodi, Federico. *Clase media: Novela*. Mexico City: Ediciones Botas, 1948.

Solís M., Leopoldo. *Economic Policy Reform in Mexico: A Case Study for Developing Countries*. New York: Pergamon Press, 1981.

Solórzano Peña, María Amelia, and Ramiro Contreras Acevedo, eds. *Derecho de consumo en México*. Guadalajara: Universidad de Guadalajara, 2005.

Sorensen, Diana. *A Turbulent Decade Remembered: Scenes from the Latin American Sixties*. Stanford, CA: Stanford University Press, 2007.

Soto Laveaga, Gabriela. "The 'Emperor' Has a New Lab Coat: How History of Science and Medicine Continue to Challenge Our Understanding of Modern Mexico." Paper presented at conference "Nuevas Fronteras: New Trends and Transformations in Modern Mexican History," Yale University, 5 June 2009.

———. "'Let's Become Fewer': Soap Operas, Contraception, and Nationalizing the Mexican Family in an Overpopulated World." *Sexuality Research and Social Policy* 4, no. 3 (2007): 19–33.

Stavans, Ilan. "A Brief Talk with Paco Ignacio Taibo II." *Literary Review* 38 (1994): 34–37.

Stepan, Alfred D. *Rethinking Military Politics: Brazil and the Southern Cone*. Princeton, NJ: Princeton University Press, 1988.

Stern, Claudio. "Notas para la deliminación de las clases medias en México." In Loaeza and Stern, *Las Clases Medias*, 19–27.

Stern, Claudio, and Joseph Kahl. "Stratification since the Revolution." In *Comparative Perspectives on Stratification: Mexico, Great Britain, Japan*, edited by Joseph Kahl, 5–30. Boston: Little, Brown, 1968.

Stiglitz, Joseph. *Globalization and Its Discontents*. New York: Norton, 2002.

Stoll, David. *Rigoberta Menchú and the Story of All Poor Guatemalans*. Boulder, CO: Westview Press, 1999.

Story, Dale. "Industrial Elites in Mexico: Political Ideology and Influence." *Journal of Interamerican Studies and World Affairs* 25, no. 3 (1983): 351–376.

Street, James H. "Can Mexico Break the Vicious Cycle of 'Stop-Go' Policy? An Institutional Overview." *Journal of Economic Issues* 20, no. 2 (June 1986): 601–612.

Taibo, Paco Ignacio, II. *Algunas nubes*. Mexico City: Leega, 1985.

———. *Cosa fácil*. Mexico City: Editorial Planeta, [1977] 1998.

———. *Días de combate*. Mexico City: Editorial Grijalbo, 1976.

———. *No habrá final feliz*. Mexico City: Editorial Planeta, [1981] 2003.

Tamayo, Sergio. "Archipiélagos de la modernidad urbana: Arquitecturas de la globalización en la Ciudad de México." In *Anuarios de Espacios Urbanos*, 189–225. Mexico City: Universidad Autónoma Metropolitana, 2001.

Tarrés, María Luisa. "Del abstencionismo electoral a la oposición política: Las clases medias en Ciudad Satélite." *Estudios Sociológicos* 4, no. 12 (1986): 361–390.

Tavera-Fenollosa, Ligia. "Social Movements and Civil Society: The Mexico City 1985 Earthquake Victim Movement." PhD diss., Yale University, 1998.

Tecla Jiménez, Alfredo. *Universidad, burguesía y proletariado*. Mexico City: Ediciones de Cultura Popular, 1976.

Teichman, Judith. "The Mexican State and the Political Implications of Economic Restructuring." *Latin American Perspectives* 19, no. 73 (1992): 88–104.

———. "Neoliberalism and the Transformation of Mexican Authoritarianism." *Mexican Studies / Estudios Mexicanos* 13, no. 1 (1997): 121–147.

Teivainen, Teivo. *Enter Economism, Exit Politics: Experts, Economic Policy and the Damage to Democracy*. London: Zed Books, 2002.

Tenorio-Trillo, Mauricio. "The Riddle of a Common History: The United States in Mexican Textbook Controversies." *Journal of Educational Media, Memory, and Society* 1, no. 1 (2009): 93–116.

Terranova, Juan. *El ignorante*. Buenos Aires: Tantalia, 2004.

Therborn, Göran. *What Does the Ruling Class Do When It Rules? State Apparatuses and State Power under Feudalism, Capitalism and Socialism*. New York: Schocken Books, 1978.

Thompson, E. P. *The Making of the English Working Class*. New York: Vintage Books, 1963.

Torres Septié, Valentina. *La educación privada en México (1903–1976)*. Mexico City: Colegio de México, 1997.

Trejo Reyes, Saúl. "Notas sobre el seminario: 'Las clases medias en la coyuntura actual.'" In Loaeza and Stern, *Las clases medias*, 103–105.

Ulloa Bornemann, Alberto. *Surviving Mexico's Dirty War: A Political Prisoner's Memoir*. Philadelphia: Temple University Press, 2007.

UNAM (Universidad Autónoma de México). *Fortaleza y debilidad de la UNAM. Respuesta de la comunidad universitaria: Propuestas y alternativas. Suplemento extraordinario.* Mexico City: UNAM, 1986.

Usigli, Rodolfo. *Ensayo de un crimen.* Buenos Aires: Centro Editor de América Latina, 1968.

———. *Medio tono: Comedia en tres actos.* Mexico City: Editorial Dialéctica, 1938.

Valés Ugalde, Francisco. "La corrupción y las transformaciones de la burguesía en México, 1940–1994." In *Vicios públicos, virtudes privadas: La corrupción en México,* edited by Claudio Lomnitz, 195–220. Mexico City: CIESAS, 2000.

Van Young, Eric. "El lugar de encuentro entre la historia económica y la historia cultural." Paper delivered at the Segundo Congreso de Historia Económica, Asociación Mexicana de Historia Económica, Universidad Nacional Autónoma de México, 27–29 October 2004.

———. "The New Cultural History Comes to Old Mexico." In "¿Una Lucha Libre?," edited by Susan Deans-Smith and Gilbert M. Joseph, special issue, *Hispanic American Historical Review* 79, no. 2 (1999): 211–248.

———. "To See Someone Not Seeing: Historical Studies of Peasants and Politics in Mexico." *Mexican Studies / Estudios Mexicanos* 6, no. 1 (1990): 133–159.

Vargas Llosa, Mario. "Mexico: The Perfect Dictatorship." *New Perspectives Quarterly* 8 (1991): 23–24.

Vaughan, Mary Kay. *Cultural Politics in Revolution: Teachers, Peasants and Schools in Mexico, 1930–1940.* Tucson: University of Arizona Press, 1997.

Veblen, Thorstein. *The Theory of the Leisure Class.* Toronto: Dover Publications, [1899] 1994.

Vernon, Raymond. *The Dilemma of Mexico's Development: The Roles of the Private and Public Sectors.* Cambridge, MA: Harvard University Press, 1963.

Villa Lever, Lorenzo. *Los libros de texto gratuitos: La disputa por la educación en México.* Guadalajara: Departamento de Investigación Científica y Superación Académica, Universidad de Guadalajara, 1988.

Viotti da Costa, Emilia. "New Publics, New Politics, New Histories: From Economic Reductionism to Cultural Reductionism—In Search of Dialectics." In *Reclaiming the Political in Latin American History: Essays from the North,* edited by Gilbert M. Joseph, 17–31. Durham, NC: Duke University Press, 2001.

Visacovsky, Sergio E., and Enrique Garguin, eds. *Moralidades, economías e identidades de clase media: Estudios históricos y etnográficos.* Buenos Aires: Antropofagia, 2009.

Volpi, Jorge. *El fin de la locura.* Barcelona: Seix Barral, 2003.

———. *Season of Ash.* Rochester, NY: Open Letter Books, 2009.

Wahrman, Dror. *Imagining the Middle Class: The Political Representation of Class in Britain, c. 1780–1840.* Cambridge: Cambridge University Press, 1995.

Wallerstein, Immanuel. "The Bourgeois(ie) as Concept and Reality." In *The Essential Wallerstein,* 324–343. New York: New Press, [1988] 2000.

———. *Open the Social Sciences: Report of the Gulbenkian Commission on the Restructuring of the Social Sciences.* Stanford, CA: Stanford University Press, 1996.

Ward, Peter M. *Mexico City.* Rev. 2nd ed. Chichester: John Wiley & Sons, 1998.

Weber, Max. *Economy and Society: An Outline of Interpretive Sociology.* New York: Bedminster Press, [1922] 1968.

Weintraub, Sidney. "Mexico's Foreign Economic Policy: From Admiration to Disappointment." In Randall, *Changing Structure of Mexico*, 43–54.

White, Luise. "Telling More: Lies, Secrets, and History." *History and Theory* 39, no. 4 (December 2000): 11–22.

Whiteford, Andrew Hunter. *Two Cities of Latin America: A Comparative Description of Social Classes.* Prospect Heights, IL: Waveland Press, 1991.

Wilkie, James W., and Paul D. Wilkins. "Quantifying the Class Structure of Mexico, 1895–1970." In *Statistical Abstract of Latin America* 21: 578–590. Los Angeles: UCLA Latin American Institute, 1981.

Williams, Heather L. *Planting Trouble: The Barzón Debtors' Movement in Mexico.* San Diego: Center for U.S.-Mexican Studies, University of California–San Diego, 1994.

———. *Social Movements and Economic Transition: Markets and Distributive Politics in Mexico.* Cambridge: Cambridge University Press, 2001.

Williams, Raymond. *Keywords: A Vocabulary of Culture and Society.* New York: Oxford University Press, 1985.

Womack, John, Jr. "Chiapas, the Bishop of San Cristóbal, and the Zapatista Revolt." In *Rebellion in Chiapas: An Historical Reader,* edited by John Womack Jr., 3–59. New York: New Press, 1999.

———. "Doing Labor History: Feelings, Work, Material Power." *Journal of the Historical Society* 5, no. 3 (2005): 255–296.

———. "The Spoils of the Mexican Revolution." *Foreign Affairs* 48, no. 4 (1970): 677–687.

———. *Zapata and the Mexican Revolution.* New York: Knopf, 1969.

Wright, Angus L. *The Death of Ramón González: The Modern Agricultural Dilemma.* Austin: University of Texas Press, 1990.

Wuhs, Steven T. *Savage Democracy: Institutional Change and Party Development in Mexico.* University Park: Penn State University Press, 2008.

Zeitlin, Maurice. *The Civil Wars in Chile, or, The Bourgeois Revolutions That Never Were.* Princeton, NJ: Princeton University Press, 1984.

Zermeño, Sergio. "Crisis, Neoliberalism, and Disorder." In Foweraker and Craig, *Popular Movements and Political Change in Mexico*, 160–180.

Žižek, Slavoj. "The Obscenity of Human Rights: Violence as Symptom." http://www.lacan.com/zizviol.htm.

Zolov, Eric. "Discovering a Land 'Mysterious and Obvious': The Renarrativizing of Post-Revolutionary Mexico." In *Fragments of a Golden Age: The Politics of Culture in Mexico since 1940,* edited by Gilbert M. Joseph, Anne Rubenstein, and Eric Zolov, 234–272. Durham, NC: Duke University Press, 2001.

———. "Expanding Our Conceptual Horizons: The Shift from an Old to a New Left in Latin America." *A Contracorriente* 5, no. 2 (2008): 47–73.

———. *Refried Elvis: The Rise of Mexican Counterculture.* Berkeley: University of California Press, 1999.

———. "Showcasing the 'Land of Tomorrow': Mexico and the 1968 Olympics." *The Americas* 61, no. 2 (2004): 159–188.

Index